The

GARDEN

OF

FRAGRANCE

بوستان سعدی

A Complete Translation of the Bustan
of Saadi (Bilingual)

Persian - English

Translated By:

G. S. DAVIE

Created by:

Hamid Eslamian

The Garden of Fragrance

Published by Persian Learning Center

Web: www.persianbell.com

Email: info@persianbell.com

ISBN: 978-1-63620-909-8

Join with Sádi and his Reflection of Magical Words

چو مشک است بی قیمت اندر ختن   همانا که در فارس انشای من

به شوخی و فلفل به هندوستان   گل آورد سعدی سوی بوستان

In Persia, my writings are, doubtless, thought nice;
As musk is in Cathay esteemed beyond price.

To the garden brought Sádi, with boldness, a rose,
As they do spice to India, where spice freely grows.

Musleh al-Din Bin Abdallah Saadi Shirazi (1210–1291), is one of the greatest classical Persian poets of all time, whose beauty of speech and eloquentness in order and prose has a worldwide reputation and is the language of all. Saadi's speeches about moral principles and Gnosticism is very beautiful and attractive, his ideas and style are highly original and so far, no one has been able to sing so beautifully. The great poet's books have also been translated into European languages, to the point that some believe that Europe recognized Persian literature with Sadi's poems. His works have long been taught in schools as a source of Persian language teaching, and many of the proverbs common in Persian have been adapted from his works.

Bustan is one of the masterpieces of Persian literature, in the old versions of Sadi Nameh. The book was written during his travels to different parts of the world and includes 183 stories in ten chapters about virtues such as justice, kindness, love, modesty, freedom, generosity, satisfaction, and happiness, and Darvish conscience practices that refer to all people for a better and happier life.

The stories of The Bustan are not the same in terms of complexity and structure, some have a more complex fictional structure and include many events and persons, while others are simple and in the same way as the story. The Bustan can be considered as a moral and educational book in which Sádi describes his utopia.

The translation appearing in this book is by G. S. Davie M.D. in 1882. Translation of poetry from one language into another is notoriously difficult. It is conceivably more demanding in the instance of classical Persian poetry than in many other traditions. Separately from the simulated loss of metre and rhyme, many of the literary devices – imagery, metaphor, punning, and so on – are also lost in the process.

Bustan is a precious learning resource for Persian language learners or Persian literature students. Not only will poems improve your Persian language, but they'll help your understanding of Persian culture and literature.

As Ralph Waldo Emerson once said: 'The word Sádi means "fortunate". He inspires in the reader a good hope.'

WWW.PERSIANBELL.COM

... So Much More Online!

✓ FREE Farsi Lessons

✓ More Farsi Learning Books!

✓ Persian Lessons

✓ Online Farsi Tutors

For a PDF Version of This Book

Please Visit www.persianbell.com

Contents

9

0

مقدمه

(Introduction)

در نیایش خداوند

Prayer of God

سرآغاز
In begin

به نام خداوند جان آفرین
In the name of the Life-giving Guardian of Earth!
حکیم سخن در زبان آفرین
The Most Wise! causing speech on the tongue to have

خداوند بخشندهٔ دستگیر
The Bountiful Giver! who aids when implored;
کریم خطا بخش پوزش پذیر
The Kind, Sin-Forgiving, Excuse-Taking Lord!

عزیزی که هر کز درش سر بتافت
So mighty, that all from His door who retired,
به هر در که شد هیچ عزت نیافت
And went to another, no honour acquired!

سر پادشاهان گردن فراز
The heads of great monarchs, with necks stretching high,
به درگاه او بر زمین نیاز
At His Court on the ground of petitioning lie.

نه گردن کشان را بگیرد به فور
He is tardy in seizing on those who rebel;
نه عذرآوران را براند به جور
And does not excuse-bringers rudely repel.

وگر خشم گیرد ز کردار زشت
If wrathful at deeds that are loathsome to sight,
چو بازآمدی ماجرا در نوشت
When you've penitent turned, "It is past? He will write.

اگر با پدر جنگ جوید کسی
Should one seek with a father in strife to engage,
پدر بی گمان خشم گیرد بسی
The father would doubtless exhibit much rage.

وگر خویش راضی نباشد ز خویش
If kinsman with kinsman should jangle and fight,
چو بیگانگانش براند ز پیش
Like an alien, he drives him away from his sight.

وگر بنده چابک نباشد به کار
If a slave who is active should useless appear,
عزیزش ندارد خداوندگار
The lord of the work will not reckon him dear.

وگر بر رفیقان نباشی شفیق

If a man towards comrades should sympathy shun,

به فرسنگ بگریزد از تو رفیق

Any comrade a league from his presence will run.

وگر ترک خدمت کند لشکری

Should a soldier decline to serve longer the State,

شود شاه لشکرکش از وی بری

The Royal Commander resigns him to Fate.

ولیکن خداوند بالا و پست

But the Lord of the Sky and the Earth's rugged skin,

به عصیان در رزق بر کس نبست

On none shuts the door of subsistence, for sin.

دو کونش یکی قطره از بحر علم

Like a drop in the ocean of knowledge, are seen

گنه بیند و پرده پوشد به حلم

Both His worlds, and the faults, He sees, kindly, He'll screen.

ادیم زمین، سفرهٔ عام اوست

The Earth's crust is His banquet, for "high" and for "low";

بر این خوان یغما چه دشمن چه دوست

At this feast free to all, what of friend? What of foe?

اگر بر جفا پیشه بشتافتی

Had He hurried in tyrannous acts to engage,

که از دست قهرش امان یافتی؟

Who would have been safe from the hand of His rage?

بری ذاتش از تهمت ضد و جنس

His Person admits not of rival nor kin;

غنی ملکش از طاعت جن و انس

His realm needs not service from man nor from Jinn

پرستار امرش همه چیز و کس

To worship His mandates all men and things vie

بنی آدم و مرغ و مور و مگس

The offspring of Adam, the bird, ant, and fly.

چنان پهن خوان کرم گسترد

So spacious a table of merciful fare

که سیمرغ در قاف قسمت خورد

He provides, that the Simargh of Kaff eats a share.

لطیف کرم گستر کارساز

The Creator is mercy-diffusing and kind,

که دارای خلق است و دانای راز

For He helps. all His creatures and knows every mind.

مر او را رسد کبریا و منی

In Him self-reliance and grandeur you see,

که ملکش قدیم است و ذاتش غنی

For His kingdom is old and His nature is free.

یکی را به سر برنهد تاج بخت

On one's head He deposits Prosperity's crown;

یکی را به خاک اندر آرد ز تخت

Another to dust from a throne He brings down.

کلاه سعادت یکی بر سرش

The head-dress of bliss may one's temples adorn;

گلیم شقاوت یکی در برش

On the breast of another Griefs blanket is worn.

گلستان کند آتشی بر خلیل

Out of fire, for the Friend, He a rose-garden makes;

گروهی بر آتش برد ز آب نیل

To Hell-fire, from the Nile, He a multitude takes.

گر آن است، منشور احسان اوست

If the former, it tokens His grace to each one;

ور این است، توقیع فرمان اوست

If the latter, it signs that His will must be done!

پس پرده بیند عملهای بد

In rear of the screen He perceives actions vile;

هم او پرده پوشد به آلای خود

With a goodness His own He conceals them, the while.

به تهدید اگر برکشد تیغ حکم

If to menace He seizes the sword of command,

بمانند کروبیان صم و بکم

The Angels around Him all deaf and dumb stand.

وگر در دهد یک صلای کرم

If He issues a notice of bountiful fare,

عزازیل گوید نصیبی برم

The Devil himself says, "I'll bear off a share."

به درگاه لطف و بزرگیش بر

On His threshold of favour and grandeur, the great

بزرگان نهاده بزرگی ز سر

Have cast from their heads Earthly splendour and state.

فروماندگان را به رحمت قریب

To those who are helpless His mercy is near;

تضرع کنان را به دعوت مجیب

And suppliants' prayers He is willing to hear.

بر احوال نابوده، علمش بصیر

The state of things hidden His knowledge lays bare;

به اسرار ناگفته، لطفش خبیر

Of secrets unspoken His insight's aware.

به قدرت، نگهدار بالا و شیب

By His power He holds HeaVn and Earth in His sway;

خداوند دیوان روز حسیب

He is Lord of the Court of the Great Judgment Day.

نه مستغنی از طاعتش پشت کس

Not a back can away from His servitude break;

نه بر حرف او جای انگشت کس

In His writings no finger can point a mistake.

قدیمی نکوکار نیکی پسند

The Eternal Well-Doer, admiring good ways,

به کلک قضا در رحم نقش بند

In the womb with Fate's pencil a figure portrays.

ز مشرق به مغرب مه و آفتاب

The moon and the sun from the East to the West

روان کرد و بنهاد گیتی بر آب

He dispatched, and spread land on the deep Ocean's crest

زمین از تب لرزه آمد ستوه

From trembling, the Earth became feeble and shocked,

فرو کوفت بر دامنش میخ کوه

Through its skirt, then, the nail-looking mountains He knocked.

دهد نطفه را صورتی چون پری

To the " Water " a fairy-like form He imparts;

که کرده‌ست بر آب صورتگری؟

Who else practised on water the sculptor's fine arts?

نهد لعل و پیروزه در صلب سنگ

In stones He sets rubies and turquoise enow,

گل و لعل در شاخ پیروزه رنگ

And the ruby-like rose on the turquoise-like bough.

ز ابر افکند قطره‌ای سوی یم

A drop He cast down from a cloud to the Deep,

ز صلب افکند نطفه‌ای در شکم

And brought seed from the loins to its uterine keep.

از آن قطره لولوی لالا کند

He makes from that drop a pearl shining so bright,

وز این، صورتی سرو بالا کند

And a form from this seed, like the cypress in height

بر او علم یک ذره پوشیده نیست

Not an atom of knowledge from Him is concealed,

که پیدا و پنهان به نزدش یکیست

For the hidden to Him is the same as revealed.

مهیاکن روزی مار و مور

He furnishes food for the snake and the ant;

اگر چند بی‌دست و پایند و زور

Though some have no limbs and of powV are but scant

به امرش وجود از عدم نقش بست

He ordered, and something from nothing arose;

که داند جز او کردن از نیست، هست؟

Who something from nothing but He could disclose?

دگر ره به کتم عدم در برد

Again to nonentity's hiding He flings us,

وز انجا به صحرای محشر برد

And thence to the plain of the Judgment He brings us.

جهان متفق بر الهیتش

A nature Divine, to Him people concede;

فرومانده از کنه ماهیتش

But His nature's true state all are helpless to read.

بشر ماورای جلالش نیافت

The extent of His glory, no mortal has found;

بصر منتهای جمالش نیافت

His exquisite beauty, no vision can bound.

نه بر اوج ذاتش پرد مرغ وهم

O'er His nature the bird of swift thought cannot fly;

نه در ذیل وصفش رسد دست فهم

To the skirt of His praise Reason's hand comes not nigh.

در این ورطه کشتی فروشد هزار

In this whirlpool have sunk ships a thousand and more,

که پیدا نشد تخته‌ای بر کنار

Of which not a plank ever got to the shore.

چه شبها نشستم در این سیر، گم

Many nights in this temple I've sat in surmise,

که دهشت گرفت آستینم که قم

When Astonishment seizing my sleeve, said, "Arise!

محیط است علم ملک بر بسیط

The Royal One's knowledge can everything clasp;

قیاس تو بر وی نگردد محیط

Your conception wants scope to take Him in its grasp.

نه ادراک در کنه ذاتش رسید

His nature, so subtle, perception can't trace;

نه فکرت به غور صفاتش رسید

The mind can't His worth by reflection embrace.

توان در بلاغت به سحبان رسید

A man with Sukban, may in eloquence vie;

نه در کنه بی چون سبحان رسید

None, the Matchless and Holy, to measure can try.

که خاصان در این ره فرس رانده‌اند

For the Chosen have driven their steeds in this race,

به لاحصی از تک فرومانده‌اند

And exceeding account, have been tired by the pace.

نه هر جای مرکب توان تاختن

One can't gallop his horse over every field,

که جاها سپر باید انداختن

For at times he is forced to surrender his shield.

وگر سالکی محرم راز گشت

When the mystical secret a traveller knows,

ببندند بر وی در بازگشت

The door that was open, behind him they close

27

کسی را در این بزم ساغر دهند

To a man in this feast they deliver the cup,

که داروی بیهوشیش در دهند

That the potion, depriving of sense, he may sup.

یکی باز را دیده بردوخته‌ست

Stitched up are the eyes of one falcon with care;

یکی دیدها باز و پر سوخته‌ست

The eyes of another are open and glare.

کسی ره سوی گنج قارون نبرد

To the treasure of Korah no traveler e'er hied,

وگر برد، ره باز بیرون نبرد

Who, if he got there, could return when he tried.

بمردم در این موج دریای خون

The wise are afraid of this ocean of blood,

کز او کس نبرده‌ست کشتی برون

For no person has yet saved his ship from its flood.

اگر طالبی کاین زمین طی کنی

If desire should allure you to travel this plain;

نخست اسب باز آمدن پی کنی

First, the horse-of-returning take care to retain!

تأمل در آیینۀ دل کنی

If within the heart's mirror reflection you make,

صفایی به تدریج حاصل کنی

Of Purity's fruit, by degrees, you'll partake

مگر بویی از عشق مستت کند

Love's perfume, perhaps, so enamours your brain,

طلبکار عهد الستت کند

That from courting the "Promise" you cannot refrain.

به پای طلب ره بدان جا بری

To the first, by the feet of Inquiring you'll hie;

وز آنجا به بال محبت پری

And from this, on the wings of Affection you'll fly.

بدرد یقین پرده‌های خیال

The curtains of Fancy are torn up by Truth;

نماند سراپرده الا جلال

A curtain, save glory, remains not, for sooth!

دگر مرکب عقل را پویه نیست

Should the charger of Wisdom fail pace to command,

عنانش بگیرد تحیر که بیست

Astonishment seizes the reins, saying, "Stand!

در این بحر جز مرد راعی نرفت

Save ' the Prophet,' no person has travelled this Deep;

گم آن شد که دنبال داعی نرفت

He was lost who in rear of the Guide did not keep.

کسانی کز این راه برگشته‌اند

All those who in error have swerved from the way,

برفتند بسیار و سرگشته‌اند

All those who in error have swerved from the way,

خلاف پیمبر کسی ره گزید

Gainst the Prophet, whoever has chosen to strive,

که هرگز به منزل نخواهد رسید

At the refuge need never expect to arrive.

محال است سعدی که راه صفا

Oh, Sádi, don't think the pure path you can tread,

توان رفت جز بر پی مصطفی

Unless by the good Mustapha you are led! "

◈⊙◈◈⊙◈

فی نعت سید المرسلین علیه الصلوة و السلام

Praise of the Chief of Created Beings (Mohamed)

کریم السجایا جمیل الشیم

Of kind disposition and nature refined!

نبی البرایا شفیع الامم

The Prophet and Pleader of all human-kind!

امام رسل، پیشوای سبیل

The Chief of the Prophets! the Guide of the road!

امین خدا، مهبط جبرئیل

Place of Gabriel's alighting! the Trusted of God!

شفیع الوری، خواجه بعث و نشر

Mediator of men! Lord of raising the dead!

امام الهدی، صدر دیوان حشر

The Chief of the Guides and the Judgment Court's Head!

کلیمی که چرخ فلک طور اوست

A communer with God, circling Heav'n in his flight;

همه نورها پرتو نور اوست

All lights that have shown are but rays from his light.

یتیمی که ناکرده قرآن درست

The orphan who showed in his reading defect,

کتب خانهٔ چند ملت بشست

Abolished the churches of many a sect

چو عزمش برآهخت شمشیر بیم

When the sabre of dread he resolved to draw out;

به معجز میان قمر زد دو نیم

With ease, he bisected the scabbard of doubt!

چو صیتش در افواه دنیا فتاد

When the mouth of the world was replete with his fame,

تزلزل در ایوان کسری فتاد

To the palace of Cyrus a shivering came.

به لا قامت لات بشکست خرد

With " la-illa " he Lat into particles crushed,

به اعزاز دین آب عزی ببرد

And before the grand faith Uza's lustre forth gushed.

نه از لات و عزی برآورد گرد

Not alone Lat and Uza beneath his feet fell,

که تورات و انجیل منسوخ کرد

He the " Gospel " and " Pentateuch " wiped out as well!

شبی بر نشست از فلک برگذشت

One night riding forth, he passed Heav'n's lofty sphere,

به تمکین و جاه از ملک درگذشت

And in glory and pomp left the angels in rear.

چنان گرم در تیه قربت براند

In the desert so warmly to God he inclined,

که بر سدره جبریل از او بازماند

That Gabriel was left in his mansion behind.

بدو گفت سالار بیت‌الحرام

To him spoke the chief of the Kaba divine:

که ای حامل وحی برتر خرام

Oh Gabriel! may higher enjoyment be thine!

چو در دوستی مخلصم یافتی

When you found honest friendship in me to exist,

عنانم ز صحبت چرا تافتی؟

Why did you the reins from my fellowship twist? "

بگفتا فراتر مجالم نماند

He answered, "To me no more power pertained;

بماندم که نیروی بالم نماند

I stopped, for no strength in my pinions remained.

اگر یک سر موی برتر پرم

If but one hair's-breadth higher to fly I presumed,

فروغ تجلی بسوزد پرم

By the blaze of your light had my wings been consumed.

نماند به عصیان کسی در گرو

From sin unredeemed not a soul can abide;

که دارد چنین سیدی پیشرو

Who has such a leader before him as guide.

چه نعت پسندیده گویم تو را؟

What suitable praises to you can I pen?

علیک السلام ای نبی الوری

Upon you be safety, oh, Prophet of men!

درود ملک بر روان تو باد

May the blessing of God on your spirit remain!

بر اصحاب و بر پیروان تو باد

On your comrades and all who belong to your train!

نخستین ابوبکر پیر مرید

First, the aged disciple, Abu-Bakar, stands;

عمر، پنجه بر پیچ دیو مرید

Second, Omar, who twisted a proud Devil's hands;

خردمند عثمان شب زنده‌دار

Third, Osman, the wise, who made vigils his rule;

چهارم علی، شاه دلدل سوار

}And fourth, Ali-Shah who rode Duldul the mule.

خدایا به حق بنی فاطمه

Oh God! by the sons who from Fatima rose!

که بر قولم ایمان کنم خاتمه

On the word of the Faith! I now draw to a close.

اگر دعوتم رد کنی ور قبول

If my prayer Thou accept or my prayer Thou shun,

من و دست و دامان آل رسول

My hand and the "prophet's" son's skirt shall be one.

چه کم گردد ای صدر فرخنده پی

Oh leader of fortunate step i what decline

ز قدر رفیعت به درگاه حی

To the height of your glory at God's holy shrine,

که باشند مشتی گدایان خیل

If a few who belong to the mendicant race,

به مهمان دارالسلامت طفیل

Should be guests and not pests at the kingdom of grace.

خدایت ثنا گفت و تبجیل کرد

The Lord has commended and raised you up so,

زمین بوس قدر تو جبریل کرد

That in front of your Power, Gabriel bows his head low.

بلند آسمان پیش قدرت خجل

Confronting your power the heavens shame display;

تو مخلوق و آدم هنوز آب و گل

You had being when Adam was water and clay.

تو اصل وجود آمدی از نخست

At first, as the root of existence you came,

دگر هرچه موجود شد فرع توست

And all who have lived, you as branches can claim.

ندانم کدامین سخن گویمت

I am doubtful what words unto you to address,

که والاتری زانچه من گویمت

For you're higher than I can find words to express.

تو را عز لولاک تمکین بس است

In your honour the glory of Laulak will do;

ثنای تو طه و یس بس است

And Tah and Yasin will be suitable too.

چه وصفت کند سعدی ناتمام؟

What praises can Sádi, the faulty, give thee?

علیک الصلوة ای نبی السلام

Oh, Prophet! may mercy and peace on you be!

❧◉❧◉❧

سبب نظم کتاب
The Reason for Composing the Book

در اقصای عالم بگشتم بسی

Very much I have travelled in many a clime;

به سر بردم ایام با هر کسی

And with many a person have utilized time.

تمتع به هر گوشه‌ای یافتم

From many a corner I pleasure have gained;

ز هر خرمنی خوشه‌ای یافتم

And from many a harvest have corn-ears obtained.

چو پاکان شیراز، خاکی نهاد

Like the pure of Shiraz with humility crowned

ندیدم که رحمت بر این خاک باد

I have never seen one, mercy be on that ground!

تولای مردان این پاک بوم

My love for the men of this sanctified part,

برانگیختم خاطر از شام و روم

From Syria and Rum made me sever my heart.

دریغ آمدم زآن همه بوستان

I regretted, from all of those gardens so fair,

تهیدست رفتن سوی دوستان

To my friends empty-handed again to repair.

به دل گفتم از مصر قند آورند

I said to myself that from Egypt they bear

بر دوستان ارمغانی برند

Sugar-candy to friends, as an offering rare.

مرا گر تهی بود از آن قند دست

If none of that candy I brought in my hand,

سخنهای شیرین‌تر از قند هست

Words sweeter than candy are mine to command.

نه قندی که مردم به صورت خورند

Not like candy in form, that for eating may serve,

که ارباب معنی به کاغذ برند

But such as the thoughtful on paper preserve

چو این کاخ دولت بپرداختم

When this palace of wealth I designed and arrayed.

بر او ده در از تربیت ساختم

Ten doors for the sake of instruction I made.

یکی باب عدل است و تدبیر و رای
First, a chapter with justice and counsels is stored
نگهبانی خلق و ترس خدای
Taking care of the people and serving the Lord.

دوم باب احسان نهادم اساس
In the Second, I've laid generosity's base;
که منعم کند فضل حق را سپاس
For he who is good for God's favours gives praise.

سوم باب عشق است و مستی و شور
The Third is on love and on rapture of mind;
نه عشقی که بندند بر خود بزور
Not the love to which profligate men are inclined.

چهارم تواضع، رضا پنجمین
Humility, Fourth. Resignation, the Fifth.
ششم ذکر مرد قناعت گزین
On those choosing contentment is chapter the Sixth.

به هفتم در از عالم تربیت
The Seventh is a chapter on discipline's sphere;
به هشتم در از شکر بر عافیت
And the Eighth will to thanking for welfare adhere.

نهم باب توبه است و راه صواب
Repentance and probity's path, the Ninth shows;
دهم در مناجات و ختم کتاب
And the Tenth brings to prayers, and the book to a close.

به روز همایون و سال سعید
In a prosperous year, on a fortunate day,
به تاریخ فرخ میان دو عید
And felicitous date that between two Eeds lay;

ز ششصد فزون بود پنجاه و پنج
When Six Hundred and Fifty and Five years had flown,
که پر در شد این نامبردار گنج
Replete with rare pearls was this treasure, well known.

الا ای خردمند پاکیزه خوی
Oh, wise One of affable nature, beware
هنرمند نشنیده‌ام عیب جوی
I've not heard that the cultured for fault-finding care.

قبا گر حریر است و گر پرنیان

Is a cloak Pdrnian? or plain silk? you will find

به ناچار حشوش بود در میان

That, of course, with a padding of cotton 'tis lined.

تو گر پرنیانی نیابی مجوش

Are you Parnian? then, to harm show not zeal!

کرم کار فرما و حشوش بپوش

Be gracious, and all my coarse padding conceal!

ننازم به سرمایهٔ فضل خویش

I do not presume on my own virtue's store;

به دریوزه آورده‌ام دست پیش

As a beggar, I come with my hands stretched before.

شنیدم که در روز امید و بیم

I have heard: "On the day full of hope and of fear,

بدان را به نیکان ببخشد کریم

To the bad and the good God in mercy is near.

تو نیز ار بدی بینیم در سخن

In my writings should you see depravity, too;

به خلق جهان آفرین کار کن

By the people God made! then, expose it to view!

چو بیتی پسند آیدت از هزار

If in one thousand couplets, of one you approve,

به مردی که دست از تعنت بدار

By manhood! in taunting, a hand do not move!

همانا که در فارس انشای من

In Persia, my writings are, doubtless, thought nice;

چو مشک است بی قیمت اندر ختن

As musk is in Cathay esteemed beyond price.

چو بانگ دهل هولم از دور بود

Like the noise of a drum, from afar was my fright;

به غیبت درم عیب مستور بود

In my heart, all my errors lay hidden from sight.

گل آورد سعدی سوی بوستان

To the garden brought Sádi, with boldness, a rose,

به شوخی و فلفل به هندوستان

As they do spice to India, where spice freely grows.

چو خرما به شیرینی اندوده پوست

They resemble the date with a sweet crusted skin,

چو بازش کنی استخوانی در اوست

Which when opened to view, has a hard stone within.

❋◉❋❋◉❋

مدح ابوبکر بن سعد بن زنگ

In praise of Atabik-Abu-Bakar-Bin-Sad-Zangi, (may the earth lie light upon him!)

مرا طبع از این نوع خواهان نبود

To desire such a nature I was not inclined;

سر مدحت پادشاهان نبود

To eulogize kings did not enter my mind;

ولی نظم کردم به نام فلان

Yet some verses I wrote, in a certain one's name,

مگر باز گویند صاحبدلان

And perhaps pious men will repeat of the same:

که سعدی که گوی بلاغت ربود

That Sa'di who Rhetoric's ball bore away,

در ایام بوبکر بن سعد بود

Was alive in Abu-Bakar-Bini-Sad's day.

سزد گر به دورش بنازم چنان

It is well I should honour his reign in my rhymes,

که سید به دوران نوشیروان

As did Sayed the poet — of Naushirwan's times

جهانبان دین پرور دادگر

A king Faith defending, to do justice sworn

نیامد چو بوبکر بعد از عمر

Since Umar, like Bu-Bakar, none has been born.

سر سرفرازان و تاج مهان

He's the chief of the noble and crown of the great;

به دوران عدلش بناز، ای جهان

In his ruling with justice, oh World, be elate!

گر از فتنه آید کسی در پناه

When a person from trouble to safe shelter goes,

ندارد جز این کشور آرامگاه

No country but this has a place for repose.

فطوبی لباب کبیت العتیق

As unto the Kaba's delightful abode,

حوالیه من کل فج عمیق

They travel by many a long valley road,

ندیدم چنین گنج و ملک و سریر

I've not seen such a Treasure, and Country, and Throne,

که وقف است بر طفل و درویش و پیر

Which on child, poor, and aged have equally shone.

نیامد برش دردناک غمی

No person approached him afflicted with grief,

که ننهاد بر خاطرش مرهمی

That he placed not a salve on his heart for relief.

طلبکار خیر است امیدوار

He's a searcher for good and is hopeful, likewise;

خدایا امیدی که دارد برآر

The hope he possesses, oh, God, realize!

کله گوشه بر آسمان برین

His cap-corner perched in the sky may be found,

هنوز از تواضع سرش بر زمین

And his head in humility still on the ground.

گدا گر تواضع کند خوی اوست

The exalted are good who humility show;

ز گردن فرازان تواضع نکوست

If a beggar be humble his Nature is so.

اگر زیردستی بیفتد چه خاست؟

A subject may fall and it matter not much;

زبردست افتاده مرد خداست

But a tyrant cast down is a man in God's clutch.

نه ذکر جمیلش نهان می‌رود

The renown of his goodness remains not concealed;

که صیت کرم در جهان می‌رود

Liberality's fame to the world is revealed

جنوبی خردمند فرخ نژاد

Like him, one so wise and so happy in soul,

ندارد جهان تا جهان است، یاد

The world does not shelter, from pole unto pole.

نبینی در ایام او رنجه‌ای

In his days, one afflicted, no eye can behold;

که نالد ز بیداد سرپنجه‌ای

Of oppression from one cruel hand, who has told?

کس این رسم و ترتیب و آیین ندید

None has seen such arrangement, such usage and rite;

فریدون با آن شکوه، این ندید

Faridun, with his pomp, did not see such a sight

از آن پیش حق پایگاهش قوی است

In the eyes of the Lord his position is strong,

که دست ضعیفان به جاهش قوی است

For the hands of the weak from his rank become long.

چنان سایه گسترده بر عالمی

On a world such abundance of favour he shows,

که زالی نیندیشد از رستمی

That a Zal from a Rustam no anxiousness knows.

همه وقت مردم ز جور زمان

Some men, on account of the harshness of Fate,

بنالند و از گردش آسمان

Are ever distressed that the sky should rotate.

در ایام عدل تو ای شهریار

Oh, friend of the city! so just is your reign,

ندارد شکایت کس از روزگار

That none against Fortune has cause to complain.

به عهد تو می‌بینم آرام خلق

In your age I see people enjoying repose;

پس از تو ندانم سرانجام خلق

After you, what may happen them God only knows!

هم از بخت فرخنده فرجام توست

It is due to your fortunate planet's bright rays,

که تاریخ سعدی در ایام توست

That the writings of Sádi appear in your days.

که تا بر فلک ماه و خورشید هست

While the sun and the moon in the sky shall remain,

در این دفترت ذکر جاوید هست

So long shall this record your merits contain.

ملوک ار نکو نامی اندوختند

If monarchs a good reputation have earned,

ز پیشینگان سیرت آموختند

The manner they have from their ancestors learned

تو در سیرت پادشاهی خویش

With qualities regal, so gifted's your mind,

سبق بردی از پادشاهان پیش

That the monarchs of yore you have left far behind

سکندر به دیوار رویین و سنگ

Alexander, with wall made of stone and of brass,

بکرد از جهان راه یأجوج تنگ

Brought Gog in the world to a difficult pass.

تو را سد یأجوج کفر از زر است

Your barrier to Gog's unbelief is of gold;

نه رویین چو دیوار اسکندر است

Not of brass, like the great Alexander's, of old

زبان آوری کاندر این امن و داد

If a poet, enjoying this justice and peace,

سپاست نگوید زبانش مباد

Does not speak in your praise, may his tongue ever cease

زهی بحر بخشایش و کان جود

What a sea of bestowing and lavishing mine!

که مستظهرند از وجودت وجود

For the poor are relieved by your presence benign.

برون بینم اوصاف شاه از حساب

Past counting, I see the king's merits remain;

نگنجد در این تنگ میدان کتاب

And their record's too large for this limited plain.

گر آن جمله را سعدی انشا کند

Were Sádi to enter the whole of them in,

مگر دفتری دیگر املا کند

A new volume he, doubtless, would have to begin.

فروماندم از شکر چندین کرم

I fail in my thanks for such generous care;

همان به که دست دعا گسترم

It is better to stretch, then, my hands out in prayer:

جهانت به کام و فلک یار باد

May the Earth and the Sky all your wishes befriend!

جهان آفرینت نگهدار باد

May the Maker of Earth to you safety extend!

بلند اخترت عالم افروخته

By your high-rising star may the world be illumed!

زوال اختر دشمنت سوخته

And the low-falling star of your foe be consumed!

غم از گردش روزگارت مباد

By grief from changed times may you never be pressed!

وز اندیشه بر دل غبارت مباد

May the dust of sad care on your heart never rest!

که بر خاطر پادشاهان غمی

(For if grief in the heart of a monarch should dwell

پریشان کند خاطر عالمی

The hearts of a world suffer anguish as well).

دل و کشورت جمع و معمور باد

May your spirit be tranquil and prosperous your realm;

ز ملکت پراکندگی دور باد

And never may ruin your state overwhelm!

تنت باد پیوسته چون دین، درست

Like the Faith, may your body for ever be sound!

بداندیش را دل چو تدبیر، سست

And your foes' hearts, as weak as their counsels be found!

درونت به تأیید حق شاد باد

May your spirit be glad by the aid of the Lord!

دل و دین و اقلیمت آباد باد

On your heart, Faith, and State be prosperity poured!

جهان آفرین بر تو رحمت کناد

May the mercy of God give repose to your mind!

دگر هرچه گویم فسانه‌ست و باد

If more I should say, It would be fable and wind.

همینت بس از کردگار مجید

From the Maker sublime, this for you should suffice,

که توفیق خیرت بود بر مزید

That His grace makes your goodness continue to rise.

نرفت از جهان سعد زنگی به درد

Sad-Zangi departed this life without care,

که چون تو خلف نامبردار کرد

For he named such a famed one as you, as his heir.

عجب نیست این فرع از آن اصل پاک

Such a branch is not strange from so holy a root;

که جانش بر اوج است و جسمش به خاک

For his soul is in Heav'n and his corpse underfoot

خدایا بر آن تربت نامدار

Oh God! on the tomb of that famous one, deign

به فضلت که باران رحمت ببار

By Thy favour, a shower of mercy to rain!

گر از سعد زنگی مثل ماند یاد

If remembrance and tales of Sdd-Zangi descend,

فلک یاور سعد بوبکر باد

May Heav'n be, forever, Sad-Bu-Bakar's friend!

❁◉❁◉❁

مدح محمد بن سعد بن ابوبکر
Praise of the Prince of Islam, S ad-Bin- Abu-Bakar- Bin-Sad

جوان جوان‌بخت روشن‌ضمیر

Oh promising youth with a luminous heart!

به دولت جوان و به تدبیر پیر

Young in fortune, but old when you counsels impart

به دانش بزرگ و به همت بلند

In knowledge profound; spirit reaching the skies;

به بازو دلیر و به دل هوشمند

Intrepid in arm, and in intellect wise.

زهی دولت مادر روزگار

Well done! the good luck of the mother of Time,

که رودی چنین پرورد در کنار

Since she nursed in her bosom a son so sublime.

به دست کرم آب دریا ببرد

With his generous hand the sea's sheen he effaced,

به رفعت محل ثریا ببرد

And, in highness, the Pleiades' mansion displaced.

زهی چشم دولت به روی تو باز

How well for the monarchs, exalted in place,

سر شهریاران گردن فراز

That the eye of their fortune is fixed on your face!

صدف را که بینی ز دردانه پر

You see that the shell which with pearls is replete,

نه آن قدر دارد که یکدانه در

With one Royal pearl can't in value compete.

تو آن در مکنون یکدانه‌ای

You are that priceless pearl in its hidden retreat,

که پیرایهٔ سلطنت خانه‌ای

And an ornament bright to the Empire's fair seat

نگه دار یارب به چشم خودش

Take care of him, Lord, with Thine own guarding eye!

بپرهیز از آسیب چشم بدش

And permit not the Evil Eye's stroke to come nigh!

خدایا در آفاق نامی کنش

Oh God! through the world make him famous appear!

به توفیق طاعت گرامی کنش

By the grace of devotion, oh render him dear!

مقیمش در انصاف و تقوی بدار

In justice and grace keep him strong by Thy will!

مرادش به دنیا و عقبی برآر

In this world and the next all his wishes fulfil!

غم از دشمن ناپسندش مباد

May he never be vexed by a rancorous foe,

ز دوران گیتی گزندت مباد

And harm from the changes of Earth never know!

بهشتی درخت آورد چون تو بار

Fruit like you the rich Paradise tree has sustained;

پسر نامجوی و پدر نامدار

The son seeks a name that the father has gained.

از آن خاندان خیر بیگانه دان

Consider them strange to that household, so fair,

که باشند بدخواه این خاندان

Who to say a bad word of this household should dare!

زهی دین و دانش، زهی عدل و داد

Well done! faith and knowledge, and justice and right;

زهی ملک و دولت که پاینده باد

Well done! realm and fortune, ne'er pass from our sight

1

(CHAPTER I)

در عدل و تدبیر و رای

ON JUSTICE, WISDOM,
AND GOVERNMENT

سرآغاز
In begin

نگنجد کرمهای حق در قیاس
The extent of God's mercies no mortal can guess;
چه خدمت گزارد زبان سپاس؟
The meed of His praises what tongue can express?

خدایا تو این شاه درویش دوست
Oh God! cause this king who befriends the distressed,
که آسایش خلق در ظل اوست
And under whose shadow the people have rest,

بسی بر سر خلق پاینده دار
On the heads of the subjects for long to survive!
به توفیق طاعت دلش زنده دار
By the grace of devotion his soul keep alive!

برومند دارش درخت امید
Keep the tree of his hope bearing fruit choice to sight!
سرش سبز و رویش به رحمت سفید
Keep his head fresh! his face, in compassion, keep bright!

به راه تکلف مرو سعدیا
In the path of pretense walk not, Sádi like some;
اگر صدق داری بیار و بیا
If you harbour sincerity, bring you, and come!

تو منزل شناسی و شه راهرو
You are pious, and walking the King's road appear;
تو حقگوی و خسرو حقایق شنو
You speak truth, and to truths of the King you give ear.

چه حاجت که نه کرسی آسمان
What loss though the footstool of Heav'n you don't put
نهی زیر پای قزل ارسلان
As a rest under K'izil Arslan's royal foot!

مگو پای عزت بر افلاک نه
Do not say, "Grandeur's foot on the highest Heav'n place!"
بگو روی اخلاص بر خاک نه
But say, "On the dust put sincerity's face!"

بطاعت بنه چهره بر آستان
In obedience, your face on the threshold place low!
که این است سر جاده راستان
For this is the highway all good people go.

اگر بنده‌ای سر بر این در بنه

If you are a slave, place your head at this gate

کلاه خداوندی از سر بنه

And take from your temples the head-dress of state.

چو طاعت کنی لبس شاهی مپوش

When serving the Lord, royal robes do not wear!

چو درویش مخلص برآور خروش

Like the Dervish sincere, let your cries fill the air!

که پروردگارا توانگر تویی

You are patron of those who in riches excel;

توانا و درویش پرور تویی

And the powerful protector of paupers, as well.

نه کشور خدایم نه فرماندهم

I am lord of no country, no mandates are mine;

یکی از گدایان این درگهم

I am one of the seekers at God's holy shrine.

تو بر خیر و نیکی دهم دسترس

Arise! oh Thou Helper! and make good my heart!

وگر نه چه خیر آید از من به کس؟

Else how can I good unto others impart?

دعا کن به شب چون گدایان به سوز

Like beggars, with zeal in the night-watches pray;

اگر می‌کنی پادشاهی به روز

If you exercise royal pursuits all the day!

کمر بسته گردن کشان بر درت

The arrogant stand at your door with loins braced,

تو بر آستان عبادت سرت

Your head on the threshold of worship is placed.

زهی بندگان را خداوندگار

How well that the slaves have a lord of this kind!

خداوند را بنده حق گزار

And the Lord has a slave who is upright in mind.

❖◉❖◉❖

حکایت نشستن مردی بر پلنگ
Story of sadi seeing a man riding on a leopard

که صاحبدلی بر پلنگی نشست
From the plain of Rudbar beheld with dismay,

همی راند رهوار و ماری به دست
Someone riding a leopard and comirig my way.

یکی گفتش: ای مرد راه خدای
I was seized with such dread at this wonderful sight,

بدین ره که رفتی مرا ره نمای
That I could not move foot from the spot, out of fright

بگفت ار پلنگم زبون است و مار
Smiling sweetly, his hand to his lip he upraised,

وگر پیل و کرکس، شگفتی مدار
Saying, " Sádi, be not at this vision amazed!

تو هم گردن از حکم داور مپیچ
From the mandates of God your own neck do not turn!

که گردن نپیچد ز حکم تو هیچ
And the orders you issue no being will spurn!"

چو حاکم به فرمان داور بود
When Cyrus obeyed the Just Monarch's commands,

خدایش نگهبان و یاور بود
The Lord was his Guardian and strengthened his hands.

محال است چون دوست دارد تو را
He cannot, since you are His friend, let you go

که در دست دشمن گذارد تو را
Away from His hand to the hand of the foe.

ره این است، روی از طریقت متاب
This truly s the road, to its tenets hold fast

بنه گام و کامی که داری بیاب
Step forward, and gain what you long for, at last!

نصیحت کسی سودمند آیدش
Admonition will profit the person, indeed,

که گفتار سعدی پسند آیدش
Who approves of the w r ords that from Sádi proceed

⟨◉⟩⟨◉⟩

حکایت نصحیت نوشیروان به هرمز
Kasra's Advice to Harmuz

شنیدم که در وقت نزع روان
Naushirwan, I have heard, ere his spirit had fled,
به هرمز چنین گفت نوشیروان
The following words to Harmuz, his son, said:

که خاطر نگهدار درویش باش
Take care of the hearts of the poor and distressed!
نه در بند آسایش خویش باش
Do not be with your own selfish pleasures possessed!

نیاید به نزدیک دانا پسند
In the view of the wise it is wrong, we are told,
شبان خفته و گرگ در گوسفند
That the shepherd should sleep and a wolf in the fold.

برو پاس درویش محتاج دار
Go you and protect all the indigent poor!
که شاه از رعیت بود تاجدار
For a king through his subjects his crown must secure.

رعیت چو بیخند و سلطان درخت
Like roots are the subjects — like trees are the kings;
درخت، ای پسر، باشد از بیخ سخت
To the tree, oh, my son! the root permanence brings.

مکن تا توانی دل خلق ریش
Do not make, while you can, people wounded in soul!
وگر می‌کنی می‌کنی بیخ خویش
If you do, you but dig your own root from its hole.

اگر جاده‌ای بایدت مستقیم
If a path that is straight it behoves you to tread,
ره پارسایان امید است و بیم
The path of the pious is hope mixed with dread.

گزند کسانش نیاید پسند
He approves not of harm to the small or the great,
که ترسد که در ملکش آید گزند
Who fears that misfortune may come to his State.

وگر در سرشت وی این خوی نیست
And if in his nature this mode is not found,
در آن کشور آسودگی بوی نیست
No odour of comfort exists in that ground

اگر پای بندی رضا پیش گیر

If your feet are encumbered, to Fate be resigned;

وگر یک سواری سر خویش گیر

If free, you can wander wherever inclined.

فراخی در آن مرز و کشور مخواه

For abundance of wealth in that realm do not pray,

که دلتنگ بینی رعیت ز شاه

Where you see subjects groaning beneath the king's sway!

ز مستکبران دلاور بترس

Be afraid of the rash and the proud self-adored!

از آن کاو نترسد ز داور بترس

Be afraid of the person who fears not the Lord!

دگر کشور آباد بیند به خواب

Other realms in his sleep he sees prosperous and blessed,

که دارد دل اهل کشور خراب

Who keeps all the hearts in his country. distressed.

خرابی و بدنامی آید ز جور

Decay and ill-fame by oppression are brought;

رسد پیش بین این سخن را به غور

The sages have found out this saying by thought

رعیت نشاید به بیداد کشت

You ought not your subjects unjustly to slay;

که مر سلطنت را پناهند و پشت

For they are the Empire's protection and stay.

مراعات دهقان کن از بهر خویش

For the sake of yourself, show the peasant respect!

که مزدور خوشدل کند کار بیش

For a labourer pleased works with greater effect.

مروت نباشد بدی با کسی

To injure a man is ungenerous and mean,

کز او نیکویی دیده باشی بسی

For his kindness you many a time may have seen."

◆⦿◆⦿◆

حکایت نصحیت خسرو به شیرویه
Khusrau's Advice to Sheroya

شنیدم که خسرو به شیرویه گفت
I have heard that Khusrau, ere his eyes closed in death,
در آن دم که چشمش زدیدن بخفت
Thus Sheroya addressed with his last parting breath:

بر آن باش تا هرچه نیت کنی
So live, that whatever may be your intent,
نظر در صلاح رعیت کنی
Your glance on the good of your subjects is bent!

الا تا نپیچی سر از عدل و رای
True wisdom and knowledge, oh son, do not spurn!
که مردم ز دستت نپیچند پای
That men from your orders their feet may not turn."

گریزد رعیت ز بیدادگر
From oppressors the subjects take refuge in flight,
کند نام زشتش به گیتی سمر
And revile them abroad in their stories at night.

بسی بر نیاید که بنیاد خود
But a very short time sees the structure effaced
بکند آن که بنهاد بنیاد بد
Of him who an evil foundation has placed.

خرابی کند مرد شمشیر زن
The tiger and swordsman can't make such a wild,
نه چندان که دود دل طفل و زن
As that from the heart-sighs of woman and child.

چراغی که بیوه زنی برفروخت
The lamp which the poor widow woman illumed,
بسی دیده باشی که شهری بسوخت
You may often have seen, has a city consumed.

از آن بهره‌ورتر در آفاق کیست
In the regions of Earth, who more favour has gained
که در ملکرانی به انصاف زیست
Than he, who in justice has lived and has reigned?

چو نوبت رسد زین جهان غریبتش
When his time for departing this life comes about,
ترحم فرستند بر تربتش
"On his tomb vouchsafe mercy "the people will shout.

بد و نیک مردم چو می‌بگذرند

Since the good and the wicked must pass as they came,

همان به که نامت به نیکی برند

It is well when with goodness they mention your name.

خداترس را بر رعیت گمار

A God-fearing man for your subjects select;

که معمار ملک است پرهیزگار

For a continent man is the realm's architect.

بد اندیش توست آن و خونخوار خلق

He who in men's harm seeks to furnish your purse,

که نفع تو جوید در آزار خلق

Is your own wicked foe and the people's worst curse.

ریاست به دست کسانی خطاست

It is wrong to bestow upon persons command,

که از دستشان دستها برخداست

From whose tyrannous acts men to God stretch their hand.

نکوکارپرور نبیند بدی

The patron of acts that are good sees no guile;

چو بد پروری خصم خون خودی

You're the foe of your life when you cherish the vile.

مکافات موذی به مالش مکن

In revenging a foe confiscation won't suit;

که بیخش برآورد باید ز بن

It behoves you to tear up his stem from the root.

مکن صبر بر عامل ظلم دوست

With a tyrannous agent you should not delay!}

که از فریبی بایدش کند پوست

For because of his fatness, his skin you must flay!

سر گرگ باید هم اول برید

It is requisite first to cut off the wolfs head,

نه چون گوسفندان مردم درید

Not after he has in the flock havoc spread.

❖◉❖◉❖

حکایت بازرگان و دزدان
Story of the merchant and robbers

چه خوش گفت بازارگانی اسیر

How well spoke the merchant, a prisoner bound,

چو گردش گرفتند دزدان به تیر

While spear-bearing robbers were standing around

چو مردانگی آید از رهزنان

When in highwaymen courage arises, ah, then!

چه مردان لشکر، چه خیل زنان

What avail troops of women and armies of men?"

شهنشه که بازارگان را بخست

The monarch who brings on a merchant distress,

در خیر بر شهر و لشکر ببست

On the city and troops shuts the door of success.

کی آن جا دگر هوشمندان روند

When again will the wise in that kingdom appear,

چو آوازهٔ رسم بد بشنوند؟

Where the noise of bad actions alone they can hear?

نکو بایدت نام و نیکی قبول

you must win a good name and must goodness elect,

نکو دار بازارگان و رسول

And the merchant and messenger, likewise, protect!

بزرگان مسافر به جان پرورند

The Great show for travelers solicitous care,

که نام نکویی به عالم برند

That their name linked with praise through the world they may bear.

تبه گردد آن مملکت عن قریب

Very soon will the kingdom experience decay,

کز او خاطر آزرده آید غریب

From which the poor stranger heart grieved comes away.

غریب آشنا باش و سیاح دوست

Be the stranger's companion and traveller's friend

که سیاح جلاب نام نکوست

For a traveler will cause a good name to extend.

نکو دار ضیف و مسافر عزیز

Show respect to a guest and the pilgrims revere;

وز آسیبشان بر حذر باش نیز

From their miseries, likewise, preserve yourself clear!

ز بیگانه پرهیز کردن نکوست

From a stranger's regard it is well to abstain;

که دشمن توان بود در زی دوست

For a foe can the look of a friend eas'ly feign.

قدیمان خود را بیفزای قدر

The rank of your aged retainers upraise-!

که هرگز نیاید ز پرورده غدر

For those you have reared never show rebel ways.

چو خدمتگزاریت گردد کهن

When the sign of old age on your servant appears,

حق سالیانش فرامش مکن

Forget not the right that is due to his years!

گر او را هرم دست خدمت ببست

If age has the hand of his usefulness bound,

تو را بر کرم همچنان دست هست

With you a rich hand showing kindness is found.

حکایت شاپور
Story of Shapur

شنیدم که شاپور دم در کشید

I have heard that Shapur very silent became,

چو خسرو به رسمش قلم در کشید

When the monarch Khusrau drew his pen through hi name.

چو شد حالش از بینوایی تباه

When his state was, from poverty, ruined and low,

نبشت این حکایت به نزدیک شاه

The following story he wrote to Khusrau:

چو بذل تو کردم جوانی خویش

Since under your shadow my youth I have passed

به هنگام پیری مرانم ز پیش

In old age, from your sight do not drive me at last!

غریبی که پر فتنه باشد سرش

The stranger, with mischievous thoughts in his head,

میازار و بیرون کن از کشورش

Do not hurt! but expel from the country, instead.

تو گر خشم بروی نگیری رواست

It is well, if to show him your wrath you are slack,

که خود خوی بد دشمنش در قفاست

For his own wicked mind is a foe at his back

وگر پارسی باشدش زاد بوم

If a native of Persia he happen to be,

به صنعاش مفرست و سقلاب و روم

Don't to Rum or Sanaa or Saklab make him flee!

هم آن جا امانش مده تا به چاشت

Even there, let his life not till breakfast time last!

نشاید بلا بر دگر کس گماشت

It is wrong an affliction on others to cast!

که گویند برگشته باد آن زمین

For they'll say, " May the land suffer ruin and rout,

کز او مردم آیند بیرون چنین

From which such a man is allowed to come out!

عمل گر دهی مرد منعم شناس

When rule you confer, a rich person secure!

که مفلس ندارد ز سلطان هراس

For no fear of the king has the man who is poor.

چو مفلس فرو برد گردن به دوش

When a needy one's neck on his shoulder must lie

از او بر نیاید دگر جز خروش

Nothing comes from him afterwards, saving a cry.

چو مشرف دو دست از امانت بداشت

When a Treasurer's hands to his trust are untrue,

بباید بر او ناظری برگماشت

You must send an Inspector to keep him in view;

ور او نیز در ساخت با خاطرش

And if he, too, a facile accomplice should prove,

ز مشرف عمل بر کن و ناظرش

The Collector and Spy from their charges remove.

خدا ترس باید امانت گزار

A man who fears God, to his charge will be just;

امین کز تو ترسد امینش مدار

The minister fearing yourself, do not trust!

بیفشان و بشمار و فارغ نشین

Give money and reckon and vigilant be!

که از صد یکی را نبینی امین

In a hundred, one faithful you rarely will see.

دو همجنس دیرینه را هم‌قلم

Two old, kindred spirits, who show the same bent,

نباید فرستاد یک به جا هم

To the same place, together, should never be sent!

چه دانی که همدست گردند و یار

How know you that they are not partners in cant;

یکی دزد باشد، یکی پرده‌دار

One a thief, and the other a thief s confidant?

چو دزدان ز هم باک دارند و بیم

When thieves among themselves, yield to terror and fear,

رود در میان کاروانی سلیم

Through the midst of them passes the caravan clear.

یکی را که معزول کردی ز جاه

If you've turned out of office a man for a crime,

چو چندی برآید ببخشش گناه

Forgive his offence, in a moderate time!

بر آوردن کام امیدوار

To accomplish the wish of a faithful one's heart,

به از قید بندی شکستن هزار

Is better than thousands of fetters to part.

نویسنده را گر سُتون عمل

Make a trusty accountant the prop of your sway;

بیفتد، نبرد طناب امل

He falls not, and cuts' not hope's tent-ropes away.

به فرمانبران بر شه دادگر

The king who is just to the Pillars of State,

پدروار خشم آورد بر پسر

Like a father with son, now and then is irate.

گهش می‌زند تا شود دردناک

t one time he beats him, till pain through him flies,

گهی می‌کند آبش از دیده پاک

At another, he brings the pure tears from his eyes.

چو نرمی کنی خصم گردد دلیر

When you exercise mildness, your foe becomes brave;

وگر خشم گیری شوند از تو سیر

And when you show ire he submits like a slave.

درشتی و نرمی به هم در به است

Severity tempered with mildness is wise;

چو رگ‌زن که جراح و مرهم نه است

Like the surgeon who cuts and the plaster applies.

جوانمرد و خوش خوی و بخشنده باش

Intrepid, good-natured, and liberal be!

چو حق بر تو پاشد تو بر خلق پاش

And sprinkle on all, since God sprinkles on thee.

همین نقش بر خوان پس از عهد خویش

When you think of the reigns of the monarchs of yore,

که دیدی پس از عهد شاهان پیش

Think the same picture yours, when your regnum is o'er.

نیامد کس اندر جهان کاو بماند

No person who entered this world has remained,

مگر آن کز او نام نیکو بماند

Save the man whose good name in the world is retained.

نمرد آن که ماند پس از وی به جای

He died not who left, as a pledge in his place,

پل و خانی و خان و مهمان سرای

A bridge, well, or alms-house, or inn for his race.

هر آن کاو نماند از پسش یادگار

When a man does not leave a memorial behind,

درخت وجودش نیاورد بار

His tree of existence you fruitless will find.

وگر رفت و آثار خیرش نماند

If he went and no offerings nor good left instead,

نشاید پس مرگش الحمد خواند

The " Al-hamd" on his dying ought not to be read!

چو خواهی که نامت بود جاودان

When you wish that your name in the world may endure,

مکن نام نیک بزرگان نهان

The renown of your ancestors do not obscure!

همین کام و ناز و طرب داشتند
The self-same desires, airs, and joys they held fast;
به آخر برفتند و بگذاشتند
They departed and left them behind them, at last.

یکی نام نیکو ببرد از جهان
One man from the world bears a name that is dear;
یکی رسم بد ماند از او جاودان
To another, vile customs forever adhere.

به سمع رضا مشنو ایذای کس
The ear of consent, to one's harm, do not lend!
وگر گفته آید به غورش برس
And if talk you should hear, think of how to befriend!

گنهکار را عذر نسیان بنه
The culprit's pretexts, to oblivion let go!
چو زنهار خواهند زنهار ده
If he asks your protection, protection bestow!

گر آید گنهکاری اندر پناه
If a sinner is able a refuge to win,
نه شرط است کشتن به اول گناه
It is unlawful to kill for the very first sin.

چو باری بگفتند و نشنید پند
If you threaten him once and he scouts all advice,
بده گوشمالش به زندان و بند
Give him prison and bonds if he dares to sin twice!

وگر بند و بندش نیاید بکار
And if bonds and advice are not likely to suit,
درختی خبیث است بیخش برآر
He's a very bad tree, dig him up by the root!

چو خشم آیدت بر گناه کسی
When you feel very angry at any one's crime,
تأمل کنش در عقوبت بسی
Before you chastise him, delay for a time!

که سهل است لعل بدخشان شکست
You can fracture a Badakhshati ruby in two,
شکسته نشاید دگرباره بست
But you cannot repair it again, if you do.

◈◉◈◉◈

حکایت در تدبیر و تأخیر در سیاست
Story on practicing delay in punishment

ز دریای عمان برآمد کسی
From the sea of Uman, once a traveler came.
سفر کرده هامون و دریا بسی
Who had crossed seas and deserts, too numerous to name.

عرب دیده و ترک و تاجیک و روم
Turk, Arab, and Persian and Greek he had seen;
ز هر جنس در نفس پاکش علوم
Every science was known to his intellect keen.

جهان گشته و دانش اندوخته
He had walked round the world and enlightenment gained;
سفر کرده و صحبت آموخته
He had wandered a deal and refinement obtained.

به هیکل قوی چون تناور درخت
Like the trunk of a tree, his appearance was strong
ولیکن فرو مانده بی برگ سخت
But, feeble from want, he could scarce crawl along.

دو صد رقعه بالای هم دوخته
Two hundred charred patches, together, are sewn,
ز حراق و او در میان سوخته
And he being burned in betwixt them is shown.

به شهری در آمد ز دریا کنار
From the side of the sea to a city he came,
بزرگی در آن ناحیت شهریار
In a land where the king bore an excellent name;

که طبعی نکونامی اندیش داشت
With a nature desirous of good he was graced,
سر عجز در پای درویش داشت
And his head at the feet of the Dervish he placed.

بشستند خدمتگزاران شاه
The royal attendants got ready a bath;
سر و تن به حمامش از گرد راه
From his body and head washed the dust of the path

چو بر آستان ملک سر نهاد
When upon the kin's threshold his forehead he pressed;
نیایش کنان دست بر بر نهاد
According him praise, with his hands on his breast;

درآمد به ایوان شاهنشهی

He entered the emperor's palace and gave:

که بختت جوان باد و دولت رهی

May your fortune be youthful! may wealth be your slave!

نرفتم در این مملکت منزلی

At each stage in the realm, where I happened to rest,

کز آسیب آزرده دیدم دلی

Not a heart did I see from affliction distressed.

ملک را همین ملک پیرایه بس

To a realm such a king is an ornament rare,

که راضی نگرد به آزار کس

For he likes not that any should suffering bear."

ندیدم کسی سرگران از شراب

Not a person I saw, with head heavy from wine,

مگر هم خرابات دیدم خراب

But the taverns, I saw in a state of decline.

سخن گفت و دامان گوهر فشاند

He discoursed and the gemmed skirt of Wisdom let loose;

به نطقی که شه آستین برفشاند

Such his speech that the king uttered praises profuse.

پسند آمدش حسن گفتار مرد

At the man's pleasant speaking much pleasure he showed;

به نزد خودش خواند و اکرام کرد

He called him beside him and honour bestowed.

زرش داد و گوهر به شکر قدوم

For his coming gave money and jewels of worth;

بپرسیدش از گوهر و زاد و بوم

Asked concerning his tribe and the place of his birth.

بگفت آنچه پرسیدش از سرگذشت

Regarding his life, he disclosed what was asked;

به قربت ز دیگر کسان برگذشت

In the king's estimation, all others he passed.

ملک با دل خویش باگفت وگو

To the mind of the monarch the thought became clear:

که دست وزارت سپارد بدو

"A person like this ought to be my vizier.

وليكن بتدريج تا انجمن

And yet, by degrees, lest the chiefs of the Court,

به سستی نخندند بر رای من

In ignorance, over my wisdom should sport.

به عقلش بباید نخست آزمود

To begin with, his skill must be tested, at least,

به قدر هنر پایگاهش فزود

And befitting his merit, his rank be increased"

برد بر دل از جور غم بارها

By oppression, he bears loads of grief on his heart,

که نا آزموده کند کارها

Who engages in schemes without knowing each part.

چو قاضی به فکرت نویسد سجل

When a judge writes with care every case that he tries,

نگردد ز دستاربندان خجل

He feels not ashamed before men who are wise.

نظر کن چو سوفار داری به شست

While the arrow is held in the thumb-stall, aim right!

نه آنگه که پرتاب کردی ز دست

Not after you've sent the winged shaft on its flight

چو یوسف کسی در صلاح و تمیز

A person like Joseph, discreet and sincere,

به یک سال باید که گردد عزیز

In the space of a year should become a vizier.

به ایام تا بر نیاید بسی

Should the strife with adversity prove to be brief,

نشاید رسیدن به غور کسی

It is needless to fret about any one's grief.

ز هر نوع اخلاق او کشف کرد

His habits he opened completely to view;

خردمند و پاکیزه دین بود مرد

Found the man to be wise and his faith to be true.

نکو سیرتش دید و روشن قیاس

He found him good-natured; sagacious, as well;

سخن سنج و مقدار مردم شناس

That he measured his words and a man's worth could tell.

به رای از بزرگان مهش دید و بیش
When in wisdom he saw not a courtier his peer,
نشاندش زیردست دستور خویش
He placed him in office above his vizier.

چنان حکمت و معرفت کار بست
Such science and knowledge he brought into play,
که از امر و نهیش درونی نخست
That a heart was not grieved by his absolute sway.

در آورد ملکی به زیر قلم
He brought under rule of the king a domain,
کز او بر وجودی نیامد الم
In a way that no person experienced a pain.

زبان همه حرف گیران ببست
On the tongues of all critics he fastened a band;
که حرفی بدش بر نیامد ز دست
For a letter corrupt did not come from his hand

حسودی که یک جو خیانت ندید
The envier who saw not one grain of deceit,
به کارش نیامد چو گندم تپید
Without benefit toiled, like the fluttering wheat

ز روشن دلش ملک پرتو گرفت
The king from his luminous heart took a ray
وزیر کهن را غم نو گرفت
Which caused in the oustd vizier fresh dismay.

ندید آن خردمند را رخنه‌ای
Not a flaw could he see in that sensible man,
که در وی تواند زدن طعنه‌ای
In order to fasten upon him a ban.

امین و بد اندیش طشتند و مور
The trusty and vile, are the basin and ant;
نشاید در او رخنه کردن به زور
The ant tries its utmost to crack it, but can't!

ملک را دو خورشید طلعت غلام
Two sunny-faced striplings the monarch possessed,
به سر بر، کمر بسته بودی مدام
Who were always at hand to obey each behest.

دو پاکیزه پیکر چو حور و پری

Like Houri and Fairy, two faces so fair;

چو خورشید و ماه از سدیگر بری

Like the sun and the moon, not a third could compare.

دو صورت که گفتی یکی نیست بیش

Two such figures, that neither could preference claim;

نموده در آیینه همتای خویش

In a mirror, appearing exactly the same.

سخنهای دانای شیرین سخن

The words of the sage of mellifluous speech,

گرفت اندر آن هر دو شمشاد بن

In the hearts of the two charming youths made a breach.

چو دیدند کاوصاف و خلقش نکوس

When they saw in his nature good qualities rise,

به طبعش هواخواه گشتند و دوست

In their hearts they became his well-wishing allies.

در او هم اثر کرد میل بشر

The love of mankind, too, on him had effect;

نه میلی چو کوتاه‌بینان به شر

Not the love the shortsighted with vileness connect.

از آسایش آنگه خبر داشتی

For whenever their faces attracted his sight,

که در روی ایشان نظر داشتی

He was conscious, at once, of a tranquil delight.

چو خواهی که قدرت بماند بلند

If you wish that your worth may not be on the wane,

دل، ای خواجه، در ساده رویان مبند

From loving smooth faces, oh master, refrain!

وگر خود نباشد غرض در میان

And although you are free from a lustful design,

حذر کن که دارد به هیبت زیان

Take care, lest your dignity suffer decline

وزیر اندر این شمه‌ای راه برد

The vizier got an inkling regarding the thing,

به خبث این حکایت بر شاه برد

And wickedly carried this tale to the king:

که این را ندانم چه خوانند و کیست

"What they call him, I know not, nor who he may be;

نخواهد به سامان در این ملک زیست

In this country he lives not as suits his degree.

سفر کردگان لاابالی زیند

All those who have travelled live fearless of fate;

که پروردهٔ ملک و دولت نیند

For they have not been nurtured by monarch or State.

شنیدم که با بندگانش سر است

I have heard that to slaves his affections incline;

خیانت پسند است و شهوت پرست

That he favours foul treason and worships lust's shrine.

نشاید چنین خیره روی تباه

It is wrong that so shameless and ruined a wretch,

که بد نامی آرد در ایوان شاه

Disgrace to the halls of the monarch should fetch.

مگر نعمت شه فرامش کنم

Of the king's gracious acts I'd forgetful remain,

که بینم تباهی و خامش کنم

Did I look on dishonour and silence maintain.

به پندار نتوان سخن گفت زود

Do not think that I could not have told you before!

نگفتم تو را تا یقینم نبود

Not a word have I said till convinced, more and more.

ز فرمانبرانم کسی گوش داشت

One among my attendants beheld what took place,

که آغوش را اندر آغوش داشت

That he clasped two, as one, in his wanton embrace.

من این گفتم اکنون ملک راست رای

I have told, and the monarch can judge for the best;

چو من آزمودم تو نیز آزمای

Such as I have examined, do you also test! "

به ناخوب تر صورتی شرح داد

In a nastier manner he argued like this:

که بد مرد را نیکروزی مباد

"May a wicked man's end have no odour of bliss!

بداندیش بر خرده چون دست یافت

When the evil disposed o'er a spark get command,

درون بزرگان به آتش بتافت

The hearts of the noble are burned with their brand.

به خرده توان آتش افروختن

You may kindle a fire with a spark from a torch;

پس آنگه درخت کهن سوختن

And when it is done, the old tree you can scorch."

ملک را چنان گرم کرد این خبر

This news made the monarch so fiery and red,

که جوشش برآمد چو مرجل به سر

That a burning, as sharp as a scythe, reached his head.

غضب دست در خون درویش داشت

Fierce Rage held its hand in the Dervish's gore

ولیکن سکون دست در پیش داشت

Yet Forbearance extended its hand out before:

که پرورده کشتن نه مردی بود

"To kill one you've reared is not manly nor bold;

ستم در پی داد، سردی بود

And oppression succeeding to justice, is cold.

میازار پروردهٔ خویشتن

Do not injure the person brought up in your sway;

چو تیر تو دارد به تیرش مزن

Smite him not with an arrow, since you are his stay!

به نعمت نبایست پروردنش

To rear him in favour is wrong, I should think,

چو خواهی به بیداد خون خوردنش

If you mean, by injustice, his life's blood to drink.

از او تا هنرها یقینت نشد

Until you were sure that his merits were sound,

در ایوان شاهی قرینت نشد

In the Royal apartments no favour he found

کنون تا یقینت نگردد گناه

So now, till his vices for certain you know,

به گفتار دشمن گزندش مخواه

Desire not his hurt, on the word of a foe! "

ملک در دل این راز پوشیده داشت

The king kept this secret concealed in his heart;

که قول حکیمان نیوشیده داشت

For he treasured the sayings which sages impart

دل است، ای خردمند، زندان راز

The prison of secrets, oh sage, is the mind!

چو گفتی نیاید به زنجیر باز

When you've spoken, you cannot the words again bind.

نظر کرد پوشیده در کار مرد

Every act of the man the king secretly spied;

خلل دید در رای هشیار مرد

In the wary one's mind a defect he descried;

که ناگه نظر زی یکی بنده کرد

For he suddenly cast on a stripling his eye,

پری چهره در زیر لب خنده کرد

And the " fairy face," furtively, smiled in reply.

دو کس را که با هم بود جان و هوش

When with soul and with life two, together, are bound,

حکایت کنانند و ایشان خموش

They are telling fine tales, though they utter no sound.

چو دیده به دیدار کردی دلیر

The lover, you know, seems, when under love's will,

نگردی چو مستسقی از دجله سیر

Like the dropsical man whom the Tigris can't fill.

ملک را گمان بدی راست شد

The king was convinced of the guilt of the sage.

ز سودا بر او خشمگین خواست شد

In a frenzy, he wished to give vent to his rage;

هم از حسن تدبیر و رای تمام

But with beauty of counsel and wisdom, the same;

به آهستگی گفتش ای نیک نام

He slowly addressed him: — " Oh man, of good name!

تو را من خردمند پنداشتم

I thought you were wise, and was perfectly sure

بر اسرار مملکت امین داشتم

That the secrets of State in your hands were secure.

گمان بردمت زیرک و هوشمند

I fancied you shrewd and intelligent, too;

ندانستمت خیره و ناپسند

I thought you not wicked and loathsome to view.

چنین مرتفع پایه جای تو نیست

You do not deserve a position so fine.

گناه از من آمد خطای تو نیس

The sin is not yours, but the blunder is mine;

که چون بدگهر پرورم لاجرم

For, no doubt, if I foster a villanous wight,

خیانت روا داردم در حرم

In my private affairs he'll think perfidy right."

برآورد سر مرد بسیاردان

The man of great knowledge erected his head,

چنین گفت با خسرو کاردان

And thus to the ruler sagacious he said:

مرا چون بود دامن از جرم پاک

"Since my skirt from the staining of guilt is quite clear,

نباشد ز خبث بداندیش باک

From wicked maligners, I harbour no fear.

به خاطر درم هرگز این ظن نرفت

My heart never nurtured a purpose so base;

ندانم که گفت آنچه بر من نرفت

I know not who told what has not taken place."

شهنشاه گفت: آنچه گفتم برت

The monarch, perplexed, said: — " Behold, the vizier!

بگویند خصمان به روی اندرت

Do not think to evade! Show no subterfuge here!

تسبم کنان دست بر لب گرفت

His hand caught his lips, as a smile on them played:

کز او هر چه آید نیاید شگفت

Whatever he states does not make me dismayed.

حسودی که بیند به جای خودم

The envious man, seeing me in his place,

کجا بر زبان آورد جز بدم

Could not say aught about me but words that disgrace.

من آن ساعت انگاشتم دشمنش

I thought him my foe at the very same hour

که بنشاند شه زیردست منش

That the monarch appointed him under my Power.

چو سلطان فضیلت نهد بر ویم

When the sultan confers on me favour, alack!

ندانی که دشمن بود در پیم؟

He is not aware of the foe at my back.

مرا تا قیامت نگیرد به دوست

Till the great resurrection, me, friend, he won't call,

چو بیند که در عز من ذل اوست

Since in my elevation he sees his own fall.

بر اینت بگویم حدیثی درست

On this subject a suitable tale I'll relate,

اگر گوش با بنده داری نخست

If you kindly will hear what your slave has to state."

❖◉❖◉❖

حکایت ابلیس در خواب یک شخص
Story of Satan appears to a man in a dream

ندانم کجا دیده‌ام در کتاب
I do not know where I saw in the book

که ابلیس را دید شخصی به خواب
Someone saw in a dream the malevolent one;

به بالا صنوبر، به دیدن چو حور
In stature a cypress; in visage a Houri.

چو خورشیدش از چهره می‌تافت نور
Light shines from her face like the sun

تو کاین روی داری به حسن قمر
He viewed him. " Oh peer of the moon," he then cried,

چرا در جهانی به زشتی سمر؟
With no news of your beauty are people supplied.

چرا نقش بندت در ایوان شاه
And depict you as ugly, on bath-chamber walls."

دژم روی کرده‌ست و زشت و تباه؟
They fancy you having a face that appals,

که ای نیکبخت این نه شکل من است
The Devil said, smiling, " My form is not so;

ولیکن قلم در کف دشمن است
But the pencil is held in the hand of my foe.

مرا همچنین نام نیک است لیک
Though I, in like manner, possess a good name,

ز علت نگوید بداندیش نیک
My foe out of malice refuses my claim.

وزیری که جاه من آبش بریخت
Since my dignity caused the vizier's overthrow,

به فرسنگ باید ز مکرش گریخت
A league from his frauds it behoves me to go.

ولیکن نیندیشم از خشم شاه
But the wrath of the king does not terrify me;

دلاور بود در سخن، بی‌گناه
For bold is the speech that from baseness is free.

اگر محتسب گردد آن را غم است
When the chief of police goes his rounds, he is sad

که سنگ ترازوی بارش کم است
Whose weighing arrangements are found to be bad."

67

چو حرفم برآید درست از قلم

Since my letters all issue correct from the pen,

مرا از همه حرف گیران چه غم؟

Why should I be grieved about fault-finding men?

ملک در سخن گفتنش خیره ماند

At his speaking the king's equanimity fled;

سر دست فرماندهی برفشاند

Snapping Sovereignty's fingers in anger, he said:

که مجرم به زرق و زبان آوری

"The culprit with cant and glib words that allure,

ز جرمی که دارد نگردد بری

From his guiltiness cannot expect to be pure.

ز خصمت همانا که نشنیده‌ام

The same that I heard from your foe with surprise,

نه آخر به چشم خودم دیده‌ام؟

At last, I have seen you perform with my eyes.

کز این زمره خلق در بارگاه

For at Court in the circle of people around,

نمی‌باشدت جز در اینان نگاه

Your gaze on these slaves, and none other, is found."

بخندید مرد سخنگوی و گفت

he man of rare eloquence smiled and thus spoke:

حق است این سخن، حق نشاید نهفت

his is true: and the truth it is needless to cloak.

در این نکته‌ای هست اگر بشنوی

There's a meaning in this, if attention you pay;

که حکمت روان باد و دولت قوی

Obeyed be your orders and strong be your sway!

نبینی که درویش بی دستگاه

Don't you see that the pauper in indigent plight,

به حسرت کند در توانگر نگاه

With regret on the opulent fixes his sight?

مرا دستگاه جوانی برفت

My vigour of youth has departed at last;

به لهو و لعب زندگانی برفت

In sporting and playing my life has been passed.

ز دیدار اینان ندارم شکیب

As I gaze on these two, no endurance have!

که سرمایه داران حسنند و زیب

For the sources of beauty and grace in them lie.

مرا همچنین چهره گلفام بود

A similar rose-coloured face I did own

بلورینم از خوبی اندام بود

Like the purest of crystal my body, once, shone.

در این غایتم رشت باید کفن

But now, it behoves me my shroud thread to spin;

که مویم چو پنبهست و دوکم بدن

For like cotton's my hair, and I'm spindle-like thin.

مرا همچنین جعد شبرنگ بود

Such night-tinted curls I at one time possessed,

قبا در بر از فریهی تنگ بود

And my elegant coat fitted tight to my breast.

دو رسته درم در دهن داشت جای

Two strings of fine pearls in my mouth held a place

چو دیواری از خشت سیمین بپای

Like a wall made of bricks with a silvery base.

کنونم نگه کن به وقت سخن

And look at me now! While to speak I make bold,

بیفتاده یک یک چو سور کهن

These have fallen one by one, like a bridge become old.

در اینان به حسرت چرا ننگرم؟

Why should I not look with regret on these two,

که عمر تلف کرده یاد آورم

Since the life I have wrecked they recall to my view?

برفت از من آن روزهای عزیز

Those days that wTere dear have away from me flown,

به پایان رسد ناگه این روز نیز

And the end of this day, too, has suddenly shown."

چو دانشور این در معنی بسفت

When this pearl, full of meaning, the sage had pierced through

بگفت این کز این به محال است گفت

"Than this," said the king, "none can utter more true."

در ارکان دولت نگه کرد شاه

The king on his Pillars of State fixed his eyes,

کز این خوبتر لفظ و معنی مخواه

Saying "Ask not for language and meaning more wise!

کسی را نظر سوی شاهد رواست

It is meet that a man on a charmer should gaze,

که داند بدین شاهدی عذر خواست

Who knows of such proofs to account for his ways.

به عقل ار نه آهستگی کردمی

By Wisdom, I swear! if I had not been slow,

به گفتار خصمش بیازردمی

I'd have punished him now, on the word of his foe.

به تندی سبک دست بردن به تیغ

He who hurriedly seizes the sword in a pet,

به دندان برد پشت دست دریغ

Bites the back of his hand with the teeth of regret.

ز صاحب غرض تا سخن نشنوی

To the talk of the interested, do not give ear!

که گر کار بندی پشیمان شوی

If you take their advice, your repentance is near.

نکونام را جاه و تشریف و مال

The position and wealth of the man of good name

بیفزود و، بدگوی را گوشمال

He increased, and the slanderer suffered more shame.

به تدبیر دستور دانشورش

By attending to what his wise counsellor said,

به نیکی بشد نام در کشورش

With goodness his name through his kingdom soon spread.

به عدل و کرم سالها ملک راند

Many years he with kindness and equity reigned;

برفت و نکونامی از وی بماند

He died and his good reputation remained.

چنین پادشاهان که دین پرورند

Such monarchs who foster the Faith in their sway,

به بازوی دین، گوی دولت برند

By the arm of the Faith, Fortune's ball bear away.

از آنان نبینم در این عهد کس

Of these in this age not a person I see;

وگر هست بوبکر سعد است و بس

If one lives — only Bu-Bakar-Sa'd he can be:

بهشتی درختی تو، ای پادشاه

Oh king, you're the tree which doth Paradise grace!

که افکنده‌ای سایه یک ساله راه

Whose shadow falls over a marvelous space!

طمع بود از بخت نیک اخترم

In my fortunate star, the desire I have fed,

که بال همای افکند بر سرم

That the wing of the Simurgh might soar o'er my head.

خرد گفت دولت نبخشد همای

Said Wisdom " The Simurgh none wealthy has made

گر اقبال خواهی در این سایه آی

If you wish to be prosperous, come under this shade! "

خدایا به رحمت نظر کرده‌ای

Oh God, a most merciful look Thou hast shown,

که این سایه بر خلق گسترده‌ای

Since over the people this shade Thou hast thrown.

دعاگوی این دولتم بنده‌وار

For this state of prosperity, slave-like, I pray:

خدایا تو این سایه پاینده دار

Oh God! never take this good shadow away! "

صواب است پیش از کشش بند کرد

It is just ere you kill to confine for a space;

که نتوان سر کشته پیوند کرد

For the head that is severed you cannot replace.

خداوند فرمان و رای و شکوه

The Lord of all wisdom and pomp and command,

ز غوغای مردم نگردد ستوه

From the clamour of man shows not weakness of hand.

سر پر غرور از تحمل تهی

To the arrogant head, of forbearance bereft,

حرامش بود تاج شاهنشهی

It is wrong that the crown of a king should be left

نگویم چو جنگ آوری پای دار

When you're warlike, I do not say, hold by your own

چو خشم آیدت عقل بر جای دار

But, when you are angry, let wisdom be shown!

تحمل کند هر که را عقل هست

Whoever has wisdom can patience display

نه عقلی که خشمش کند زیردست

Not the wisdom that anger can hold in its sway.

چو لشکر برون تاخت خشم از کمین

When the army drove Anger, from ambush to light,

نه انصاف ماند نه تقوی نه دین

Faith, Justice and Piety vanished from sight.

ندیدم چنین دیو زیر فلک

Such a demon as this, I've not seen 'neath the sky,

که از وی گریزند چندین ملک

From whom such an army of angels should fly.

گفتار اندر بخشایش بر ضعیفان
Story on mercy to the weak

نه بر حکم شرع آب خوردن خطاست
To drink water is wrong should the law not permit;
وگر خون به فتوی بریزی رواست
And if blood you should shed by the law, it is fit.

که را شرع فتوی دهد بر هلاک
If the law should decide that 'tis proper to slay,
الا تا نداری ز کشتنش باک
Take care, that in killing no fear you display!

وگر دانی اندر تبارش کسان
If some of the criminal's household you know,
بر ایشان ببخشای و راحت رسان
Award to them freely, and comfort bestow!

گنه بود مرد ستمکاره را
For the man who committed the crime is to blame
چه تاوان زن و طفل بیچاره را؟
What have wife and poor children done, meriting shame?

تنت زورمند است و لشکر گران
Though your body be strong and your army be great,
ولیکن در اقلیم دشمن مران
Do not march with your troops through an enemy's state

که وی بر حصاری گریزد بلند
For he to a strong, lofty fortress will fly,
رسد کشوری بی گنه را گزند
And harm to the guiltless dominion comes nigh.

نظر کن در احوال زندانیان
Examine the men who in dungeons are bound!
که ممکن بود بی‌گنه در میان
For among them an innocent man may be found.

چو بازارگان در دیارت بمرد
If a merchant should happen to die in your land,
به مالش خساست بود دستبرد
It would be meanness to lay on his riches a hand!

کز آن پس که بر وی بگریند زار
For afterwards those who lament for him sore,
به هم باز گویند خویش و تبار
His household and friends, will repeat o'er and o'er:

که مسکین در اقلیم غربت بمرد

This luckless one died in a far distant land,

متاعی کز او ماند ظالم ببرد

And his chattels were seized by the tyrant's mean hand."

بیندیش از آن طفلک بی پدر

Let that fatherless child of your thoughts have a share

وز آه دل دردمندش حذر

Of the sighs from his heart, full of anguish, beware!

بسا نام نیکوی پنجاه سال

There are many good names with a fifty years' root,

که یک نام زشتش کند پایمال

That one mention of evil will hurl under foot.

پسندیده کاران جاوید نام

Agreeable rulers, with permanent names,

تطاول نکردند بر مال عام

On the people's effects make no tyrannous claims.

بر آفاق اگر سر به سر پادشاست

Should a man rule the world from the East to the West,

چو مال از توانگر ستاند گداست

And plunder the rich, he's a beggar at best.

بمرد از تهیدستی آزاد مرد

The generous man went, from poverty, hence;

ز پهلوی مسکین شکم پر نکرد

He filled not his paunch at the pauper's expense.

◆◉◆◆◉◆

در معنی شفقت بر حال رعیت
Story on sympathy for subjects

شنیدم که فرماندهی دادگر
I have heard that a king who was just and devout,
قبا داشتی هر دو روی آستر
Had a cloak, having lining both inside and out.

یکی گفتش ای خسرو نیکروز
One addressed him: — " Oh monarch of fortunate reign!
ز دیبای چینی قبایی بدوز
A cloak of brocade, brought from China, obtain! "

بگفت این قدر ستر و آسایش است
He replied, "This for cov'ring and comfort will do;
وز این بگذری زیب و آرایش است
And if this you exceed, 'tis for people to view.

نه از بهر آن می‌ستانم خراج
From my subjects I do not the taxes collect,
که زینت کنم بر خود و تخت و تاج
That my person, my throne, and my crown may be decked.

چو همچون زنان حله در تن کنم
Were I in the clothes of a woman to dress,
به مردی کجا دفع دشمن کنم؟
By manhood! when would I the foeman repress?

مرا هم ز صد گونه آز و هواست
I also have longings, a hundred and more,
ولیکن خزینه نه تنها مراست
But not solely for me is the treasury's store."

خزاین پر از بهر لشکر بود
For the sake of the army, are treasuries full;
نه از بهر آذین و زیور بود
Not for purchasing trinkets and toys, as a rule.

سپاهی که خوشدل نباشد ز شاه
The soldier whose heart with the king is irate,
ندارد حدود ولایت نگاه
Is slow in protecting the bounds of the State.

چو دشمن خر روستایی برد
When the foe bears the villager's ass from his Power,
ملک باج و ده یک چرا می‌خورد؟
The king should not taxes, and tithes, too, devour.

مخالف خرش برد و سلطان خراج

The foe stole his ass, and the king levied tax;

چه اقبال ماند در آن تخت و تاج؟

Could a State show prosperity, cursed with such racks?

مروت نباشد بر افتاده زور

It is ungenerous to trample on one you supplant;

برد مرغدون دانه از پیش مور

The miserly bird takes the grain from the ant

رعیت درخت است اگر پروری

The subject's a tree, unto which, if you tend,

به کام دل دوستان بر خوری

The fruit you will eat to the joy of your friend.

به بی‌رحمی از بیخ و بارش مکن

With cruelty, dig it not up fruit and root;

که نادان کند حیف بر خویشتن

For the fool on himself places tyranny's foot

کسان بر خورند از جوانی و بخت

Those have tasted the pleasures of fortune and youth,

که بر زیردستان نگیرند سخت

Who towards their subjects have exercised ruth.

اگر زیردستی در آید ز پای

If a subject should chance from his station to fall,

حذر کن ز نالیدنش بر خدای

Take care! lest to God for redress he should call.

چو شاید گرفتن به نرمی دیار

When a state can be peacefully gained for the king,

به پیکار خون از مشامی میار

By war, the red blood from a pore do not bring.

به مردی که ملک سراسر زمین

By manhood! the realm with a world in its bound,

نیرزد که خونی چکد بر زمین

Is not worth, that a blood-drop should fall to the ground

❀◉❀◉❀

حکایت در شناختن دوست و دشمن را
Story (About Darius and his housekeeper)

شنیدم که دارای فرخ تبار

I have heard that Darius, of fortunate race,

ز لشکر جدا ماند روز شکار

Got detached from his suite, on the day of the chase.

دوان آمدش گله‌بانی به پیش

Before him came running a horse-tending lout

شهنشه برآورد یغلق ز کیش

The king from his quiver an arrow pulled out

به صحرا در از دشمنان دار باک

In the desert, 'tis well to show terror of foes,

که در خانه باشد گل از خار پاک

For at home not a thorn will appear on the rose;

برآورد چوپان در آن دم خروش

The terrified horse-keeper uttered a cry,

که دشمن نیم در هلاکم مکوش

Saying: " Do not destroy me! no foeman am I.

من آنم که اسبان شه پرور

I am he who takes care of the steeds of the king;

به خدمت بدین مرغزار اندرم

In this meadow, with zeal to my duty I cling."

ملک را دل رفته آمد به جای

The king's startled heart found composure again;

بخندید و گفت: ای نکوهیده رای

He smiled and exclaimed: — "Oh most foolish of men

تو را یاوری کرد فرخ سروش

Some fortunate angel has succoured you here

وگر نه زه آورده بودم به گوش

Else the string of my bow, I'd have brought to my ear."

نگهبان مرعی بخندید و گفت

The guard of the pasturage smiled and replied:

نصیحت ز منعم نباید نهفت

Admonition, from friends, it becomes not to hide.

نه تدییر محمود و رای نکوست

The arrangements are bad and the counsels unwise,

که دشمن نداند شهنشه ز دوست

When the king can't a friend from a foe recognize.

چنان است در مهتری شرط زیست

The condition of living in greatness is so,

که هر کهتری را بدانی که کیست

That every dependent you have you should know.

مرا بارها در حضر دیده‌ای

You often have seen me when present at Court,

ز خیل و چراگاه پرسیده‌ای

And inquired about horses and pastures and sport

کنونت به مهر آمدم پیشباز

And now that in love I have met you again,

نمی‌دانیم از بداندیش باز

Me you cannot distinguish from rancorous men.

توانم من، ای نامور شهریار

As for me, I am able, oh name-bearing king!

که اسبی برون آرم از صد هزار

Any horse ouit of one hundred thousand to bring.

مرا گله‌بانی به عقل است و رای

With wisdom and judgment as herdsman I serve;}

تو هم گلهٔ خویش باری، بپای

o you, in like manner, your own flock preserve!"

در آن تخت و ملک از خلل غم بود

In that capital anarchy causes distress,

که تدبیر شاه از شبان کم بود

Where the plans of the king than the herdsman's are less

◈◉◈◈◉◈

حکایت در مورد جمشید
Story about Jamshed

شنیدم که جمشید فرخ سرشت
I have heard that fanshed? whose good nature was known,
به سرچشمه ای بر به سنگی نبشت
On the head of a fountain inscribed with a stone:

بر این چشمه چون ما بسی دم زدند
At this fountain great numbers, like us, have drawn breath,
برفتند چون چشم بر هم زدند
Who, within an eye's twinkle, have tasted of death.

گرفتیم عالم به مردی و زور
I have conquered a world by my manhood and strength;
ولیکن نبردیم با خود به گور
And yet, to the grave cannot bear it at length."

چو بر دشمنی باشدت دسترس
When over a foe you can Power exercise,
مرنجانش کو را همین غصه بس
Do not gall him! the sorrow for him should suffice.

عدو زنده سرگشته پیرامنت
A living foe near you, whose mind is a wreck,
به از خون او کشته در گردنت
Is better by far, than his blood on your neck.

◈◉◈◉◈

گفتار اندر نظر در حق رعیت مظلوم
Story on hearing complaints

تو کی بشنوی نالهٔ دادخواه
When will you give ear to a suppliant's cry?

به کیوان برت کلهٔ خوابگاه؟
Your bed-chamber roof is in Saturn, on high.

چنان خسب کآید فغانت به گوش
So sleep, that lamenting may come to your ear,

اگر دادخواهی برآرد خروش
Should a suppliant carry his clamouring near.

که نالد ز ظالم که در دور توست
He complains of the tyrant who lives in your reign;

که هر جور کاو می‌کند جور توست
For each wrong he commits unto you will pertain.

نه سگ دامن کاروانی درید
The skirt of the traveler, the dog did not tear,

که دهقان نادان که سگ پرورید
But the ignorant peasant who reared him with care.

دلیر آمدی سعدیا در سخن
Oh Sádi I in speech you have shown yourself bold;

چو تیغت به دست است فتحی بکن
The victory win i since the sabre you hold

بگو آنچه دانی که حق گفته به
Declare what you know! for truth spoken is best;

نه رشوت ستانی و نه عشوه ده
You do not take bribes; pious frauds you detest.

طمع بند و دفتر ز حکمت بشوی
From the volume wash sense, if you keep your tongue still

طمع بگسل و هرچه دانی بگوی
Let craving be snapped and declare what you will.

❖◉❖◉❖

داستان پادشاه و گدا
Story of a King and the Beggar

خبر یافت گردن‌کشی در عراق
A king of Irak with the news was supplied,
که می‌گفت مسکینی از زیر طاق
That under his palace a mendicant cried:

تو هم بر دری هستی امیدوار
You, too, at a door sit with hope in your eyes;
پس امید بر در نشینان برآر
Hence, the hope of the poor at your door, realize!

نخواهی که باشد دلت دردمند
The afflicted in heart, from their bondage relieve!
دل دردمندان برآور ز بند
That your own heart may never have reason to grieve.

پریشانی خاطر دادخواه
The implorer for justice, heart-broken from grief,
براندازد از مملکت پادشاه
By the state of the provinces measures the chief.

تو خفته خنک در حرم نیمروز
You have slept cool at noon in your private retreat";
غریب از برون گو به گرما بسوز
To the poor out of door say, ' Be burned in the heat!'

ستاننده داد آن کس خداست
The Lord for that person will justice obtain,
که نتواند از پادشه دادخواست
Who has justice implored from the monarch in vain."

حکایت در معنی شفقت

Story of ibn-abdul-aziz, and his signet ring

یکی از بزرگان اهل تمیز

Of people discreet, one among the grandees,

حکایت کند ز ابن عبدالعزیز

A story relates of Ibn- Abdul- Aziz:

که بودش نگینی در انگشتری

His ring had a stone in its centre, so rare,

فرو مانده در قیمتش جوهری

That the jeweller could not its value declare.

به شب گفتی از جرم گیتی فروز

At night, you'd have said that that world-lighting ray,

دری بود از روشنایی چو روز

Was a gem that in brightness resembled the day.

قضا را درآمد یکی خشک سال

It happened one year that a famine set in,

که شد بدر سیمای مردم هلال

And full-moon-like men as the crescent grew thin.

چو در مردم آرام و قوت ندید

When of comfort and strength he saw men dispossessed,

خود آسوده بودن مروت ندید

He thought it unmanly that he should have rest.

چو بیند کسی زهر در کام خلق

When in everyone's mouth one sees poison, alas!

کیش بگذرد آب نوشین به حلق

Adown his own throat when will sweet water pass?

بفرمود و بفروختندش به سیم

He ordered, they bartered the jewel for gold,

که رحم آمدش بر غریب و یتیم

For he pitied the orphan, the poor, and the old.

به یک هفته نقدش به تاراج داد

For the space of a week he gave money, like spoil,

به درویش و مسکین و محتاج داد

To the poor and the needy and weak of the soil.

فتادند در وی ملامت کنان

The censurers blamed him for doing amiss,

که دیگر به دستت نیاید چنان

Saying, " Hope not again for a jewel like this! "

شنیدم که می‌گفت و باران دمع

I have heard that he said — and a shower of tears

فرو می‌دویدش به عارض چو شمع

Trickled down his pale cheeks, as a candle appears

که زشت است پیرایه بر شهریار

Very ugly an ornament shows on the king,

دل شهری از ناتوانی فگار

Whose subjects are tortured by Poverty's sting.

مرا شاید انگشتری بی‌نگین

A ring without gems is becoming to me;

نشاید دل خلقی اندوهگین

A ring without gems is becoming to me;

خنک آن که آسایش مرد و زن

He is happy who tries man and woman to please,

گزیند بر آرایش خویشتن

And prefers others' joy to his own selfish ease

نکردند رغبت هنرپروران

Those cherishing virtue no eagerness show

به شادی خویش از غم دیگران

For delight to themselves, wrung from other men's woe.

اگر خوش بخسبد ملک بر سریر

If the monarch sleeps happy, reclined on his throne,

نپندارم آسوده خسبد فقیر

To the poor, J suspect, soothing sleep is unknown.

وگر زنده دارد شب دیر باز

And if through the night-long he vigils should keep,

بخسبند مردم به آرام و ناز

In comfort and pleasure his subjects will sleep.

بحمدالله این سیرت و راه راست

And, praise be to God! this right nature and road,

اتابک ابوبکر بن سعد راست

On At&bak-Bu-Bakar-Bin-Sdd are bestowed.

کس از فتنه در پارس دیگر نشان

Of tumult in Persia, one sees not a trace,

نبیند مگر قامت مهوشان

Excepting the moon-visaged's figure and face.

یکی پنج بیتم خوش آمد به گوش

A song of five couplets I heard with delight,

که در مجلسی می‌سرودند دوش

That was sung at a musical party last night

مرا راحت از زندگی دوش بود

Last night I had pleasure in life for a space,

که آن ماهرویم در آغوش بود

For that moon-visaged maiden was in my embrace.

مر او را چو دیدم سر از خواب مست

On perceiving that sleep had bewildered her head,

بدو گفتم ای سرو پیش تو پست

"Oh slumber transported, beloved one!" I said;

دمی نرگس از خواب نوشین بشوی

"Wash slumber away from your eyes, for a while!

چو گلبن بخند و چو بلبل بگوی

Like the nightingale sing! like the rose-blossom smile!

چه می‌خسبی ای فتنه روزگار؟

Oh plague of the world! why thus, sleeping, recline?

بیا و می لعل نوشین بیار

Come and bring with you some of last night's ruby wine!

نگه کرد شوریده از خواب و گفت

Bewildered through sleep, she beheld me and spake:

مرا فتنه خوانی و گویی مخفت

You call me a trouble, and say, ' Keep awake! '

در ایام سلطان روشن نفس

In the days of the monarch of luminous mind,

نبیند دگر فتنه بیدار کس

None again will the nuisance of wakefulness rind.

❖◉❖◉❖

حکایت اتابک تکله

Story of Atabak Tukla

در اخبار شاهان پیشینه هست

In the records of monarchs of yore,

که چون تکله بر تخت زنگی نشست

it is shown That when Tukla succeeded to Zangi's great throne

به دورانش از کس نیازرد کس

In his reign not a person another could touch

سبق برد اگر خود همین بود و بس

He excelled if he only accomplished this much

چنین گفت یک ره به صاحبدلی

He once to a pious believer thus spoke:

که عمرم به سر رفت بی حاصلی

My life to the present has ended in smoke.

بخواهم به کنج عبادت نشست

When country, position, and throne disappear,

که دریابم این پنج روزی که هست

From the world none takes riches, except the Fakir,

چو می‌بگذرد جاه و ملک و سریر

To sit in the corner of worship I'm fain,

نبرد از جهان دولت الا فقیر

And turn to account the l Jive days ' that remain."

چو بشنید دانای روشن نفس

When the wise man of luminous soul heard this stuff,

به تندی برآشفت کای تکله بس

In a towering rage, he said, "Tukla, enough!

طریقت به جز خدمت خلق نیست

Save in ruling your subjects, no path you possess;

به تسبیح و سجاده و دلق نیست

Not in rosaries, carpets, nor mendicant's dress.'

تو بر تخت سلطانی خویش باش

On your own royal throne you must tarry secure,

به اخلاق پاکیزه درویش باش

And the rank of a Dervish by virtues procure.

به صدق و ارادت میان بسته‌دار

In intention and truth with your loins girt be found;

ز طامات و دعوی زبان بسته‌دار

Let your tongue 'gainst desires and pretensions be bound!

قدم باید اندر طریقت نه دم

It is right to advance in the Faith and not boast;

که اصلی ندارد دم بی‌قدم

For to brag and not act, is a wind-bag, at most.

بزرگان که نقد صفا داشتند

The nobles, who Purity's money possessed,

چنین خرقه زیر قبا داشتند

In tatters, like these, under mantles were dressed."

◀◉▸◀◉▸

حکایت ملک روم با دانشمند
Story op the sultan of rum

شنیدم که بگریست سلطان روم

have heard that Rurrts Sultan with tears in his eyes,

بر نیکمردی ز اهل علوم

Said in presence of one who was pious and wise:

که پایایم از دست دشمن نماند

"By the hand of my foe of all strength I'm bereft,

جز این قلعه و شهر با من نماند

There is nought, save this city and fort, with me left

بسی جهد کردم که فرزند من

I have worked very hard that my child in my stead,

پس از من بود سرور انجمن

Should be chief of the Council as soon as I'm dead.

کنون دشمن بدگهر دست یافت

Now the foe of base breeding has put me to rout,

سر دست مردی و جهدم بتافت

And my fingers of manhood are twisted about

چه تدبیر سازم، چه درمان کنم؟

What course shall I follow? what remedy prove,

که از غم بفرسود جان در تنم

That from body and soul I may sorrow remove?"

بگفت ای برادر غم خویش خور

The sage became vexed, saying, "Why do you cry?

که از عمر بهتر شد و بیشتر

At such wisdom and pluck, it becomes one to sigh!

تو را این قدر تا بمانی بس است

This much is sufficient for you, to live on;

چو رفتی جهان جای دیگر کس است

The world is another's as soon as you're gone.

اگر هوشمند است و گر بی‌خرد

Your son may be wise or he may be a muff

غم او مخور کاو غم خود خورد

Do not bother! he'll bear his own grief well enough!

مشقت نیرزد جهان داشتن

It repays not the trouble to be the Earth's head

گرفتن به شمشیر و بگذاشتن

To seize with the sword and let go when you're dead.

تو تدبیر خود کن که آن پر خرد

Take care of yourself! that as sapience shows;

که بعد از تو باشد غم خود خورد

And he who succeeds you will bear his own woes.

بدین پنج روزه اقامت مناز

With the "five days of grace that are left, do not play!

به اندیشه تدبیر رفتن بساز

By reflection, arrange to depart on your way.

که را دانی از خسروان عجم

Of the monarchs of Persia, whom now do you know?

ز عهد فریدون و ضحاک و جم

For they practised oppression on high and on low.

که بر تخت و ملکش نیامد زوال؟

Whose kingdom and throne will not suffer decay?

نماند به جز ملک ایزد تعال

No kingdom, except the Almighty's, will stay.

که را جاودان ماندن امید ماند

No person need hope to remain here secure,

چو کس را نبینی که جاوید ماند؟

For even the earth will not always endure.

که را سیم و زر ماند و گنج و مال

If a person has silver and gold and supplies,

پس از وی به چندی شود پایمال

Under foot they'll be trodden, soon after he dies.

وز آن کس که خیری بماند روان

Hence, mercy incessantly reaches the soul

دمادم رسد رحمتش بر روان

Of the person, whose goodness continues to roll.

بزرگی کز او نام نیکو نماند

The man of distinction, who left a good name,

توان گفت با اهل دل کاو نماند

Since he died not, could unto the pious exclaim:

الا تا درخت کرم پروری

That you nurse Liberality's tree, have a care! '

گر امیدواری کز او بر خوری

And Felicity's fruit you will certainly share.

کرم کن که فردا که دیوان نهند

Bestow! that, to-morrow, when justice they mete,

منازل به مقدار احسان دهند

Becoming your kindness, they give you a seat'

یکی را که سعی قدم پیشتر

The man who, in running, has striven the most,

به درگاه حق، منزلت بیشتر

At the Court of the Lord gets the loftiest post.

یکی باز پس خائن و شرمسار

If a man be a traitor and conscious of shame,

بترسد همی مرد ناکرده کار

He conceals it as though he possessed a good name.

بهل تا به دندان گزد پشت دست

Till his teeth bite the back of his hand, let him sin!

تنوری چنین گرم و نانی نبست

An oven so hot and no bread shut within!

بدانی گه غله برداشتن

At the time of removing the grain, you will read

که سستی بود تخم ناکاشتن

That it argues neglect, not to sow any seed."

❖◉❖◉❖

حکایت مرزبان ستمگار با زاهد
Story of a Syrian recluse

خردمند مردی در اقصای شام
On the border of Syria a famed man of God,
گرفت از جهان کنج غاری مقام
Apart from the world, made a cave his abode.

به صبرش در آن کنج تاریک جای
Resigned in that corner a gloomy retreat
به گنج قناعت فرو رفته پای
On Contentment's rich treasure, he planted his feet.

بزرگان نهادند سر بر درش
The notables laid their proud heads at his door,
که در می‌نیامد به درها سرش
For inside their portals his head did not- soar.

تمنا کند عارف پاکباز
The fair-dealing hermit has this in his eye,
به دریوزه از خویشتن ترک آز
That in beggary, greed from his spirit may fly.

چو هر ساعتش نفس گوید بده
When his breath evry moment says — "Give me, in haste!"
به خواری بگرداندش ده به ده
They direct him from village to village disgraced.

در آن مرز کاین پیر هشیار بود
In the land where this prudent recluse had his cell,
یکی مرزبان ستمکار بود
A tyrannical governor happened to dwell;

که هر ناتوان را که دریافتی
Who by violence twisted the fingers behind,
به سرپنجگی پنجه برتافتی
Of all the poor men he was able to find.

جهان سوز و بی‌رحمت و خیره‌کش
A tyrant unmerciful, void of all fear;
ز تلخیش روی جهانی ترش
By his harshness a world's faces frowning appear.

گروهی برفتند از آن ظلم و عار
A multitude fled from that outrage and shame,
ببردند نام بدش در دیار
And disclosed to the world his iniquitous name.

گروهی بماندند مسکین و ریش

A number, heart- wounded and wretched, remained,

پس چرخه نفرین گرفتند پیش

And in rear of their spinning-wheels, curses they rained.

ید ظلم جایی که گردد دراز

In the place where the hand of Oppression goes far,

نبینی لب مردم از خنده باز

You behold not men's lips, from their laughing, ajar.

به دیدار شیخ آمدی گاه گاه

To see the old Saint, oft the chief would repair;

خدادوست در وی نکردی نگاه

But the Pietest looked as if no one were there.

ملک نوبتی گفتش: ای نیکبخت

The chief once addressed him — " Oh favoured by Fate!

به نفرت ز من در مکش روی سخت

Do not harden your face on account of your hate!

مرا با تو دانی سر دوستی است

That it is my design to befriend you, you know

تو را دشمنی با من از بهر چیست؟

On my account, therefore, why enmity show?

گرفتم که سالار کشور نیم

I do not presume to be chief in the land,

به عزت ز درویش کمتر نیم

But in honour, not less than the Dervish I stand

نگویم فضیلت نهم بر کسی

To be ranked above others I do not lay claim;

چنان باش با من که با هر کسی

As to others you are, unto me, be the same! "

شنید این سخن عابد هوشیار

The intelligent worshipper heard this remark;

بر آشفت و گفت: ای ملک، هوش دار

He was angry and answered, "Oh governor, hark!

وجودت پریشانی خلق از اوست

By your presence, distress to the people extends;

ندارم پریشانی خلق دوست

I reckon not scourges of people my friends.

تو با آن که من دوستم، دشمنی

You are hostile to those who are friendly to me;

نپندارمت دوستدار منی

That you are my friend, I'm unable to see.

چرا دوست دارم به باطل منت

Supposing I did on you friendship bestow;

چو دانم که دارد خدا دشمنت؟

What then? Since by God you are counted a foe! "

خدادوست را گر بدرند پوست

If from one of God's chosen the skin they should rend,

نخواهد شدن دشمن دوست، دوست

The enemy will not be friend of the Friend.

عجب دارم از خواب آن سنگدل

I'm amazed how that hard-hearted person can sleep,

که خلقی بخسبند از او تنگدل

Since a city through him lies in misery deep

الا گر هنر داری و عقل و هوش

If virtue and wisdom and sense in you dwell,

بفضل و ترحم میان بند و کوش

Be ready in liberal acts to excel!

❖◉❖◉❖

گفتار اندر نگه داشتن خاطر درویشان
Story on oppressing the weak

مها زورمندی مکن با کهان
Oh tyrant! from crushing the helpless refrain!
که بر یک نمط می‌نماند جهان
For the world in one mode does not always remain.

سر پنجهٔ ناتوان بر مپیچ
The fingers of one who is weak, do not twist!
که گر دست یابد برآیی به هیچ
For should he prevail, you will cease to exist

عدو را به کوچک نباید شمرد
Degrade not a man from his rank, I repeat!
که کوه کلان دیدم از سنگ خرد
For weak you will be, if you fall from your seat.

دل دوستان جمع بهتر که گنج
The hearts of friends, happy, are better than gold,
خزینه تهی به که مردم به رنج
And a treasury, empty, than men in Griefs hold.

مینداز در پای کار کسی
With another's affairs do not meddle at all!
که افتد که در پایش افتی بسی
For it may be that, oft, at his feet you will fall

تحمل کن ای ناتوان از قوی
Oh weak one! be patient with one who is strong!
که روزی تواناتر از وی شوی
For you may be more powerful than he is ere long.

به همت برآر از ستیهنده شور
Bring destruction by prayer from the tyrannous wight!
که بازوی همت به از دست زور
For prayer's arm is better than hands that have might

لب خشک مظلوم را گو بخند
Bid not smile, the dry lips of the people oppressed!
که دندان ظالم بخواهند کند
For the tyrant's foul fangs from their sockets they'll wrest.

به بانگ دهل خواجه بیدار گشت
At the sound of the drum the rich man woke, at last;
چه داند شب پاسبان چون گذشت؟
Does he know how the night of the watchman has passed?

خورد کاروانی غم بار خویش

The traveler shows for his own load concern;

نسوزد دلش بر خر پشت ریش

For his ass's galled back, his hard heart does not yearn.

گرفتم کز افتادگان نیستی

I admit you are none of the down-fallen band;

چو افتاده بینی چرا نیستی؟

When you see one has fallen why impotent stand?

براینت بگویم یکی سرگذشت

On this topic I'll tell you a story I know;

که سستی بود زین سخن درگذشت

For to pass from the subject would negligence show

◈◉◈◈◉◈

حکایت در معنی رحمت با ناتوانان در حال توانایی
Story on the kindness to the poor when you have plenty

چنان قحط سالی شد اندر دمشق
Such a famine, one year, in Damascus arose,
که یاران فراموش کردند عشق
That friends passed each other, as if they were foes.

چنان آسمان بر زمین شد بخیل
The sky had so miserly been to the ground,
که لب تر نکردند زرع و نخیل
That moisture on fields or on palms was not found

بخوشید سرچشمه‌های قدیم
The fountains, that long had existed, were dry;
نماند آب، جز آب چشم یتیم
No water, save that in the orphan boy's eye

نبودی به جز آه بیوه زنی
If smoke from a chimney arose to the sky,
اگر برشدی دودی از روزنی
It was only the poor widow woman's sad sigh.

چو درویش بی رنگ دیدم درخت
I saw that the trees, like the poor, were stripped bare;
قوی بازوان سست و درمانده سخت
That the strong armed were weak and in wretched despair.

نه در کوه سبزی نه در باغ شخ
The hills showed no verdure, the gardens no shoots;
ملخ بوستان خورده مردم ملخ
The locusts ate gardens, and men ate those brutes.

در آن حال پیش آمدم دوستی
I met an old friend, in this season of moans;
از او مانده بر استخوان پوستی
His body had shrivelled to skin and to bones.

وگر چه به مکنت قوی حال بود
I was greatly surprised, for his means were not small
خداوند جاه و زر و مال بود
He had rank, and had money, and stores at his call.

بدو گفتم: ای یار پاکیزه خوی
I said: "Oh companion! of character pure,
چه درماندگی پیشت آمد؟ بگوی
Explain the affliction you have to endure!

بغرید بر من که عقلت کجاست؟

He roared at me, saying, "Oh where is your sense?

چو دانی و پرسی سؤالت خطاست

When you know and you ask, you commit an offence.

نبینی که سختی به غایت رسید

Don't you see that affliction has reached to excess;

مشقت به حد نهایت رسید؟

That no bounds can restrict the amount of distress.

نه باران همی آید از آسمان

From the heavens there descends not a shower of rain;

نه بر می‌رود دود فریاد خوان

Not a sigh goes aloft from the poor who complain, "

بدو گفتم: آخر تو را باک نیست

I replied: "You at least have no reason to fear

کشد زهر جایی که تریاک نیست

The poison destroys when no antidote's near

گر از نیستی دیگری شد هلاک

If another through want has been vanquished by death,

تو را هست، بط را ز طوفان چه باک؟

You have food; does the duck heed the hurricane's breath? "

نگه کرد رنجیده در من فقیه

The holy man gave me a look, full of pain;

نگه کردن عالم اندر سفیه

Like the look of the wise on the ignorant swain;

که مرد ار چه بر ساحل است، ای رفیق

Saying, "Friend! though a man the sea-shore may have found,

نیاساید و دوستانش غریق

He does not rejoice, when his comrades are drowned.

من از بینوایی نیم روی زرد

Not from absence of means has my face become pale;

غم بینوایان رخم زرد کرد

Concern for the starving has made my heart quail.

نخواهد که بیند خردمند، ریش

do not desire that a wise man should scan

نه بر عضو مردم، نه بر عضو خویش

A wound on his limbs, or the limbs of a man.

یکی اول از تندرستان منم

And praise be to God; though from wounds I am free,

که ریشی ببینم بلرزد تنم

My body still shakes, if a wound I should see.

منغص بود عیش آن تندرست

Imbittered's the joy of a man who is well,

که باشد به پهلوی بیمار سست

Who alongside a paralyzed patient must dwell.

چو بینم که درویش مسکین نخورد

When I see the necessitous poor go unfed,

به کام اندرم لقمه زهر است و درد

On my palate, like poison and dregs is my bread.

یکی را به زندان درش دوستان

If you carry one's friends to a dungeon and chains,

کجا ماندش عیش در بوستان؟

What pleasure for him in the garden remains?

حکایت نگرانی برای دیگران
Story on concern for others

شبی دود خلق آتشی برفروخت

The sighs of the people one night raised a fire;

شنیدم که بغداد نیمی بسوخت

Half Baghdad, I have heard, was consumed in its ire.

یکی شکر گفت اندران خاک و دود

A person gave thanks, midst the smoke and the dust,

که دکان ما را گزندی نبود

Saying, "Harm has not come to my shop from the gust'

جهاندیده‌ای گفتش ای بوالهوس

A man of experience said: "Mine of disgrace!

تو را خود غم خویشتن بود و بس؟

In you, not a grief but for self, has a place.

پسندی که شهری بسوزد به نار

That a town should be burned up by fire, you delight,

اگر چه سرایت بود بر کنار؟

Although at the border there wanders a blight.

به جز سنگدل ناکند معده تنگ

Who his stomach would stuff but the heartless, alone,

چو بیند کسان بر شکم بسته سنگ

When he sees others' stomachs compressed with a stone?

توانگر خود آن لقمه چون می‌خورد

Will the rich man himself eat that morsel, so sweet,

چو بیند که درویش خون می‌خورد؟

When he sees that the poor their own blood have to eat?

مگو تندرست است رنجوردار

Do not say that the sick nurse is hearty and whole:

که می‌پیچد از غصه رنجوروار

For he twists like a patient, from anguish of soul.

تنکدل چو یاران به منزل رسند

When the friends of " Kind Heart " the wished resting- place find,

نخسبد که واماندگان از پسند

He sleeps not, for others are struggling behind.

دل پادشاهان شود بارکش

The hearts of good kings become burdened, alas!

چو بینند در گل خر خارکش

When they see in the quagmire the thorn-bearing ass.

اگر در سرای سعادت کس است

If a man in Felicity's mansion reside,

ز گفتار سعدیش حرفی بس است

One letter from Sádi suffices to guide

همینت بسنده‌ست اگر بشنوی

It suffices for you, if observance you show

که گر خار کاری سمن ندروی

You cannot reap jasmines if briars you sow."

◈◉◈◉◈

حکایت در مورد ستم
Story on oppression

یکی بر سر شاخ، بن می برید
One was cutting the branches and trunk of a tree

خداوند بستان نگه کرد و دید
The lord of the garden his doings did see.

بگفتا گر این مرد بد می کند
He said, If the work of this person is vile,

نه با من که با نفس خود می کند
Himself, and not me, he is hurting, the while."

نصیحت بجای است اگر بشنوی
Advice is salvation, if taken aright

ضعیفان میفکن به کتف قوی
Overthrow not the weak with the shoulder of might!

که فردا به داور برد خسروی
For, tomorrow, to God as a king will be borne

گدایی که پیشت نیرزد جوی
The beggar, that now, you'd not value one corn.

چو خواهی که فردا بوی مهتری
Since you wish that you may on the morrow be great,

مکن دشمن خویشتن، کهتری
Do not sink your own foe to a humble estate!

که چون بگذرد بر تو این سلطنت
For when this dominion shall pass from your grasp,

بگیرد به قهر آن گدا دامنت
That beggar your skirt, out of malice, will clasp.

مکن، پنجه از ناتوانان بدار
At oppressing the feeble, take care not to aim

که گر بفکنندت شوی شرمسار
For, should they prevail, you'll be covered with shame.

که زشت است در چشم آزادگان
In the view of the noble of mind, it is base

بیفتادن از دست افتادگان
At the hand of the fallen to suffer disgrace.

بزرگان روشندل نیکبخت
Enlightened and fortunate men of renown,

به فرزانگی تاج بردند و تخت
Have obtained by their wisdom the throne and the crown.

به دنباله راستان گژ مرو

In the wake of the true, do not crookedly steer!

وگر راست خواهی ز سعدی شنو

And if Truth you desire, unto Sádi give ear!

سخنی در مورد عدل و ظلم و ثمره آن
Discourse ON oppression

خبرداری از خسروان عجم

Of the Persian Khusraus do you knowledge possess?

که کردند بر زیردستان ستم؟

For all 'neath their sway, they did sorely oppress.

نه آن شوکت و پادشایی بماند

Their splendour and royalty suffered decay;

نه آن ظلم بر روستایی بماند

Their oppression of villagers vanished away.

خطا بین که بر دست ظالم برفت

Observe the mistake which the tyrant's hand sped:

جهان ماند و با او مظالم برفت

The world lives and he, with his foul deeds, is dead.

خنک روز محشر تن دادگر

Oh blessed is the king on the great Judgment Day,

که در سایهٔ عرش دارد مقر

Who within the throne's shade is permitted to stay!

به قومی که نیکی پسندد خدای

To the tribe who appreciate goodness, the Lord

دهد خسروی عادل و نیک رای

Gives a king who with justice and wisdom is stored.

چو خواهد که ویران شود عالمی

When He wishes to change to a desert the land,

کند ملک در پنجهٔ ظالمی

He delivers the State to the tyrant's harsh hand.

سگالند از او نیکمردان حذر

Pious men, full of cautiousness, therefore, suppose

که خشم خدای است بیدادگر

That the anger of God, through the tyrant's hand shows.

بزرگی از او دان و منت شناس

From Him know that greatness and gratitude spring;

که زایل شود نعمت ناسپاس

If ungrateful for favours, they'll quickly take wing.

اگر شکر کردی بر این ملک و مال

If you've tendered your thanks for your riches and state,

به مالی و ملکی رسی بی زوال

You'll get wealth and a kingdom that will not abate.

وگر جور در پادشایی کنی

And should you be tyrannous during your reign,

پس از پادشایی گدایی کنی

A beggar's estate, after empire, you'll gain.

حرام است بر پادشه خواب خوش

It becomes not a king, in soft slumber, to rest,

چو باشد ضعیف از قوی بارکش

While the weak by the strong are unjustly oppressed.

میازار عامی به یک خردله

On the people one grain of distress do not bring!

که سلطان شبان است و عامی گله

For they are the flock and the shepherd's the king.

چو پرخاش بینند و بیداد از او

When war and injustice through him they sustain,

شبان نیست، گرگ است، فریاد از او

He's a wolf, not a shepherd; of him they complain.

بد انجام رفت و بد اندیشه کرد

The king who, on subjects, Oppression's hand laid,

که با زیردستان جفا، پیشه کرد

Departed unhappy and malice displayed.

نخواهی که نفرین کنند از پست

If you wish not that men should behind you revile,

نکوباش تا بد نگوید کست

Be good, so that none can declare you have guile!

❮◉❯❮◉❯

صفت جمعیت اوقات درویشان راضی

Story on the happy times of the contented poor

مگو جاهی از سلطنت بیش نیست

Do not say that no rank is than empire more great;

که ایمن‌تر از ملک درویش نیست

For the Dervish's realm is the happiest state!

سبکبار مردم سبک‌تر روند

The man lightly burdened will swifter proceed;

حق این است و صاحبدلان بشنوند

This is truth, and the good to the saying give heed.

تهیدست تشویش نانی خورد

The grief of a loaf, the poor beggar sustains;

جهانبان به قدر جهانی خورد

To a world, the distress of a monarch attains.

گدا را چو حاصل شود نان شام

When food for the evening the beggar has found,

چنان خوش بخسبد که سلطان شام

As the king of Damascus, he'll slumber as sound.

غم و شادمانی به سر می‌رود

Both sorrow and gladness to end are inclined,

به مرگ این دو از سر به در می‌رود

And will vanish together at death, from the mind.

چه آن را که بر سر نهادند تاج

What matters it then, whom the multitude crowned?

چه آن را که بر گردن آمد خراج

What matters it then, who the tax money found?

اگر سرفرازی به کیوان بر است

If a noble should soar over Saturn on high,

وگر تنگدستی به زندان در است

Or a destitute man in a dungeon should lie;

چو خیل اجل بر سر هر دو تاخت

When both are attacked by the Army of Fate,

نمی شاید از یکدگرشان شناخت

Which is one which the other no mortal can state.

◈◉◈◉◈

101

حکایت عابد و استخوان پوسیده
Story on the transitoriness of greatness

شنیدم که یک بار در حله‌ای
I have heard that a skull in the Tigris, one day,
سخن گفت با عابدی کله‌ای
Conversed with a servant of God, in this way:

که من فر فرماندهی داشتم
The splendour of monarchy, once, I possessed;
به سر بر کلاه مهی داشتم
By the head-dress of greatness my temples were pressed.

سپهرم مدد کرد و نصرت وفاق
The sky gave assistance and Vict'ry was pleased;
گرفتم به بازوی دولت عراق
With the arm of Good Fortune, I Babylon seized.

طمع کرده بودم که کرمان خورم
I had cherished a longing to conquer Kirman?-
که ناگه بخوردند کرمان سرم
But the worms ate my head and so thwarted my plan.

بکن پنبهٔ غفلت از گوش هوش
From your mind's lug, the cotton of negligence clear!
که از مردگان پندت آید به گوش
For advice from the dead now arrives at your ear."

◈◉◈◉◈

گفتار اندر نکوکاری و بدکاری و عاقبت آنها
On Doing Good and Evil, and the Result

نکوکار مردم نباشد بدش

A man who does good has no evil to fear;

نورزد کسی بد که نیک افتدش

No person does evil that good may appear.

شر انگیز هم بر سر شر شود

The promoters of sin, also, wickedly roam,

چو کژدم که با خانه کمتر شود

Like scorpions, that seldom get back to their home.

اگر نفع کس در نهاد تو نیست

f your nature is such that it benefits none;

چنین گوهر و سنگ خارا یکی است

The jewel and stone, in like manner are one.

غلط گفتم ای یار شایسته خوی

I am wrong, oh companion, of temp'rament sweet!

که نفع است در آهن و سنگ و روی

In a face, stone and iron, you profit will meet.

چنین آدمی مرده به ننگ را

Such a man's better dead than enduring the shame,

که بر وی فضیلت بود سنگ را

That a stone can than him greater excellence claim.

نه هر آدمی زاده از دد به است

Not each son sprung from Adam surpasses the beast;

که دد ز آدمی زادهٔ بد به است

For a brute is less vile than a villain, at least.

به است از دد انسان صاحب خرد

A man who is wise, leaves the beast far behind

نه انسان که در مردم افتد چو دد

Not the being who, brute-like, attacks his own kind.

چو انسان نداند به جز خورد و خواب

When a man knows of eating and sleeping alone,

کدامش فضیلت بود بر دواب؟

Over beasts, in what way is his excellence shown?

سوار نگون بخت بی راهرو

From the ill-fated horseman, who galloped astray,

پیاده برد ز او به رفتن گرو

The footman, in walking, the prize bore away.

کسی دانهٔ نیکمردی نکاشت

No person has sown generosity's seed,

کز او خرمن کام دل برنداشت

Who reaps not, in harvest, befitting his need.

نه هرگز شنیدیم در عمر خویش

I never have heard, since my lifetime began,

که بدمرد را نیکی آمد به پیش

That goodness comes forth to reward the bad man.

حکایت شحنه مردم آزار

Story of an oppressing chief

گزیری به چاهی در افتاده بود

Down a well, once, had fallen a champion of fame,

که از هول او شیر نر ماده بود

From whose dread the male tiger a tigress became.

بداندیش مردم به جز بد ندید

An ill-wisher of men, nought but evil could see;

بیافتاد و عاجزتر از خود ندید

He fell; and observed none more helpless than he.

همه شب ز فریاد و زاری نخفت

The night-long, from wailing and weeping, awake;

یکی بر سرش کوفت سنگی و گفت

Someone battered his head with a stone, and thus spake::

تو هرگز رسیدی به فریاد کس

Did you ever the wrongs of a person redress,

که می‌خواهی امروز فریادرس؟

That to-day you are asking for aid in distress?

همه تخم نامردمی کاشتی

You have sown all the seed, in atrocity steeped;

ببین لاجرم بر که برداشتی

Take a look at the fruit you've in consequence reaped!

که بر جان ریشت نهد مرهمی

To your soul, sad and wounded, who salve would apply,

که دلها ز ریشت بنالد همی؟

When hearts from your wounding still, suffering, cry?

تو ما را همی چاه کندی به راه

Since you dug for our service a pit in the way,

به سر لاجرم در فتادی به چاه

Down into a well you have fallen, to-day."

دو کس چه کنند از پی خاص و عام

Two people dig wells for the high and the low;

یکی نیک محضر، دگر زشت نام

One of good disposition, the other a foe.

یکی تشنه را تا کند تازه حلق

One to moisten the throats of the thirsty, withal;

دگر تا به گردن در افتند خلق

The other that people down headlong may fall.

اگر بد کنی چشم نیکی مدار

If you sin, do not hope any goodness to see!

که هرگز نیارد گز انگور بار

For grapes will not grow from a Tamarisk tree!

نپندارم ای در خزان کشته جو

Oh you who in Autumn your barley will sow,

که گندم ستانی به وقت درو

I don't think you'll reap wheat when the time comes to mow!

درخت زقوم ار به جان پروری

If the thorny Zakum with your life you should train,

مپندار هرگز کز او بر خوری

Do not think that a quince from its boughs you'll obtain!

رطب ناورد چوب خرزهره بار

The rare, luscious date, or the colocynth fruit

چو تخم افکنی، بر همان چشم دار

In the seed which you scatter, your hope you should put.

❖◉❖◉❖

حکایت حجاج یوسف
Story of Hajaj and the righteous man

حکایت کنند از یکی نیکمرد

Of one of the God-fearing people, they say

که اکرام حجاج یوسف نکرد

That he did not respect to Hajaj- Yusuf 'pay.

به سرهنگ دیوان نگه کرد تیز

He gave the court headsman a look of command,

که نطعش بینداز و خونش بریز

Saying, "Spread out his leather and sprinkle his sand!"

چو حجت نماند جفا جوی را

When argument fails the tyrannical wight,

به پرخاش در هم کشد روی را

He draws up his face into wrinkles, for fight.

بخندید و بگریست مرد خدای

The hard-hearted dullard astonished appears

عجب داشت سنگین دل تیره رای

He asked, "Why these smiles and these tears in your eye?"

چو دیدش که خندید و دیگر گریست

When Hajaj saw him smile and again saw him cry,

بپرسید کاین خنده و گریه چیست؟

He asked, "Why these smiles and these tears in your eye?"

بگفتا همی‌گریم از روزگار

He replied, "I am weeping, for Fate's at my door,

که طفلان بیچاره دارم چهار

And of helpless young children, I'm bringing up four.

همی‌خندم از لطف یزدان پاک

I smile, that by favour of God, the most pure,

که مظلوم رفتم نه ظالم به خاک

I die the oppressed, not the heartless pursuer."

پسر گفتش: ای نامور شهریار

Someone said, "Oh illustrious king of the land,

یکی دست از این مرد صوفی بدار

Beware! and withdraw from this peasant your hand!

که خلقی بر او روی دارند و پشت

For a family in him have their succour and stay;

نه رای است خلقی به یک بار کشت

It is wrong that a tribe, all at once, you should slay.

بزرگی و عفو و کرم پیشه کن

Magnanimity, pardon, and kindness pursue!

ز خردان اطفالش اندیشه کن

Keep the innocent age of his children in view!

مگر دشمن خاندان خودی

Perhaps you've become your own family's foe,

که بر خاندان ها پسندی بدی

Since, when harm comes to families, pleasure you show!

مپندار و دلها به داغ تو ریش

Do not think that with hearts sorely scorched by your brand,

که روز پسین آیدت خیر پیش

When the ' last day ' arrives you will justified stand!

شنیدم که نشنید و خونش بریخت

I have heard that he list not and caused him to die;

ز فرمان داور که داند گریخت؟

From the orders of God, who can know how to fly?

بزرگی در آن فکرت آن شب بخفت

At night, a wise man in that thought went to bed,

به خواب اندرش دید و پرسید و گفت

And saw in a dream the poor martyr, who said:

دمی بیش بر من سیاست نراند

His torture of me, in a moment was passed;

عقوبت بر او تا قیامت بماند

But torture on him, till the 'Judgment' will last"

نترسی که پاک اندرونی شبی

You fear not lest one of the holy, one night,

برآرد ز سوز جگر یا ربی؟

From his hot, burning liver should cry, 'Lord, requite!

نخفته‌ست مظلوم از آهش بترس

The oppressed has not slept; of his sobs have a care!

ز دود دل صبحگاهش بترس

Of the sighs of his heart in the morning, beware!

بسودا چنان بر وی افشاند دست

In passion he flourished his hands on him, so,

که حجاج را دست حجت ببست

That the arguing hand of Hajaj was bound low.

نه ابلیس بد کرد و نیکی ندید؟

Did not Satan do ill and no good on him smiled?

بر پاک ناید ز تخم پلید

Pure fruit will not spring from a seed that's defiled.

مدر پرده کس به هنگام جنگ

In the season of war, tear not any one's screen!

که باشد تو را نیز در پرده ننگ

For to you may belong some dishonour, unseen.

مزن بانگ بر شیرمردان درشت

Against tiger-like men do not enter the lists,

چو با کودکان بر نیابی به مشت

When you cannot prevail over boys with your fists!

شنیدم که نشنید و خونش بریخت

I have heard that he list not and caused him to die;

ز فرمان داور که داند گریخت

From the orders of God, who can know how to fly?

بزرگی در آن فکرت آنشب بخفت

At night, a wise man in that thought went to bed,

به خواب اندرون دید درویش و گفت

And saw in a dream the poor martyr, who said:

دمی بیش بر من سیاست نراند

" His torture of me, in a moment was passed;

عقوبت بر او تا قیامت بماند

But torture on him, till the 'Judgment' will last"

حکایت جور و ستم

Story on oppression

یکی پند می‌داد فرزند را

A person was giving advice to his son:

نگه دار پند خردمند را

The counsels of those who are wise, do not shun!

مکن جور بر خردکان ای پسر

Oh son! do not trample on those who are small!

که یک روزت افتد بزرگی به سر

For a giant, someday, on your own head may fall.

نمی‌ترسی ای کودک کم خرد

Oh short-witted boy! do you feel no dismay,

که روزی پلنگیت بر هم درد؟

Lest a tiger should tear you to pieces some day?

به خردی درم زور سرپنجه بود

In the days of my youth I was powerful in arm,

دل زیردستان ز من رنجه بود

And the hearts of my subjects through me suffered harm.

بخوردم یکی مشت زورآوران

I encountered a blow from one strong among men,

نکردم دگر زور بر لاغران

And the weak have not felt my oppression again."

◈◉◈◉◈

در نواخت رعیت و رحمت بر افتادگان
On the responsibility of rulers

الا تا به غفلت نخفتی که نوم

Take care, lest you carelessly slumber! for sleep

حرام است بر چشم سالار قوم

Is forbid to the chief, with the tribe in his keep.

غم زیردستان بخور زینهار

Take care, that the grief of your subjects you share!

بترس از زیردستی روزگار

And fear, lest the vengeance of Time you should bear!

نصیحت که خالی بود از غرض

Advice that, devoid of self-int'rest, one sees,

چو داروی تلخ است، دفع مرض

Is like drugs that are bitter, repelling disease.

◈◉◈◉◈

حکایت پادشاه با محبت
Story of the king afflicted with tapeworm

یکی را حکایت کنند از ملوک
Of one of the monarchs, a tale they relate,

که بیماری رشته کردش چو دوک
Who by worms was reduced to a spindle-like state.

چنانش در انداخت ضعف جسد
His weakness of body had lowered him, so,

که می‌برد بر زیردستان حسد
That he envied the meanest of those who are low.

که شاه ار چه بر عرصه نام آور است
Though the king has a name that is famous in chess,

چو ضعف آمد از بیدق کمتر است
When weakness arrives, than the pawn he is less.

ندیمی زمین ملک بوسه داد
A courtier salaamed l to the monarch, and said:

که ملک خداوند جاوید باد
"May the life of the sovereign forever be sped

در این شهر مردی مبارک دم است
There lives in this city a man of blest life

که در پارسایی چنوبی کم است
Among men who are pious, his peers are not rife,

نبردند پیشش مهمات کس
Not a person his burden before him has brought,

که مقصود حاصل نشد در نفس
Who, at once, has not gained the intention he sought.

بخوان تا بخواند دعایی بر این
Bid him come! that a suitable prayer he may try;

که رحمت رسد ز آسمان برین
For mercy descends to the earth. from the sky."

بفرمود تا مهتران خدم
He so ordered, that servants exalted in place,

بخواندند پیر مبارک قدم
Went and summoned the Elder of fortunate pace.

بگفتا دعایی کن ای هوشمند
"Oh sage" said the monarch, "a prayer repeat!

که در رشته چون سوزنم پای‌بند
With the tapeworm I'm, needle-like, bound by the feet."

شنید این سخن پیر خم بوده پشت
The crook-backed philosopher heard this remark;

به تندی برآورد بانگی درشت
With harshness he uttered a shout, saying, "Hark!

که حق مهربان است بر دادگر
God favours the man who from justice won't swerve,

ببخشای و بخشایش حق نگر
Grant pardon and God's own forgiveness observe!

دعای منت کی شود سودمند
In my praying for you, when would profit be found?

اسیران محتاج در چاه و بند؟
You hold captives oppressed, and in dark dungeons bound

تو ناکرده بر خلق بخشایشی
No act of forgiveness to men your life shows;

کجا بینی از دولت آسایشی؟
By riches, when will you experience repose?

ببایدت عذر خطا خواستن
Ask pardon, you must, for the laws you've transgressed,

پس از شیخ صالح دعا خواستن
And then, from Sheikh-Salih a prayer request!

کجا دست گیرد دعای ویت
How can his beseeching be useful to you,

دعای ستمدیدگان در پیت؟
While the prayers of the wretched your footsteps pursue? "

شنید این سخن شهریار عجم
The Monarch of Persia heard all this discourse,

ز خشم و خجالت بر آمد بهم
And from anger and shame felt an ireful remorse;

برنجید و پس با دل خویش گفت
He was vexed, and then turned the affair in his head

چه رنجم؟ حق است این که درویش گفت
Why grieve I? 'tis true what the Dervish has said! "

بفرمود تا هر که در بند بود
He commanded, and all whom in bonds they could see,

به فرمانش آزاد کردند زود
By his order were quickly allowed to go free.

111

جهاندیده بعد از دو رکعت نماز

The sage, after two inclinations in prayer,

به داور برآورد دست نیاز

The hands of beseeching, to God, thus laid bare:

که ای برفرازندهٔ آسمان

"Oh Thou who supportest the sky in Thy hand!

به جنگش گرفتی به صلحش بمان

Thou hast seized him in war, now in peace let him stand! "

ولی همچنان بر دعا داشت دست

He was still in this attitude, praying profound,

که شه سر برآورد و بر پای جست

When the fallen sick man jumped erect on the ground.

تو گفتی ز شادی بخواهد پرید

You'd have said that from gladness he wished to take wing

چو طاووس، چون رشته در پا ندید

Like the Peacock, who saw not his leg in a string.

بفرمود گنجینهٔ گوهرش

He commanded; and treasure and jewels they spread

فشاندند در پای و زر بر سرش

On the ground at his feet, also under his head.

حق از بهر باطل نشاید نهفت

The true for the sake of the false, do not hide

از آن جمله دامن بیفشاند و گفت

He emptied his skirt of the whole, and then cried:

مرو با سر رشته بار دگر

"Do not travel, hereafter, in Tyranny's train,

مبادا که دیگر کند رشته سر

That you may not be seized by the tapeworm again!

چو باری فتادی نگهدار پای

When once you have fallen, look after your feet!

که یک بار دیگر بلغزد ز جای

That you may not again tumble down from your seat

ز سعدی شنو کاین سخن راست است

To Sa'di give ear! in this saying truth lies

نه هر باری افتاده برخاستهست

The man who falls down, does not always arise."

◈◉◈◉◈

گفتار اندر بی‌وفائی دنیا
On the Transitoriness of the World

جهان ای پسر ملک جاوید نیست
The world is a realm that is transient, oh son!

ز دنیا وفاداری امید نیست
Do not hope for fidelity here, for there's none!

نه بر باد رفتی سحرگاه و شام
Did not Solomon's throne, on the wind swiftly fly,

سریر سلیمان علیه‌السلام؟
Both morning and evening (on him safety lie!),

به آخر ندیدی که بر باد رفت؟
And have you not seen that it vanished at last?

خنک آن که با دانش و داد رفت
Happy he, who with knowledge and justice has passed

کسی زین میان گوی دولت ربود
From the center, the man bore Prosperity's ball,

که در بند آسایش خلق بود
Who laboured to comfort the great and the small.

به کار آمد آنها که برداشتند
The people were useful who held the fruit fast

نه گرد آوریدند و بگذاشتند
Not those who collected and left it, at last.

◈◉◈◉◈

در تغیر روزگار و انتقال مملکت
Story of an Egyptian King

شنیدم که در مصر میری اجل
I have heard that in Egypt a king who was great,

سپه تاخت بر روزگارش اجل
Was attacked in his prime by the army of Fate.

جمالش برفت از رخ دل فروز
In his cheek, heart-illuming, the beauty decayed;

چو خور زرد شد بس نماند ز روز
Pale as bread he became, and then Fate he obeyed.

113

گزیدند فرزانگان دست فوت

Philosophers learned bit the hand of Regret,

که در طب ندیدند داروی موت

For in Physic, no medicine for death could they get.

همه تخت و ملکی پذیرد زوال

Every kingdom and throne must submit to decay,

به جز ملک فرمانده لایزال

Save the kingdom of God, which will not pass away.

چو نزدیک شد روز عمرش به شب

When the day of his life was approaching to night,

شنیدند می‌گفت در زیر لب

They heard, as he spoke in a voice very slight:

که در مصر چون من عزیزی نبود

There has not been in Egypt a monarch like me;

چو حاصل همین بود چیزی نبود

Since the upshot is this, it was nothing, you see.

جهان گرد کردم نخوردم برش

I conquered the world, but no fruit did I find:

برفتم چو بیچارگان از سرش

I go, like a pauper, and leave it behind! "

پسندیده رایی که بخشید و خورد

One of praiseworthy wisdom, who gave and enjoyed,

جهان از پی خویشتن گرد کرد

The world, for the sake of himself, has employed.

در این کوش تا با تو ماند مقیم

Strive for that which will always beside you appear!

که هرچ از تو ماند دریغ است و بیم

For all that is left you, is sorrow and fear.

کند خواجه بر بستر جان گداز

The Magnate, reclined on the life-melting bed,

یکی دست کوتاه و دیگر دراز

Shows one hand contracted, the other outspread;

در آن دم تو را می‌نماید به دست

When his tongue was by terror from speaking confined,

که دهشت زبانش ز گفتن ببست

The meaning he then with his hands to you signed:

که دستی به جود و کرم کن دراز

"One hand in bestowing and kindness make long!

دگر دست کوته کن از ظلم و آز

And the other contract, in oppression and wrong! "

کنونت که دست است خاری بکن

Now that you have a hand, others' sorrow delete!

دگر کی بر آری تو دست از کفن؟

For when will your hand leave the white winding sheet?

بتابد بسی ماه و پروین و هور

The Sun, Moon and Pleiades long will illume,

که سر بر نداری ز بالین گور

Ere. you raise up your head from its prop in the tomb.

حکایت قزل ارسلان با دانشمند

Story of Kizil-Arslan and his fort

قزل ارسلان قلعه‌ای سخت داشت

King Kizil-Arslan a strong castle once held,

که گردن به الوند بر می‌فراشت

The height of whose head that of Alwand excelled.

نه اندیشه از کس نه حاجت به هیچ

No concern for a soul, not a want did betide

چو زلف عروسان رهش پیچ پیچ

Its path was all twists, like the curls of a bride.

چنان نادر افتاده در روضه‌ای

It stood in a garden, attractive and rare,

که بر لاجوردی طبق بیضه‌ای

Like an egg on a platter of blue earthenware.

شنیدم که مردی مبارک حضور

A person of presence benign, I've heard say,

به نزدیک شاه آمد از راه دور

To visit the king, came a long, tedious way.

حقایق شناسی، جهاندیده‌ای

A man of experience and versed in the true

هنرمندی، آفاق گردیده‌ای

A person of skill, who had roamed the Earth through.

قزل گفت چندین که گردیده‌ای

Kizil said, " among the places in which you have been,

چنین جای محکم دگر دیده‌ای؟

Such another strong fortress as this, have you seen? "

بخندید کاین قلعه‌ای خرم است

He, smiling, replied—" True, this fort lovely shows,

ولیکن نپندارمش محکم است

But that it is strong, I by no means suppose.

نه پیش از تو گردن کشان داشتند

Did not chiefs of renown hold it previous to you?

دمی چند بودند و بگذاشتند؟

For a time they existed, then vanished from view!

نه بعد از تو شاهان دیگر برند

After you, in like mode, other kings will have sway,

درخت امید تو را بر خورند؟

And the fruit of the tree of your hope take away.

ز دوران ملک پدر یاد کن

Remember the time of your own father's reign,

دل از بند اندیشه آزاد کن

And your heart from the bonds of concern free again!

چنان روزگارش به کنجی نشاند

Fortune forces him so in a corner to sit,

که بر یک پشیزش تصرف نماند

That he has not the spending of one copper bit.

چو نومید ماند از همه چیز و کس

When hopeless of persons and things he had grown,

امیدش به فضل خدا ماند و بس

In the favour of God was his hope set alone.

بر مرد هشیار دنیا خس است

In a wise man's opinion, the Earth is a weed

که هر مدتی جای دیگر کس است

That remains with each man but a moment, indeed."

⟨◉⟩⟨◉⟩

حکایت مرد دیوانه
Story of a Madman

چنین گفت شوریده‌ای در عجم

A madman in Persia, the following said

به کسری که ای وارث ملک جم

To Cyrus: " Oh heir, of the realm of Jamshed!

اگر ملک بر جم بماندی و بخت

If kingdom and fortune with Jam had remained,

تو را کی میسر شدی تاج و تخت؟

The crown and the throne, when would you have obtained?

اگر گنج قارون به دست آوری

If the wealth of Karun you were able to save,

نماند مگر آنچه بخشی، بری

It remains not; you take what in bounty you gave."

◈◉◈◉◈

حکایت پدر ارسلان
Story of Kizil-Arsalan's father

چو الب ارسلان جان به جان‌بخش داد

When the spirit of Alp-Arsalan to God fled,

پسر تاج شاهی به سر برنهاد

His son placed the Imperial Crown on his head.

به تربت سپردندش از تاجگاه

Alp was borne from the throne to the tomb and there shut;

نه جای نشستن بد آماجگاه

He had no sitting-place and no archery-butt

چنین گفت دیوانه‌ای هوشیار

A madman sagacious, was heard, thus, to say,

چو دیدش پسر روز دیگر سوار

When he saw the son riding a charger next day

زهی ملک و دوران سر در نشیب

Well done! State and Reign of the head the tomb mews

پدر رفت و پای پسر در رکیب

The father has gone and the son's in his shoes."

چنین است گردیدن روزگار

The revolving of Time has but one tale to tell

سبک سیر و بدعهد و ناپایدار

It is fleeting, unstable and lying, as well.

چو دیرینه روزی سرآورد عهد

When the man, full of days, brought his life to a close,

جوان دولتی سر برآرد ز مهد

The promising youth from his cradle arose.

منه بر جهان دل که بیگانه‌ای است

Put no trust in the world! for a stranger it roams,

چو مطرب که هر روز در خانه‌ای است

Like the minstrel, who, daily, resides in fresh homes.

نه لایق بود عیش با دلبری

Unfit is the pleasure a sweetheart supplies,

که هر بامدادش بود شوهری

With whom, every morning, a fresh husband lies.

نکویی کن امسال چون ده تو راست

Show kindness this year, while the village is thine

که سال دگر دیگری دهخداست

To another, the village, next year, you resign.

حکایت پادشاه غور با روستایی

The Tyrannical King and the Villager

بزرگی جفا پیشه در حد غور

In the confines of Ghor an oppressor held sway,

گرفتی خر روستایی به زور

Who by force, took the villagers' asses away.

خران زیر بار گران بی علف

The asses, unfed, under burdens of weight,

به روزی دو مسکین شدندی تلف

After two days of hardship, submitted to Fate.

چو منعم کند سفله را، روزگار

When Fortune has wealth on a caitiff bestowed,

نهد بر دل تنگ درویش، بار

On the heart of the poor she deposits a load.

چو بام بلندش بود خودپرست

If a self-lover's roof should some altitude show,

کند بول و خاشاک بر بام پست

He throws rubbish and pisses on roofs that are low.

شنیدم که باری به عزم شکار

I have heard that intending to hunt, round about,

برون رفت بیدادگر شهریار

The tyrannical ruler one morning set out.

تکاور به دنبال صیدی براند

In pursuit of his quarry he galloped amain,

شبش در گرفت از حشم باز ماند

And night overtook him, remote from his train.

به تنها ندانست روی و رهی

Unattended, he knew not the place nor the way,

بینداخت ناکام شب در دهی

And was forced, for the night, in a village to stay.

خری دید پوینده و کارگر

He saw a fleet ass, that was fit for the road,

توانا و زورآور و باربر

That was willing and strong and could bear a good load.

یکی مرد کرد استخوانی بدست

A man with a bone in his hand was so thrashing

چنان میزدش کاستخوان می شکست

And beating the beast, that its bones he was smashing.

شهنشه برآشفت و گفت ای جوان!

The king waxing wroth, said, "Oh youth! I beseech!

زحد رفت جورت بر این بی زبان

You are harsh beyond bounds to this brute without speech;

چو زورآوری خودنمایی مکن

Because you have strength, do not show yourself vain!

بر افتاده زور آزمایی مکن

And from testing your might on the fallen, refrain! "

پسندش نیامد فرومایه قول

The ignorant swain did not like this remark,

یکی بانگ بر پادشه زد بهول

And shouting with awe at the monarch, said, "Hark!

که بیهوده نگرفتم این کار پیش

In adopting this measure I have an intent;

برو چون ندانی بی کار خویش

Since you know not, be off! and pursue your own bent!

بسا کس که پیش تو معذور نیست

Many men, at first sight, whom you would not excuse,

چو وا بینی از مصلحت دور نیست

On inquiry, are found to be right in their views.

ملک را درشت آمد از وی خطاب

The reproof he administered ruffled the king;

بگفتا بیا تا چه بینی صواب

He said to him, "Come! are you right in this thing?

که پندارم از عقل بیگانه ای

I'm afraid you're a stranger to wisdom, my lad:

نه مستی همانا دیوانه ای

You do not seem drunk, but you look as if mad."

بخندید کای ترک نادان! خموش

He smiled, saying " Ignorant Turk, not a word!

مگر حال خضرت نیامد بگوش

The story of Khizir you may not have heard?

نه دیوانه خواند کس او را نه مست

Not a man called him mad, no one said he was drunk,

چرا کشتی ناتوان شکست؟

Then why were the poor people's boats by him sunk? "

جهان جوی گفت ای ستمکار مرد!

The monarch replied," Oh tyrannical one!

چه دانی که خضر آن برای چه کرد؟

Do you know why that action by Khizir was done?

در آن بحر مردی جفاپیشه بود

A tyrannical man had his residence there,

که دلها ازو بحر اندیشه بود

From whom, people's hearts were an ocean of care.

جزایر ز کردار او پر خروش

At his actions, the isles in lamenting engaged;

جهانی ز دستش چو دریا بجوش

A world at his hand, like the ocean enraged.

پس آنرا ز بهر مصالح شکست

Out of policy Khizir the boats all destroyed,

که سالار ظالم نگیرد بدست

That they by the tyrant might not be employed.

شکسته متاعی که در دست توست

To have property, damaged, within your control,

ار آن به که در دست دشمن درست

Is better than that, with your enemy whole."

بخندید دهقان روشن ضمیر

The peasant of luminous mind smiled, and said:

که پس حق بدست من است ای امیر

Oh Chief! then, the truth is with me on this head.

نه از جهل می بشکنم پای خر

I break not, from folly, the legs of the ass,

که از جور سلطان بیدادگر

But because of a tyrant's oppression, alas!

خر این جایگه لنگ و تیمار کش

A lame ass in this place, though enduring Care's sting,

از آن به که پیش ملک بارکش

Is better than that, bearing loads for the king.

تو آنرا نبینی که کشتی گرفت

That he seized all the boats, you've omitted to say,

که چون تا ابد نام زشتی گرفت

And acquired a bad name, that will haunt him for aye.

تفو بر چنان ملک و دولت که راند

Oh fie! such a king and the State where he reigns!

که شنعت بر او تا قیامت بماند

For a curse on his head till the Judgment remains.

ستمگر جفا بر تن خویش کرد

Upon his own body, the tyrant works ill,

نه بر جان مسکین درویش کرد

And not on the poor who submit to his will.

که فردا در آن محفل نام و ننگ

In To-morrow's assembly for all, when he stands,

بگیرد گریبان و ریشش به چنگ

He will seize on his collar and beard with his hands;

نهد بار او زار بر گردنش

On his neck the vast load of his crimes he will place,

نیارد سر از عار بر گردنش

And he wont raise his head on account of disgrace.

گرفتم که خر بارش اکنون کشد

His burden the ass carries now, I admit;

در آن روز بار خران چون کشد؟

How on him, on that day, will the ass's load sit?

اگر انصاف پرسی بداختر کس است

If you ask for the truth, then, ill-fated is he,

که در راحتش رنج دیگر کس است

Who in others' distress his own comfort can see.

همین پنج روزش تنعم بود

But a few days of pleasure to him will pertain,

که شادیش در رنج مردم بود

Whose gladness depends on his fellow-men's pain.

اگر من نبینم مر او را هلاک

If that heart without life did not rise, it were good;

شب گور چشمم نخسبد به خاک

For because of him, men sleep in sorrowful mood."

شه این جمله بشنید و چیزی نگفت

The king heard it all but no answer expressed;

ببست اسپ و سر بر نمد زین بخفت

Tied his horse, laid his head on his Numda to rest.

همه شب ز بیداری اختر شمرد

He was wakeful all night, counting stars in the skies;

ز سودا و اندیشه خوابش نبرد

From passion and thinking, sleep closed not his eyes.

چو آواز مرغ سحر گوش کرد

When he heard the cock crow, at the dawning of day,

پریشانی شب فراموش کرد

The distress of the night quickly vanished away.

سواران همه شب یزک تاختند

The horsemen, all night, kept patrolling around,

سحرگه پی اسب بشناختند

And at dawn saw his horse's hoof-prints on the ground.

بر آن عرصه بر اسپ دیدند و شاه

They beheld the king riding his steed on the plain;

پیاده دویدند یکسر سپاه

To his presence, on foot, ran the whole of his train.

به خدمت نهادند سر بر زمین

In devotion they bowed their heads low on the sand;

چو دریا شد از موج لشکر، زمین

From the surging of troops, like the sea was the land.

بزرگان نشستند و خوان خواستند

The courtiers sit down and refreshments demand;

بخوردند و مجلس بیاراستند

They ate and a festive assembly they planned.

چو شور و طرب در نهاد آمدش

When the sound of the mirth on the king had effect,

ز دهقان دوشینه یاد آمدش

On the swain of last night, he began to reflect.

بفرمود و جستند و بستند سخت

He commanded, they searched for and bound him apace;

به خواری فکندند در پای تخت

At the foot of the throne, threw him down in disgrace.

سیه دل برآهیخت شمشیر تیز

The headsman unsheathed his dire sabre, so keen;

ندانست بیچاره روی گریز

By the doomed one, no way of escape could be seen.

شنیدم آندم از زندگی آخرش

He reckoned that moment of life as his last,

بگفت آنچه گردید در خاطرش

And boldly disclosed what within his mind passed.

نبینی که چون کارد بر سر بود

Don't you see, when the knife to the summit is laid,

قلم را زبانش روان تر بود

That the tongue of the pen far more fluent is made.

چو دانست کز شه نتوان گریخت

When one knows that he cannot escape from his foe,

به ناپاکی او تیر ترکش بریخت

From his quiver, the arrows he, fearless, will strew.

سر نا امیدی برآورد و گفت

He raised up his head in despair, and thus said:

شب گور در ده محالست خفت

"In the thorp you can't sleep, on the night you are dead.

ز نامهربانی که در دور تست

On account of the heartlessness seen in your age,

همه عالم آوازه جور تست

The world knows the violence in which you engage.

نه من کردم از دست جورت نفیر

I alone do not curse your tyrannical reign,

که خلقی ز خلقی یکی کشته گیر

But the people; of them, see in me but one slain!

عجب کز منت بر دل آمد درشت

It is strange that my words should have rankled your will;

بکش گر توانی همه خلق کشت

Kill away, if the whole of mankind you can kill!

وگر سخت آمد نکوهش ز من

And if my reproaches come harsh to your mind,

بانصاف بیخ نکوهش بکن

With justice, uproot all oppression you find!

ترا چاره از ظلم برگشتن است

Your work is to drive all injustice away;

نه بیچاره بیگنه کشتن است

Not, a helpless and innocent person, to slay.

چو بیداد کردی توقع مدار

When you practise injustice, the hope do not hold

که نامت به نیکی رود در دیار

That your name through the world will with goodness be told.

ندانم که چون خسپدت دیدگان

I cannot conceive how you manage to sleep;

نخفته ز دستت ستمدیدگان

For those you oppressed have had vigils to keep.

بدان کی ستوده شود پادشاه؟

Know! when will a monarch be honestly praised,

که خلقش ستایند در بارگاه

In whose court, all the people have flatt'ry's voice raised?

چه سودآفرین بر سر انجمن؟

What avails the assembly's demonstrative praise!

پس چرخه نفرین کنان مرد و زن

While spinning their wheels, people malisons raise? "

گرفت این سخن شاه ظالم بگوش

The tyrannical king, to this lecture inclined

ز سرمستی غفلت آمد بهوش

From the maze of neglect, he recovered his mind.

بزرگیش بخشید و فرماندهی

In the village, where Fortune the truth to him showed,

ز شاخ امیدش برآمد بهی

He the office of chief on that peasant bestowed.

بیاموزی از عاقلان حسن خوی

Such wisdom and manners, you cannot procure

نه چندان که از غافل عیب جوی

From the learned, as you can from the fault-finding boor.

ز دشمن شنو سیرت خود که دوست

From foes hear your qualities; not from allies;

هر آنچه ار تو آید بچشمش نکوست

For whatever you do will seem good in their eyes.

ستایش سرایان نه یار تو اند

Those singing your praises are friends, but in name;

ملامت کنان دوستدار تو اند

And those who reprove you, true. friendship can claim.

ترش روی بهتر کند سرزنش

A sour-visaged person much better rebukes,

که یاران خوش طبع شیرین منش

Than a good-natured friend, who has sweet-smiling looks.

ازین به نصیحت نگوید کست

Than this, none can tender you better advice;

اگر عاقلی یک اشارت بست

And if you have wisdom, a hint will suffice.

حکایت مأمون با کنیزک
Story of Mamun and his Slave

چو دور خلافت به مأمون رسید

When the turn of Mamun to be Caliph arrived,

یکی ماه پیکر کنیزک خرید

To purchase a beautiful maid he contrived

به چهر آفتابی، به تن گلبنی

In body a rosebush, in visage a sun,

به عقل خردمند بازی کنی

With the wisdom of sages, a frolicsomeone.

به خون عزیزان فرو برده چنگ

On the blood of beloved ones, her ringers impinged;

سر انگشتها کرده عناب رنگ

Her nails with the juice of the jujube were tinged.

بر ابروی عابد فریبش خضاب

There appeared on her saint-luring eyebrows a dye,

چو قوس قزح بود بر آفتاب

Like a rainbow arched over the sun in the sky.

شب خلوت آن لعبت حور زاد

In the night-time, that idol, celestial in race,

مگر تن در آغوش مأمون نداد

Would not yield herself up to Mamun's fond embrace

گرفت آتش خشم در وی عظیم

Within him, the burning of rage mighty grew;

سرش خواست کردن چو جوزا دو نیم

Her head, like the twins, he would fain cut in two.

بگفتا سر اینک به شمشیر تیز

She exclaimed, "Lo! my head, with the sword strike it free!

بینداز و با من مکن خفت و خیز

But indulge not in sleeping and rising with me! "

بگفت از چه بر دل گزند آمدت؟

He asked her, "By whom has your mind been distressed?

چه خصلت ز من ناپسند آمدت؟

What habit have I, that you seem to detest? "

بگفت ار کشی ور شکافی سرم

She replied, " If you kill me or split up my head,

ز بوی دهانت به رنج اندرم

From the smell of your mouth I am sick and in dread;

کشد تیر پیکار و تیغ ستم

The arrow of war, and oppression's sword hit

به یک بار و بوی دهن دم به دم

In a moment, a foul breath destroys bit by bit"-

شنید این سخن سرور نیکبخت

The fortunate chief heard this honest address:

برآشفت تند و برنجید سخت

He was greatly afflicted and writhed, in distress.

دلش گرچه در حال از او رنجه شد

Though his heart, for the time, at her speaking was pained,

دوا کرد و خوشبوی چون غنچه شد

He took drugs and a breath sweet as rose-blossoms gained.

پری چهره را همنشین کرد و دوست

He made comrade and friend of the fairy-faced maid;

که این عیب من گفت، یار من اوست

"For my faults she has told and a friend's part has played."

به نزد من آن کس نکوخواه توست

To me, it appears that the man is your friend,

که گوید فلان خار در راه توست

Who points out the thorns on the way you must wend.

به گمراه گفتن نکو می‌روی

You succeed very well by declaring what's wrong;

جفایی تمام است و جوری قوی

Oppression is perfect and tyranny.strong!

هر آن گه که عیبت نگویند پیش

Whenever they tell not your faults to your face,

هنر دانی از جاهلی عیب خویش

You in ignorance reckon your fault as a grace!

مگو شهد شیرین شکر فایق است

Do not say that sweet honey's a drug, that will suit

کسی را که سقمونیا لایق است

Any person, requiring some scammony root.

چه خوش گفت یک روز دارو فروش

How well spoke the man, who had medicines to sell —

شفا بایدت داروی تلخ نوش

You must drink bitter draughts if you wish to get well,

به پرویزن معرفت بیخته

Well strained through the sieve of the knowledge divine,

به شهد ظرافت برآمیخته

With the honey of Piety blended up fine."

حکایت درویش صادق و پادشاه بیدادگر
The Fakir and the King

شنیدم که از نیکمردی فقیر

A Fakir, I have heard, who was holy and kind,

دل آزرده شد پادشاهی کبیر

Vexed the soul of a king, who was haughty in mind.

مگر بر زبانش حقی رفته بود

Very likely, a truth from his tongue had transpired

ز گردن‌کشی بر وی آشفته بود

Concerning his pride, and his fury was fired.

به زندان فرستادش از بارگاه

From the Court to a dungeon he sent him away;

که زورآزمای است بازوی جاه

For the arm of a monarch is able to slay.

ز یاران کسی گفتش اندر نهفت

A friend sought his cell and, in secret, thus spoke:

مصالح نبود این سخن گفت، گفت

The sayings you uttered could only provoke ".

رسانیدن امر حق طاعت است

Devotion's fulfilling God's orders," he said,

ز زندان نترسم که یک ساعت است

"I fear not the dungeon — an hour and 'tis fled "

همان دم که در خفیه این راز رفت

The moment this secret, in secret got vent,

حکایت به گوش ملک باز رفت

Straight back to the ears of the monarch it went.

بخندید کاو ظن بیهوده برد

With a smile, he replied, "His assumption is wrong;.

نداند که خواهد در این حبس مرد

Does he know that he'll die in that dungeon ere long "?

غلامی به درویش برد این پیام

This message, a serf to the holy man gave;

بگفتا به خسرو بگو ای غلام

He replied, "Give this answer to Cyrus, oh slave

مرا بار غم بر دل ریش نیست

The world, too, for more than an hour won't remain

که دنیا همین ساعتی بیش نیست

Grief and Joy, in the holy no footing obtain.

نه گر دستگیری کنی خرمم

If you grant me release, you'd not make me feel glad;

نه گر سر بری بر دل آید غمم

If my head you should sever, my heart won't be sad.

تو گر کامرانی به فرمان و گنج

If to you troops and empire and treasure pertain,

دگر کس فرومانده در ضعف و رنج

And I have my children, hopes blighted, and pain,

به دروازهٔ مرگ چون در شویم

When we come in our wand'ring to Death's open gate,

به یک هفته با هم برابر شویم

Together, as equals, a week we shall wait.

منه دل بر این دولت پنج روز

On the realm of five days do not let your heart dwell!

به دود دل خلق، خود را مسوز

Do not foolishly burn your own body in hell!

نه پیش از تو بیش از تو اندوختند

Did not rulers before you more treasure obtain!

به بیداد کردن جهان سوختند؟

By injustice they burned up the world in their reign.

چنان زی که ذکرت به تحسین کنند

So live! that your name may be mentioned with praise;

چو مردی، نه بر گور نفرین کنند

That when dead, on your tomb none may malisons raise.

نباید به رسم بد آیین نهاد

A law to bad customs you should not apply!

که گویند لعنت بر آن، کاین نهاد

For, 'A curse on that nature depraved! ' they will cry.

وگر بر سرآید خداوند زور

And if the strong man to dominion should rise,

نه زیرش کند عاقبت خاک گور؟

Won't the dust of the grave keep him down when he dies "?

بفرمود دلتنگ روی از جفا

For Oppression's sad victim, the tyrant decreed

که بیرون کنندش زبان از قفا

That his innocent tongue from its root should be freed.

چنین گفت مرد حقایق شناس

The truth-recognizing philosopher said:

کز این هم که گفتی ندارم هراس

About this, too, you mention, I cherish no dread

من از بی زبانی ندارم غمی

My having no tongue will not cause me a woe;

که دانم که ناگفته داند همی

For I'm sure, what's unspoken, the Maker will know.

اگر بینوایی برم ور ستم

If want or oppression I'm fated to bear,

گرم عاقبت خیر باشد چه غم؟

And at last I am happy, why foster a care?

عروسی بود نوبت ماتمت

The season of grief is a bridal to you,

گرت نیکروزی بود خاتمت

If, when your end comes, you have gladness in view ",

❖◉❖◉❖

حکایت زورآزمای تنگدست
Story of a hard-up pugilist

یکی مشت زن بخت و روزی نداشت
A pugilist's means of support were not good

نه اسباب شامش مهیا نه چاشت
For supper or breakfast no suitable food:

ز جور شکم گل کشیدی به پشت
From his stomach's demands, he bore clay on his back,

که روزی محال است خوردن به مشت
For his fists could not find him in rations, alack!

مدام از پریشانی روزگار
He had ever, because of his sorrowful plight,

دلش حسرت آورد و تن سوگوار
A load on his heart, on his body a blight.

گهش جنگ با عالم خیره‌کش
At one time, he warred with the world's wicked power;

گه از بخت شوریده، رویش ترش
At another, harsh Fate caused his face to look sour.

گه از دیدن عیش شیرین خلق
From observing, again, the sweet pleasure of all,

فرو می‌شدی آب تلخش به حلق
The large, bitter tears down his gullet would fall.

گه از کار آشفته بگریستی
Again at his wretched affairs he would cry —

که کس دید از این تلخ‌تر زیستی؟
Has anyone seen such a live wretch as I?

کسان شهد نوشند و مرغ و بره
On honey and chickens and kids, some are fed;

مرا روی نان می‌نبیند تره
Not a pot-herb is seen on the face of my bread.

گر انصاف پرسی نه نیکوست این
If you ask about justice, it must be a slur,

برهنه من و گربه را پوستین
That, whereas I am naked, a cat has its fur.

چه بودی که پایم در این کار گل
Alas! if the Sky had such sympathy shown,

به گنجی فرو رفتی از کام دل
As into my keeping some wealth to have thrown;

131

مگر روزگاری هوس راندمی

For a time, I would, likely, have revelled in lust,

ز خود گرد محنت بیفشاندمی

And brushed from my body Adversity's dust"

شنیدم که روزی زمین می‌شکافت

I have heard that one day he was digging the ground,

عظام زنخدان پوسیده یافت

When a lower jaw-bone, that was rotten, he found.

به خاک اندرش عقد بگسیخته

The links of the chain were divided, throughout,

گهرهای دندان فرو ریخته

And the fine pearly teeth were all scattered about.

دهان بی زبان پند می‌گفت و راز

The mouth, without tongue, truth and secrets thus spoke:

که ای خواجه با بینوایی بساز

Oh sir! you must bear Disappointment's sad stroke!

نه این است حال دهن زیر گل

Is this not the state of the mouth under mud?

شکر خورده انگار یا خون دل

It may have eat sugar or drunk its heart's blood.

غم از گردش روزگاران مدار

On account of the changes of Time, do not grieve!

که بی ما بگردد بسی روزگار

For Time oft will change and not say, By your leave

همان لحظه کاین خاطرش روی داد

The moment his conscience this meaning divined,

غم از خاطرش رخت یک سو نهاد

Grief carried her baggage away from his mind.

که ای نفس بی رای و تدبیر و هش

Oh spirit," he said, "void of wisdom and will,

بکش بار تیمار و خود را مکش

Endure sorrow's load, but yourself do not kill!"

اگر بنده‌ای بار بر سر برد

If a slave has a load on his head to support,

وگر سر به اوج فلک بر برد

Or his head at the top of the sky he should sport,

در آن دم که حالش دگرگون شود

t the moment his state becomes altered by death,

به مرگ از سرش هر دو بیرون شود

Both conditions will go from his head, at a breath.

غم و شادمانی نماند ولیک

Grief and gladness are fleeting, and yet it is sure

جزای عمل ماند و نام نیک

That good names, and the meed of all actions endure

کرم پای دارد، نه دیهیم و تخت

Beneficence lasts, not the crown and the throne;

بده کز تو این ماند ای نیکبخت

Oh lucky one, give! for this lasts when you're gone.

مکن تکیه بر ملک و جاه و حشم

Put your trust not in kingdom nor troops and display!

که پیش از تو بوده‌ست و بعد از تو هم

For before you they were and behind you will stay.

زرافشان، چو دنیا بخواهی گذاشت

Scatter gold! since the world you will have to forego;

که سعدی در افشاند اگر زر نداشت

For Sádi strewed pearls, if no gold he could strew.

◈◉◈◈◉◈

حکایت در معنی خاموشی از نصیحت کسی که پند نپذیرد
Story of an Oppressor

حکایت کنند از جفاگستری
Of a wicked oppressor, a tale they relate,
که فرماندهی داشت بر کشوری
That he exercised sovereignty over a State.

در ایام او روز مردم چو شام
In his reign people's days were as dark as the night;
شب از بیم او خواب مردم حرام
And at night, people slept not, from terror and fright.

همه روز نیکان از او در بلا
At his hand, pious men were all day in despair;
به شب دست پاکان از او بر دعا
The holy, at night, held their hands up in prayer.

گروهی بر شیخ آن روزگار
In front of the sheikh of that period, a band
ز دست ستمگر گرستند زار
Said, weeping, because of the tyrant's harsh hand,

که ای پیر دانای فرخنده رای
" Oh guide I in whom learning and wisdom appear,
بگوی این جوان را بترس از خدای
Advise this young man that the Lord he should fear!"

بگفتا دریغ آیدم نام دوست
He replied, "I am loath to declare the Friend's name;
که هر کس نه در خورد پیغام اوست
For all are not worthy His message to claim."

کسی را که بینی ز حق بر کران
When you find that a man thinks the truth is not right,
منه با وی، ای خواجه، حق در میان
Oh sir! do not talk about truth to that wight!

حقت گفتم ای خسرو نیکرای
The Truth, oh wise king! I explained to you well;
توان گفت حق پیش مرد خدای
To a God-fearing person, the Truth you can tell.

دریغ است با سفله گفت از علوم
At teaching fools knowledge, I care not to toil;
که ضایع شود تخم در شوره بوم
For the seed I but waste in a profitless soil.

چو در وی نگیرد عدو داندت

They think me a foe when it fails to take root,

برنجد به جان و برنجاندت

Oh monarch! your aim is to do what is right

تو را عادت، ای پادشه، حق روی است

Oh monarch! your aim is to do what is right

دل مرد حق گوی از این جا قوی است

Hence the heart of the truth-speaking person has might.

نگین خصلتی دارد ای نیکبخت

Oh favoured a seal has a feature well known

که در موم گیرد نه در سنگ سخت

It makes an impression on wax, not on stone.

عجب نیست گر ظالم از من به جان

No wonder the tyrant through me suffers grief,

برنجد که دزد است و من پاسبان

Since I am the watchman and he is the thief!

تو هم پاسبانی به انصاف و داد

You, too, are a watchman in justice and right;

که حفظ خدا پاسبان تو باد

May the watching of God be your guard day and night!

تو را نیست منت ز روی قیاس

Not yours is the favour, comparison says;

خداوند را من و فضل و سپاس

To the Maker be thanksgiving, merit, and praise!

که در کار خیرت به خدمت بداشت

That in doing good works, He has kept you employed;

نه چون دیگرانت معطل گذاشت

And not left you, like others, with effort destroyed,

همه کس به میدان کوشش درند

Everyone in the plain of exertion may play,

ولی گوی بخشش نه هر کس برند

But, the ball-of-bestowing, each bears not away.

تو حاصل نکردی به کوشش بهشت

By striving, you did not obtain Paradise;

خدا در تو خوی بهشتی بهشت

God caused a good nature within you to rise.

دلت روشن و وقت مجموع باد

May your heart be enlightened and tranquil your time!

قدم ثابت و پایه مرفوع باد

May your footing be sure and your rank be sublime!

حیاتت خوش و رفتنت بر صواب

May your lifetime be happy! your going be fair!

عبادت قبول و دعا مستجاب

Received be your worship! and answered your prayer!

گفتار اندر رای و تدبیر ملک و لشکرکشی
Remarks on dealing with enemies

همی تا برآید به تدبیر کار

Until your diplomacy terminates right,

مدارای دشمن به از کارزار

It is better to natter your foe, than to fight.

چو نتوان عدو را به قوت شکست

When, by force, you're unable to vanquish your foes,

به نعمت بباید در فتنه بست

By favours, the portal of strife you must close!

گر اندیشه باشد ز خصمت گزند

If you fear lest you be by an enemy stung,

به تعویذ احسان زبانش ببند

With the charm of munificence, tie up his tongue!

عدو را به جای خسک زر بریز

Give your enemy money! not thorns from a hedge!

که احسان کند کند، دندان تیز

For munificence blunts all the teeth that have edge.

چو دستی نشاید گزیدن، ببوس

The hand you can't bite, it is proper to kiss!

که با غالبان چاره زرق است و لوس

By skill, you can coax and enjoy earthly bliss;

به تدبیر رستم در آید به بند

By management, Rustam will come to the noose,

که اسفندیارش نجست از کمند

From whose coil, Asfandyar could not cast himself loose.

عدو را به فرصت توان کند پوست

You can find the occasion your foe's skin to rend;

پس او را مدارا چنان کن که دوست

Take care of him! then, as you would of a friend.

حذر کن ز پیکار کمتر کسی

Be cautious in fighting with one you despise!

که از قطره سیلاب دیدم بسی

From a drop, I have oft seen a torrent arise.

مزن تا توانی بر ابرو گره

While you can, let not knots on your eyebrows be seen!

که دشمن اگرچه زبون، دوست به

An opponent is best as a friend, although mean.

بود دشمنش تازه و دوست ریش

His foe shows delight, and his friend shows distress,

کسی کش بود دشمن از دوست بیش

Whose friends are, in count, than his enemies less.

مزن با سپاهی ز خود بیشتر

With an army exceeding your own, do not fight!

که نتوان زد انگشت بر نیشتر

For you can't with your finger a lancet's point smite.

وگر زو تواناتری در نبرد

And should you be stronger in war than your foe;

نه مردی است بر ناتوان زور کرد

To the weak, 'tis unmanly oppression to show!

اگر پیل زوری وگر شیر چنگ

Though you've lion-like hands and an elephant's force,

به نزدیک من صلح بهتر که جنگ

Peace is better than war, as a matter of course.

چو دست از همه حیلتی درگسست

When the hand has by every deception been torn,

حلال است بردن به شمشیر دست

The hand to the sword may be lawfully borne.

اگر صلح خواهد عدو سر مپیچ

Should your foe wish for peace, his request do not spurn!

وگر جنگ جوید عنان بر مپیچ

And should he seek battle, the reins do not turn!

که گر وی ببندد در کارزار

For should he resolve to resist in the field,

تو را قدر و هیبت شود یک، هزار

The strength and the awe of a thousand you'll wield.

ور او پای جنگ آورد در رکاب

If his foot he has placed in the stirrup of war,

نخواهد به حشر از تو داور حساب

You won't be arraigned at the Great Judgment Bar.

تو هم جنگ را باش چون کینه خواست

Be prepared, too, for war, should sedition awake!

که با کینه ور مهربانی خطاست

For kindness to blackguards is quite a mistake.

چو با سفله گویی به لطف و خوشی

If you talk in an affable way to a wretch,

فزون گرددش کبر و گردن کشی

His presumption and arrogance higher will stretch.

به اسبان تازی و مردان مرد

When your enemy, vanquished, approaches your gate;

بر آر از نهاد بداندیش گرد

Cast revenge from your heart and cast ire from your pate!

چو زنهار خواهد کرم پیشه کن

You should kindness bestow when he asks for your care;

ببخشای و از مکرش اندیشه کن

Be gracious! and of his deceptions, beware!

ز تدبیر پیر کهن بر مگرد

From an aged man's counselling turn not away!

که کارآزموده بود سالخورد

For he knows his work well who has lived to be grey!

در آرند بنیاد رویین ز پای

And should they remove from its site the strong-hold

جوانان به نیروی و پیران به رای

The youth with the sword and with wisdom the old

بیندیش در قلب هیجا مفر

In the thick of the fight, bear a refuge in mind!

چه دانی که زان که باشد ظفر؟

What know you which side will the victory find?

چو بینی که لشکر ز هم دست داد

When you see that your army has lost in the strife,

به تنها مده جان شیرین به باد

Alone, do not cast to the wind your sweet life!

اگر بر کناری به رفتن بکوش

Should your place be the border, make running your care!

وگر در میان لبس دشمن بپوش

And if in the middle, the foe's raiment wear!

وگر خود هزاری و دشمن دویست

If you number two thousand two hundred your foe,

چو شب شد در اقلیم دشمن مایست

When night has arrived from his clime you should go!

شب تیره پنجه سوار از کمین

At night, Fifty horsemen from lying in wait,

چو پانصد به هیبت بدرد زمین

Like Five Hundred, a noise on the ground will create.

چو خواهی بریدن به شب راهها

When you wish to accomplish some marches by night,

حذر کن نخست از کمینگاهها

First, look for the ambushes, hidden from sight!

میان دو لشکر چو یک روز راه

When one of two armies has marched for a day,

بماند، بزن خیمه بر جایگاه

The strength from his hands will have dwindled away;

تو آسوده بر لشکر مانده زن

At your leisure the army exhausted attack!

که نادان ستم کرد بر خویشتن

For the fool has himself placed a load on his back.

چو دشمن شکستی بیفکن علم

When you've vanquished your foe, do not lower your flag!

که بازش نیاید جراحت به هم

Lest again he should gather his forces, and brag.

بسی در قفای هزیمت مران

In pursuit of the fugitives, go not too far!

نباید که دور افتی از یاوران

For you should not lose sight of your comrades in war.

هوا بینی از گرد هیجا چو میغ

When the air, from war's dust, like a cloud to you shows,

بگیرند گردت به زوبین و تیغ

Around you, with spears and with swords, they will close.

به دنبال غارت نراند سپاه

From searching for plunder, the soldier refrains,

که خالی بماند پس پشت شاه

Who, alone, at the back of the monarch remains.

سپه را نگهبانی شهریار

To an army, the duty of guarding the king,

به از جنگ در حلقهٔ کارزار

Is better than fight in the battle-field's ring.

◀◉▶◀◉▶

گفتار اندر نواخت لشکریان در حالت امن
Remarks on cherishing the army

دلاور که باری تهور نمود

If once a brave man should courageousness show,

بباید به مقدارش اندر فزود

Befitting his merits, promotion bestow!

که بار دگر دل نهد بر هلاک

That again upon death he may hazard his life,

ندارد ز پیکار یأجوج باک

And not fear to contend against Gog, in war's strife.

سپاهی در آسودگی خوش بدار

During peace, keep the welfare of soldiers in view!

که در حالت سختی آید به کار

That in times of emergency, good may ensue.

کنون دست مردان جنگی ببوس

It is now, you should kiss the defender's rough hand,

نه آنگه که دشمن فرو کوفت کوس

And not when the foe beats his drum in your land.

سپاهی که کارش نباشد به برگ

If a soldier's profession should fail to give bread,

چرا روز هیجا نهد دل به مرگ؟

Why should he, when war happens, sport with his head?

نواحی ملک از کف بدسگال

The bounds of your realm, from the enemy's hold,

به لشکر نگه دار و لشکر به مال

With your army preserve! and your army with gold!

ملک را بود بر عدو دست، چیر

The king has the mastery over his foes,

چو لشکر دل آسوده باشند و سیر

When his troops are content and their hearts have repose.

بهای سر خویشتن می‌خورد

The price of his head, the brave soldier but eats;

نه انصاف باشد که سختی برد

It is very unjust, then, when hardship he meets.

چو دارند گنج از سپاهی دریغ

When they think it a pity to give him their gold,

دریغ آیدش دست بردن به تیغ

His hand from the sword he is apt to withhold.

چه مردی کند در صف کارزار

What pluck will he show, when for battle arrayed,

که دستش تهی باشد و کار، زار

Whose hand contains nought, and whose works are decayed?

◈ ◈

گفتار اندر تقویت مردان کار آزموده
Remarks on the selection of troops and leaders

به پیکار دشمن دلیران فرست

Send men who are brave to encounter the foe!

هژبران به ناورد شیران فرست

And lions, to fight against tigers, should go!

به رای جهاندیدگان کار کن

The wisdom of persons experienced, apply!

که صید آزموده‌ست گرگ کهن

For the wolf that is aged, in hunting is sly.

مترس از جوانان شمشیر زن

Of youths who can handle the sword, have no fear!

حذر کن ز پیران بسیار فن

Of veterans grounded in science, keep clear!

جوانان پیل افکن شیرگیر

Young men, who can tigers and elephants hold,

ندانند دستان روباه پیر

Do not know all the tricks of the fox become old.

خردمند باشد جهاندیده مرد

The man who has travelled has knowledge in store,

که بسیار گرم آزموده‌ست و سرد

For abundance of heat and exposure he bore.

جوانان شایستهٔ بخت ور

Young men who are worthy, whom Fortune has sped,

ز گفتار پیران نپیچند سر

From the words of the aged avert not their head.

گرت مملکت باید آراسته

If you wish to arrange the affairs of a realm,

مده کار معظم به نوخاسته

Appoint not a novice to manage the helm.

سپه را مکن پیشرو جز کسی

Let no one as chief of your army be seen,

که در جنگها بوده باشد بسی

Who shall not in many a battle have been.

نتابد سگ صید روی از پلنگ

The sporting-dog shrinks from the fierce leopard's sight

ز روبه رمد شیر نادیده جنگ

The fox cows the tiger who never saw fight.

چو پرورده باشد پسر در شکار

When a boy has been tutored to follow the chase,

نترسد چو پیش آیدش کارزار

He does not feel frightened when war shows its face.

به کشتی و نخجیر و آماج و گوی

By boating and hunting and polo and butts,

دلاور شود مرد پرخاشجوی

The war-seeking man, like a dare-devil struts.

به گرمابه پرورده و عیش و ناز

One in warm-baths and pleasure and blandishments trained,

برنجد چو بیند در جنگ باز

When the portal of battle is opened, is pained

دو مردش نشانند بر پشت زین

To support him in saddle, two men must be found;

بود کش زند کودکی بر زمین

And a boy, with a spindle, could beat him to ground

یکی را که دیدی تو در جنگ پشت

If in battle a run-away's back meets your gaze,

بکش گر عدو در مصافش نکشت

Take his life, if the foe should not finish his days!

مخنث به از مرد شمشیر زن

A pederast surpasses the swordsman by far,

که روز وغا سر بتابد چو زن

Who, woman-like, runs in the season of war.

❁◉❁◉❁

حکایت شجاعت

On Bravery

چه خوش گفت گرگین به فرزند خویش

ow well spoke Gurghin to his son, on the day

چو قربان پیکار بربست و کیش

That he bound on his quiver and sword, for the fray.

اگر چون زنان جست خواهی گریز

If you harbour a thought, like a woman, of flight,

مرو آب مردان جنگی مریز

Do not go! and defame not war's heroes of might "

سواری که در جنگ بنمود پشت

The horseman who showed in the battle his back,

نه خود را که نام آوران را بکشت

Not himself, but brave warriors extinguished, alack!

شجاعت نیاید مگر زآن دو یار

No valour, except in those two comrades, shows,

که افتند در حلقهٔ کارزار

Who right in the centre of battle deal blows

دو همجنس همسفرهٔ همزبان

Two messmates, of similar language and race,

بکوشند در قلب هیجا به جان

To their utmost will strive, in the fight's centre place;

که تنگ آیدش رفتن از پیش تیر

For the one feels ashamed from the arrows to go,

برادر به چنگال دشمن اسیر

While his brother is seized, in the hands of the foe.

چو بینی که یاران نباشند یار

When you find that your friends are unwilling to aid,

هزیمت ز میدان غنیمت شمار

Let arrangements for flight, and not plunder, be made!

گفتار اندر دلداری هنرمندان
On Cherishing the Army

دو تن، پرور ای شاه کشور گشای

Two persons, oh conquering king, patronize!

یکی اهل رزم و دگر اهل رای

The man who has strength and the man who is wise.

ز نام آوران گوی دولت برند

Those bear Fortune's ball off, from persons renowned,

که دانا و شمشیر زن پرورند

Who cherishing sages and warriors are found.

هر آن کاو قلم را نورزید و تیغ

If a man has not handled the pen or the sword,

بر او گر بمیرد مگو ای دریغ

Over him, should he die, say no sorrowing word!

قلم زن نکودار و شمشیر زن

Look after the writer and swordsman, with care;

نه مطرب که مردی نیاید ز زن

Not the minstrel! for bravery in woman is rare!

نه مردی است دشمن در اسباب جنگ

It is unmanly that you, with the enemy armed,

تو مدهوش ساقی و آواز چنگ

Should with Bearers of wine and lute music be charmed.

بسا اهل دولت به بازی نشست

Many prosperous people who sat down to play,

که دولت برفتش به بازی ز دست

By gambling, have squandered their fortunes away.

❖◉❖◉❖

گفتار اندر حذر کردن از دشمنان

On being always Prepared for an Enemy

نگویم ز جنگ بد اندیش ترس

I don't bid you fear to wage war with a foe;

در آوازهٔ صلح از او بیش ترس

Of his talk about peace, greater fear you should show!

بسا کس به روز آیت صلح خواند

Many persons by day have the verse of peace read,

چو شب شد سپه بر سر خفته راند

Who, at night, marched their troops on the sleeping foe's head.

زره پوش خسبند مرد اوژنان

The conquering men sleep in armour complete;

که بستر بود خوابگاه زنان

For a woman, a couch is a sleeping-place meet.

به خیمه درون مرد شمشیر زن

Does not sleep, as a woman at home does, undressed.

برهنه نخسبد چو در خانه زن

For the foe to attack you in secret will dare.

بباید نهان جنگ را ساختن

It behoves you, in secret, for war to prepare!

که دشمن نهان آورد تاختن

For the foe to attack you in secret will dare.

حذر کار مردان کار آگه است

Taking care, is the business of men of good stamp;

یزک سد رویین لشکر گه است

The advanced guard's the brazen defence of the camp.

◉ ◉

گفتار اندر دفع دشمن به رای و تدبیر

Remarks on plotting and mutual quarrels

میان دو بد خواه کوتاه دست

Between two malevolent men, of short hand,

نه فرزانگی باشد ایمن نشست

To settle secure, does not wisdom command.

که گر هر دو باهم سگالند راز

For should they, together, in secret conspire,

شود دست کوتاه ایشان دراز

The short hands of both will extension acquire.

یکی را به نیرنگ مشغول دار

By deception, keep one of them fully employed

دگر را برآور ز هستی دمار

Let the other's existence be quickly destroyed!

اگر دشمنی پیش گیرد ستیز

If an enemy makes his arrangements for strife,

به شمشیر تدبیر خونش بریز

With the sword of contrivance, deprive him of life!

برو دوستی گیر با دشمنش

To his enemy go, and your friendship declare!

که زندان شود پیرهن بر تنش

For a dungeon would be like a shirt for his wear.

چو در لشکر دشمن افتد خلاف

In your enemy's army, when factiousness shows,

تو بگذار شمشیر خود در غلاف

You can let your own sword in its scabbard repose.

چو گرگان پسندند بر هم گزند

When wolves are determined each other to harm,

بر آساید اندر میان گوسفند

Between them, the flock rests secure from alarm.

چو دشمن به دشمن بود مشتغل

When your enemies, grappling each other, you find,

تو با دوست بنشین به آرام دل

You may sit with your friends in composure of mind

گفتار اندر ملاطفت با دشمن از روی عاقبت اندیشی
On aiming at Peace while engaged in War

چو شمشیر پیکار برداشتی

When you've flourished the sabre of battle on high,

نگه دار پنهان ره آشتی

On the pathway to peace keep, in secret, your eye!

که لشکر شکوفان مغفر شکاف

For subduers of hosts, who have helmets destroyed,

نهان صلح جستند و پیدا مصاف

In secret seek peace, while in fighting employed.

دل مرد میدان نهانی بجوی

In secret, the heart of the warrior entreat,

که باشد که در پایت افتد چو گوی

For, perhaps, he may fall like a ball at your feet

چو سالاری از دشمن افتد به چنگ

When an enemy's general falls in your way,

به کشتن درش کرد باید درنگ

Before you extinguish him, practise delay;

که افتد کز این نیمه هم سروری

For it may be, that one of your leaders is found

بماند گرفتار در چنبری

In the enemy's circle, a prisoner bound.

اگر کشتی این بندی ریش را

And should you this sore -wounded captive have slain,

نبینی دگر بندی خویش را

You never will see your own captive again.

نترسد که دورانش بندی کند

The man who on captives gives vent to his hate,

که بر بندیان زورمندی کند؟

Is not frightened that Time will himself captivate.

کسی بندیان را بود دستگیر

person to succour poor prisoners strains,

که خود بوده باشد به بندی اسیر

Who himself shall have been, once, a captive in chains

اگر سر نهد بر خطت سروری

If a leader should tender submission to you,

چو نیکش بداری، نهد دیگری

And you treat him politely, another comes, too.

اگر خفیه ده دل بدست آوری

If you secretly gather ten hearts to your aid,

از آن به که صد ره شبیخون بری

It is better than hundreds of night-attacks made.

◀◉▸◀◉▸

گفتار اندر حذر از دشمنی که در طاعت آید
On the Treatment of a Foe who has become friendly

گرت خویش دشمن شود دوستدار

Should a foe, of himself, to you friendliness show,

ز تلبیسش ایمن مشو زینهار

From his frauds you will never security know.

که گردد درونش به کین تو ریش

From the hatred he bears you, heart-wounded, he sighs

چو یاد آیدش مهر پیوند خویش

When thoughts of his "Love" and relations arise.

بد اندیش را لفظ شیرین مبین

To the sweet words of enemies never attend

که ممکن بود زهر در انگبین

They're the same as when poison with honey you blend.

کسی جان از آسیب دشمن ببرد

He saves not his life from the enemy's blow,

که مر دوستان را به دشمن شمرد

Who looks on the man who informs as a foe.

نگه دارد آن شوخ در کیسه در

That robber, his pearl in a bag will conceal,

که بیند همه خلق را کیسه بر

When he sees all the people accustomed to steal.

سپاهی که عاصی شود در امیر

The soldier who will not his leader obey,

ورا تا توانی به خدمت مگیر

You should never admit to your service and pay!

ندانست سالار خود را سپاس

His former commander he failed to revere!

تو را هم ندارد، ز غدرش هراس

Of you, too, from malice, he will not show fear.

به سوگند و عهد استوارش مدار

To bind him by promise and oath do not try!

نگهبان پنهان بر او بر گمار

But a watchman, in secret, despatch as a spy!

نو آموز را ریسمان کن دراز

You must give to a novice a good deal of rein;

نه بگسل که دیگر نبینیش باز

If you snap it, you never will see him again.

چو اقلیم دشمن به جنگ و حصار

When a foe's land and fortress by war you obtain,

گرفتی، به زندانیانش سپار

Hand him over to those who in dungeons have lain!

که بندی چو دندان به خون در برد

Since the prisoner's teeth in his heart's blood were stuck,

ز حلقوم بیدادگر خون خورد

From the throat of the tyrant, the blood he will suck.

چو بر کندی از دست دشمن دیار

Seize the land for yourself, when you've cleared out the foe,

رعیت به سامان تر از وی بدار

And on all of the subjects, more freedom bestow!

که گر باز کوبد در کارزار

For should he attempt to knock War's door again,

بر آرند عام از دماغش دمار

The people will tear ruin out of his brain.

وگر شهریان را رسانی گزند

And if on the citizens, harm you impose,

در شهر بر روی دشمن مبند

Do not shut the town gates in the face of your foes!

مگو دشمن تیغ زن بر در است

Do not say that the sword- wielding foe's at your gate;

که انباز دشمن به شهر اندر است

For the enemies' friends in the city await.

به تدبیر جنگ بد اندیش کوش

In arranging for war with a foe, work with zeal!

مصالح بیندیش و نیت بپوش

Consider affairs; but your object conceal!

منه در میان راز با هر کسی

Divulge not your secret to each passerby;

که جاسوس هم کاسه دیدم بسی

For I've oft seen a person hob-nob with a spy.

سکندر که با شرقیان حرب داشت

Alexander, who war upon Easterns once pressed,

در خیمه گویند در غرب داشت

Had the door of his tent, they say, facing the West

چو بهمن به زاولستان خواست شد

When to march into Zawilistan Bahman meant,

چپ آوازه افکند و از راست شد

He rumoured the left, by the right hand he went.

اگر جز تو داند که عزم تو چیست

If you cannot your purpose from any one keep,

بر آن رای و دانش بباید گریست

As a consequence, Wisdom and Knowledge will weep.

کرم کن، نه پرخاش و کین‌آوری

Be generous, and war and revenge from you fling!

که عالم به زیر نگین آوری

And under your signet, the world you will bring.

چو کاری بر آید به لطف و خوشی

When a work can be settled by kindness and peace,

چه حاجت به تندی و گردن کشی؟

Why should you rebellion and outrage release?

نخواهی که باشد دلت دردمند

If you wish that your heart be not burdened with grief,

دل درمندان بر آور ز بند

From their bonds, give the hearts of the wretched relief!

به بازو توانا نباشد سپاه

In the arm of a soldier, for strength do not seek!

برو همت از ناتوانان بخواه

Go and pray for a blessing from those who are weak!

دعای ضعیفان امیدوار

The prayers of the weak who are hopeful and free,

ز بازوی مردی به آید به کار

Are more efficacious than man's arm can be.

هر آن کاستعانت به درویش برد

Whoever seeks aid at a holy man's feet,

اگر بر فریدون زد از پیش برد

If he fought Faridun? would not suffer defeat.

2

(CHAPTER II)

در احسان

ON BENEFICENCE

سرآغاز

In begin

اگر هوشمندی به معنی گرای

To affairs of the spirit incline; if you've sense;

که معنی بماند ز صورت به جای

For the spirit remains when the body goes hence.

که را دانش و جود و تقوی نبود

The man without knowledge, free-giving and grace,

به صورت درش هیچ معنی نبود

Does not have in his body for conscience a place

کسی خسبد آسوده در زیر گل

The person sleeps tranquilly under the ground,

که خسبند از او مردم آسوده دل

Through whom, people sleeping in comfort are found.

غم خویش در زندگی خور که خویش

Endure your own grief during life! for your friends

به مرده نپردازد از حرص خویش

"Will neglect you when dead, for their own selfish ends.

زر و نعمت اکنون بده کان تست

Gold and affluence give! while you have them in hand;

که بعد از تو بیرون ز فرمان تست

For after you die, they're not yours to command.

نخواهی که باشی پراکنده دل

If you wish not hereafter affliction to find,

پراکندگان را ز خاطر مهل

Never let the afflicted escape from your mind!

پریشان کن امروز گنجینه چست

You should scatter your treasure in bounty to-day;

که فردا کلیدش نه در دست تست

For to-morrow, the key will have passed from your sway.

تو با خود ببر توشه خویشتن

In almsgiving, bear off your stores during life!

که شفقت نیاید ز فرزند و زن

For no sympathy comes from a son and a wife!

کسی گوی دولت ز دنیا برد

Prosperity's ball, from the world he will bear,

که با خود نصیبی به عقبی برد

Who carries away to the future a share.

به غمخوارگی چون سرانگشت من

In compassion, excepting my own nail's, alack!

نخارد کس اندر جهان پشت من

Not a soul in this world thinks of scratching my back.

مکن، بر کف دست نه هر چه هست

On the palm of your hand, all your wealth do not set!

که فردا به دندان بری پشت دست

Lest, to-morrow, you gnaw at the hand of Regret.

به پوشیدن ستر درویش کوش

In concealing, the veil of the pious poor try!

که ستر خدایت بود پرده پوش

For the curtain Divine hides from every eye.

مگردان غریب از درت بی نصیب

Do not portionless turn the poor man from your door!

مبادا که گردی به درها غریب

Lest begging at gates should for you be in store.

بزرگی رساند به محتاج خیر

On the needy, a noble will favours bestow,

که ترسد که محتاج گردد به غیر

For he fears he'll be poor, if he fails to do so.

به حال دل خستگان در نگر

The state of the broken in heart, keep in view!

که روزی تو دلخسته باشی مگر

Lest you should, hereafter, be heart-broken, too.

درون فروماندگان شاد کن

To the hearts of the wretched, some gladness impart!

ز روز فروماندگی یاد کن

And let not the day of distress leave your heart!

نه خواهنده‌ای بر در دیگران؟

As a beggar, at other men's doors you don't wait

به شکرانه خواهنده از در مران

In gratitude, drive not the poor from your gate!

گفتار اندر نواخت ضعیفان
Story on the cherishing of orphans and showing mercy on their condition

پدرمرده را سایه بر سر فکن
A shade o'er the head of the orphan boy put!

غبارش بیفشان و خارش بکن
Disperse all his sighs and his sorrows uproot!

ندانی چه بودش فرو مانده سخت؟
You know not why he has this helplessness seen?

بود تازه بی بیخ هرگز درخت؟
Does a tree without root ever show itself green?

چو بینی یتیمی سر افکنده پیش
When you see the sad head of an orphan bent low,

مده بوسه بر روی فرزند خویش
On the face of your son, do not kisses bestow!

یتیم ار بگرید که نازش خرد؟
If an orphan should weep, who will purchase relief?

وگر خشم گیرد که بارش برد؟
And should he be vexed, who will share in his grief?

الا تا نگرید که عرش عظیم
Take care! lest he weeps, for the great throne on high

بلرزد همی چون بگرید یتیم
Will tremble and shake, should an orphan child cry!

به رحمت بکن آبش از دیده پاک
By kindness, the tears from his pure eyes displace!

به شفقت بیفشانش از چهره خاک
By compassion, disperse all the dust from his face!

اگر سایه خود برفت از سرش
If his own sheltering shadow has gone from his head,

تو در سایه خویشتن پرورش
Take him under your own fostering shadow, instead!

من آنگه سر تاجور داشتم
I at that time the head of a monarch possessed,

که سر بر کنار پدر داشتم
When I let it recline on my own father's breast;

اگر بر وجودم نشستی مگس
If a fly on my body made bold to alight,

پریشان شدی خاطر چند کس
The hearts of a number were grieved at the sight

156

کنون دشمنان گر برندم اسیر

If now, to a dungeon they captive me bear,

نباشد کس از دوستانم نصیر

Not one of my friends to assist me would care.

مرا باشد از درد طفلان خبر

The sufferings of poor orphan children I know;

که در طفلی از سر برفتم پدر

In my childhood, my father to God had to go

❖◉❖◉❖

حکایت ثمره نیکوکاری

Story on the fruits of well-doing

یکی خار پای یتیمی بکند

A thorn, that had stuck in an orphan boy's foot

به خواب اندرش دید صدر خجند

In a dream Khojand's chief saw a person out-root

همی گفت و در روضه‌ها می‌چمید

He was saying — and strutting in Paradise, free:

کز آن خار بر من چه گلها دمید

"What roses have grown from that thorn over me?"

مشو تا توانی ز رحمت بری

While you can, from the practice of mercy don't go!

که رحمت برندت چو رحمت بری

For on you they'll have mercy, if mercy you show.

چو انعام کردی مشو خودپرست

When you do one a favour, don't swell with conceit!

که من سرورم دیگران زیردست

Saying, " I am supreme with all else at my feet I"

اگر تیغ دورانش انداخته‌ست

If the sword of his Time has been driven beneath,

نه شمشیر دوران هنوز آخته‌ست؟

Is the dread sword of Time not still out of its sheath?

چو بینی دعاگوی دولت هزار

When a thousand men blessing your fortune, you see,

خداوند را شکر نعمت گزار

To God, for His gifts, let your thankfulness be!

که چشم از تو دارند مردم بسی
For with hope fixed on you, a vast multitude stand;
نه تو چشم داری به دست کسی
And you are not hopeful at any one's hand.

کرم» خوانده‌ام سیرت سروران»
Liberality's special to kings, I've expressed;
غلط گفتم، اخلاق پیغمبران
I've said wrong; it's a nature by prophets possessed

حکایت ابراهیم علیه‌السلام
Story the Nature of Prophets (Abraham and the fire-worshipper)
شنیدم که یک هفته ابن‌السبیل
I have heard: for a week not a son of the road,
نیامد به مهمانسرای خلیل
At the liberal guest-house of Abraham showed

ز فرخنده خویی نخوردی بگاه
From his sociable nature, he broke not his fast,
مگر بینوایی در آید ز راه
Hoping some needy traveller might share his repast.

برون رفت و هر جانبی بنگرید
Out he went and most carefully looked all around;
بر اطراف وادی نگه کرد و دید
His gaze travelled over the valley r he found

به تنها یکی در بیابان چو بید
One alone in the wild, like a willow to sight;
سر و مویش از گرد پیری سپید
With his head and his hair, from the snow of age, white

به دلداریش مرحبایی بگفت
By way of consoling, "You're welcome t" he said;
به رسم کریمان صلایی بگفت
In the mode of the generous, invitement he made:

که ای چشمهای مرا مردمک
"My eye f s tender pupil,, oh stranger! thou art;
یکی مردمی کن به نان و نمک
Be generous, and of my provisions, take part! "

158

نعم گفت و برجست و برداشت گام

u With pleasure' he said, then arose and progressed,

که دانست خلقش، علیه‌السلام

For he knew the "friend's" nature (on him safety rest!).

رقیبان مهمانسرای خلیل

The attendants of Abraham's charity Khan

به عزت نشاندند پیر ذلیل

In dignity seated the humble old man.

بفرمود و ترتیب کردند خوان

He ordered, they sorted the trays on the ground,

نشستند بر هر طرف همگنان

And seated themselves in their places around.

چو بسم الله آغاز کردند جمع

When all at trie board, the "bismillah" began,

نیامد ز پیرش حدیثی به سمع

He heard not the phrase from the feeble old man.

چنین گفتش: ای پیر دیرینه روز

He spoke to him, thus: " Oh old man, full of days!

چو پیران نمی‌بینمت صدق و سوز

I see not the old's faith and warmth in your ways.

نه شرط است وقتی که روزی خوری

Before you eat bread, does the rule not hold good,

که نام خداوند روزی بری؟

That you mention the name of the Giver of food? "

بگفتا نگیرم طریقی به دست

He answered, "I keep not the custom, at least;

که نشنیدم از پیر آذرپرست

For it never was taught me by Magian priest."

بدانست پیغمبر نیک فال

Then the prophet, of prosperous lot, could detect

که گبر است پیر تبه بوده حال

That the old week belonged to the Magian sect.

به خواری براندش چو بیگانه دید

He instantly drove him away in disgrace;

که منکر بود پیش پاکان پلید

For in front of the holy, the vile have no place.

سروش آمد از کردگار جلیل

An angel came down from the Maker adored,

به هیبت ملامت کنان کای خلیل

And with awe thus rebuked him: " Oh friend of the Lord!

منش داده صد سال روزی و جان

Food and life I have given him for one hundred years;

تو را نفرت آمد از او یک زمان

Your dislike for the man, in a moment, appears.

گر او می‌برد پیش آتش سجود

Though a person should show adoration for fire,

تو وا پس چرا می‌بری دست جود؟ "

Why cause Liberality's hand to retire? "

گفتار اندر احسان با نیک و بد

On Well-doing

گره بر سر بند احسان مزن

On the purse-mouth of charity, tie not a knot!

که این زرق و شید است و آن مکر و فن

Calling this, fraud and folly, and that, tricks and plot

زیان می‌کند مرد تفسیردان

The religious expounder makes injury spread,

که علم و ادب می‌فروشد به نان

Who barters his knowledge and culture for bread

کجا عقل یا شرع فتوی دهد

How can wisdom with law give decision, indeed!

که اهل خرد دین به دنیا دهد؟

When a man who is wise, to the world sells the creed?

ولیکن تو بستان که صاحب خرد

And yet you should purchase, for he who is wise,

از ارزان فروشان به رغبت خرد

From those who sell cheap, with avidity buys

حکایت عابد با شوخ دیده
Story of the holy man and the impudent poet

زباندانی آمد به صاحبدلی
To a good-hearted man came a poet, one day,

که محکم فروماندهام در گلی
And said, " I am helplessly stuck in the clay

یکی سفله را ده درم بر من است
Ten direms I owe to so squeezing a dun,

که دانگی از او بر دلم ده من است
That one dang from his hand, on my back is a ton.

همه شب پریشان از او حال من
At night, on account of him, wretched my state;

همه روز چون سایه دنبال من
Like a shadow, all day at my heels he's in wait.

بکرد از سخنهای خاطر پریش
He has made, by harsh language which nature resents,

درون دلم چون در خانه ریش
The core of my heart, like my house door, all rents.

خدایش مگر تا ز مادر بزاد
Perhaps God, to him, since the day he was born,

جز این ده درم چیز دیگر نداد
Beside those ten coins, has not given a corn.

ندانسته از دفتر دین الف
To A in Fate's volume, he could not attain;

نخوانده به جز باب لاینصرف
He has read nothing else than the chapter on gain.

خور از کوه یک روز سر بر نزد
Not a day does the sun from the hills upwards soar,

که آن قلتبان حلقه بر در نزد
That that infamous sneak does not knock at my door.

در اندیشهام تا کدامم کریم
The kind benefactor I'm anxious to know,

از آن سنگدل دست گیرد به سیم
Who will save me with coin from that hard-hearted foe."

شنید این سخن پیر فرخ نهاد
The kind-natured man heard him chatter and grieve,

درستی دو، در آستینش نهاد
And loosened two gold pieces inside his sleeve.

161

زر افتاد در دست افسانه گوی

The gold reached the hand of that rare, fabling one;

برون رفت از آنجا چو زر تازه روی

Out he went with his face shining bright, like the sun.

یکی گفت: شیخ! این ندانی که کیست؟

Someone said to the sheikh — "You don't know this black sheep?

بر او گر بمیرد نباید گریست

Over him, when he dies, it would be folly to weep.

گدایی که بر شیر نر زین نهد

The beggar who saddles the tiger, indeed!

ابو زید را اسب و فرزین نهد

Gives the Knight and the Queen to the famed Abuzid

بر آشفت عابد که خاموش باش

The servant of God, in a rage, said, "Desist!

تو مرد زبان نیستی، گوش باش

You are scarcely a preacher; attentively, list!

اگر راست بود آنچه پنداشتم

If what I imagined, should prove to be right,

ز خلق آبرویش نگه داشتم

I have guarded his honour from people of spite;

وگر شوخ چشمی و سالوس کرد

If he practiced deception and impudence, yet,

الا تا نپنداری افسوس کرد

Take care not to think I experience regret!

که خود را نگه داشتم آبروی

For my honour I've saved, by the money I gave,

ز دست چنان گربزی یاوه گوی

From such a deceitful and talkative knave."

بد و نیک را بذل کن سیم و زر

On the good and the bad, lavish silver and gold!

که این کسب خیر است و آن دفع شر

One's an excellent work, the other vice will withhold.

خنک آن که در صحبت عاقلان

Oh happy is he who with wise men remains,

بیاموزد اخلاق صاحبدلان

And the virtues of those who are pious, obtains!

گرت عقل و رای است و تدبیر و هوش

If wisdom and knowledge within you appear,

به عزت کنی پند سعدی به گوش

With reverence to Sádi's advice you'll give ear;

که اغلب در این شیوه دارد مقال

For in this manner, chiefly, his eloquence rolls;

نه در چشم و زلف و بناگوش و خال

Not on eyes nor on curls, not on ears nor on moles.

❖◉❖◉❖

حکایت ممسک و فرزند ناخلف

Story of the miserly father and the generous son

یکی رفت و دینار از او صد هزار

One departed and left earthly treasure behind;

خلف برد صاحبدلی هوشیار

His successor was generous and prudent in mind.

نه چون ممسکان دست بر زر گرفت

He did not, like misers, clutch greedily gold;

چو آزادگان دست از او بر گرفت

Over it, like the free, he relinquished his hold.

ز درویش خالی نبودی درش

His palace was filled with the needy and poor,

مسافر به مهمانسرای اندرش

And travellers lived in his guest-house secure.

دل خویش و بیگانه خرسند کرد

He made kinsmen and strangers, in spirit, content;

نه همچون پدر سیم و زر بند کرد

And was not, like his father, on hoarding-up bent.

ملامت کنی گفتش ای باد دست

A reprover addressed him Oh squandering hand!

به یک ره پریشان مکن هر چه هست

Do not scatter, at once, all you have in command!

به سالی توان خرمن اندوختن

In a year you can one harvest, only, obtain;

به یک دم نه مردی بود سوختن

It is silly to burn, in one moment, the grain!

چو در تنگدستی نداری شکیب

If you do not have patience in times of distress,

نگه دار وقت فراخی حسیب

Look to your accounts when you plenty possess"!

⟨◉⟩⟨◉⟩

پندها و اندرزها
Maxims and Remarks

به دختر چه خوش گفت بانوی ده

To her daughter, how well spoke a village-chiefs wife

که روز نوا برگ سختی بنه

"Prepare for distress when provisions are rife!

همه وقت بر دار مشک و سبوی

At all times, a pitcher and cup brimful show!

که پیوسته در ده روان نیست جوی

For the stream in the village will not always flow

به دنیا توان آخرت یافتن

With the world, you can doubtless Futurity gain,

به زر پنجه شیر نر تافتن

And the claws of the Devil, with gold you can sprain

به دست تهی بر نیاید امید

From a hand that is empty, no hope will arise;

به زر برکنی چشم دیو سپید

With gold, you can gouge out the White Devil's eyes.

اگر تنگدستی مرو پیش یار

Do not visit your Love, if you own not a thing!

وگر سیم داری بیا و بیار

And if you have silver, oh come thou, and bring!

تهی دست در خوبرویان مپیچ

Do not turn empty handed the door of the Fair!

که بی سیم مردم نیرزند هیچ

For a man without money is valueless there!

وگر هرچه یابی به کف بر نهی

If you place on your palm all the wealth you possess,

کفت وقت حاجت بماند تهی

Your palm will be bare, in the time of distress.

گدایان به سعی تو هرگز قوی

By your efforts, weak beggars will never get strong,

نگردند، ترسم تو لاغر شوی

And I fear, you yourself will get weak before long.

◈◉◈◉◈

ادامه ی حکایت ممسک و فرزند ناخلف
Continuation of the Story of the Miser's Son

چو مناع خیر این حکایت بگفت

When this story, discouraging good, he had told,

ز غیرت جوانمرد را رگ نخفت

Chagrin made the blood in the youth's veins run cold.

پراکنده دل گشت از آن عیب جوی

By these callous remarks, his kind heart was unstrung,

بر آشفت و گفت ای پراکنده گوی

He was vexed and exclaimed, " Incoherent of tongue!

مرا دستگاهی که پیرامن است

My father once said that the wealth I've obtained,

پدر گفت میراث جد من است

As a heritage from my forefathers remained;

نه ایشان به خست نگه داشتند

Did they not, before that, protect it with care?

به حسرت بمردند و بگذاشتند؟

They died, with regret, and left all to their heir.

به دستم نیفتاد مال پدر

The wealth of my father has fallen to me,

که بعد از من افتد به دست پسر

So that, after my exit, my son's it should be.

همان به که امروز مردم خورند

It is better that men should consume it to-day,

که فردا پس از من به یغما برند

For, to-morrow, they'll bear it as plunder away."

خور و پوش و بخشای و راحت رسان

Eat and dress and bestow, and remove others' care!

نگه می چه داری ز بهر کسان؟

And know that your wealth is for others to share!

برند از جهان با خود اصحاب رای
From the world it is borne by possessors of mind;
فرو مایه ماند به حسرت بجای
Mean wretches regretfully leave it behind.

زر و نعمت اکنون بده کان توست
Give gold and life's joys, while you have them in hand,
که بعد از تو بیرون ز فرمان توست
For after you die, they're beyond your command!

به دنیا توانی که عقبی خری
With the world, you can surely Futurity get,
بخر، جان من، ور نه حسرت بری
Then purchase, my soul! or you'll suffer regret.

❖◉❖◉❖

حکایت محبت به همسایگان
Story on showing kindness to neighbors

بزارید وقتی زنی پیش شوی
A wife, shedding tears, to her husband thus said
که دیگر مخر نان ز بقال کوی
"From the merchant nearby, do not purchase more bread

به بازار گندم فروشان گرای
Henceforth, to the market of wheat-sellers go!
که این جو فروشیست گندم نمای
For he sells only barley, though wheat he may show.

نه از مشتری کز زحام مگس
Not from customers, but from the number of flies,
به یک هفته رویش ندیده‌ست کس
His face, for a week, has been hid from men's eyes."

به دلداری آن مرد صاحب نیاز
In consoling, the husband, a master of prayer,
به زن گفت کای روشنایی، بساز
Replied to his wife, " Roshanai forbear!

به امید ما کلبه اینجا گرفت
Expecting our favour he opened shop there;
نه مردی بود نفع از او واگرفت
To withdraw now our custom would scarcely be fair'

ره نیکمردان آزاده گیر

The path of the good, and the gen rous, select!

چو استاده‌ای دست افتاده گیر

And since you have a footing, the fallen protect!

ببخشای کآنان که مرد حقند

Be forgiving! for people who study the Lord;

خریدار دکان بی رونقند

Are buyers at shops where no glitter is stored.

جوانمرد اگر راست خواهی ولیست

If truly you wish to know one generous mind,

کرم پیشهٔ شاه مردان علیست

It's the liberal Alt, the chief of mankind!

حکایت زائر مکه
Story of the pilgrim to Mecca

شنیدم که پیری به راه حجاز

I have heard that a man did to Mecca repair,

به هر خطوه کردی دو رکعت نماز

And made, at each step, two prostrations in prayer.

چنان گرم رو در طریق خدای

So zealous a walker in God's path, to boot,

که خار مغیلان نکندی ز پای

That he plucked not the Acacia thorn from his foot

به آخر ز وسواس خاطر پریش

At last, by a conscience deluded inspired,

پسند آمدش در نظر کار خویش

His own foolish doings he greatly admired.

به تلبیس ابلیس در چاه رفت

By the Devil deceiving, he walked to a pit,

که نتوان از این خوب تر راه رفت

For he could not discover a pathway more fit.

گرش رحمت حق نه دریافتی

If he had not been found by the mercy of God,

غرورش سر از جاده برتافتی

His pride would have made his head swerve from the road.

یکی هاتف از غیبش آواز داد

In this manner, a voice from above, him addressed:—

که ای نیکبخت مبارک نهاد

"Oh man of good fortune! whose nature is blessed!

مپندار اگر طاعتی کردهای

Do not think that because you have worshipped so fine,

که نزلی بدین حضرت آوردهای

You have carried a gift to this Presence Divine!

به احسانی آسوده کردن دلی

To soothe by a kindness one heart has more grace,

به از الف رکعت به هر منزلی

Than a thousand prostrations at. each halting place."

حکایت روزه داری

Story on fasting

به سرهنگ سلطان چنین گفت زن

The wife of a government officer said:

که خیز ای مبارک در رزق زن

Rise Mabarak and knock at the door of life's bread.

برو تا ز خوانت نصیبی دهند

Go, and ask them to give you a share from the tray!

که فرزندکانت نظر بر رهند

For your children are in a deplorable way ".

بگفتا بود مطبخ امروز سرد

He answered, The kitchen to-day will be cold.,

که سلطان به شب نیت روزه کرد

For the Sultan, last night, said a fast he would hold,.

زن از ناامیدی سر انداخت پیش

The wife in despair dropped her head on her breast;

همی گفت با خود دل از فاقه ریش

With heart sore from hunger herself she addressed:

که سلطان از این روزه گویی چه خواست؟

When the king talks of fasts, does he gain in the least?

که افطار او عید طفلان ماست

The breaking of his fast is my children's feast ".

خورنده که خیرش برآید ز دست

The eaters r who have a beneficent hand,

به از صائم الدهر دنیا پرست

Beat the constantly fasting and. world-serving, band.

مسلم کسی را بود روزه داشت

It is right for the person to keep up a fast,

که درمانده‌ای را دهد نان چاشت

Who gives bread to the poor, for their morning repast.

وگرنه چه لازم که سعی بری

If not! why should trouble be suffered by you?

ز خود بازگیری و هم خود خوری؟

You withhold from yourself, and consume yourself, too!

خیالات نادان خلوت نشین

The ignorant fancies of hermits must tend

بهم بر کند عاقبت کفر و دین

To confound unbelief and the Faith,, in the end."

صفائیست در آب و آئینه نیز

There is clearness in water, and mirrors, as well;

ولیکن صفا را بباید تمیز

But the clearness of each you should know how to tell.

◈◉◈◉◈

حکایت کرم مردان صاحبدل

Story of the kind poor man and the debtor

یکی را کرم بود و قوت نبود

A man had no power, but was generous inclined;

کفافش به قدر مروت نبود

His means did not equal his liberal mind.

که سفله خداوند هستی مباد

May a miser the owner of wealth never be!

جوانمرد را تنگدستی مباد

May a generous man never poverty see

کسی را که همت بلند اوفتد

The person whose spirit soars lofty and loose,

مرادش کم اندر کمند اوفتد

Will find that his projects fall short of his noose.

چو سیلاب ریزان که در کوهسار

Like the wild, rushing flood, in a mountainous place,

نگیرد همی بر بلندی قرار

Which, while on high ground, cannot stop its mad pace.

نه در خورد سرمایه کردی کرم

He was generous beyond what his means would allow

تنک مایه بودی از این لاجرم

And, thus, his resources were shallow enow.

برش تنگدستی دو حرفی نبشت

One poverty-stricken, a note to him sent —:

که ای خوب فرجام نیکو سرشت

"Oh thou happy of end, and of nature content!

یکی دست گیرم به چندین درم

Assist me with so many direms, pray!

که چندی است تا من به زندان درم

For I've lain in a dungeon for many a day ".

به چشم اندرش قدر چیزی نبود

He could not the value of anything see

ولیکن به دستش پشیزی نبود

And yet, in his hand not a copper had he.

به خصمان بندی فرستاد مرد

To the foes of the debtor a person he sent,

که ای نیکنامان آزاد مرد

Saying, " Men of good name who are free, oh, relent!

بدارید چندی کف از دامنش

Permit that he may for a short time be free!

وگر می‌گریزد ضمان بر منش

And if he runs off, I'll security be ".

وز آنجا به زندانی آمد که خیز

Prom thence to the dungeon he went, and said, "Rise!

وز این شهر تا پای داری گریز

And run from this city, while strength in you lies"!

چو گنجشک در باز دید از قفس

When. an open cage door met the poor sparrow's view

قرارش نماند اندر آن یک نفس

For a moment, thereafter, no patience he knew.

چو باد صبا زآن میان سیر کرد

Like the breeze of the morning, he fled from that place,

نه سیری که بادش رسیدی به گرد

Not a flight that the wind with his dust could keep pace.

گرفتند حالی جوانمرد را

They instantly seized on the generous man,

که حاصل کن این سیم یا مرد ر

Saying, "Bring forth the debtor or coin, if you can

به بیچارگی راه زندان گرفت

Like the helpless, the road to the jail he was brought;

که مرغ از قفس رفته نتوان گرفت

For a bird that has flown from its cage can't be caught

شنیدم که در حبس چندی بماند

For a time, I have heard, in confinement he lay;

نه شکوت نوشت و نه فریاد خواند

He wrote not a line, nor for help did he pray.

زمانها نیاسود و شبها نخفت

He was restless by day, from his nights slumber fled;

بر او پارسایی گذر کرد و گفت

A holy man passed him, and thus to him said:

نپندارمت مال مردم خوری

"You don't seem to have lived on the substance of men;

چه پیش آمدت تا به زندان دری؟

What has happened, that you are a prisoner, then"?

171

بگفت ای جلیس مبارک نفس

Oh spirit auspicious! " he said, " you are right J

نخوردم به حیلتگری مال کس

No one's wealth have I eaten by baseness or sleight.

یکی ناتوان دیدم از بند ریش

I saw a poor wretch who from fetters was sore;

خلاصش ندیدم به جز بند خویش

But by taking his place, could I ope Freedom's door.

ندیدم به نزدیک رایم پسند

It appeared to me loathsome to reason, that!

من آسوده و دیگری پایبند

Should be free, and another in fetters should lie ".

بمرد آخر و نیکنامی ببرد

He died in the end, and he bore a good name;

زهی زندگانی که نامش نمرد

Oh happy's the life that has permanent fame!

تنی زنده دل، خفته در زیر گل

A living soul's body, with clay round it spread,

به از عالمی زندهٔ مرده دل

Is better than bodies alive, with souls dead.

دل زنده هرگز نگردد هلاک

To a living soul, Death will not dare to come near;

تن زنده دل گر بمیرد چه باک؟

If a living soul's body should die, what's the fear?

حکایت معنی محبت

Story on the meaning of kindness

یکی در بیابان سگی تشنه یافت

Someone crossing the desert a thirsty dog found;

برون از رمق در حیاتش نیافت

The last breath was just left in the life of the hound

کله دلو کرد آن پسندیده کیش

That Faith-approved man used as bucket his hat,

چو حبل اندر آن بست دستار خویش

And in place of a rope, tied Ijis turban to that

به خدمت میان بست و بازو گشاد

He bared both his arms and made ready to save;

سگ ناتوان را دمی آب داد

To the poor, helpless animal, water he. gave.

خبر داد پیغمبر از حال مرد

The Prophet, the state of that person explained,.

که داور گناهان از او عفو کرد

And release for his sin from the Maker obtained.

الا گر جفاکاری اندیشه کن

If you are a tyrant,, beware and reflect!

وفا پیش گیر و کرم پیشه کن

The path of the generous and faithful, select!

کسی با سگ نیکویی گم نکرد

He, in saving a dog, did not sympathy waste;

کجا گم شود خیر با نیکمرد؟

When is goodness in keeping, of good men effaced?

کرم کن چنان کت برآید ز دست

Be as- generous as ever you possibly can!

جهانبان در خیر بر کس نبست

God shuts not the portal of joy upon man;.

گرت در بیابان نباشد چهی

If you have not a well in the desert to show,

چراغی بنه در زیارتگهی

Put a lamp in the place unto which pilgrims go

به قنطار زر بخش کردن ز گنج

Gold bestowed from a treasure in sackfuls, like spoil.

نباشد چو قیراطی از دسترنج

Does not match one diiar? from the hard hand of Toil.

برد هر کسی بار در خورد زور

A man in accord with his strength carries weight;

گران است پای ملخ پیش مور

In front of an emmet, a locust's leg's great!

تو با خلق سهلی کن ای نیکبخت

Oh fortunate, man! keep men's welfare in view,

که فردا نگیرد خدا با تو سخت

That, to-morrow, the Lord deal not harshly with you! '

گر از پا در آید، نماند اسیر

He who does not from helping the fallen refrain,

که افتادگان را بود دستگیر

Should he tumble himself, will not captive remain.

به آزار فرمان مده بر رهی

On a slave, do not exercise harshly command!

که باشد که افتد به فرماندهی

For it may be that empire will, fall to his hand;

چو تمکین و جاهت بود بر دوام

When, your grandeur and pomp are established secure,

مکن زور بر ضعف درویش عام

Be not harsh to your subjects, although they are poor!

که افتد که با جاه و تمکین شود

For grandeur and pomp they may, someday, possess —

چو بیدق که ناگاه فرزین شود

Like the pawn that, at once, takes the Queen's place in chess.

نصیحت شنو مردم دوربین

Men who see what is good, and to counsels give heed,

نپاشند در هیچ دل تخم کین

In any one's heart will not sow hatred's seed.

خداوند خرمن زیان می‌کند

The harvest's praud owner but does himself harm,

که بر خوشه‌چین سر گران می‌کند

When haughty to gleaners who visit his farm.

نترسد که نعمت به مسکین دهند

He fears, lest the Lord show the poor gleaner grace,

وزآن بار غم بر دل این نهند؟

And, therefore, Griefs load on his conscience should place.

بسا زورمندا که افتاد سخت

Full many a strong one has drained Ruin's cup;

بس افتاده را یاوری کرد بخت

And Fortune has helped many ruined men up.

دل زیر دستان نباید شکست

It is wrong, then, the hearts of your subjects to break,

مبادا که روزی شوی زیردست

For as subject, one morn, you may chance to awake.

حکایت در معنی رحمت بر ضعیفان و اندیشه در عاقبت
Story of the dervish and the rich man

بنالید درویشی از ضعف حال
A Dervish complained of his state, so distressed,

بر تندرویی خداوند مال
To a hot-tempered person who riches possessed.

نه دینار دادش سیه دل نه دانگ
Not a rap did the black-hearted miser bestow;

بر او زد به سر باری از طیره بانگ
But, in arrogance, angrily bawled at him, so

دل سائل از جور او خون گرفت
That the poor beggar's heart, at his tyranny, bled;

سر از غم بر آورد و گفت ای شگفت
He from grief raised his head, and, "Oh wonderment said;

توانگر ترش روی، باری، چراست؟
"Why at least should one opulent sour-visaged be?

مگر می‌نترسد ز تلخی خواست؟
From the terror of begging, perhaps, he is free!

بفرمود کوته نظر تا غلام
The short-sighted ordered; the slave, in due course,

براندش به خواری و زجر تمام
Expelled him in perfect disgrace, and by force.

به ناکردن شکر پروردگار
As he failed to give thanks to the cherishing Lord,

شنیدم که برگشت از او روزگار
I have heard that good fortune away from him soared.

بزرگیش سر در تباهی نهاد
The head of his greatness, on ruin he placed;

عطارد قلم در سیاهی نهاد
And Mercury's pen, his fair fortune effaced.

شقاوت برهنه نشاندش چو سیر
Like a garlic clove, Wretchedness seated him nude;

نه بارش رها کرد و نه بارگیر
He saved not his baggage nor pack-horses, good.

فشاندش قضا بر سر از فاقه خاک
On his head Fate the dust of starvation then brought;

مشعبد صفت، کیسه و دست پاک
His purse and his hand, like the juggler's, held nought.

سراپای حالش دگرگونه گشت

His state was completely inverted at last;

بر این ماجرا مدتی برگذشت

With affairs in this pickle, a period passed.

غلامش به دست کریمی فتاد

To a kind-hearted person his slave was consigned;

توانگر دل و دست و روشن نهاد

Rich of heart and of hand, and enlightened in mind.

به دیدار مسکین آشفته حال

At the sight of a pauper, in sorrowful plight,

چنان شاد بودی که مسکین به مال

He was glad as the poor, to whom wealth gives delight.

شبانگه یکی بر درش لقمه جست

At night, someone asked for a bit at his door

ز سختی کشیدن قدمهاش سست

Weak in step from the burden of hardship he bore.

بفرمود صاحب نظر بنده را

he clear-sighted man, thus, his servant addressed —:

که خشنود کن مرد درمنده را

"Go and gladden the heart of that beggar, distressed"!

چو نزدیک بردش ز خوان بهرهای

When the slave carried near him a share from the tray,

برآورد بی خویشتن نعرهای

He uttered a cry, he was helpless to stay;

شکسته دل آمد بر خواجه باز

And when he returned to his master again,

عیان کرده اشکش به دیباجه راز

The tears on his cheeks made his secret quite plain.

بپرسید سالار فرخنده خوی

The chief of the happy in nature, then, said

که اشکت ز جور که آمد به روی؟

"Whose tyranny causes those tears to be shed "?

بگفت اندرونم بشورید سخت

He answered, " My heart grieves as much as it can,

بر احوال این پیر شوریده بخت

At the state of this aged, unfortunate man.

که مملوک وی بودم اندر قدیم

For I was his slave in the good days of old;

خداوند املاک و اسباب و سیم

He was owner of property, silver and gold;

چو کوتاه شد دستش از عز و نا

When, in grandeur and pride, his hand ceased to be

کند دست خواهش به درها دراز

In dbor-to-door begging, his hand became long ", strong,

بخندید و گفت ای پسر جور نیست

He smiled, saying, "This is not harshness, oh son!

ستم بر کس از گردش دور نیست

The changes of Time bring oppression to none.

نه آن تندروی است بازارگان

Is this wretch not that merchant of days long gone by,

که بردی سر از کبر بر آسمان؟

Who, in haughtiness, carried his head to the sky?

من آنم که از آن روزم از در براند

I am he whom that day he expelled from his gate —

به روز منش دور گیتی نشاند

The revolving of Time has placed him in my state.

نگه کرد باز آسمان سوی من

The Sky once again took a look at my case,

فرو شست گرد غم از روی من

And washed all the traces of dust from my face.

خدای ار به حکمت ببندد دری

If God in His wisdom one portal should close,

گشاید به فضل و کرم دیگری

By His favour another wide-open He throws.

بسا مفلس بینوا سیر شد

Full many a pauper has satisfied grown;

بسا کار منعم زبر زیر شد

Many rich men's affairs have become overthrown "-

❖◉❖◉❖

177

حکایت شبلی و مورچه
Story of Shibli and the ant

یکی سیرت نیکمردان شنو

O a virtue of one of the pious give ear,

اگر نیکبختی و مردانه رو

If you're pious yourself, and your conduct is clear

که شبلی ز حانوت گندم فروش

When Shibli the saint, from a wheat-seller's store,

به ده برد انبان گندم به دوش

To his thorp, on his shoulder, a bag of wheat bore

نگه کرد و موری در آن غله دید

He looked, and an ant in the wheat caught his eye,

که سرگشته هر گوشه‌ای می‌دوید

Which hither and thither, bewildered, did hie.

ز رحمت بر او شب نیارست خفت

In grief at its state, he all night kept awake

به مأوای خود بازش آورد و گفت

He carried it back to its dwelling, and spake:

مروت نباشد که این مور ریش

It is far from humane that this ant, forced to roam,

پراکنده گردانم از جای خویش

I should cause to be wretched, away from its home."

درون پراکندگان جمع دار

Keep tranquil the people distracted in heart,

که جمعیتت باشد از روزگار

So that Fortune to you may composure impart!

چه خوش گفت فردوسی پاک زاد

How well spoke Fardusi? of origin pure,

که رحمت بر آن تربت پاک باد

On his sanctified tomb may God's mercy endure,

میازار موری که دانه کش است

"The ant that bears grain r you ought not to oppress!

که جان دارد و جان شیرین خوش است

It has life, and sweet life is a joy to possess!"

سیاه اندرون باشد و سنگدل

He's a merciless man, and hard-hearted, at best,

که خواهد که موری شود تنگدل

Who harbours the wish that an ant be distressed

مزن بر سر ناتوان دست زور

With the hand of oppression, the weak, do not beat!

که روزی به پایش در افتی چو مور

For ant-like, one day, you may fall at their feet

نبخشود بر حال پروانه شمع

For the moth's state, the candle all sympathy spurned;

نگه کن که چون سوخت در پیش جمع

Before the assembly, observe how it burned!

گرفتم ز تو ناتوان تر بسی است

I admit there are many more feeble than you;

تواناتر از تو هم آخر کسی است

Than you, at least One is more puissant, too.

گفتار اندر ثمره جوانمردی

Remarks on generosity

ببخش ای پسر کآدمی زاده صید

Show kindness, oh son! since all human in name,

به احسان توان کرد و، وحشی به قید

By kindness can evry wild animal tame'!

عدو را به الطاف گردن ببند

Round your enemy's neck, fasten favours profuse

که نتوان بریدن به تیغ این کمند

With the sabre, he cannot divide such a noose.

چو دشمن کرم بیند و لطف و جود

When a foe" sees abundance and favour and grace,

نیاید دگر خبث از او در وجود

Not again will his wickedness dare to show face.

مکن بد که بد بینی از یار نیک

Do not sin, though a comrade should wickedness show!

نروید ز تخم بدی بار نیک

Good fruit from a seed that is bad will not grow

چو با دوست دشخوار گیری و تنگ

When you deal with a friend in a miserly way,

نخواهد که بیند تو را نقش و رنگ

He desires not to witness you prosp'rous and gay.

و گر خواجه با دشمنان نیکخوست

If a ruler, to foes, a kind manner extends,

بسی بر نیاید که گردند دوست

In a very short time, all the foes become friends.

⟨◉⟩⟨◉⟩

حکایت در معنی صید کردن دلها به احسان

Story on Gaining Hearts by Kindness

به ره بر یکی پیشم آمد جوان

On the road, there came running my way a young man;

به تک در پیش گوسفندی دوان

Behind him a sheep with alacrity ran.

بدو گفتم این ریسمان است و بند

a Have you hold of a rope or a tether?" I said,

که می‌آرد اندر پیت گوسفند

By which the poor creature is after you led "?

سبک طوق و زنجیر از او باز کرد

The collar and chain he removed from it, deft,

چپ و راست پوییدن آغاز کرد

And then scampered about, from the right to the left

هنوز از پیش تازیان می‌دوید

Immediately after him hurried the pet,

که جو خورده بود از کف مرد و خوی

As if barley and grass from his fingers it ate.

چو باز آمد از عیش و شادی به جای

On returning from sporting and playing, again,

مرا دید و گفت ای خداوند رای

He looked at me, saying, " Oh wise among men

نه این ریسمان می‌برد با منش

This tether, it is not that'hrings it with me,

که احسان کمندی است در گردنش

But the noose on its neck is kind treatment] you see."

به لطفی که دیده‌ست پیل دمان

The elephant wanton, from kindness enjoyed,

نیارد همی حمله بر پیلبان

Attacks not the man, as his keeper employed.

بدان را نوازش کن ای نیکمرد

To the bad be indulgent, oh thou who art good

که سگ پاس دارد چو نان تو خورد

For the dog will keep watch when he eats of your food.

بر آن مرد کند است دندان یوز

To the man the Pard's teeth become blunt by degrees,

که مالد زبان بر پنیرش دو روز

Who rubs on its tongue, for a day or two, cheese.

◈◉◈◉◈

حکایت درویش با روباه
Story of the Dervish and the Pox

یکی روبهی دید بی دست و پای

A man saw a fox that had paralyzed feet;

فرو ماند در لطف و صنع خدای

At God's work he was lost in amazement complete

که چون زندگانی به سر می‌برد؟

Saying, "Since he was able to live in a way,

بدین دست و پای از کجا می‌خورد؟

With members so useless when ate he each day? "

در این بود درویش شوریده رنگ

The Dervish was puzzling his brains very much,

که شیری در آمد شغالی به چنگ

When a lion appeared with a jackal in's clutch;

شغال نگون بخت را شیر خورد

He fed on the jackal, of fortune bereft,

بماند آنچه روباه از آن سیر خورد

And the fox ate his fill from the portion he left

دگر روز باز اتفاق اوفتاد

It happened next morn, in a similar way,

که روزی رسان قوت روزش بداد

That Providence gave him his food for the day.

یقین، مرد را دیده بیننده کرد

Truth enabled the eyes of the man, then, to see;

شد و تکیه بر آفریننده کرد

He went, and his hope on the Maker placed he.

کز این پس به کنجی نشینم چو مور

Like an ant, in a corner I'll sit, from this hour,

که روزی نخوردند پیلان به زور

For elephants get not subsistence by power."

زنخدان فرو برد چندی به جیب

With his chin on his breast, for a little, he stood,

که بخشنده روزی فرستد ز غیب

That the Giver might from the unseen send him food.

نه بیگانه تیمار خوردش نه دوست

Neither stranger nor friend to relieve him took pains;

چو چنگش رگ و استخوان ماند و پوست

There remained of him, harp-like, but skin, bone and veins.

چو صبرش نماند از ضعیفی و هوش

hen of patience and sense, due to weakness, deprived,

ز دیوار محرابش آمد به گوش

A voice at his ear from the Mosque niche arrived: —

برو شیر درنده باش، ای دغل

"Go, copy the fierce, tearing tiger, oh cheat!

مینداز خود را چو روباه شل

And ape not the fox with the paralyzed feet!

چنان سعی کن کز تو ماند چو شیر

So strive that you have, like the lion, to spare;

چه باشی چو روبه به وامانده سیر؟

Like the fox, why be pleased with ' remains ' for your fare?

چو شیر آن که را گردنی فربه است

Should a man, like a tiger, a fat neck possess,

گر افتد چو روبه، سگ از وی به است

And fall like a fox, than a dog, he is less.

به چنگ آر و با دیگران نوش کن

Make use of your hands! with your peers eat and drink!

نه بر فضلهٔ دیگران گوش کن

And from eating the leavings of other men, shrink!

بخور تا توانی به بازوی خویش

By your own arm, while fit, let your food be supplied!

که سعیت بود در ترازوی خویش

For your efforts will by your own balance be tried.

چو مردان ببر رنج و راحت رسان

Like a man, bear your trouble, and happiness give!

مخنث خورد دسترنج کسان

On the labour of others let Pcederasts live!

بگیر ای جوان دست درویش پیر

Go thou and assist! oh advice-taking man!

نه خود را بیفکن که دستم بگیر

Do not cast thyself down! saying, "Help! if you can."

خدا را بر آن بنده بخشایش است

That servant from God will forgiveness obtain,

که خلق از وجودش در آسایش است

Through the presence of whom people happy remain.

کرم ورزد آن سر که مغزی در اوست

Kind acts are performed by that head that has mind;

که دون همتانند بی مغز و پوست

The mean, like a skin, without brains, you will find.

کسی نیک بیند به هر دو سرای

The good of both worlds the kind person enjoys

که نیکی رساند به خلق خدای

Who in bettering people, his moments employs

◈◉◈◉◈

حکایت بنده مخلص خدا
Story of a miserly servant of God

شنیدم که مردی است پاکیزه بوم

I heard that a pure-natured man, knowing God,

شناسا و رهرو در اقصای روم

And walking His ways, had in Rum his abode.

من و چند سیاح صحرانورد

I and some desert-traversing travelers, free,

برفتیم قاصد به دیدار مرد

Departed, resolved that the man we should see.

سر و چشم هر یک ببوسید و دست

He kissed each one's eyes, head and hands after that

به تمکین و عزت نشاند و نشست

With deference and honour he placed us, and sat.

زرش دیدم و زرع و شاگرد و رخت

His servants and vines, stores and fields, I could see;

ولی بی مروت چو بی بر درخت

Like a tree without fruit, most ungenerous was he.

به لطف و سخن گرم رو مرد بود

In politeness of manner, his warmth I'll uphold;

ولی دیگدانش عجب سرد بود

But in other respects, he was bitterly cold.

همه شب نبودش قرار و هجوع

In the night time, we neither could slumber nor rest,

ز تسبیح و تهلیل و ما را ز جوع

He, from telling his beads; we, by hunger oppressed.

سحرگه میان بست و در باز کرد

He dressed in the morning and opened the door,

همان لطف و پرسیدن آغاز کرد

And repeated the fuss of the evening before.

یکی بد که شیرین و خوش طبع بود

A good-natured fellow, with wit at command,

که با ما مسافر در آن ربع بود

Was a traveler, together with us, in that land.

مرا بوسه گفتا به تصحیف ده

He said: "You're mistaken, in giving a kiss!

که درویش را توشه از بوسه به

For food to the needy would yield greater bliss.

به خدمت منه دست بر کفش من

Do not carry, in service, your head to my shoes!

مرا نان ده و کفش بر سر بزن

Give me food! beat with slippers my head, if you choose!"

به ایثار مردان سبق برده‌اند

By alms-giving, people will others excel;

نه شب زنده داران دل مرده‌اند

Not the dead-hearted men who on night vigils dwell.

همین دیدم از پاسبان تتار

The watchmen of Tartary showed me the sight;

دل مرده و چشم شب زنده‌دار

Dead of heart, but wide open their eyes all the night.

کرامت جوانمردی و نان دهی است

From kindness and bread-giving, greatness will come;

مقالات بیهوده طبل تهی است

And meaningless words are a big, empty drum.

قیامت کسی بینی اندر بهشت

At the Judgment, the man will in Paradise stay,

که معنی طلب کرد و دعوی بهشت

Who has searched for the truth cast pretension away.

به معنی توان کرد دعوی درست

One can with reality make his claim just;

دم بی قدم تکیه گاهی است سست

Mere talk, without acts, is a weak prop to trust.

❖◉❖◉❖

حکایت حاتم طائی و صفت جوانمردی او
Story of Hatim Tai and his generosity

شنیدم در ایام حاتم که بود

I have heard that in Htim Tai's days, there appeared

به خیل اندرش بادپایی چو دود

In his stables a smoke-coloured horse he had reared;

صبا سرعتی، رعد بانگ ادهمی

As the morning breeze rapid — a thunder-voiced steed,

که بر برق پیشی گرفتی همی

That was more than a match for the lightning in speed.

به تک ژاله می‌ریخت بر کوه و دشت

While he ran, he showered hail over mountain and plain

تو گفتی مگر ابر نیسان گذشت

You'd have said that a cloud had, in passing, dropped rain.

یکی سیل رفتار هامون نورد

A crosser of deserts and torrent-like fleet

که باد از پیش باز ماندی چو گرد

For the wind lagged behind, like the dust, from his feet

ز اوصاف حاتم به هر مرز و بوم

Men, famed for their knowledge, were talking in praise

بگفتند برخی به سلطان روم

With the Sultan of Rum, about Hatim kind ways.

185

که همتای او در کرم مرد نیست

They remarked that, in kindness, he beat everyone;

چو اسبش به جولان و ناورد نیست

Like his horse in careering and war, there was none:

بیابان نوردی چو کشتی بر آب

Desert traveling, resembling a ship on the deep;

که بالای سیرش نپرد عقاب

No crow on the wing, o'er his running could keep.

به دستور دانا چنین گفت شاه

The king thus addressed his enlightened vizier:

که دعوی خجالت بود بی گواه

A claim without proof sounds absurd in my ear.

من از حاتم آن اسب تازی نژاد

From Hatim that charger, of pure Arab breed,

بخواهم، گر او مکرمت کرد و داد

I will ask, and if, kindly, he gives me the steed,

بدانم که در وی شکوه مهی است

Of the grandeur of greatness, I'll know he's possessed;

وگر رد کند بانگ طبل تهی است

If not, he's a loud-sounding drum, at the best.

رسولی هنرمند عالم به طی

A messenger, wise and accomplished, he sent

روان کرد و ده مرد همراه وی

To Tat and ten men in his retinue went.

زمین مرده و ابر گریان بر او

On the ground, dry and lifeless, the clouds had wept rain

صبا کرده بار دگر جان در او

And the cool morning breeze made its life fresh again.

به منزلگه حاتم آمد فرود

To the rest-house of Hatim, he came as a guest;

برآسود چون تشنه بر زنده رود

Like the thirsty by Zindas cool stream, he took rest.

سماطی بیفکند و اسبی بکشت

Hatim spread the food-trays and a charger he killed;

به دامن شکر دادشان زر به مشت

He put sweets in their laps and with gold their hands filled.

شب آن جا ببودند و روز دگر
They remained for the night, and, the following day,

بگفت آنچه دانست صاحب خبر
What the messenger knew, he proceeded to say.

همی گفت حاتم پریشان چو مست
Then Hatim replied — while he raved as if drunk

به دندان ز حسرت همی کند دست
And the teeth of Regret, in his hand deeply sunk

که ای بهره ور موبد نیک نام
Oh sharer in. wisdom, and happy in name!

چرا پیش از اینم نگفتی پیام؟
Why did you not sooner this message proclaim?

من آن باد رفتار دلدل شتاب
That courser, so choice, swift as Duldul in flight,

ز بهر شما دوش کردم کباب
On account of your coming, I roasted last night.

که دانستم از هول باران و سیل
For I knew, that because of the floods and the rain,

نشاید شدن در چراگاه خیل
To the stud-grazing ground, none could access obtain.

به نوعی دگر روی و راهم نبود
In no other way could provision be planned,

جز او بر در بارگاهم نبود
For only this horse, at the time, was at hand.

مروت ندیدم در آیین خویش
It appeared to me mean, by the customs I keep,

که مهمان بخسبد دل از فاقه ریش
That guests, with their hearts sore from hunger, should sleep.

مرا نام باید در اقلیم فاش
My name in the regions about must be known,

دگر مرکب نامور گو مباش
Though another famed steed I may never more own."

کسان را درم داد و تشریف و اسب
He gave the men gold, steeds and dresses of state —

طبیعی است اخلاق نیکو نه کسب
Kind actions are never acquired, but innate.

خبر شد به روم از جوانمرد طی

To Rum went the news of the liberal Tai;

هزار آفرین گفت بر طبع وی

The Sultan applauded his nature, so high.

ز حاتم بدین نکته راضی مشو

With this one trait of Hatim, remain not content!

از این خوب تر ماجرایی شنو

But hear me relate a more noble event!

◈◈◈◈

حکایت در آزمودن پادشاه یمن حاتم را به آزاد مردی
The testing of Hatim Tai's generosity by the King of Yemen

ندانم که گفت این حکایت به من

I forget who narrated this story to me,

که بوده‌ست فرماندهی در یمن

That in Yemen, a monarch there happened to be.

ز نام آوران گوی دولت ربود

Fortune's ball he abducted from others renowned,

که در گنج بخشی نظیرش نبود

For in scattering treasure his peer was not found.

توان گفت او را سحاب کرم

Generosity's cloud, you might call him, with gain,

که دستش چو باران فشاندی درم

For his hand sprinkled direms, like showers of rain.

کسی نام حاتم نبردی برش

If one spoke in his presence of Hatim good name,

که سودا نرفتی از او بر سرش

Towards Hatim, wild rage to his head quickly came.

که چند از مقالات آن بادسنج

How long will you talk of that wind-weigher, pray!

که نه ملک دارد نه فرمان نه گنج

Who neither has country, nor treasure, nor sway?"

شنیدم که جشنی ملوکانه ساخت

For a banquet, I've heard that he issued behests;

چو چنگ اندر آن بزم خلقی نواخت

At the feast, like a harp, he delighted his guests.

در ذکر حاتم کسی باز کرد

Someone started the mention of Hatim Tai's fame,

دگر کس ثنا گفتن آغاز کرد

And another continued his praise to proclaim.

حسد مرد را بر سر کینه داشت

In the monarch, vile Envy a wicked thought hatched,

یکی را به خون خوردنش بر گماشت

And a person to shed Hatim's blood he dispatched.

که تا هست حاتم در ایام من

For he said, "While this Hatim exists, in my days,

نخواهد به نیکی شدن نام من

My name will not travel, united with praise,"

بلا جوی راه بنی طی گرفت

On the road to the Tat tribe the hireling set out,

به کشتن جوانمرد را پی گرفت

And to kill the kind Hatim, went searching about;

جوانی به ره پیشباز آمدش

Before him a young man approached on the road

کز او بوی انسی فراز آمدش

From whose visage, the odour of heartiness flowed.

نکو روی و دانا و شیرین زبان

He was handsome and wise; a sweet tongue he possessed;

بر خویش برد آن شبش میهمان

He took the man home for the night, as his guest.

کرم کرد و غم خورد و پوزش نمود

He was kind, sympathized and apologies made,

بد اندیش را دل به نیکی ربود

And by goodness, the fiend in the wretch's heart laid!

نهادش سحر بوسه بر دست و پای

He kissed in the morning his hands and his feet;

که نزدیک ما چند روزی بپای

Saying, "Tarry some days with me here, I entreat"

بگفتا نیارم شد اینجا مقیم

He answered, "I cannot now halt in this spot,

که در پیش دارم مهمی عظیم

For before me, a work of importance I've got!"

بگفت ار نهی با من اندر میان

" If you mention the business to me,' lie then said.

چو یاران یکدل بکوشم به جان

Like friends of one heart, with my life I will aid."

به من دار گفت، ای جوانمرد، گوش

Oh liberal man! to my statement give ear

که دانم جوانمرد را پرده پوش

For I know that the generous can secrets revere.

در این بوم حاتم شناسی مگر

Perhaps, in this district you know Hatim Tat,

که فرخنده رای است و نیکو سیر؟

Of fortunate name and of qualities high?

سرش پادشاه یمن خواسته ست

The monarch of Yemen has asked for his head;

ندانم چه کین در میان خاسته ست

I know not what hate has between them been bred

گرم ره نمایی بدان جا که اوست

To where he resides, will you kindly direct?

همین چشم دارم ز لطف تو دوست

This much from your favour, oh friend! I expect."

بخندید برنا که حاتم منم

The youth, smiling, said, "I am Hatim and lo!

سر اینک جدا کن به تیغ از تنم

Here's my head — cut it off with your sword, at a blow!

نباید که چون صبح گردد سفید

It is wrong that when morning dissolves into day,

گزندت رسد یا شوی ناامید

You should suffer a wrong, or go hopeless away."

چو حاتم به آزادگی سر نهاد

When Hatim so generously offered to die,

جوان را برآمد خروش از نهاد

There arose from the soul of the youth a loud cry.

به خاک اندر افتاد و بر پای جست

He fell to the earth; jumped again on the ground

گهش خاک بوسید و گه پای و دست

Kissed his feet and his hands and the dust all around.

بینداخت شمشیر و ترکش نهاد
He threw down his sword; cast his quiver away,

چو بیچارگان دست بر کش نهاد
And with hands, slave-like, folded, proceeded to say,

که من گر گلی بر وجودت زنم
Did I dare but to strike against your body a rose,

به نزدیک مردان نه مردم، زنم
I'd be woman, not man, as our noble faith shows. "

دو چشمش ببوسید و در بر گرفت
He kissed Hatim's eyes; gave a parting embrace,

وز آنجا طریق یمن بر گرفت
And went towards Yemen y away from that place.

ملک در میان دو ابروی مرد
By the face of the man, the king instantly knew

بدانست حالی که کاری نکرد
That he had not performed what he said he would do.

بگفتا بیا تا چه داری خبر
He said, "Come along, now! what news do you bring?

چرا سر نبستی به فتراک بر؟
You did not his head with your saddle-strap sling?

مگر بر تو نام‌آوری حمله کرد
Perhaps the renowned one attacked you, instead?

نیاوردی از ضعف تاب نبرد؟
And, from weakness, you failed in the combat, and fled?"

جوانمرد شاطر زمین بوسه داد
The clever, magnanimous man kissed the ground;

ملک را ثنا گفت و تمکین نهاد
Praised the monarch and rendered obeisance profound.

بدو گفت کای شاه با داد و هوش
"Oh king! full of justice and reason, I pray!

ازین در سخنهای حاتم نیوش
Give ear unto what about Hatim I say!

که دریافتم حاتم نامجوی
In him I discovered a generous youth;

هنرمند و خوش منظر و خوبروی
Accomplished, kind-visaged and handsome, forsooth!

جوانمرد و صاحب خرد دیدمش

I saw he was liberal, and wise notions held;

به مردانگی فوق خود دیدمش

And found that in courage myself he excelled.

مرا بار لطفش دو تا کرد پشت

The load of his favour, my back crooked made

به شمشیر احسان و فضلم بکشت

He killed me with kindness and Favour's keen blade.

بگفت آنچه دید از کرمهای وی

He told what he saw of his generous ways.

شهنشه ثنا گفت بر آل طی

On the household of Hatim, the king showered praise.

فرستاده را داد مهری درم

He gave silver and gold to the messenger chaste;

که مهر است بر نام حاتم کرم

Saying, "Bounty's a seal upon 'Hatim' s name placed."

مر او را سزد گر گواهی دهند

If people bear witness, this much he can claim,

که معنی و آوازهاش همرهند

That his acts and the rumour thereof, are the same

◈◉◈◉◈

حکایت دختر حاتم در روزگار پیغمبر(ص)
Story of Hatim's Daughter in the Time of the Prophet (On him be safety!)

شنیدم که طی در زمان رسول

I have heard that the Tat, in the Prophet's own time.,

نکردند منشور ایمان قبول

Refused to receive the religion sublime.

فرستاد لشکر بشیر نذیر

His enlightening and threatening army he sent,

گرفتند از ایشان گروهی اسیر

And captured a number who would not repent.

بفرمود کشتن به شمشیر کین

He ordered them all to be put to the sword;

که ناپاک بودند و ناپاک دین

For reverence they lacked and their faith was abhorred

زنی گفت من دختر حاتمم

I'm a daughter of Hatim" a woman exclaimed,

بخواهید از این نامور حاکمم

They request my release from this governor famed.

کرم کن به جای من ای محترم

Oh revered one! have mercy upon me, I pray!

که مولای من بود از اهل کرم

For my father was generous enough, in his day"!

به فرمان پیغمبر نیک رای

Obeying the pure-minded Prophet's commands,

گشادند زنجیرش از دست و پای

They severed the chains from her feet and her hands.

در آن قوم باق نهادند تیغ

They put all the rest of the tribe to the sword

که راند سیلاب خون بی دریغ

And a torrent of blood, without pity, outpoured.

به زاری به شمشیر زن گفت زن

To a soldier, the woman in agony said

مرا نیز با جمله گردن بزن

As you've done to the others, cut off, too, my head!

مروت نبینم رهایی ز بند

For I feel it ungenerous, that I should be loose

به تنها و یارانم اندر کمند

By myself, and my friends all confined in the noose ".

همی گفت و گریان بر احوال طی

To the brothers of Tai she was speaking through tears,When the sound of her

به سمع رسول آمد آواز وی

voice reached the "prophet's "sharp ears.

ببخشود آن قوم و دیگر عطا

He gave her the tribe and some presents of note;

که هرگز نکرد اصل و گوهر خطا

"A pure nature," he said, " will not error promote ".

❖◉❖◉❖

حکایت حاتم طائی
On the generosity of Hatim, and Praise of the King of Islam (Hatim Tai and his wife)

ز بنگاه حاتم یکی پیرمرد

At Hatim's store tent, an old pauper, distressed,

طلب ده درم سنگ فانید کرد

For ten direm's weight of kanlz made request

ز راوی چنان یاد دارم خبر

From a writer, I thus recollect the event,

که پیشش فرستاد تنگی شکر

That a sackful of sugar before him he sent.

زن از خیمه گفت این چه تدبیر بود؟

From the tent, Hatims wife shouted, "What is this plan?

همان ده درم حاجت پیر بود

But the weight of ten direms required the old man ".

شنید این سخن نامبردار طی

This remark reached the ears of the chieftain of Tai

بخندید و گفت ای دلارام حی

Who smiling, replied, "Oh heart-soother from Hat!

گر او در خور حاجت خویش خواست

If he asked in accordance with what was his need,

جوانمردی آل حاتم کجاست؟

Where is Hatim s magnanimous nature, indeed"?

چو حاتم به آزادمردی دگر

Like Hatim, in true liberality, none

ز دوران گیتی نیامد مگر

Through the changes of Time has appeared, except one

ابوبکر سعد آن که دست نوال

Abu-Bakar-Sdd, whose reward-giving hand,

نهد همتش بر دهان سؤال

Places prayers for himself in the mouth of Demand.

رعیت پناها دلت شاد باد

Oh protector of subjects, may joy fill your heart!

به سعیت مسلمانی آباد باد

To Islam may your labours fresh glory impart!

سرافرازد این خاک فرخنده بوم

By your efforts, the dust of this fortunate home,

ز عدلت بر اقلیم یونان و روم

Excels the dominions of Greece and of Rome.

194

چو حاتم، اگر نیستی کام وی

If you cannot to Hatim! s unique fame come nigh,

نبردی کس اندر جهان نام طی

None has borne in the world a renown like to Tai.

ثنا ماند از آن نامور در کتاب

That famed person's praises in records remain

تو را هم ثنا ماند و هم ثواب

Your praise and good works, too, will mention obtain.

که حاتم بدان نام و آوازه خواست

Then Hatim's desire was a popular name,;

تو را سعی و جهد از برای خداست

Your zeal has the glory of God for its aim.

تکلف بر مرد درویش نیست

There is nothing to make the poor suffer distress,

وصیت همین یک سخن بیش نیست

And in stating your fame, not a word's in excess.

که چندان که جهدت بود خیر کن

Be useful, so long as you're able to strive!

ز تو خیر ماند ز سعدی سخن

For your goodness and SddVs discourse will survive

◈◉◈◈◉◈

حکایت همدردی پادشاهان

On the Sympathy of Kings (the King, and the Peasant and his ass)

یکی را خری در گل افتاده بود

A certain one's donkey had sunk in the mud;

ز سوداش خون در دل افتاده بود

From anger the blood reached his heart like a flood.

بیابان و باران و سرما و سیل

There were desert and rain, cold and torrents, around!

فرو هشته ظلمت بر آفاق ذیل

And the black skirt of Darkness hung over the ground.

همه شب در این غصه تا بامداد

From night until morning his rage he let loose;

سقط گفت و نفرین و دشنام داد

He reviled and reproached and indulged in abuse.

195

نه دشمن برست از زبانش نه دوست

Neither kindred nor foe from his tongue got away;

نه سلطان که این بوم و بر زآن اوست

Nor the sultan who over the country held sway.

قضا را خداوند آن پهن دشت

The king of that region, a person renowned,

در آن حال منکر بر او بر گذشت

Was playing chaugdn on the exercise-ground;

شنید این سخنهای دور از صواب

He heard those remarks, so remote from the truth,

نه صبر شنیدن، نه روی جواب

And neither could listen nor answer, forsooth.

نگه کرد سالار اقلیم دید

The man saw the chief of the country, and found

که بر پشتهٔ ماجرا می شنید

That he heard all he said from a neighbouring mound.

به چشم سیاست در او بنگریست

The monarch abashed, turned his eyes on his train:

که سودای این بر من از بهر چیست؟

Can any, the anger he bears me, explain?

یکی گفت شاها به تیغش بزن

Someone answered, " Oh king! with the sword take his life!

که نگذاشت کس را نه دختر نه زن

For he spared none not even his daughter and wife."

نگه کرد سلطان عالی محل

The monarch sublime looked about him in ire;

خودش در بلا دید و خر در وحل

Saw the man in distress and his ass in the mire.

ببخشود بر حال مسکین مرد

He pitied the poor, wretched villager's plight,

فرو خورد خشم سخنهای سرد

And swallowed his rage, at the words full of spite;

زرش داد و اسب و قبا پوستین

Gave him gold and a horse and fur cloak of his own:

چه نیکو بود مهر در وقت کین

How comely is kindness when rancour is shown!

یکی گفتش ای پیر بی عقل و هوش

Oh old man void of wisdom and sense," someone cried,

عجب رستی از قتل، گفتا خموش

"You've evaded death, strangely! " "Desist!" he replied;

اگر من بنالیدم از درد خویش

"If I sorely lamented because of my grief,

وی انعام فرمود در خورد خویش

Becoming his station, he gave me relief."

بدی را بدی سهل باشد جزا

Rendering evil for evil is easy to do;

اگر مردی احسن الی من اسا

If you're manly, do good to the man who wronged you!

◈ ◉ ◈ ◈ ◉ ◈

حکایت مرد ثروتمند و مرد فقیر
Story of the rich man and the noble poor man

شنیدم که مغروری از کبر مست

A haughty one, drunk with the pride of high place,

در خانه بر روی سائل ببست

Shut the door of his house in a poor beggar's face.

به کنجی فرو ماند و بنشست مرد

The pauper sat down in a corner, distressed;

جگر گرم و آه از تف سینه سرد

Liver hot and sighs cold, from the fire in his breast.

شنیدش یکی مرد پوشیده چشم

His sobs reached the ears of a man who was blind:

بپرسیدش از موجب کین و خشم

What has vexed you and caused you this fury of mind"?

فرو گفت و بگریست بر خاک کوی

He told shedding tears on the dust of the road

جفایی کز آن شخصش آمد به روی

Of the cruel oppression that proud person showed

بگفت ای فلان ترک آزار کن

He replied, "Oh unknown one! abandon your care!

یک امشب به نزد من افطار کن

For the night share my dwelling and break your fast there"!

به خلق و فریبش گریبان کشید

By kindness and coaxing he made him subdued

به خانه در آوردش و خوان کشید

Took him home to his house and regaled him with food.

بر آسود درویش روشن نهاد

The Dervish of luminous nature reposed, closed"!

بگفت ایزدت روشنایی دهاد

And said, "May the Lord ope your eyes that are

شب از نرگسش قطره چندی چکید

Some drops, in the night, from his eyes trickled free;

سحر دیده بر کرد و دنیا بدید

He oped them at dawn and the world he could see!

حکایت به شهر اندر افتاد و جوش

Through the city the story was told with surprise,

که آن بی بصر دیده بر کرد دوش

That the man who was blind in the night oped his eyes.

شنید این سخن خواجه سنگدل

The hard-hearted tyrant was told the affair}

که برگشت درویش از او تنگدل

From whom the poor man had gone off in despair.

بگفتا حکایت کن ای نیکبخت

He said, "Oh thou favoured of Fate, tell me true!

که چون سهل شد بر تو این کار سخت؟

How has this hard affair become easy to you?

که بر کردت این شمع گیتی فروز؟

Who caused your earth-lighting-up candle to blaze"?

بگفت ای ستمکار آشفته روز

He answered: "Oh tyrant, of burdensome days!

تو کوته نظر بودی و سست رای

Your vision was short and your wisdom depraved;

که مشغول گشتی به جغد از همای

With the sad-visaged owl, not the Phoenix, you slaved.

به روی من این در کسی کرد باز

With the sad-visaged owl, not the Phoenix, you slaved.

که کردی تو بر روی وی در، فراز

In my face, the same person has opened the door,

اگر بوسه بر خاک مردان زنی
If you kiss but the dust of the feet of such men
به مردی که پیش آیدت روشنی
By manhood! the light will approach you again.

کسانی که پوشیده چشم دلند
Those people whose heart's eyes are totally blind,
همانا کز این توتیا غافلند
Appear to neglect this eye-salve in their mind

چو برگشته دولت ملامت شنید
When the man of changed fortune this censuring met,
سر انگشت حیرت به دندان گزید
At his fingers he gnawed with the teeth of Regret;

که شهباز من صید دام تو شد
My falcon," he said, " fell to your snare as game;
مرا بود دولت به نام تو شد
The good fortune was mine, but it went to your name ".

کسی چون به دست آورد جره باز
When has any one brought the male hawk to his net.
فرو برده چون موش دندان آز؟
Who has, mouse-like, his teeth upon avarice set?

الا گر طلبکار اهل دلی
Beware, if the path of the good you select!
ز خدمت مکن یک زمان غافلی
Do not show in your service a moment's neglect!

خورش ده به گنجشک و کبک و حمام
Feed the partridge, the quail, and the pigeon with care,
که یک روزت افتد همایی به دام
For some day the griffin may fall to your snare.

چو هر گوشه تیر نیاز افکنی
When Humility's arrow you everywhere cast,
امید است ناگه که صیدی زنی
You may hope to bring game to your keeping, at last.

دری هم بر آید ز چندین صدف
But one pearl will be found in a number of shells;
ز صد چوبه آید یکی بر هدف
On the target, but one, in a hundred shafts, tells.

❁◉❁◉❁

حکایت مردی که پسرش را گم کرد

Story of the man and his lost son

یکی را پسر گم شد از راحله

A man lost his son off a pack-camel's back,

شبانگه بگردید در قافله

And, at night, searched the whole caravan for his track.

ز هر خیمه پرسید و هر سو شتافت

He asked at each tent, and to every side hied

به تاریکی آن روشنایی نیافت

In the darkness, the light shining bright he espied.

چو آمد بر مردم کاروان

When again he returned to the caravan folk,

شنیدم که می‌گفت با ساروان

To a driver of camels, I heard, he thus spoke: —

ندانی که چون راه بردم به دوست

Do you know how this gem was recovered by me

هر آن کس که پیش آمدم گفتم اوست

Whoever approached me, I said, 'It is he!'"

از آن اهل دل در پی هر کسند

The holy, with life, ask each person they can,

که باشد که روزی به مردی رسند

In the hope that they sometime may get the right man.

برند از برای دلی بارها

For the sake of one heart, many griefs they oppose,

خورند از برای گلی خارها

And endure many thorns, for the sake of one rose.

◈◉◈◉◈

حکایت گوهر تاج ملک زاده
Story of the prince's crown jewel

ز تاج ملکزاده‌ای در مناخ
From the crown of a prince, in a stony camp-ground,

شبی لعلی افتاد در سنگلاخ
A gem fell at night, among the pebbles around.

پدر گفتش اندر شب تیره رنگ
Said his father, " The night has so very dark grown,

چه دانی که گوهر کدام است و سنگ؟
How can you distinguish the gem from a stone?

همه سنگها پاس دار ای پسر
Preserve, oh my son, all the stones lying here!

که لعل از میانش نباشد به در
That the ruby may not from their midst disappear."

در اوباش، پاکان شوریده رنگ
Among the rabble, the holy of rapturous face,

همان جای تاریک و لعلند و سنگ
Are the ruby among stones, in a dark, dreary place.

به رغبت بکش بار هر جاهلی
The load of the foolish with dignity bear!

که افتی به سر وقت صاحبدلی
For, at last, the reward of the pious you'll share.

کسی را که با دوستی سرخوش است
You can see that the person in love with a friend,

نبینی که چون بار دشمن کش است؟
Bears the enemy's troubles that on him descend;

بدرد چو گل جامه از دست خار
Tears his robes, like a rose at the hand of a thorn;

که خون در دل افتاده خندد چو نار
For the warm lover smiles, like the pomegranate torn.

غم جمله خور در هوای یکی
For the love you bear one, sympathize with the whole!

مراعات صد کن برای یکی
Take care of a hundred, because of one soul!

گرت خاک پایان شوریده سر
If the humble in gait and distracted in mind,

حقیر و فقیرند اندر نظر
Debased and in poverty steeped, you should find,

تو هرگز مبین شان بچشم پسند
Never view them as though they delighted your eyes!
که ایشان پسندیدۀ حق بسند
That they are approved of by God, will suffice.

کسی را که نزدیک ظنت بد اوست
The person who may in your judgment be vile,
چه دانی که صاحب ولایت خود اوست؟
May be Powerless to guide his own actions, the while.

در معرفت بر کسانی است باز
The door of God's knowledge is open to those
که درهاست بر روی ایشان فراز
In the faces of whom, people other doors close.

بسا تلخ عیشان تلخی چشان
Many bitter delights of the tasters of woe,
که آیند در حله دامن کشان
On the Last Day, as awful accusers will show.

ببوسی گرت عقل و تدبیر هست
If wisdom and judgment within you are found,
ملکزاده را در نواخانه دست
Kiss the king's grandson's hand, in the dark dungeon bound!

که روزی برون آید از شهربند
He will someday go free through the state-prison gate,
بلندیت بخشد چو گردد بلند
And confer on you rank, when he comes to be great.

مسوزان درخت گل اندر خریف
Do not burn up that rose-bush in autumn, though sere!
که در نوبهارت نماید ظریف
For to you in the spring, it will precious appear.

حکایت پدر بخیل و پسر لاابالی
Story of a miserly father and his prodigal son

یکی زهرهٔ خرج کردن نداشت
A man to spend money lacked courage and will;

زرش بود و یارای خوردن نداشت
He had gold but no stomach for eating his fill.

نه خوردی، که خاطر بر آسایدش
He ate not, in order to comfort his mind;

نه دادی، که فردا بکار آیدش
Nor gave, that to-morrow release he might find.

شب و روز در بند زر بود و سیم
He was thinking of silver and gold, night and day;

زر و سیم در بند مرد لئیم
The silver and gold in the miser's hand lay.

بدانست روزی پسر در کمین
The son, in concealment, one day saw the spot

که ممسک کجا کرد زر در زمین
Where the father had hidden his money, ill-got.

ز خاکش بر آورد و بر باد داد
From the ground he removed it and spent it apace;

شنیدم که سنگی در آن جا نهاد
I have heard that he buried a stone in its place.

جوانمرد را زر بقایی نکرد
The gold with the generous youth did not last

به یک دستش آمد، به دیگر بخورد
It came to one hand, through the other it passed.

کز این کم زنی بود ناپاکرو
For this reason, a spendthrift than woman is less

کلاهش به بازار و میزر گرو
His cap's in the market, in pawn is his dress.

نهاده پدر چنگ در نای خویش
The father had seized his own throat in his gripe;

پسر چنگی و نایی آورده پیش
The son had brought forward the lute and the pipe.

پدر زار و گریان همه شب نخفت
From weeping, the father at night kept awake;

پسر بامدادان بخندید و گفت
The son in the morning laughed loudly, and Spake:

زر از بهر خوردن بود ای پدر

or enjoying, oh father! our money we own;

ز بهر نهادن چه سنگ و چه زر

For treasuring, gold is not better than stone ".

زر از سنگ خارا برون آورند

From adamant gold is extracted with care,

که با دوستان و عزیزان خورند

To clothe and bestow and provide proper fare;

زر اندر کف مرد دنیاپرست

And gold in the grasp of a miser's close fist,

هنوز ای برادر به سنگ اندرست

In the stone, still, oh brother! appears to exist.

چو در زندگانی بدی با عیال

If you over your children in life tyrannize,

گرت مرگ خواهند، از ایشان منال

Complain not of them, if they wish your demise!

چو خشم آری آن گه خورند از تو سی

Like a charm, they'll their longing for food satisfy,

که از بام پنجه گز افتی به زیر

When you fall from a roof that is fifty yards high.

بخیل توانگر به دینار و سیم

If a miser has plenty of gold in his hands,

طلسمی است بالای گنجی مقیم

As a talisman, over his treasure he stands.

از آن سالها میبماند زرش

And his gold will remain for a number of years,

که لرزد طلسمی چنین بر سرش

For a talisman, such, o'er it trembling appears.

به سنگ اجل ناگهش بشکنند

With the dread stone of death, him, they quickly destroy,

به اسودگی گنج قسمت کنند

And in sharing his wealth, heirs their leisure employ.

پس از بردن و گرد کردن چو مور

Hence, rather than carry and store, like the ant,

بخور پیش از آن کهت خورد کرم گور

Enjoy, while you can! when worms eat you, you can't!

سخنهای سعدی مثال است و پند

Sádi's sayings, both proverbs and maxims, comprise;

به کار آیدت گر شوی کار بند

By them, he will profit who honestly tries.

دریغ است از این روی برتافتن

To avert from these sayings your face, it is sad!

کز این روی دولت توان یافتن

For prosperous wealth in this way can be had.

حکایت نتایج سودمند کار نیک کوچک
On the Beneficial Results of a Small Favour

جوانی به دانگی کرم کرده بود

A youth, with a Dang, had a kindness supplied;

تمنای پیری بر آورده بود

An old man's desire, he had once gratified.

به جرمی گرفت آسمان ناگهش

By Heaven, for a crime, he was suddenly bound

فرستاد سلطان به کشتنگهش

The king sent him off to the gibbeting-ground.

تکاپوی ترکان و غوغای عام

From doors, streets and roofs, folk were viewing in groups

تماشاکنان بر در و کوی و بام

The clamouring mob and careering of troops.

چو دید اندر آشوب، درویش پیر

When, in midst of the tumult, the old Dervish saw

جوان را به دست خلایق اسیر

The youth the crowd's captive and doomed by the law,

دلش بر جوانمرد مسکین بخست

His heart for the poor, generous victim was grieved,

که باری دل آورده بودش به دست

For once by his hand had his heart been relieved.

برآورد زاری که سلطان بمرد

He uttered a wail that the king was no more;

جهان ماند و خوی پسندیده برد

"The world he has left — a good nature he bore"

به هم بر همی‌سود دست دریغ

He was wringing his hands, in apparent distress;

شنیدند ترکان آهخته تیغ

The troops with their sabres drawn, heard his address.

به فریاد از ایشان بر آمد خروش

A noise of lamenting from all of them rose;

تپانچه زنان بر سر و روی و دوش

On their heads, face, and shoulders, they dealt them -selves blows.

پیاده به سر تا در بارگاه

They hurried on foot to the Royal Court door,

دویدند و بر تخت دیدند شاه

And saw the king sit on his throne, as before.

جوان از میان رفت و بردند پیر

The young man escaped and the old man was drawn

به گردن بر تخت سلطان اسیر

By the neck, as a captive, before the king's throne.

به ولش بپرسید و هیبت نمود

With daunting and threatening, the sultan inquired —:

که مرگ منت خواستن بر چه بود؟

In reporting me dead, by what aim were you fired?

چو نیک است خوی من و راستی

In my nature both goodness and uprightness lie,

بد مردم آخر چرا خواستی؟

In spite of that, why did you wish me to die"?

برآورد پیر دلاور زبان

The courageous old man raised his voice, in this way —:

که ای حلقه در گوش حکمت جهان

On thou, whom the whole of the world must obey!

به قول دروغی که سلطان بمرد

By the statement, untrue, that the sultan was dead,

نمردی و بیچاره‌ای جان ببرد

You yet live, and one, helpless, escaped with his head ".

ملک زین حکایت چنان بر شکفت

This story so greatly astonished the king,

که چیزش ببخشید و چیزی نگفت

That he gave him a present and said not a thing.

وز این جانب افتان و خیزان جوان

Then, stumbling and rising, the helpless young man,

همی رفت بیچاره هر سو دوان

Away in a state of bewilderment ran.

یکی گفتش از چار سوی قصاص

A man from the square of requital, thus spake —

چه کردی که آمد به جانت خلاص؟

"How did you deliver your life from the stake"?

به گوشش فرو گفت کای هوشمند

"Oh intelligent asker!" he breathed in his ear,

به جانی و دانگی رهیدم ز بند

"By a man and a Dang from the noose I got clear ".

یکی تخم در خاک از آن می‌نهد

For this reason a man in the ground casts the seed;

که روز فرو ماندگی بر دهد

That he may gather fruit, in the season of need.

جوی باز دارد بلایی درشت

One grain may the greatest misfortune restrain;

عصایی شنیدی که عوجی بکشت

Great Ogg, you perceive, was by Moses' staff slain.

حدیث درست آخر از مصطفاست

The Chosen One's saying is true, you can tell,

که بخشایش و خیر دفع بلاست

That bestowing and goodness misfortune repel.

عدو را نبینی در این بقعه پای

You won't see an enemy's foot in this place,

که بوبکر سعد است کشور خدای

Where the conquering Bu-Bakar-Sad shows his face.

بگیر ای جهانی به روی تو شاد

A world gets delight through your presence and grace;

جهانی، که شادی به روی تو باد

A world, saying, "Joy ever be in your face I"

کس از کس به دور تو باری نبرد

Not a man in your reign on another can tread;

گلی در چمن جور خاری نبرد

The thorn does not harass the rose in its bed.

تویی سایهٔ لطف حق بر زمین

You're the shade of the favour of God o'er the ground;

پیمبر صفت رحمة العالمین

You resemble the prophet, in mercy profound.

تو را قدر اگر کس نداند چه غم؟

What although a man may not your worth realize?

شب قدر را می‌ندانند هم

The Great Night of Power, too, he can't recognize.

حکایت در معنی ثمرات نکوکاری در آخرت
Story on the fruits of well-doing

کسی دید صحرای محشر به خواب

A man saw the Great Judgment Plain in a dream

مس تفته روی زمین ز آفتاب

The Earth's face like sun-heated copper did seem.

همی بر فلک شد ز مردم خروش

The cries of mankind rose to Heav'n's lofty seat;

دماغ از تبش می‌برآمد به جوش

Their brains, too, were boiling, because of the heat.

یکی شخص از این جمله در سایه‌ای

A man, midst the throng, in the shade was at rest;

به گردن بر از خلد پیرایه‌ای

A Paradise ornament showed on his breast.

بپرسید کای مجلس آرای مرد

Oh assembly adorner! " the dreaming man said,

که بود اندر این مجلست پایمرد؟

In this mighty assembly, who granted you aid?"

رزی داشتم بر در خانه، گفت

He answered, " A vine at my house door I kept;

به سایه درش نیکمردی بخفت

A good man came under its shadow and slept.

در این وقت نومیدی آن مرد راست

That pure, upright saint, in this time of despair,

گناهم ز دادار داور بخواست

Asked my sins from the just-dealing God, in this prayer:

که یارب بر این بنده بخشایشی

Deliver, oh God, this poor slave from his woes!

کز او دیده‌ام وقتی آسایشی

For once by his means I enjoyed sweet repose.'"

چه گفتم چو حل کردم این راز را؟

I was glad when I found out the mystery's cause,

بشارت خداوند شیراز را

And told the good news to the lord of Shiraz;

که جمهور در سایهٔ همتش

For the world, in the shade of his eminent mind,

مقیمند و بر سفرهٔ نعمتش

Secure at his table of bounty, you'll find.

درختی است مرد کرم، باردار

A liberal man is a fruit-bearing tree,

وز او بگذری هیزم کوهسار

And if you neglect it, Hell's firewood you'll be.

حطب را اگر تیشه بر پی زنند

If they lay the sharp axe to the wither'd tree's root,

درخت برومند را کی زنند؟

When will they attack the good tree, bearing fruit?

بسی پای دار، ای درخت هنر

Oh tree, full of merit, long, long may you live!

که هم میوه‌داری و هم سایه‌ور

For you freely bear fruit and a shade you can give

گفتار اندر حکومت عدل

Remarks on the fear of Kings and the government of a country

بگفتیم در باب احسان بسی

In connexion with favour, enough, I have said;

ولیکن نه شرط است با هر کسی

Yet it need not be showered on everyone's head.

بخور مردم آزار را خون و مال

Eat the blood and the wealth of tyrannical kings!

که از مرغ بد کنده به پر و بال

For a bad cock is best, with plucked plumage and wings.

یکی را که با خواجهٔ توست جنگ

If a man to be fighting your master is known,

به دستش چرا می‌دهی چوب و سنگ؟

Why strengthen his hands with a stick and a stone?

بر انداز بیخی که خار آورد

Destroy, without sorrow, the thorn-bearing root!

درختی بپرور که بار آورد

And carefully cherish the tree that bears fruit!

کسی را بده پایهٔ مهتران

On a person the rank of a noble bestow,

که بر کهتران سر ندارد گران

Who to the distressed will not arrogance show!

مبخشای بر هر کجا ظالمی است

Show no grace to the spot where a tyrant's lines fall!

که رحمت بر او جور بر عالمی است

For mercy to him is oppression on all!

جهان‌سوز را کشته بهتر چراغ

Much better extinguish the world-burner's flame!

یکی به در آتش که خلقی به داغ

Better one man on fire than a people in shame.

هر آن کس که بر دزد رحمت کند

Whenever you pity the fierce robbing-man,

به بازوی خود کاروان می‌زند

With your own arm you rifle the rich caravan.

جفاپیشگان را بده سر بباد

Throw tyrannical heads to the wind in its flight!

ستم بر ستم پیشه عدل است و داد

Oppression on tyrants, is justice and right!

حکایت مهربانی با افراد نالایق
On Kindness to the Unworthy

شنیدم که مردی غم خانه خورد

I have heard that a man some home sorrow endured,

که زنبور بر سقف او لانه کرد

For bees in his roof had their dwelling secured.

ز بانو طلب کرد ساطور را

He asked for a big butcher's-knife from his dame

که ویران کند خان زنبور را

To demolish the nest of the bees was his aim.

زنش گفت از اینان چه خواهی؟ مکن

His wife said, "Oh, do not effect your design!

که مسکین پریشان شوند از وطن

For the poor bees, dispersed from their dwelling, will pine."

بشد مرد نادان پس کار خویش

The foolish man yielded and went his own way;

گرفتند یک روز زن را به نیش

His wife with their stings was assaulted one day.

بیامد ز دگان سوی خانه مرد

The man from his shop to his dwelling returned;

بران بی خرد زن بسی طیره کرد

At his wife's stupid folly, with anger he burned.

زن بی خرد بر در و بام و کوی

The ignorant woman, from door, street and roof,

همی کرد فریاد و می گفت شوی

Was shouting complaints, while the man gave reproof!

مکن روی بر مردم ای زن ترش

Do not make your face sour in men's presence, oh wife!

تو گفتی که زنبور مسکین مکش

Deprive not you said, ' the poor bees of their life! "

کسی با بدان نیکویی چون کند؟

On behalf of the bad, why beneficence show?

بدان را تحمل، بد افزون کند

Forbear with the bad and you make their sins grow.

چو اندر سری بینی آزار خلق

When oppression of men, in a ruler, you note,

به شمشیر تیزش بیازار حلق

With a sharp-cutting sword you should tickle his throat.

سگ آخر که باشد که خوانش نهند؟

That a dog should have " food-trays," what worth has he shown?

بفرمای تا استخوانش دهند

Give orders, so that they may toss him a bone!

چه نیکو زده‌ست این مثل پیر ده

The village priest, nicely, this proverb expressed:

ستور لگدزن گران بار به

For the pack-horse that kicks, heavy burdens are best"

اگر نیکمردی نماید عسس

When the night-watch, patrolling, civility shows,

نیارد به شب خفتن از دزد، کس

At night, from the thieves, not a soul gets repose.

نی نیزه در حلقهٔ کارزار

In the centre of battle the cane of one spear

بقیمت تر از نیشکر صد هزار

Is, than thousands of sugar-canes, reckoned more dear.

نه هر کس سزاوار باشد به مال

That all are not worthy of riches, is clear;

یکی مال خواهد، یکی گوشمال

One needs riches, another a box on the ear.

چو گربه نوازی کبوتر برد

When you rear up a cat, off your pigeons it bears;

چو فربه کنی گرگ، یوسف درد

If a wolf you should fatten, your Joseph it tears.

بنایی که محکم ندارد اساس

The building whose base is not stable and true,

بلندش مکن ور کنی زو هراس

Raise not lofty! or show for it dread, if you do

❖◉❖◉❖

گفتار اندر آینده نگری و مشعیت الهی
Remarks on foresight and providence

چه خوش گفت بهرام صحرانشین
How well spoke Bihram of the desert renowned,

چو یکران توسن زدش بر زمین
When thrown by an obstinate horse to the ground:

دگر اسبی از گله باید گرفت
"From the pasture another horse must be obtained;

که گر سرکشد باز شاید گرفت
For when one is rebellious he must be restrained."

سرچشمه شاید گرفتن به بیل
You may stop, with a bodkin, the fountain's weak source;

چو پر شد نشاید گرفتن به پیل
When flooded, an elephant can't stem its course.

ببند ای پسر دجله در آب کاست
Dam the Tigris, oh son! when the water is scant;

که سودی ندارد چو سیلاب خاست
For when it increases in volume, you can't!

چو گرگ خبیث آمدت در کمند
When the wicked old wolf puts his head in the noose,

بکش ور نه دل بر کن از گوسفند
Take his life! or your heart from your flocks you may loose.

از ابلیس هرگز نیاید سجود
Adoration from Satan's a thing quite unknown;

نه از بد گهر نیکوئی در وجود
Good actions have never by villains been shown.

بد اندیش را جاه و فرصت مده
Of a fit place and time, let no foe be possessed!

عدو در چه و دیو در شیشه به
A foe in a well, and fiend bottled, are best

مگو شاید این مار کشتن به چوب
Do not say that this snake, with a stick, you must slay;

چو سر زیر سنگ تو دارد بکوب
When you have its head under a stone, pound away!

قلم زن که بد کرد با زیردست
When a writer has injured his poor fellow men,

قلم بهتر او را به شمشیر دست
A sword for his hands is more fit than a pen

213

مدبر که قانون بد می‌نهد

The vizier who imposes the bad laws he frames,

تو را می‌برد تا به دوزخ دهد

Will carry you on till he gives you to flames.

مگو ملک را این مدبر بس است

Do not say, "This vizier is befitting the state.

مدبر مخوانش که مدبر کس است

Do not call him vizier; he's the people's bad fate.

سعید آورد قول سعدی به جای

To the sayings of Sádi the fortunate list;

که ترتیب ملک است و تدبیر رای

For in them growth of state, sense and wisdom exist

3

باب سوم

(CHAPTER III)

 در عشق و مستی و شور

ON LOVE

سرآغاز

In begin

خوشا وقت شوریدگان غمش

Oh blest are the days of those rilled with God's love!

اگر زخم بینند وگر مرهمش

Whether meeting with wounds, or His salve, from above!

گدایانی از پادشاهی نفور

They are beggars, who all Earthly Royalty shun;

به امیدش اندر گدایی صبور

Who, hopeful, in beggary patience have won.

دمادم شراب الم در کشند

Every moment they swallow the wine-draught of pain;

وگر تلخ بینند دم در کشند

And although they taste bitterness, do not complain.

بلای خمار است در عیش مل

In the pleasure of wine, as a curse, sickness shows;

سلحدار خار است با شاه گل

The thorn is a guard on the stem of the rose.

نه تلخ است صبری که بر یاد اوست

Not bitter's the patience with Him for its end;

که تلخی شکر باشد از دست دوست

For the bitter is sweet, from the hand of a friend.

ملامت کشانند مستان یار

They are bearers of censure enamoured of God

سبک تر برد اشتر مست بار

The camel excited bears swifter his load.

اسیرش نخواهد رهایی ز بند

His captive desires not from bonds to be loose;

شکارش نجوید خلاص از کمند

His prey does not seek to escape from His noose.

سلاطین عزلت، گدایان حی

They are kings in retirement; God's mendicants, crossed;

منازل شناسان گم کرده پی

They are versed in God's ways and their footsteps are lost.

به سر وقتشان خلق ره کی برند

When will men, to their doings, discover the way,

که چون آب حیوان به ظلمت درند

Since, like water of life, in deep darkness they stay?

216

چو بیت‌المقدس درون پر قباب

Like Jerusalem's temple, interior all light,

رها کرده دیوار بیرون خراب

But outside, the walls are in ruinous plight.

چو پروانه آتش به خود در زنند

Like moths, they deliver themselves up to fire;

نه چون کرم پیله به خود برتنند

They're not dressed, like the silkworm, in silken attire.

دلارام در بر، دلارام جوی

With their loves in their bosom, for sweethearts they look;

لب از تشنگی خشک، بر طرف جوی

From thirst, their lips dry by the side of a brook!

نگویم که بر آب قادر نیند

I don't say that they cannot some water command;

که بر شاطی نیل مستسقیند

But, beside the Nile's bank, like the dropsied, they stand.

❖◉❖◉❖

تقریر عشق مجازی و قوت آن
On the Power of True and Metaphorical Love

تو را عشق همچون خودی ز آب و گل

Your love of one, made out of water and clay

رباید همی صبر و آرام دل

Like yourself, steals all patience and calmness away.

به بیداریش فتنه بر خد و خال

While awake, you're bewitched with her cheek and her mole;

به خواب اندرش پای بند خیال

While dreaming, the thought of her fetters your soul.

به صدقش چنان سر نهی در قدم

In devotion, your head on her feet you've so placed,

که بینی جهان با وجودش عدم

That when with her, you look on the world as effaced.

چو در چشم شاهد نیاید زرت

When the longing for gold in your sweetheart is slight,

زر و خاک یکسان نماید برت

Gold and dust are exactly the same in your sight

دگر با کست بر نیاید نفس

Your soul with another one cannot be bound,

که با او نماند دگر جای کس

For, with her, not a place for another is found.

تو گویی به چشم اندرش منزل است

You say that her dwelling exists in your eyes;

وگر دیده بر هم نهی در دل است

If your eyelids you close, in your heart, then, it lies.

نه اندیشه از کس که رسوا شوی

You've no care lest dishonour should reach you, at length;

نه قوت که یک دم شکیبا شوی

To be patient, one moment, you have not the strength.

گرت جان بخواهد به لب بر نهی

If she asks for your life, on your palm, you it lay;

ورت تیغ بر سر نهد سر نهی

If she places a sword on your head, you say, "Slay!"

چو عشقی که بنیاد آن بر هواست

Since the love whose foundation, on lust, has its stand,

چنین فتنه‌انگیز و فرمانرواست

Is such a disturber and wields such command,

عجب داری از سالکان طریق

Do you wonder that travelers in God's path are found

که باشند در بحر معنی غریق؟

In the ocean of spiritual consciousness, drowned?

به سودای جانان ز جان مشتعل

In love for the Sweetheart, they care not for life;

به ذکر حبیب از جهان مشتغل

In the thought of the Friend, they have shunned Earthly strife

به یاد حق از خلق بگریخته

In remembrance of God, from the, people they've fled;

چنان مست ساق که می ریخته

With the Cup-bearer charmed, all the wine they have shed.

نشاید به دارو دوا کردشان

One cannot with medicine establish their cure,

که کس مطلع نیست بر دردشان

For no one can tell the disease they endure.

الست از ازل همچنانشان به گوش

Forever, "Am I not thy God?" they so hear,

به فریاد قالوا بلی در خروش

That in clamouring "Yes!" they excited appear

گروهی عمل دار عزلت نشین

A group of Directors in lonely retreat

قدمهای خاکی، دم آتشین

With their breath full of fire, although earthy their feet

به یک نعره کوهی ز جا بر کنند

They root up a hill from its site, with a cry,

به یک ناله شهری به هم بر زنند

And demolish a kingdom, at once, with a sigh.

چو بادند پنهان و چالاک پوی

Like the wind, they're unseen and of hurricane speed;

چو سنگند خاموش و تسبیح گوی

Like stone they are silent, and rosaries read.

سحرها بگریند چندان که آب

In the mornings, so much do they weep, that their tears,

فرو شوید از دیده‌شان کحل خواب

From their eyes wash the ointment of sleep, that appears.

فرس کشته از بس که شب رانده‌اند

The horse has been killed, for they drove him all night;

سحرگه خروشان که وامانده‌اند

And they clamour at dawn, at their wearied-out plight.

شب و روز در بحر سودا و سوز

Night and day, in the sea of love's burning, they stay;

ندانند ز آشفتگی شب ز روز

From amazement, they know not the night from the day.

چنان فتنه بر حسن صورت نگار

For the great Artist's beauty, so great is their craze

که با حسن صورت ندارند کار

That the picture's rare beauty attracts not their gaze.

ندادند صاحبدلان دل به پوست

Saints yield not their hearts to an elegant skin;

وگر ابلهی داد بی مغز کاوست

If a fool has done so, he has no brains within.

می صرف وحدت کسی نوش کرد

That person the pure wine of Unity drank,

که دنیا و عقبی فراموش کرد

Who this world and the next, in oblivion, sank

❧◉❧◉❧

حکایت در معنی تحمل محب صادق

Story of the beggar's son and the king's son

شنیدم که وقتی گدازاده‌ای

I have heard that the son of a beggar, one time,

نظر داشت با پادشازاده‌ای

Fell in love with the son of a monarch sublime.

همی‌رفت و می‌پخت سودای خام

He went and encouraged a passion insane;

خیالش فرو برده دندان به کام

Fancy made him believe that his wish he would gain.

ز میدانش خالی نبودی چو میل

He always remained, like a post, on his course —

همه وقت پهلوی اسبش چو پیل

Like the elephant, always alongside the horse.

دلش خون شد و راز در دل بماند

His heart became blood and the secret there lay,

ولی پایش از گریه در گل بماند

Yet his feet, from his weeping, remained in the clay.

رقیبان خبر یافتندش ز درد

The attendants discovered the cause of his pain,

دگرباره گفتندش اینجا مگرد

And said to him, "Wander not hither again

دمی رفت و یاد آمدش روی دوست

For a moment he went, but the thought of his face

دگر خیمه زد بر سر کوی دوست

Made him settle again near his friend's dwelling place.

غلامی شکستش سر و دست و پای

A slave smashed his head and his feet and his hands,

که باری نگفتیمت ایدر مپای

Saying, "Did we not warn you away from these lands?"

دگر رفت و صبر و قرارش نبود

He departed, with patience and rest at an end;

شکیبایی از روی یارش نبود

No endurance, away from the face of his friend.

مگس وارش از پیش شکر به جور

Like flies from the sugar, they drove him by force,

براندندی و بازگشتی بفور

But he quickly reverted again to his course.

کسی گفتش ای شوخ دیوانه رنگ

One addressed him: " Oh rashling! with reason astray,

عجب صبر داری تو بر چوب و سنگ

Neath the rod and the stone you much patience display!"

بگفت این جفا بر من از دست اوست

At his hand," he replied, "I this harshness sustain;

نه شرطیست نالیدن از دست دوست

At the hand of a friend it is wrong to complain.

من اینک دم دوستی می‌زنم

The spirit of friendship I breathe, you must know

گر او دوست دارد وگر دشمنم

Whether, me, he accepts as a friend, or a foe.

ز من صبر بی او توقع مدار

When away from him, ask not for patience of mind!

که با او هم امکان ندارد قرار

For even when with him, no rest can I find.

نه نیروی صبرم نه جای ستیز

No strength to be patient; no strife-ground have I

نه امکان بودن نه پای گریز

No power to remain and no courage to fly.

مگو زین در بارگه سر بتاب

Do not say, 'Move your head from this Court-door of hope

وگر سر چو میخم نهد در طناب

Though he pull at my head, like a peg in a rope!

نه پروانه جان داده در پای دوست

Is the moth not who gives to his mistress life's spark

به از زنده در کنج تاریک اوست؟

Better off, than alive in his own nook so dark?"

بگفت ار خوری زخم چوگان اوی؟

He asked, "If a wound from his club you should meet?"

بگفتا به پایش در افتم چو گوی

He replied, "I will drop like a ball at his feet"

بگفتا سرت گر ببرد به تیغ؟

He said, "Should he cut off your head with a sword?"

بگفت این قدر نبود از وی دریغ

He replied, "Even that, I will freely afford.

مرا خود ز سر نیست چندان خبر

Regarding my head, I am ignorant, quite,

که تاج است بر تارکم یا تبر

Whether on it a crown or a hatchet may light

مکن با من ناشکیبا عتیب

At me, without patience, reproaches don't fling!

که در عشق صورت نبندد شکیب

For patience in love's an impossible thing.

چو یعقوبم ار دیده گردد سپید

If, like Jacob's, my eyes become whiten'd and blind,

نبرم ز دیدار یوسف امید

To see Joseph, the hope will not pass from my mind."

یکی را که سر خوش بود با یکی

If a man has a sweetheart, beloved in his eyes,

نیازارد از وی به هر اندکی

He's not vexed at each trifle that happens to rise.

رکابش ببوسید روزی جوان

I have heard that the youth kissed his stirrup, one day

برآشفت و برتافت از وی عنان

He was angry and twisted the reins from his way.

بخندید و گفتا عنان برمپیچ

He said, smiling, "From twisting your reins round, desist

که سلطان عنان برنپیچد ز هیچ

For the king, without reason, his reins does not twist

مرا با وجود تو هستی نماند

While near you, I am of existence bereft;

به یاد توام خودپرستی نماند

In thinking of you, no self-worship is left

گرم جرم بینی مکن عیب من

If you see in me crime, do not blame on me bring!

تویی سر بر آورده از جیب من

Your own head, you have caused from my collar to spring!

بدان زهره دستت زدم در رکاب

Hence, boldly, my hand to your stirrup I brought,

که خود را نیاوردم اندر حساب

For I reckoned myself in the matter as nought

کشیدم قلم در سر نام خویش

I have taken the pen and erased my own name;

نهادم قدم بر سر کام خویش

I have planted my feet on my own ardent flame

مرا خود کشد تیر آن چشم مست

I am killed by the glance of that love-kindling eye;

چه حاجت که آری به شمشیر دست؟

What need, then, to flourish your sabre on high? "

تو آتش به نی در زن و در گذر

Set fire to the reeds, and then go from the ground!

که نه خشک در بیشه ماند نه تر

For nor withered nor moist, in the forest, is found.

◈◈◈

حکایت در معنی اهل محبت
On the frailty of lovers

شنیدم که بر لحن خنیاگری

I have heard that a minstrel's sweet notes so entranced

به رقص اندر آمد پری پیکری

A fairy-faced maid that she gracefully danced.

ز دلهای شوریده پیرامنش

Her, the hearts of admirers so closely begirt,

گرفت آتش شمع در دامنش

That the flame of a candle set fire to her skirt

پراکنده خاطر شد و خشمناک

Distracted in spirit, she anger displayed,

یکی گفتش از دوستداران، چه باک؟

When one of her lovers said, " Why be afraid?

تو را آتش ای دوست دامن بسوخت

The fire has, oh friend! set your skirt in a blaze

مرا خود به یک بار خرمن بسوخت

It has burned, in a moment, the hope of my days."

اگر یاری از خویشتن دم مزن

If you are a friend, do not boast of the fact!

که شرک است با یار و با خویشتن

To serve God and yourself, is an impious act.

◈◉◈◉◈

حکایت عشاق
Story on the occupation of lovers

چنین دارم از پیر داننده یاد

From an old man of learning, I thus bear in mind,

که شوریده‌ای سر به صحرا نهاد

That a zealot his head to the desert inclined.

پدر در فراقش نخورد و نخفت

At his absence, his father could eat not nor rest;

پسر را ملامت بکردند و گفت

The boy they rebuked; thus, himself he expressed:

از انگه که یارم کس خویش خواند

Inasmuch as the Friend deigned to call me His own,

دگر با کسم آشنایی نماند

From everyone else my affection has flown.

به حقش که تا حق جمالم نمود

By Truth! until God showed His beauty to me,

دگر هر چه دیدم خیالم نمود

All else I had seen was but fancy set free."

نشد گم که روی از خلایق بتافت

He's not lost who averted his face from mankind;

که گم کرده خویش را باز یافت

But his " Lost One" again, he has managed to find.

پراکندگانند زیر فلک

Those enraptured of God, who beneath the sky dwell,

که هم دد توان خواندشان هم ملک

May be said to be angels and wild beasts, as well.

ز یاد ملک چون ملک نارمند

In remembrance of God, like the angels, they're high;

شب و روز چون دد ز مردم رمند

Night and day from mankind, like the wild beasts, they fly

قوی بازوانند کوتاه دست

Strong in arm, though their hands are, from helplessness,; shrunk

خردمند شیدا و هشیار مست

Philosophers frantic; sagacious men drunk

گه آسوده در گوشه‌ای خرقه دوز

Now patching their clothes in a corner, content;

گه آشفته در مجلسی خرقه سوز

Then engaged in the assembly, on burning them bent.

نه سودای خودشان، نه پروای کس

No regard for themselves and of others no thought;

نه در کنج توحیدشان جای کس

In their nook of God's "Oneness" for others, no spot

پریشیده عقل و پراکنده هوش

Bewildered in reason; intelligence lost

ز قول نصیحتگر آکنده گوش

To the words of admonishers deaf as a post!

به دریا نخواهد شدن بط غریق

There's no chance of a duck, in the sea, being drowned;

سمندر چه داند عذاب حریق؟

In the cold salamander what dread of fire's found?

تهیدست مردان پر حوصله

They are full of ambition, no wealth do they own;

بیابان نوردان پی قافله

They fearlessly travel the desert alone.

ندارند چشم از خلایق پسند

They expect not mankind to be pleased with their ways;

که ایشان پسندیده حق بسند

They're approved of by God, and that amply repays.

عزیزان پوشیده از چشم خلق

They are dear ones, concealed from the people's dim eyes;

نه زنار داران پوشیده دلق

No Brahminical thread 'neath their tattered clothes lies.

پر از میوه و سایه ور چون رزند

Full of fruit and of shade and, if like the grape too,

نه چون ما سیهکار و ازرق رزند

They're not wicked, like us, and dyed over with blue.

به خود سر فرو برده همچون صدف

Like shell-fish, they're silent within their own home,

نه مانند دریا بر آورده کف

And not like the ocean when lashed into foam.

نه مردم همین استخواناند و پوست

Skin and bone put together may not be mankind;

نه هر صورتی جان معنی در اوست

In each figure a soul, knowing God, you can't find

نه سلطان خریدار هر بندهای است

The king does not buy every slave in the mart;

نه در زیر هر ژندهای زندهای است

Each old, tattered robe does not hide a live heart!

اگر ژاله هر قطرهای در شدی

Were a pearl to be formed from each globule of hail,

چو خرمهره بازار از او پر شدی

Thick as shells they would be in the market, for sale.

چو غازی به خود بر نبندند پای

They do not, like rope-dancers, wooden clogs wear

که محکم رود پای چوبین ز جای

Wooden shoes render walking an uphill affair.

حریفان خلوت سرای الست.

Companions of God's private mansion on high;

به یک جرعه تا نفخهٔ صور مست

By a draught, till the last trump, oblivious they lie.

به تیغ از غرض بر نگیرند چنگ

For the sword, they won't part from the object they own;

که پرهیز و عشق آبگینهست و سنگ

For chasteness and love, are the crystal and stone.

❀⊙❀⊙❀

حکایت در معنی غلبه وجد و سلطنت عشق
Story on the power of ecstacy and empire of love

یکی شاهدی در سمرقند داشت
In fair Samarkand, one a mistress possessed;
که گفتی به جای سمر قند داشت
You'd have said that her speech was like sugar expressed

جمالی گرو برده از آفتاب
Her loveliness bore off the palm from the sun;
ز شوخیش بنیاد تقوی خراب
By her merriness, piety's base was undone.

تعالی الله از حسن تا غایتی
The Almighty upon her such beauty bestowed,
که پنداری از رحمت است آیتی
That you'd fancy a sign of His mercy He showed

همی رفتی و دیدهها در پیش
She would walk with the eyes of a crowd in her wake
دل دوستان کرده جان برخیش
Friends sacrificed hearts for her sweet nature's sake.

نظر کردی این دوست در وی نهفت
In concealment, this lover the fair lady spied;
نگه کرد باری به تندی و گفت
She gave him a withering glance, once, and cried:

که ای خیره سر چند پویی پیم
Oh block-head! how long will you after me sweat?
ندانی که من مرغ دامت نیم؟
Do you know not that I'm not the bird for your net?

گرت بار دیگر ببینم به تیغ
If I see you again, with the sword, at a blow,
چو دشمن ببرم سرت بی دریغ
I'll not scruple to cut off your head, like a foe."

کسی گفتش اکنون سر خویش گیر
A person addressed him " Now go your own way!
از این سهل تر مطلبی پیش گیر
And find a more facile ' beloved as your prey

نپندارم این کام حاصل کنی
I don't think you will gain the desire of your mind;
مبادا که جان در سر دل کنی
God forbid, that you cast your sweet life to the wind!"

چو مفتون صادق ملامت شنید

Like a lover sincere, the reproof he heard through;

بدرد از درون ناله‌ای برکشید

A cold sigh from his heart, full of anguish, he drew;

که بگذار تا زخم تیغ هلاک

Saying, " Stop! till the sabre of death does its worst,

بغلطاندم لاشه در خون و خاک

And my corpse, from its wound, rolls in blood and in dust!

مگر پیش دشمن بگویند و دوست

To foe and to friend they, perhaps, will explain,

که این کشته دست و شمشیر اوست

That I by her hand with the sabre was slain.

نمی‌بینم از خاک کویش گریز

To fly from her quarter, I see not my way;

به بیداد گو آبرویم بریز

Do not scatter my honour unjustly, I pray!

مرا توبه فرمایی ای خودپرست

You bid me repent, oh self-worshipping man!

تو را توبه زین گفت اولی ترست

To repent of your words, were a worthier plan!

ببخشای بر من که هرچ او کند

Forgive me! for all that she does, I can tell —

وگر قصد خون است نیکو کند

Even if it is shedding of blood —she does well

بسوزاندم هر شبی آتشش

Her fire, through the night, makes my poor body burn;

سحر زنده گردم به بوی خوشش

Her fragrance makes life, in the morning, retura

اگر میرم امروز در کوی دوست

If, to-day, in my love's street my life I should end,

قیامت زنم خیمه پهلوی دوست

At the Judgment, my tent I will pitch by my friend"

مده تا توانی در این جنگ پشت

While able, do not in love's war suffer rout;

که زنده‌ست سعدی که عشقش بکشت

Is not Sádi alive, though his love is put out?

❖◉❖◉❖

حکایت در فدا شدن اهل محبت و غنیمت شمردن
On Lovers Sacrificing Themselves and Considering Destruction a Boon

یکی تشنه می‌گفت و جان می‌سپرد
While yielding his life up, a thirsty one cried:

خنک نیکبختی که در آب مرد
Oh happy's the man who in cool water died"!

بدو گفت نابالغی کای عجب
Oh strange! " a raw youth, in reply to him, said;

چو مردی چه سیراب و چه خشک لب.
What are water and lips that are dry, when you're dead"?

بگفتا نه آخر دهان تر کنم
He replied, "I, at least, will not moisten my lips,

که تا جان شیرینش در سر کنم؟
That for Him my dear life may experience eclipse."

فتد تشنه در آبدان عمیق
One, thirsty, will into a deep cistern bound,

که داند که سیراب میرد غریق
For he knows he'll die sated with water, if drowned.

اگر عاشقی دامن او بگیر
If you are a lover, His skirt you should seize!

وگر گویدت جان بده، گو بگیر
If He asks for your life, say, "It is Yours when You please!"

بهشت تن آسانی آنگه خوری
Your body in Paradise, happy, will dwell,

که بر دوزخ نیستی بگذری
When you cross safely over nonentity's hell.

دل تخم کاران بود رنج کش
The hearts of the sowers of seed are distressed;

چو خرمن برآید بخسبند خوش
But when harvest arrives, they in happiness rest.

در این مجلس آن کس به کامی رسید
In this meeting, the person his object has found,

که در دور آخر به جامی رسید
Who gets hold of the cup at the finishing round.

❁◉❁◉❁

حکایت صبر و ثبات روندگان
On the Patience and Firmness of the Godly

چنین نقل دارم ز مردان راه

I thus have a tale from the men of the way —

فقیران منعم، گدایان شاه

Beneficent poor; king-like beggars are they.

که پیری به در یوزه شد بامداد

In the morning, to beg, an old pauper set out;

در مسجدی دید و آواز داد

And on seeing the door of a mosque gave a shout

یکی گفتش این خانهٔ خلق نیست

This house," someone answered, "belongs not to men

که چیزی دهندت، بشوخی مایست

Who are wont to give alms; wait not impudent, then!"

بدو گفت کاین خانه کیست پس

He inquired of him, "Who is the lord of this place

که بخشایشش نیست بر حال کس؟

Where no mercy is shown towards any one's case?"

بگفتا خموش، این چه لفظ خطاست

Be silent," he said, " such false words to let fall!

خداوند خانه خداوند ماست

The lord of this house is the Lord over all!"

نگه کرد و قندیل و محراب دید

The lamps and the prayer-niche, the old person eyed;

به سوز از جگر نعرهای بر کشید

In warmth, from the depths of his heart, he replied:

که حیف است از این جا فراتر شدن

What a pity it is to go on, from this place!

دریغ است محروم از این در شدن

Disappointed to go from this door's a disgrace.

نرفتم به محرومی از هیچ کوی

Not a street have I quitted, despairing, before;

چرا از در حق شوم زردروی؟

Why should I, in shame, go away from this door?

هم این جا کنم دست خواهش دراز

Here, too, I will stretch out the hand of demand,

که دانم نگردم تهیدست باز

For I know that I will not return, with bare hand."

شنیدم که سالی مجاور نشست

He sat for a year as a worshipper, there;

چو فریاد خواهان برآورده دست

As a suppliant, lifted his hands up in prayer.

شبی پای عمرش فرو شد به گل

The feet of his life sank, one night, in the mud,

تپیدن گرفت از ضعیفیش دل

And his heart took to throbbing, from poorness of blood.

سحر برد شخصی چراغش به سر

In the morning, a lamp at his head someone laid,

رمق دید از او چون چراغ سحر

And saw his last breath, like the morning lamp, fade.

همی‌گفت غلغل کنان از فرح

He was raving and saying in accents of pride:

و من دق باب الکریم انفتح

Who f er knocked at the Bounteous One's door, it oped wide!"

طلبکار باید صبور و حمول

To a searcher, endurance and patience are good;

که نشنیده‌ام کیمیاگر ملول

I've not heard of an Alchymist, doleful in mood.

چه زرها به خاک سیه در کنند

Much gold he converts into ashes, alas!

که باشد که روزی مسی زر کنند

In the hope that, one day, he'll make gold out of brass.

زر از بهر چیزی خریدن نکوست

In purchasing, gold is a good thing to spend;

نخواهی خریدن به از یاد دوست

You can't better buy, than the smiles of the " friend."

گر از دلبری دل به تنگ آیدت

If your heart, through a mistress, should suffer distress,

دگر غمگساری به چنگ آیدت

Another grief soother you'll get to caress.

مبر تلخ عیشی ز روی ترش

Don't embitter your joy through a sour face, accursed!

به آب دگر آتشش باز کش

With another one's beauty, extinguish the first!

ولی گر به خوبی ندارد نظیر

And yet, if in beauty she has not a peer,

به اندک دل آزار ترکش مگیر

For a little annoyance, desert not the dear!

توان از کسی دل بپرداختن

One can sever his heart from a person, 'tis true

که دانی که بی او توان ساختن

When he finds he is able, without him, to do.

حکایت جستجو کننده واقعی تحت ستم
Story on a true searcher persevering under oppression

شنیدم که پیری شبی زنده داشت

one pious, who kept up his vigils all night,

سحر دست حاجت به حق بر فراشت

Raised his hands up in prayer, at the first dawn of light

یکی هاتف انداخت در گوش پیر

A voice from the sky reached the aged man's ear,

که بی حاصلی، رو سر خویش گیر

Saying, "Go on your way, you are portionless here!

بر این در دعای تو مقبول نیست

Your petition has not been received at this gate;

به خواری برو یا به زاری بایست

Go away, in disgrace! If you don't, weeping wait"!

شب دیگر از ذکر و طاعت نخفت

Next night, he, in worshipping God, kept awake;

مریدی ز حالش خبر یافت، گفت

A disciple got news of his case and, thus, spake:

چو دیدی کز آن روی بسته‌ست در

"Since you've seen that the door on that side is shut to,

به بی حاصلی سعی چندین مبر

Disappointment, so zealously, do not pursue

به دیباچه بر اشک یاقوت فام

Adown his pale cheeks, from repentance, there ran

به حسرت ببارید و گفت ای غلام

The tears ruby coloured; he said, " Oh young man!

به نومیدی آنگه بگردیدمی

In hopelessness, I would have wandered away

از این ره، که راهی دگر دیدمی

From this road, had I seen where another path lay.

مپندار گر وی عنان بر شکست

That my hands from His saddle-straps I will unclose!

که من باز دارم ز فتراک دست

That my hands from His saddle-straps I will unclose!

چو خواهنده محروم گشت از دری

When a beggar returns from a door unrelieved,

چه غم گر شناسد در دیگری؟

And knows of another, why should he feel grieved?

شنیدم که راهم در این کوی نیست

I have heard that my path in this street does not lie,

ولی هیچ راه دگر روی نیست

And yet, I can no other pathway descry ".

در این بود سر بر زمین فدا

Thus engaged, on the ground of devotion his head;

که گفتند در گوش جانش ندا

In the ear of his soul the pure Angel, thus, said:

قبول است اگر چه هنر نیستش

He's accepted, although without worth of his own,

که جز ما پناهی دگر نیستش

For excepting in Me, no protection is known ".

حکایت حکیم و پسرش

Story of the sage and his son

یکی در نشابور دانی چه گفت

In Nishapur? what did an enlightened man say,

چو فرزندش از فرض خفتن بخفت؟

When sleep bore his son, at night prayers, away?

توقع مدار ای پسر گر کسی

"Oh son! do not hope, if you have any soul,

که بی سعی هرگز به جایی رسی

That you ever will reach, without striving, the goal!

سمیلان چو می بر نگیرد قدم

The barley cut early will not come to aught;

وجودی است بی منفعت چون عدم

It is a profitless body, as if it were naught.

طمع دار سود و بترس از زیان

Be desirous of gain, and for loss show alarm!

که بی بهره باشند فارغ زیان

For share-less is he who is careless of harm ".

حکایت در صبر بر جفای آن که از او صبر نتوان کرد
Story of patience under oppression

شکایت کند نوعروسی جوان

A young, recent bride to her old father ran

به پیری ز داماد نامهربان

And to tell of his son-in-law's harshness, began:

که مپسند چندین که با این پسر

The oppression is such, while this boy I obey,

به تلخی رود روزگارم به سر

That my sweet life, in bitterness, passes away.

کسانی که با ما در این منزلند

The people who near me reside, in this part,

نبینم که چون من پریشان دلند

I see not, like me, much afflicted in heart.

زن و مرد با هم چنان دوستند

Men and women, together, so loving are found —

که گویی دو مغز و یکی پوستند

Two brains in one skin, you would say, had been bound

ندیدم در این مدت از شوی من

I've not seen that my husband has, during this space,

که باری بخندید در روی من

For once, condescended to smile in my face ".

شنید این سخن پیر فرخنده فال

This oration was heard by the good omened sage —

سخندان بود مرد دیرینه سال

An eloquent man was the man of old age —

یکی پاسخش داد شیرین و خوش

How like an old man was his answer, so fair!

که گر خوبروی است بارش بکش

"If he's handsome, endeavour his burden to bear!

دریغ است روی از کسی تافتن

It is sad to avert from a person your face,

که دیگر نشاید چنو یافتن

For you mayn't get another as good, in his place.

چرا سر کشی زان که گر سر کشد

Why against him rebel? should he cease to love, then

به حرف وجودت قلم در کشد؟

Why against him rebel? should he cease to love, then

رضا ده بفرمان حق بنده وار

With the orders of God, slave-like, satisfied be!

که چون او نبینی خداوندگار

For a lord like to him, you will not again see ".

یکم روز بر بنده‌ای دل بسوخت

Once my heart, on account of a slave, suffered pain,

که می‌گفت و فرماندهش می‌فروخت

Who, when sold by his master, remarked, in this strain:

تو را بنده از من به افتد بسی

Slaves better than I am will fall to your lot;

مرا چون تو دیگر نیفتد کسی

But a master like you will not eas'ly be got."

❖◉❖◉❖

حکایت بیمار و طبیب

Story on Preferring the Pain to the Cure for the Sake of the Friend (The patient and the doctor)

طبیبی پری چهره در مرو بود

A doctor, sweet-faced, had in Merv his abode;

که در باغ دل قامتش سرو بود

Within the heart's garden, he cypress-like showed.

نه از درد دلهای ریشش خبر

For the grief of hearts wounded by him, not a care;

نه از چشم بیمار خویشش خبر

Of the hopes of those ailing through him, unaware.

حکایت کند دردمندی غریب

A sufferer tells a good tale of his case —:

که خوش بود چندی سرم با طبیب

With the doctor my head was much pleased, for a space;

نمی‌خواستم تندرستی خویش

To recover my health I had little desire,

که دیگر نیاید طبیبم به پیش

For the Doctor would, then, from attending, retire ".

بسا عقل زورآور چیردست

Many powerful in wisdom and valiant in hand,

که سودای عشقش کند زیردست

By the passion of love are brought under command

چو سودا خرد را بمالید گوش

When Passion gives Wisdom a box on the ear,

نیارد دگر سر برآورد هوش

Understanding can never again its head rear.

❖◉❖◉❖

حکایت در معنی استیلای عشق بر عقل
Story on the domination of love over wisdom

یکی پنجهٔ آهنین راست کرد
One adjusted his iron-like ringers for fight,

که با شیر زورآوری خواست کرد
Being anxious to test on a tiger his might

چو شیرش به سرپنجه در خود کشید
When the brute with his claws pulled him into his clutch,

دگر زور در پنجه در خود ندید
The strength of his fingers, he found, was not much.

یکی گفتش آخر چه خسبی چو زن؟
One asked him, "Why sleep like a woman? at least,

به سرپنجه آهنینش بزن
With your iron-like fingers, let drive at the beast! "

شنیدم که مسکین در آن زیر گفت
The poor man, I have heard, 'neath the tiger, said low:

نشاید بدین پنجه با شیر گفت
With these fingers, one can't strike a tiger a blow."

چو بر عقل دانا شود عشق چیر
When love a philosopher's wisdom o'erthrows;

همان پنجه آهنین است و شیر
Like the iron-like fingers and tiger it shows.

تو در پنجه شیر مرد اوژنی
n the claws of a hero-like tiger retained,

چه سودت کند پنجهٔ آهنی؟
With your iron-like fingers, what good can be gained?

چو عشق آمد از عقل دیگر مگوی
When love rises, talk not of wisdom, again!

که در دست چوگان اسیر است گوی
In Polo, the ball must the club's slave remain.

❖◉❖◉❖

حکایت در معنی عزت محبوب در نظر محب
Story of the young married cousins

میان دو عم زاده وصلت فتاد

Between two young cousins a marriage took place

دو خورشید سیمای مهتر نژاد

Two sun-like in aspect and noble in race —

یکی را به غایت خوش افتاده بود

The union to one gave the greatest delight;

دگر نافر و سرکش افتاده بود

The other indulged in aversion and spite.

یکی خلق و لطف پریوار داشت

One fairy-like neatness and nature possessed;

یکی روی در روی دیوار داشت

The other with face to the wall stood distressed

یکی خویشتن را بیاراستی

One decked out her fairy-like figure with care;

دگر مرگ خویش از خدا خواستی

The other sought death from the Lord in each prayer.

پسر را نشاندند پیران ده

The youth was reproved by the village old men:

که مهرت بر او نیست مهرش بده

"You love her not! give her her dower, again! "

بخندید و گفتا به صد گوسفند

He, smiling, replied, " With an hundred sheep, see!

تغابن نباشد رهایی ز بند

He, smiling, replied, " With an hundred sheep, see!

به ناخن پری چهره می‌کند پوست

With her nails, the fair beauty her soft skin would flay,

که هرگز بدین کی شکیبم ز دوست؟

Saying, When will this soothe, while my lover's away?

کند ترک مهر و وفا و وصول

He may friendship and faith and sweet union forsake;

مرا زان چه گر رد کند ور قبول

If he spurn or accept it, what odds will it make?

بتا همچنین زندگانی کنم

Come along! I am willing to live in this style;

جفا بینم و مهربانی کنم

I will harshness endure and reply with a smile.

نه صد گوسفندم که سیصد هزار

I'm not one hundred sheep! five score thousand by three,

نباید به نادیدن روی یار

For not seeing my love would not recompense me! '

تو را هر چه مشغول دارد ز دوست

Whatever employs you away from " the Friend,"

اگر راست خواهی دلارامت اوست

If you ask for the truth,. it's your sweatheart, depend!

یکی پیش شوریده حالی نبشت

Someone wrote to a person demented, like this:

که دوزخ تمنا کنی یا بهشت؟

Do you wish to see Hell or to gain Heavenly bliss? "

بگفتا مپرس از من این ماجرا

Do not ask me concerning this point! " he replied;

پسندیدم آنچ او پسندد مرا

"I'll be pleased with whichever the Lord may decide! "

حکایت مجنون و صدق محبت او

On the Sincerity of Majnun's Love for Laila

به مجنون کسی گفت کای نیک پی

Someone said to Majriun " Oh auspicious in pace!

چه بودت که دیگر نیایی به حی؟

Why is it you never in Hai show your face?

مگر در سرت شور لیلی نماند

Perhaps love for Laila has gone from your head?

خیالت دگر گشت و میلی نماند؟

Your fancy has changed and your passion has fled "?

چو بشنید بیچاره بگریست زار

When the helpless one heard this, he burst into tears,

که ای خواجه دستم ز دامن بدار

And answered, "Oh master! desist from your jeers!

مرا خود دلی دردمند است ریش

My own heart is afflicted with sorrow; away!

تو نیزم نمک بر جراحت مریش

Do not you, too, rub salt on my ulcer, I pray!

نه دوری دلیل صبوری بود

No proof is remoteness, of patience in me

که بسیار دوری ضروری بود

For distance may oft a necessity be ".

بگفت ای وفادار فرخنده خوی

Oh faithful and good-natured one! " said the friend,

پیامی که داری به لیلی بگوی

Say! have you a message for Laila, to send"?

بگفتا مبر نام من پیش دوست

"Near my loved one," he said, "do not carry my name!

که حیف است نام من آنجا که اوست

In her presence to name me, would be a great shame "!

◀◉▶◀◉▶

حکایت سلطان محمود و سیرت ایاز
On Sultan Mahmud and Ayaz

یکی خرده بر شاه غزنین گرفت

A person in Guzni thus slandered the king:

که حسنی ندارد ایاز ای شگفت

Ayaz has no beauty; oh wonderful thing!

گلی را که نه رنگ باشد نه بوی

On a rose that has neither got colour nor smell,

غریب است سودای بلبل بر اوی

It is strange that the nightingale's passion should dwell! "

به محمود گفت این حکایت کسی

By someone the tale to Mahmud had been brought,

بپیچید از اندیشه بر خود بسی

And he showed himself greatly distressed at the thought.

که عشق من ای خواجه بر خوی اوست

Oh master! my love's for his nature," he said,

نه بر قد و بالای نیکوی اوست

By his height or fine figure it has not been bred."

شنیدم که در تنگنایی شتر

I have heard that a camel fell down in a pass,

بیفتاد و بشکست صندوق در

And shattered a box, full of jewels, alas!

به یغما ملک آستین برفشاند

These the king in his favour as plunder bestowed,

وز آنجا به تعجیل مرکب براند

And swiftly away on his charger then rode.

سواران پی در و مرجان شدند

On picking up pearls all the horsemen were bent;

ز سلطان به یغما پریشان شدند

For the booty, away from the monarch they went.

نماند از وشاقان گردن فراز

Of the noble attendants, no person there was

کسی در قفای ملک جز ایاز

In rear of the monarch, excepting Ayaz.

نگه کرد کای دلبر پیچ پیچ

The king looked and said, "Oh my curly haired one!

ز یغما چه آورده‌ای؟ گفت هیچ

Of the booty, what share have you brought? " He said, " None!

من اندر قفای تو می‌تاختم

I straightway in rear of you galloped my steed;

ز خدمت به نعمت نپرداختم

I left not attendance for plunder, indeed."

گرت قربتی هست در بارگاه

If a confidant's place in the court you possess,

به خلعت مشو غافل از پادشاه

Neglect not the king for the sake of a dress!

خلاف طریقت بود کاولیا

It iis opposed to religion that saints, in their line,

تمنا کنند از خدا جز خدا

Should desire ought of God but the spirit divine.

گر از دوست چشمت بر احسان اوست

Should your hope in a friend on his kindness depend,

تو در بند خویشی نه در بند دوست

You are serving yourself at the cost of the friend

تو را تا دهن باشد از حرص باز

While avarice keeps your two lips wide apart,

نیاید به گوش دل از غیب راز

The Secret from God shuns the ear of your heart.

حقیقت سرایی است آراسته
The Truth is a mansion, embellished with care;
هوی و هوس گرد برخاسته
Lust and Passion are dust that has risen up there.

نبینی که جایی که برخاست گرد
Don't you see that wherever the dust clouds arise,
نبیند نظر گرچه بیناست مرد
A man sees no object, although he has eyes?

حکایت عابد و کشتی
Story of the Saint and the ferry-boat

قضا را من و پیری از فاریاب
It occurred that a saint from Faryab once, and I
رسیدیم در خاک مغرب به آب
In the land of the west to a river came nigh.

مرا یک درم بود برداشتند
I possessed but one direm, so me they took o'er
به کشتی و درویش بگذاشتند
In the vessel, and left the poor man on the shore.

سیاهان براندند کشتی چو دود
Fast as smoke was the boat by the wicked crew rowed,
که آن ناخدا نا خدا ترس بود
For the Master no fear of the "Great Master n showed.

مرا گریه آمد ز تیمار جفت
I wept at thus having my friend to forsake.
بر آن گریه قهقه بخندید و گفت
At my weeping he heartily laughed and, thus, spake:

مخور غم برای من ای پر خرد
Oh wise one! let sorrow for me be remote!
مرا آن کس آرد که کشتی برد
He will carry me over Who carries the boat "!

بگسترد سجاده بر روی آب
His carpet he spread on the face of the stream;
خیال است پنداشتم یا به خواب
Was it merely a fancy, or was it a dream?

ز مدهوشیم دیده آن شب نخفت

On account of amazement, I slept not that night;

نگه بامدادان به من کرد و گفت

He viewed me and said — at the first dawn of light —

تو لنگی به چوب آمدی من به پای

"You wondered! oh comrade, of fortunate thought!

تو را کشتی آورد و ما را خدای

The boat carried you and by God I was brought"!

چرا اهل معنی بدین نگروند

People chained to the world do not credit this talk,

که ابدال در آب و آتش روند؟

That the holy through fire and through water can walk.

نه طفلی کز آتش ندارد خبر

The child, of the mischief of fire unaware,

نگه داردش مادر مهرور؟

The mother protects with the greatest of care.

پس آنان که در وجد مستغرقند

Hence, know, that the people in ecstasy drown'd,

شب و روز در عین حفظ حقند

In the eyes of the Lord special favour have found!

نگه دارد از تاب آتش خلیل

He watches the " friend " in the fierce burning pile!

چو تابوت موسی ز غرقاب نیل

What of Moses' small ark being sunk in the Nile?

چو کودک به دست شناور برست

When a youth has escaped who is able to swim,

نترسد وگر دجله پهناورست

The Tigris though broad has no terror for him.

تو بر روی دریا قدم چون زنی

When will you step out on the face of the sea?

چو مردان که بر خشک تردامنی؟

You're like men on the land, as defiled as can be.

❖◉❖◉❖

گفتار در معنی فنای موجودات در معرض وجود باری

On the Frailty of Creatures and the Grandeur of God. (may his name be glorified!)

ره عقل جز پیچ بر پیچ نیست

The pathway to wisdom is twist upon twist;

بر عارفان جز خدا هیچ نیست

For the holy, the Maker alone can exist.

توان گفتن این با حقایق شناس

You can tell this to people who truths recognize;

ولی خرده گیرند اهل قیاس

But people of theory will criticize;

که پس آسمان و زمین چیستند؟

Saying, "What is the sky and the earth, do you say?

بنی آدم و دام و دد کیستند؟

Who are men? what are game and the wild beasts of prey"?

پسندیده پرسیدی ای هوشمند

Oh intelligent man! Your inquiry is well;

بگویم گر آید جوابت پسند

If the answer is pleasing to you, I will tell.

که هامون و دریا و کوه و فلک

The desert and ocean, the hills and the sky;

پری و آدمی‌زاد و دیو و ملک

The fairies, mankind, fiends, and angels on high;

همه هرچه هستند از آن کمترند

All things that exist, for this reason are less,

که با هستیش نام هستی برند

That only through Him they existence possess.

عظیم است پیش تو دریا به موج

The sea in a storm is sublime in your eye;

بلند است خورشید تابان به اوج

And lofty's the vault. of the rotating sky.

ولی اهل صورت کجا پی برند

But when will mere surface observers obtain

که ارباب معنی به ملکی درند

A glimpse of where spiritual persons remain?

که گر آفتاب است یک ذره نیست

For if it's the sun, not a speck they descry;

وگر هفت دریاست یک قطره نیست

If the whole seven seas, not a drop can they spy.

چو سلطان عزت علم بر کشد

When the Sultan of Glory His flag has unfurl'd,

جهان سر به جیب عدم در کشد

Into Nullity's collar collapses the world!

◉ ◉

حکایت دهقان در لشکر سلطان

Story of the villager and the army of the sultan

رئیس دهی با پسر در رهی

An old village chief with his son, on their way,

گذشتند بر قلب شاهنشهی

Passed a king's mighty army, in battle array.

پسر چاوشان دید و تیغ و تبر

The son looked on heralds and weapons untold;

قباهای اطلس، کمرهای زر

On mantles of satin and girdles of gold;

یلان کماندار نخجیر زن

On bow-bearing heroes, the slayers of game;

غلامان ترکش کش تیرزن

On slaves, quiver-bearing, and archers of fame.

یکی در برش پرنیانی قباه

Parnian silken mantles the breasts of some graced;

یکی بر سرش خسروانی کلاه

On the temples of others are coronets placed.

پسر کان همه شوکت و پایه دید

When the son all this splendour and grandeur had seen,

پدر را به غایت فرومایه دید

He saw that his father was humble and mean;

که حالش بگردید و رنگش بریخت

That his manner had changed and his colour had fled;

ز هیبت به بیغوله‌ای در گریخت

That he hurried away to a corner, from dread.

پسر گفتش آخر بزرگ دهی

You are chief of a village, at least?" the son said;

به سرداری از سر بزرگان مهی

In chiefship you're over the great people's head!

چه بودت که ببریدی از جان امید

What occurred, that the hope of your life you forsook?

بلرزیدی از باد هیبت چو بید؟

That at sight of a king, like a willow you shook"?

بلی، گفت سالار و فرماندهم

He said, " I'm a ruler and chief, as you state;

ولی عزتم هست تا در دهم

But my dignity stops at my own village gate"!

بزرگان از آن دهشت آلوده‌اند

Overwhelmed with amazement the holy are seen,

که در بارگاه ملک بوده‌اند

Because in the court of the king they have been.

تو، ای بی خبر، همچنان در دهی

In the village, oh careless one! such is your case,

که بر خویشتن منصبی می‌نهی

That you on yourself a high estimate place!

نگفتند حرفی زبان آوران

Men of eloquence have not delivered a speech,

که سعدی نگوید مثالی بر آن

That Sádi some proverb, thereon, does not teach

مگر دیده باشی که در باغ و راغ

Perhaps you have seen that in garden and swamp,

بتابد به شب کرمکی چون چراغ

The glow-worm shines brightly at night, like a lamp.

یکی گفتش ای کرمک شب فروز

One inquired, thus, "Oh moth, lighting night with your ray!

چه بودت که بیرون نیایی به روز؟

Why is it you do not appear in the day? "

ببین کآتشی کرمک خاکزاد

Observe what the earth-nurtured, fire-giving fly,

جواب از سر روشنایی چه داد

From its head of enlightenment, said, in reply:

که من روز و شب جز به صحرا نیم

In the plains day and night I am present, always;

ولی پیش خورشید پیدا نیم

But never apparent before the sun's rays! "

❖◉❖◉❖

حکایت اتابک و مرد روشن ضمیر
Story of the Wise Man and Atabak-Sad Bin- Zangi (May the favour of God be on him)

ثنا گفت بر سعد زنگی کسی

A person gave Sad, son of Zangi, great praise.

که بر تربتش باد رحمت بسی

On his tomb be abundance of mercy always.

درم داد و تشریف و بنواختش

He gave direms, a robe, and respect to him showed,

به مقدار خود منزلت ساختش

And becoming his merit position bestowed.

چو الله و بس دید بر نقش زر

When " God is enough" in gold lines, met his view,

بشورید و برکند خلعت ز بر

He raved, and the robe from his bosom he threw.

ز سوزش چنان شعله در جان گرفت

From the heat, such a flame in his conscience began,

که برجست و راه بیابان گرفت

Up he jumped and away to the wilderness ran.

یکی گفتش از همنشینان دشت

A desert companion said, "Kindly relate

چه دیدی که حالت دگرگونه گشت

What sight you have seen that has altered your state!

تو اول زمین بوسه دادی به جای

The ground, to begin with, three times you did kiss;

نبایستی آخر زدن پشت پای

It did not become you to change after this!

بخندید کاول ز بیم و امید

"He smiled, saying, "Firstly, from hope and from dread,

همی لرزه بر تن فتادم چو بید

Through my body a willow-like shivering spread;

به آخر ز تمکین الله و بس

Thereafter, ' the Glory of God will suffice

نه چیزم به چشم اندر آمد نه کس

Removed every person and thing from my eyes."

❖◉❖◉❖

حکایت مرد حق شناس
Story of a duty-knowing man

به شهری در از شام غوغا فتاد
In a city of Syria a tumult began;

گرفتند پیری مبارک نهاد
They had put into bonds a good-natured, old man.

هنوز آن حدیثم به گوش اندر است
That saying of his — in my ears still remains —

چو قیدش نهادند بر پای و دست
When they fastened his hands and his ankles in chains:

که گفت ار نه سلطان اشارت کند
If the Sultan" he said, " does not furnish the sign,

که را زهره باشد که غارت کند؟
What person can me to destruction consign?

بباید چنین دشمنی دوست داشت
It is proper to treat as a friend such a foe,

که می‌دانمش دوست بر من گماشت
For the Friend has despatched him to hurt me, I know.

اگر عز و جاه است وگر ذل و قید
Be it honour and rank or if bonds and disgrace,

من از حق شناسم، نه از عمرو و زید
From God Til acknowledge it, not Adam's race!

ز علت مدار، ای خردمند، بیم
About your disease, oh wise man! do not quake!

چو داروی تلخت فرستد حکیم
When the Doctor sends drugs that are bitter, to take.

بخور هرچه آید ز دست حبیب
All that comes from the hand of the ' Friend,' then, endure!

نه بیمار داناتر است از طبیب
A patient's not skilled, like a doctor, to cure."

❖◉❖◉❖

حکایت صاحب نظر پارسا

Story of an abstinent, pious man

یکی را چو من دل به دست کسی

One like me, with his heart in another one's hand,

گرو بود و می‌برد خواری بسی

Was a captive and had much abasement to stand.

پس از هوشمندی و فرزانگی

He had, previously, wisdom and knowledge displayed

به دف بر زدندش به دیوانگی

Yet, because of his madness, a butt he was made.

ز دشمن جفا بردی از بهر دوست

From his intimate friends many thumpings he bore,

که تریاک اکبر بود زهر دوست

Like a peg, with his forehead projecting before.

قفا خوردی از دست یاران خویش

On the head of misfortune, by fancy so put,

چو مسمار پیشانی آورده پیش

That the roof of his brain was well kicked under foot

خیالش چنان بر سر آشوب کرد

From the foe, for the friend, he submitted to wrong;

که بام دماغش لگدکوب کرد

For poison from friends is an antidote strong.

نبودش ز تشنیع یاران خبر

No knowledge had he of his friend's chiding strains;

که غرقه ندارد ز باران خبر

For the man who is drowned does not know when it rains.

کرا پای خاطر بر آمد به سنگ

The person whose heart has grown callous to blame,.

نیندیشد از شیشهٔ نام و ننگ

Does not care for the mirror of honour and shame.

شبی دیو خود را پریچهره ساخت

The devil appeared as a beauty, one night,

در آغوش آن مرد و بر روی بتاخت

In that holy man's bosom, and worried him, quite.

سحرگه مجال نمازش نبود

In the morning he had not the Power to say prayer;

ز یاران کس آگه ز رازش نبود

Of his secret not one of his friends was aware.

به آبی فرو رفت نزدیک بام

He plunged into water as far as the chin

بر او بسته سرما دری از رخام

And like marble, was soon by the cold frozen in.

نصیحتگری لومش آغاز کرد

A reprover began to upbraid him and scold:

که خود را بکشتی در این آب سرد

You are killing yourself in this water, so cold."

ز برنای منصف بر آمد خروش

The judicious young man raised a clamour and said:

که ای یار چند از ملامت؟ خموش

Beware! and be dumb on this infamous head!

مرا پنج روز این پسر دل فریفت

For a little, this youth so enraptured my heart,

ز مهرش چنانم که نتوان شکیفت

That my love for him made all my patience depart.

نپرسید باری به خلق خوشم

In my good disposition no interest he showed;

ببین تا چه بارش به جان می‌کشم

See how far with my life I am bearing his load!

پس آن را که شخصم ز خاک آفرید

Hence, He who created my body from dust,

به قدرت در او جان پاک آفرید

By His Power has consigned a pure soul to its trust.

عجب داری ار بار امرش برم

You're amazed that His load of commands I sustain!

که دایم به احسان و فضلش درم؟

In His kindness and favour I always remain! "

گفتار اندر سماع اهل دل و تقریر حق و باطل آن
On the Ecstasy of Pious People, and its Truth and Folly

اگر مرد عشقی کم خویش گیر
If a lover you are, keep yourself less in view

وگر نه ره عافیت پیش گیر
If you're not; then, Futurity's pathway pursue!

مترس از محبت که خاکت کند
Lest love should reduce you to dust, do not fear!

که باقی شوی گر هلاکت کند
For should it destroy, you'll immortal appear.

نروید نبات از حبوب درست
Green plants do not grow from the grains that are sound,

مگر حال بر وی بگردد نخست
Unless they are first covered up in the ground.

تو را با حق آن آشنایی دهد
With God such abundance of friendship you gain,

که از دست خویشت رهایی دهد
That release from the hands of yourself you obtain.

که تا با خودی در خودت راه نیست
You've no road in yourself, while to self you are wed;

وز این نکته جز بی خود آگاه نیست
The enraptured alone are informed on this head.

نه مطرب که آواز پای ستور
Not the minstrel alone, but the horse's hoofs sound

سماع است اگر عشق داری و شور
Is music, if rapture within you is found.

مگس پیش شوریده دل پر نزد
To the lover distracted a fly comes not nigh,

که او چون مگس دست بر سر نزد
For he beats at his head with his hands like a fly.

نه بم داند آشفته سامان نه زیر
Bass and treble are one to a crazed lover's ear

به آواز مرغی بنالد فقیر
At a bird's cheerful singing, laments the Fakir

سراینده خود می‌نگردد خموش
The minstrel himself does not stop in his strain;

ولیکن نه هر وقت باز است گوش
But he cannot, at all times, a hearing obtain.

چو شوریدگان می پرستی کنند

When rapturous men are adorers of wine,

به آواز دولاب مستی کنند

At a water-wheel's sound they to rapture incline.

به چرخ اندر آیند دولاب وار

They circle and dance, like a watering wheel,

چو دولاب بر خود بگریند زار

And like water-wheels, weep on themselves a great deal.

به تسلیم سر در گریبان برند

In submission, their heads 'neath their collars they bear;

چو طاقت نماند گریبان درند

When endurance remains not, their collars they tear.

مکن عیب درویش مدهوش مست

What the song is, oh brother! to you I'll explain,

که غرق است از آن می‌زند پا و دست

If I know who the person is hearing the strain!

نگویم سماع ای برادر که چیست

If his flight be from spirituality's dome,

مگر مستمع را بدانم که کیست

To the height of his soaring no angel can roam.

گر از برج معنی پرد طیر او

And if he be mirthful and playful and vain,

فرشته فرو ماند از سیر او

His follies become more confirmed in his brain.

وگر مرد لهو است و بازی و لاغ

What adorer of lust in pure songs will rejoice?

قوی تر شود دیوش اندر دماغ

Those asleep, not the drunk, rise to hear a fine voice!

چو مرد سماع است شهوت پرست

By the breeze of the morning expands the sweet rose

به آواز خوش خفته خیزد، نه مست

Not firewood, which only an axe can unclose.

پریشان شود گل به باد سحر

The Earth's full of melody, drunkenness and cries;

نه هیزم که نشکافدش جز تبر

And yet, in a glass, what see men without eyes?

جهان پر سماع است و مستی و شور

Find not fault with a Dervish, bewildered and drunk;

ولیکن چه بیند در آیینه کور؟

He with hands and feet struggles because he has sunk.

نبینی شتر بر نوای عرب

At the Arab's ha-da-ing the camel, you see,

که چونش به رقص اندر آرد طرب؟

Goes dancing along in the greatest of glee.

شتر را چو شور طرب در سر است

Since the rapture of mirth in a camel is shown,

اگر آدمی را نباشد خر است

If 'tis not in a man, as an ass he is known.

◈ ◉ ◈ ◈ ◉ ◈

حکایت مرد نی زن

Story of the flute-player

شکر لب جوانی نی آموختی

A sugar-lipped youth on a flute could so play,

که دلها در آتش چو نی سوختی

That like reeds in the fire tender hearts burned away.

پدر بارها بانگ بر وی زدی

His father would frequently scold him in ire,

به تندی و آتش در آن نی زدی

And set the soft flute that offended on fire.

شبی بر ادای پسر گوش کرد

To his son's sweet performance he listened one night;

سماعش پریشان و مدهوش کرد

The music perplexed and confounded him, quite.

همی گفت و بر چهره افکنده خوی

He was saying, while sweat down his face trickled free,

که آتش به من در زد این بار نی

The flute has, at last, raised a burning in me! "

ندانی که شوریده حالان مست

You know not why rapturous men, in a trance,

چرا بر فشانند در رقص دست؟

Keep snapping their fingers whenever they dance?

گشاید دری بر دل از واردات

A door opens wide by God's grace in their mind,

فشاند سر دست بر کاینات

And their fingers they snap at all human in kind.

حلالش بود رقص بر یاد دوست

They may lawfully dance in the thought of the Friend,

که هر آستینیش جانی در اوست

For each of their sleeves does a soul comprehend.

گرفتم که مردانه‌ای در شنا

I admit that in swimming you're clever and neat,

برهنه توانی زدن دست و پا

And when nude can strike out with your hands and your feet.

بکن خرقه نام و ناموس و زرق

Let the robes of deceit, name and fame be dispersed!

که عاجز بود مرد با جامه غرق

For a man becomes weak if in garments immersed.

تعلق حجاب است و بی حاصلی

Worldly love is a veil by which nothing is gained;

چو پیوندها بگسلی واصلی

When you snap the attachments, the Lord is obtained.

حکایت پروانه و صدق محبت او
Story of the moth and the candle

کسی گفت پروانه را کای حقیر

Someone said to a moth, "Oh, contemptible mite!

برو دوستی در خور خویش گیر

Go! love one who will your affection requite!

رهی رو که بینی طریق رجا

A road you should walk in which hope's path you see;

تو و مهر شمع از کجا تا کجا؟

Between you and the candle no friendship can be!

سمندر نه‌ای گرد آتش مگرد

You are no Salamander; don't flit round the light!

که مردانگی باید آنگه نبرد

You must courage display when you purpose to fight!

ز خورشید پنهان شود موش کور

The mole lies concealed from the light of the sun,

که جهل است با آهنین پنجه زور

For against iron claws it is folly to run.

کسی را که دانی که خصم تو اوست

When for certain you find that a man is your foe,

نه از عقل باشد گرفتن به دوست

It would not be right, for him friendship to show.

تو را کس نگوید نکو می‌کنی

No one tells you, ' Your conduct is perfectly right

که جان در سر کار او می‌کنی

In destroying your life for the love of the light!

گدایی که از پادشه خواست دخت

The beggar who wished he a princess might wed,

قفا خورد و سودای بیهوده پخت

Nursed a passion absurd, and got beaten, instead!

کجا در حساب آرد او چون تو دوست

Will the candle include one like you as a friend,

که روی ملوک و سلاطین در اوست؟

When to look at her sultans and kings condescend?

مپندار کاو در چنان مجلسی

Do not think, that with such an assembly in view,

مدارا کند با چو تو مفلسی

She will cherish regard for a creature, like you!

وگر با همه خلق نرمی کند

And if to mankind she is gentle and sweet,.

تو بیچارهای با تو گرمی کند

Your are helpless, and therefore she shows you her heat."

نگه کن که پروانهٔ سوزناک

Observe what the moth, full of hot anguish, said:

چه گفت، ای عجب گر بسوزم چه باک؟

"If I burn, oh astonishing! What is the dread?

مرا چون خلیل آتشی در دل است

As occurred to the "friend," in my heart a fire glows,

که پنداری این شعله بر من گل است

Hence, I fancy the flame is a beautiful rose!

نه دل دامن دلستان میکشد

My heart does not pull my heart-ravisher's tails;

که مهرش گریبان جان میکشد

But, rather, her friendship my life's collar hales.

نه خود را بر آتش به خود میزنم

I set not myself out of pleasure on fire,

که زنجیر شوق است در گردنم

For circling my neck is the chain of desire.

مرا همچنان دور بودم که سوخت

While still at a distance her heat to me came,

نه این دم که آتش به من در فروخت

Not now that my body is burned by her flame —

نه آن میکند یار در شاهدی

In the smiles of a mistress a friend acts not so

که با او توان گفتن از زاهدی

That he can, by her side, aught of piety show —

که عیبم کند بر تولای دوست؟

At my love for my friend, who on me casts a slur,

که من راضیم کشته در پای دوست

Since I gladly accept immolation from her?

مرا بر تلف حرص دانی چراست؟

Why I long to be killed, are you able to tell?

چو او هست اگر من نباشم رواست

If she live, although I am no more, it is well!

بسوزم که یار پسندیده اوست

I am burning — for she is a ravishing friend—

که در وی سرایت کند سوز دوست

In the hope that my burning to her may extend.

مرا چند گویی که در خورد خویش

How long will you say: In accord with your state,

حریفی به دست آر همدرد خویش

Secure a companion who'll pity your fate!

بدان ماند اندرز شوریده حال

Your advice to a lover distracted, comes nigh

که گویی به کژدم گزیده منال

To telling a scorpion-stung man not to cry."

کسی را نصیحت مگو ای شگفت

Oh wonder! a man for advice don't select,

که دانی که در وی نخواهد گرفت

On whom you are sure it will have no effect!

ز کف رفته بیچاره‌ای را لگام

When the reins from a helpless one's palm chance to go,

نگویند کآهسته را ای غلام

They say not: "Oh boy, drive a little more slow! "

چه نغز آمد این نکته در سندباد

How well in the Sindbad is mentioned this truth:

که عشق آتش است ای پسر پند، باد

"Love is truly a fire, may it teach you, oh youth! "

به باد آتش تیز برتر شود

A fire, by the wind is increased much in strength;

پلنگ از زدن کینه ور تر شود

By attacking, a leopard grows fiercer, at length.

چو نیکت بدیدم بدی می‌کنی

When I saw you were good, you have wickedness shown,

که رویم فرا چون خودی می‌کنی

For you force my face downwards, the same as your own.

ز خود بهتری جوی و فرصت شمار

Than yourself, seek a better! and deem it a joy

که با چون خودی گم کنی روزگار

That with one like yourself, you the time can destroy.

پی چون خودی خودپرستان روند
After those, like themselves, self-conceited folk stalk;

به کوی خطرناک مستان روند
In a street, full of danger, inebriates walk.

من اول که این کار سر داشتم
When first to engage in this work I agreed,

دل از سر به یک بار برداشتم
My heart from the head of existence I freed.

سر انداز در عاشقی صادق است
He who risks life in war, as a lover is true;

که بدزهره بر خویشتن عاشق است
The cowardly man keeps his self-love in view.

اجل ناگهی در کمینم کشد
Fate will suddenly kill me, while lying in wait;

همان به که آن نازنینم کشد
I would rather that dear one would slaughter me, straight.

چو بی شک نبشته‌ست بر سر هلاک
On the head of destruction when, doubtless, is writ,

به دست دلارام خوشتر هلاک
To death, at the hand of a mistress, submit!

نه روزی به بیچارگی جان دهی؟
Won't you helplessly, one day, your life give away?

همان به که در پای جانان دهی
For the sake of your love, better give it to-day!

❖◉❖❖◉❖

مخاطبه شمع و پروانه
Conversation between the Candle and the Moth

شبی یاد دارم که چشمم نخفت
I remembered one night lying sleepless in bed,

شنیدم که پروانه با شمع گفت
That I heard what the moth to the fair candle said:

که من عاشقم گر بسوزم رواست
A lover am I, if I burn it is well!

تو را گریه و سوز باری چراست؟
Why you should be weeping and burning, do tell."

بگفت ای هوادار مسکین من
Oh my poor humble lover! " the candle replied,

برفت انگبین یار شیرین من
My friend, the sweet honey, away from me hied.

چو شیرینی از من به در می‌رود
When sweetness away from my body departs,

چو فرهادم آتش به سر می‌رود
A fire like Farhad's to my summit then starts'

همی گفت و هر لحظه سیلاب درد
Thus she spoke and, each moment, a torrent of pain

فرو می‌دویدش به رخسار زرد
Adown her pale cheeks trickled freely, like rain.

که ای مدعی عشق کار تو نیست
Oh suitor! with love you have nothing to do,

که نه صبر داری نه یارای ایست
Since nor patience nor power of standing have you.

تو بگریزی از پیش یک شعله خام
Oh crude one! a flame makes you hasten away;

من استاده‌ام تا بسوزم تمام
But I, till completely consumed, have to stay.

تو را آتش عشق اگر بر بسوخت
If the burning of love makes your wings feel the heat,

مرا بین که از پای تا سر بسوخت
See how I am consumed, from the head to the feet! "

نرفته ز شب همچنان بهره‌ای
But a very small portion had passed of the night,

که ناگه بکشتش پری‌چهره‌ای
When a fairy-faced maiden extinguished her light

259

همی گفت و می‌رفت دودش به سر

She was saying, while smoke from her head curled above,

که این است پایان عشق، ای پسر

Thus ends, oh my boy, the existence of love!"

اگر عاشقی خواهی آموختن

If the love-making science you wish to acquire,

به کشتن فرج یابی از سوختن

You're more happy extinguished than being on fire.

مکن گریه بر گور مقتول دوست

Do not weep o'er the grave of the slain for the Friend!

برو خرمی کن که مقبول اوست

Be glad! for to him He will mercy extend.

اگر عاشقی سر مشوی از مرض

If a lover, don't wash the complaint from your head!

چو سعدی فرو شوی دست از غرض

Like Sádiy wash selfishness from you, instead!

فدایی ندارد ز مقصود چنگ

From his object, a faithful one will not refrain,

و گر بر سرش تیر بارند و سنگ

Although on his head stones and arrows they rain!

به دریا مرو گفتمت زینهار

I have told you: don't enter this ocean at all!

وگر می‌روی تن به طوفان سپار

If you do yield your life to the hurricane squall!

❖◉❖◉❖

4

باب چهارم

(CHAPTER IV.)

در تواضع

On Humility

سرآغاز
In begin

ز خاک آفریدت خداوند پاک

From the dust, the Pure God to you entity gave;

پس ای بنده افتادگی کن چو خاک

Be humble! resembling the dust, then, oh, slave!

حریص و جهان سوز و سرکش مباش

Shun pride and oppression, and sordid desire!

ز خاک آفریدندت آتش مباش

Out of dust they created you, do not be fire!

چو گردن کشید آتش هولناک

When the terrible Fire raised its arrogant crown,

به بیچارگی تن بینداخت خاک

The Earth cast its body in helplessness down.

چو آن سرفرازی نمود، این کمی

When Fire haughtiness showed; Earth submissiveness, then,

از آن دیو کردند، از این آدمی

From That they made demons, from This they made men!

حکایت مروارید
Story of the Pearl

یکی قطره باران ز ابری چکید

From a cloud there descended a droplet of rain;

خجل شد چو پهنای دریا بدید

It was ashamed when it saw the expanse of the main,

که جایی که دریاست من کیستم؟

Saying, "Who may I be, where the sea has its run?

گر او هست حقا که من نیستم

If the sea has existence, I, truly, have none!"

چو خود را به چشم حقارت بدید

I Since in its own eyes the drop humble appeared,

صدف در کنارش به جان پرورید

I In its bosom, a shell with its life the drop reared;

سپهرش به جایی رسانید کار

The sky brought the work with success to a close,

که شد نامور لؤلؤ شاهوار

And a famed royal pearl from the rain-drop arose.

بلندی از آن یافت کاو پست شد

I Because it was humble it excellence gained;

در نیستی کوفت تا هست شد

Knocked at Nullity's door till it being obtained.

❖◉❖◉❖

حکایت در معنی نظر مردان در خود به حقارت

On Men of God viewing Themselves with Contempt

جوانی خردمند پاکیزه بوم

A wise youth with a nature from wickedness free,

ز دریا بر آمد به دربند روم

Arrived at the harbour of Rum, from the sea.

در او فضل دیدند و فقر و تمیز

Devoutness, discernment and wisdom he showed;

نهادند رختش به جایی عزیز

They placed his effects in a holy abode.

سر صالحان گفت روزی به مرد

The chief-of-the-pious addressed him, one day:

که خاشاک مسجد بیفشان و گرد

From the mosque, brush the dust and the rubbish away

همان کاین سخن مرد رهرو شنید

The instant the wanderer heard this affair,

برون رفت و بازش کس آنجا ندید

He departed and no one again saw him there.

بر آن حمل کردند یاران و پیر

From that the companions and elders opined,

که پروای خدمت نبودش فقیر

That the needy young man was to work disinclined.

دگر روز خادم گرفتش به راه

A servant next day met him walking along,

که ناخوب کردی به رأی تباه

And said, " Through your folly you did very wrong!

ندانستی ای کودک خودپسند
You were not aware, oh self-satisfied swain!
که مردان ز خدمت به جایی رسند
That people by service their wishes obtain."

گرستن گرفت از سر صدق و سوز
With sincereness and warmth he began tears to shed:
که ای یار جان پرور دلفروز
"Oh heart-lighting, life-guarding comrade," he said;

نه گرد اندر آن بقعه دیدم نه خاک
Neither rubbish nor dust in that spot could I trace;
من آلوده بودم در آن جای پاک
I alone was defiled in that sanctified place.

گرفتم قدم لاجرم باز پس
I therefore determined my feet to withdraw;
که پاکیزه به مسجد از خاک و خس
For a mosque, pure, is better than rubbish and straw."

طریقت جز این نیست درویش را
No pathway, save this, for the Dervish is seen —
که افکنده دارد تن خویش را
He must count his own body as humble and mean.

بلندیت باید تواضع گزین
Humility choose, if you wish to be high;
که آن بام را نیست سلم جز این
For that ladder, alone, to this roof can come nigh!

◀◉▶◀◉▶

حکایت بایزید بسطامی
On the Humility of Bayazid

شنیدم که وقتی سحرگاه عید

have heard that one morning, the day being Eed?

ز گرمابه آمد برون بایزید

There came from a warm-bath the good Bayazid.

یکی طشت خاکسترش بی‌خبر

Without knowing, a basin of ashes, 'tis said,

فرو ریختند از سرایی به سر

Someone threw from a house on the top of his head.

همی گفت شولیده دستار و موی

He was saying — disordered his turban and hair

کف دست شکرانه مالان به روی

And rubbing his face with his palms, as in prayer —

که ای نفس من در خور آتشم

"Oh spirit of mine, I am worthy of fire,

به خاکستری روی در هم کشم؟

Since for ashes, I wrinkle my features in ire! "

بزرگان نکردند در خود نگاه

The great do not look on themselves as select;

خدابینی از خویشتن بین مخواه

From a selfish man, piety, do not expect!

بزرگی به ناموس و گفتار نیست

True greatness, with fame and fine speech is not bound,

بلندی به دعوی و پندار نیست

With pretensions- and fancies, high place is not found.

قیامت کسی بینی اندر بهشت

At the Judgment in Paradise, him you will find,

که معنی طلب کرده ودعوی بهشت

Who searched for the truth and put claims from his mind.

تواضع سر رفعت افرازدت

Humility raises sublimity's crown,

تکبر به خاک اندر اندازدت

And arrogance, under the dust casts you down.

به گردن فتد سرکش تند خوی

The hot-tempered rebel falls headlong below

بلندیت باید بلندی مجوی

If you wish to be great, do not arrogance show!

گفتار در عجب و عاقبت آن و شکستگی و یرکت آن
On Pride and its Result, and Sadness and its Blessing.

ز مغرور دنیا ره دین مجوی

Do not ask for the Faith from one proud of his pelf!

خدابینی از خویشتن بین مجوی

Do not piety seek from a lover of self!

گرت جاه باید مکن چون خسان

If rank you desire do not copy the base!

به چشم حقارت نگه در کسان

With the eye of humility limit your gaze!

گمان کی برد مردم هوشمند

When will an intelligent person surmise,

که در سرگرانی است قدر بلند؟

That power exalted in arrogance lies?

از این نامورتر محلی مجوی

For a nobler position than this, do not seek!

که خوانند خلقت پسندیده خوی

That in praise of your nature the multitude speak!

نه گر چون تویی بر تو کبر آورد

When a man, like yourself, makes you feel his pride's weight,

بزرگش نبینی به چشم خرد؟

With wisdom's clear eye, can you view him as great?

تو نیز ار تکبر کنی همچنان

You also from haughtiness do just the same;

نمایی، که پیشت تکبر کنان

You resemble the proud who preceding you came.

چو استاده‌ای بر مقامی بلند

When in station exalted, securely you stand,

بر افتاده گر هوشمندی مخند

Do not laugh at the fallen, if sense you command!

بسا ایستاده در آمد ز پای

Many persons established have suffered disgrace,

که افتادگانش گرفتند جای

And those who were fallen have seized on their place.

گرفتم که خود هستی از عیب پاک

I admit, that from faults you are perfectly free!

تعنت مکن بر من عیب‌ناک

Do not curse me! Of faults I'm as full as can be.

یکی حلقهٔ کعبه دارد به دست

The Kaba's ring-knocker, one holds in his hand;

یکی در خراباتی افتاده مست

In a tavern, another's so drunk, he can't stand.

گر آن را بخواند، که نگذاردش؟

If He wills that the former may near Him remain,

ور این را براند، که باز آردش؟

And drives off the latter, to call him again;

نه مستظهر است آن به اعمال خویش

The first is not helped by his own acts of grace,

نه این را در توبه بستهست پیش

And the door is not shut in the other one's face.

حکایت عیسی (ع) و عابد و ناپارسا
Story of Jesus — On him be safety! — and the Pharisee

شنیدستم از راویان کلام

have heard the narrators of history tell,

که در عهد عیسی علیهالسلام

That when Jesus was living (may peace on Him dwell),

یکی زندگانی تلف کرده بود

A person had wasted his life in vile ways,

به جهل و ضلالت سر آورده بود

He was froward and sinful, for heartlessness famed:

دلیری سیه نامهای سخت دل

At his vileness, the Devil himself was ashamed!

ز ناپاکی ابلیس در وی خجل

At his vileness, the Devil himself was ashamed!

به سر برده ایام، بی حاصلی

He had brought, without profit, his days to a close;

نیاسوده تا بوده از وی دلی

As long as he lived, not a soul had repose.

سرش خالی از عقل و از احتشام

His head, void of wisdom, was full of conceit,

شکم فربه از لقمههای حرام

And his stomach was stuffed with prohibited meat

267

به ناراستی دامن آلوده‌ای

His skirt was polluted by practices vile,

به نداشتی دوده اندوده‌ای

And his household was crusted with deeds that defile.

نه پایی چو بینندگان راست رو

Not a footing had he, like beholders upright;

نه گوشی چو مردم نصیحت شنو

Not an ear, like the men who hear truths with delight.

چو سال بد از وی خلایق نفور

As from famine, the people away from him fly;

نمایان به هم چون مه نو ز دور

All pointing, as at the new moon in the sky.

هوی و هوس خرمنش سوخته

Foul lust had so set all his harvest on fire,

جوی نیکنامی نیندوخته

That a grain of good name he had failed to acquire.

سیه نامه چندان تنعم براند

He was vile, and so freely had pleasure's cup drained,

که در نامه جای نبشتن نماند

That for writing, no place in his reccrd remained.

گنهکار و خودرای و شهوت پرست

A sinner self-willed and adoring lust's sight;

به غفلت شب و روز مخمور و مست

In negligence stupid and drunk day and night.

شنیدم که عیسی در آمد ز دشت

Jesus Christ, I have heard, from the wilderness came,

به مقصوره عابدی برگذشت

And passed by the hut of a hermit of fame.

به زیر آمد از غرفه خلوت نشین

The hermit came down from his room at the sound,

به پایش در افتاد سر بر زمین

And fell at his feet, with his head on the ground.

گنهکار برگشته اختر ز دور

The sinner, ill-starred, from afar saw the sight;

چو پروانه حیران در ایشان ز نور

Like the moth, he was greatly amazed at their light.

تأمل به حسرت کنان شرمسار

Ashamed and reflecting, because of regret;

چو درویش در دست سرمایه‌دار

Like a pauper in front of a wealthy man set;

خجل زیر لب عذرخواهان به سوز

Asking, pardon, abashed, in words fervent and low,

ز شبهای در غفلت آورده روز

For the nights of neglect into day-light let go.

سرشک غم از دیده باران چو میغ

Tears of grief as from clouds showered down from his eyes;

که عمرم به غفلت گذشت ای دریغ

Ah! my life in neglect has been wasted," he cries;

بر انداختم نقد عمر عزیز

The coin of dear life, to the wind I have thrown,

به دست از نکویی نیاورده چیز

And have brought not one atom of goodness my own.

چو من زنده هرگز مبادا کسی

May no person be able to live, such as I;

که مرگش به از زندگانی بسی

Than like me to be living, 'twere better to die!

برست آن که در عهد طفلی بمرد

He was saved who in infancy passed to the dead,

که پیرانه سر شرمساری نبرد

For to manhood he bore not a shame-laden head

گناهم ببخش ای جهان آفرین

Oh, Creator of Earth! from my sins set me free;

که گر با من آید فبئس القرین

For I'm badly allied if they travel with me!"

در این گوشه نالان گنهکار پیر

In this corner, lamenting, the sinful old man —

که فریاد حالم رس ای دستگیر

Crying, "Aid my sad plight! for, oh helper, you can!"

نگون مانده از شرمساری سرش

Was standing, ashamed, with his head bent before,

روان آب حسرت به شیب و برش

While over his bosom repentant tears pour.

وز آن نیمه عابد سری پر غرور

And the worshipper there, with his head full of pride,

ترش کرده بر فاسق ابرو ز دور

From afar, at the profligate frowning, thus cried:

که این مدبر اندر پی ما چراست؟

"Why does this apostate our footsteps pursue?

نگون بخت جاهل چه در خورد ماست؟

What kindred has this ruined wretch with us two?

به گردن در آتش در افتاده‌ای

One worthy to fall headlong down into fire,

به باد هوی عمر بر داده‌ای

Having yielded his life up to lustful desire.

چه خیر آمد از نفس تر دامنش

From his foul skirted spirit, what goodness has come,

که صحبت بود با مسیح و منش؟

That with the Messiah and me, he should chum?

چه بودی که زحمت ببردی ز پیش

It were well, had he carried his troubles off, first,

به دوزخ برفتی پس کار خویش

And followed to hell all his actions accursed!

همی رنجم از طلعت ناخوشش

I grieve, on account of his villainous face,

مبادا که در من فتد آتشش

Lest the fire of his guilt should in me find a place.

به محشر که حاضر شوند انجمن

When the meeting is called, on the Last Judgment Day,

خدایا تو با او مکن حشر من

Do not raise me, oh God! with this creature I pray! "

در این بود و وحی از جلیل الصفات

Thus speaking, a voice from the glorious God

در آمد به عیسی علیه الصلوة

Came to Jesus (on Whom be all blessings bestowed!:

که گر عالم است این و گر وی جهول

If that one is learned, and, if ignorant this,

مرا دعوت هر دو آمد قبول

The petitions of both have not reached Me amiss

270

تبه کرده ایام برگشته روز

He who wrecked all his prospects and ruined his days,

بنالید بر من به زاری و سوز

With weeping and fervour to Me humbly prays.

به بیچارگی هر که آمد برم

Whoever in humbleness seeks for My face,

نیندازمش ز آستان کرم

I will not expel from the threshold of grace.

عفو کردم از وی عملهای زشت

I have pardoned the horrible sins he has wrought;

به انعام خویش آرمش در بهشت

By My favour, to Paradise will he be brought.

وگر عار دارد عبادت پرست

And should the Adorer of Worship ' feel shame

که در خلد با وی بود هم نشست

Lest he should in Paradise fellowship claim,

بگو ننگ از او در قیامت مدار

Say, Blush not for him, at the Last Judgment Morn,

که آن را به جنت برند این به نار

For they'll bear him to Heav'n and to Hell you'll be borne

که آن را جگر خون شد از سوز و درد

That one's liver turned blood through his burning and grief,

گر این تکیه بر طاعت خویش کرد

If the other relied on himself for relief.

ندانست در بارگاه غنی

He was not aware that at God's justice seat,

که بیچارگی به ز کبر و منی

Humility's better than pride and conceit"

کرا جامه پاک است و سیرت پلید

For the man, whose clothes clean and soul filthy, you see,

در دوزخش را نباید کلید

The gate of hell-fire has no need for a key.

بر این آستان عجز و مسکینیت

At this threshold, infirmness and scantness of pelf,

به از طاعت و خویشتن بینیت

Are better than worship and fondness of self.

چو خود را ز نیکان شمردی بدی

When you count yourself one of the good, you are bad;

نمی‌گنجد اندر خدایی خودی

Conceit, in divinity never was clad!

اگر مردی از مردی خود مگوی

If manly, don't boast of your manliness here!

نه هر شهسواری به در برد گوی

The ball is not captured by each cavalier.

پیاز آمد آن بی هنر جمله پوست

That mean one appeared, like an onion, all skin,

که پنداشت چون پسته مغزی در اوست

Who thought he had brains, like a pista within.

از این نوع طاعت نیاید به کار

This sort of devotion's a profitless thing;

برو عذر تقصیر طاعت بیار

Go, and pleas for defects in your worshipping, bring!

نخورد از عبادت بر آن بی خرد

No fruit for his worship that fool ever had,

که با حق نکو بود و با خلق بد

Who was good before God and with people was bad.

سخن ماند از عاقلان یادگار

Speech exists as a monument over the wise;

ز سعدی همین یک سخن یاد دار

From Sádi one word in your memory prize!

گنهکار اندیشناک از خدای

A sinner who thinks about God, now and then

به از پارسای عبادت نمای

Excels the adorer, devout before men."

◆◉◆◉◆

حکایت دانشمند

Story of the poor theologian and the proud cazi

فقیهی کهن جامهٔ تنگدست

A poor theologian in old raiment dressed,

در ایوان قاضی به صف بر نشست

Sat down in the hall of a judge, with the best

نگه کرد قاضی در او تیز تیز

The Cazi beheld him with ire in his eyes;

معرف گرفت آستینش که خیز

The mace-bearer tugged at his sleeve, saying, " Rise!

ندانی که برتر مقام تو نیست

It does not become you, the best place to seize;

فروتر نشین، یا برو، یا بایست

Sit lower or leave, or stand up if you please!

بجای بزرگان دلیری مکن

In the ranks of the great, do not haughtily crow!

چو سر پنجهات نیست شیری مکن

Since you do not have claws, tiger tricks do not show!

نه هر کس سزاوار باشد به صدر

Everyone is not worthy to fill the chief seat;

کرامت به جاه است و منزل به قدر

You see greatness with rank, rank with merit you meet.

دگر ره چه حاجت ببیند کست؟

What need have you, then, of a person's advice?

همین شرمساری عقوبت بست

The shame, as a punishment, ought to suffice!

به عزت هر آن کاو فروتر نشست

The man who sits lower, with honour to show,

به خواری نیفتد ز بالا به پست

Does not tumble disgraced from above down below."

چو آتش برآورد بیچاره دود

From the breast of the Dervish, like fire the smoke welled;

فروتر نشست از مقامی که بود

He sat lower down than the place he first held

فقیهان طریق جدل ساختند

The divines, in their way of disputing then pranced;

لم و لا اسلم درانداختند

The " Why " and " We do not admit" they advanced.

گشادند بر هم در فتنه باز

They together the portal of discord oped wide,

به لا و نعم کرده گردن دراز

And extended their necks, as they " Yes" and "No" cried.

تو گفتی خروسان شاطر به جنگ

You'd have said that bold cocks, as not seldom occurs,

فتادند در هم به منقار و چنگ

Were fighting together with beaks and with spurs.

یکی بی خود از خشمناکی چو مست

As if drunk one beside himself passionate stands;

یکی بر زمین می‌زند هر دو دست

Another is beating the floor with his hands.

فتادند در عقدهٔ پیچ پیچ

They fell into knots of an intricate kind,

که در حل آن ره نبردند هیچ

And a way to undo them were helpless to find

کهن جامه در صف آخرترین

The man in old clothes on the very last seat,

به غرش در آمد چو شیر عرین

Like a fierce roaring lion vexed, sprang to his feet.

دلایل قوی باید و معنوی

"Proofs clear and convincing are needed," he yelled,

نه رگهای گردن به حجت قوی

Not the veins of the neck with wild arguments swelled!

مرا نیز چوگان لعب است و گوی

The club and the ball, too, of letters I hold."

بگفتند اگر نیک دانی بگوی

They said, " If proficient, your knowledge unfold! "

به کلک فصاحت بیانی که داشت

With rhetoric's pen the clear proofs he possessed,

به دلها چو نقش نگین بر نگاشت

On their hearts as if graved on a seal he impressed.

سر از کوی صورت به معنی کشید

From substance to spirit his head he out-drew;

قلم بر سر حرف دعوی کشید

Their lines of pretension he passed his pen through.

274

بگفتندش از هر کنار آفرین

From every corner applause they proclaimed;

که بر عقل و طبعت هزار آفرین

At his wisdom and nature, "Well done!" they exclaimed.

سمند سخن تا به جایی براند

He the dun horse of eloquence urged to such pass,

که قاضی چو خر در وحل باز ماند

That the Cazi remained in the mud, like an ass.

برون آمد از طاق و دستار خویش

His robe and the turban he wore on his head,

به اکرام و لطفش فرستاد پیش

In honour and kindness he sent him and said:

که هیهات قدر تو نشناختم

Alas! that I failed your great merits to know,

به شکر قدومت نپرداختم

And thanks for your coming neglected to show!

دریغ آیدم با چنین مایه‌ای

I am sorry, that having such wisdom in store,

که بینم تو را در چنین پایه‌ای

You appear in a state I am forced to deplore."

معرف به دلداری آمد برش

To console him the mace-bearer near to him sped;

که دستار قاضی نهد بر سرش

The Cazfs rich turban to place on his head.

به دست و زبان منع کردش که دور

With his hand and his tongue he opposed him: " Away

منه بر سرم پایبند غرور

The fetters of pride on my head do not lay!

که فردا شود بر کهن میزران

For to-morrow to those with old. turbans you'd see,

به دستار پنجه گزم سر گران

With a fifty-yard turban, me proud as could be.

چو مولام خوانند و صدر کبیر

When they call me a lord and a mighty Ameer,

نمایند مردم به چشمم حقیر

Other men in my eyes will like rubbish appear.

تفاوت کند هرگز آب زلال

Does it make any diff erence if water quite pure,

گرش کوزه زرین بود یا سفال؟

Is held in a golden or earthenware ewer?

خرد باید اندر سر مرد و مغز

In the head of a man brains and wisdom should be,

نباید مرا چون تو دستار نغز

A turban like yours is unsuited to me.

کس از سر بزرگی نباشد به چیز

From bigness of head no one benefit gains;

کدو سر بزرگ است و بی مغز نیز

A pumpkin's big-headed but does not have brains.

میفراز گردن به دستار و ریش

For turban and beard raise your neck not, alas!

که دستار پنبه‌ست و سبلت حشیش

For your turban is cotton, your whiskers dry grass.

به صورت کسانی که مردم وشند

All those who a human appearance possess,

چو صورت همان به که دم در کشند

Do well if like idols they silence profess!

به قدر هنر جست باید محل

A rank must be sought in accordance with worth;

بلندی و نحسی مکن چون زحل

Do not, Saturn-like, greatness and troubles bring forth!

نی بوریا را بلندی نکوست

The merit of cane, used for matting, is size;

که خاصیت نیشکر خود در اوست

In its substance, the virtue of sugar-cane lies.

بدین عقل و همت نخوانم کست

With such wisdom and spirit, I call you not man!

وگر می‌رود صد غلام از پست

Although hundreds of slaves in your following ran!

چه خوش گفت خرمهره‌ای در گلی

How well spoke the Cowrie? bespattered with mire,

چو برداشتش پر طمع جاهلی

When a fool picked it up, full of eager desire:

مرا کس نخواهد خریدن به هیچ

To buy me for anything, none will aspire,

به دیوانگی در حریرم مپیچ

Do not, madly, bedeck me in silken attire! '

نه منعم به مال از کسی بهتر است

A rich man by his wealth does not others surpass;

خر ار جل اطلس بپوشد خر است

Clothe a donkey in satin and still he's an ass! ''

بدین شیوه مرد سخنگوی چست

In this manner, the clever and eloquent sage,

به آب سخن کینه از دل بشست

With the water of speech washed his mouth free from rage.

دل آزرده را سخت باشد سخن

The words of a person heart-grieved are severe;

چو خصمت بیفتاد سستی مکن

When your enemy falls, do not lazy appear!

چو دستت رسد مغز دشمن بر آر

Remove your foe's brain, when he comes in your Power!

که فرصت فرو شوید از دل غبار

For, fit time will all dust from the heart surely scour.

چنان ماند قاضی به جورش اسیر

So subdued by his harshness the Cazi remained,

که گفت ان هذا لیوم عسیر

That he said, "To a hard day, indeed, I've attained."

به دندان گزید از تعجب یدین

He gnawed at his hands with the teeth of surprise;

بماندش در او دیده چون فرقدین

Like the two polar stars, he fixed on him his eyes

وز آنجا جوان روی همت بتافت

The youth turned his face of resolve from that place;

برون رفت و بازش نشان کس نیافت

Out he hurried and no one again found his trace.

غریو از بزرگان مجلس بخاست

Among the chiefs of the assembly a clamour arose:

که گویی چنین شوخ چشم از کجاست؟

Where this speaker so forward belongs to, who knows?"

نقیب از پیش رفت و هر سو دوید

The mace-bearer after him everywhere hied;

که مردی بدین نعت و صورت که دید؟

"Who has seen one who suits this description?" he cried.

یکی گفت از این نوع شیرین نفس

Someone said, "Such a man, whose sweet temper is known,

در این شهر سعدی شناسیم و بس

In this city I recognize Sádi, alone."

بر آن صد هزار آفرین کاین بگفت

Five score thousands of praises on him I invoke,

حق تلخ بین تا چه شیرین بگفت

For he said bitter truths, yet how sweetly he spoke!

⟨◉⟩⟨◉⟩

حکایت توبه کردن ملک زادهٔ گنجه
Story on the repentance of the prince of Gunja

یکی پادشه زاده در گنجه بود

In the city of Gunja a prince chanced to dwell;

که دور از تو ناپاک و سرپنجه بود

A nobody, filthy and cruel, as well

به مسجد در آمد سرایان و مست

He came singing to mosque, having tippled too much,

می اندر سر و ساتکینی به دست

With wine in his head and a cup in his clutch.

به مقصوره در پارسایی مقیم

A pietist lived in the holiest part,

زبانی دلاویز و قلبی سلیم

With tongue heart-suspending and pitying heart.

تنی چند بر گفت او مجتمع

Some people had gathered to hear his address —

چو عالم نباشی کم از مستمع

When you fail to be learned than the hearer you're less —

چو بی عزتی پیشه کرد آن حرون

When that obstinate scapegrace dishonour professed,

شدند آن عزیزان خراب اندرون

These pious men's hearts became greatly distressed.

چو منکر بود پادشه را قدم

When the feet of a king from the path of truth stray,

که یارد زد از امر معروف دم؟

Who is able to boast of his virtuous sway?

تحکم کند سیر بر بوی گل

The odour of garlic drowns that of the rose;

فرو ماند آواز چنگ از دهل

The sound of a lute near a drum weakness shows.

گرت نهی منکر بر آید ز دست

If orders prohibiting crime you emit;

نشاید چو بی دست و پایان نشست

Like paralysed people, you ought not to sit!

وگر دست قدرت نداری، بگوی

And if you possess not command over speech,

که پاکیزه گردد به اندرز خوی

Who becomes pure in soul by the doctrines you teach?

چو دست و زبان را نماند مجال

When away from the hand and the tongue pow has fled,

به همت نمایند مردی رجال

Men exhibit their manhood in prayers, instead.

یکی پیش دانای خلوت نشین

One in front of the hermit, of knowledge profound,

بنالید و بگریست سر بر زمین

Lamented and wept, with his head on the ground;

که باری بر این رند ناپاک و مست

Saying, " Once, on the part of this drunk debauchee,

دعا کن که ما بی زبانیم و دست

Say a prayer! for speechless and powMess are we."

دمی سوزناک از دلی با خبر

From a heart well-informed one sigh fervent and long,

قوی تر که هفتاد تیغ و تبر

Is than seventy swords and war-axes more strong.

بر آورد مرد جهاندیده دست

he experienced person then raised his hands high;

چه گفت ای خداوند بالا و پست

What said he? " Oh Lord of the earth and the sky!

خوش است این پسر وقتش از روزگار

The Fates have made pleasant the time of this boy

خدایا همه وقت او خوش بدار

Oh God! throughout life may he pleasure enjoy!"

کسی گفتش ای قدوهٔ راستی

A person addressed him, "Oh guide to the truth!

بر این بد چرا نیکویی خواستی؟

Why asked you that good might befall this vile youth?

چو بد عهد را نیک خواهی ز بهر

Why do you wish well for an infidel pest?

چه بد خواستی بر سر خلق شهر؟ "

On the city and people, why evil request? "

چنین گفت بینندهٔ تیز هوش

The cautious observer replied in this way:

چو سر سخن در نیابی مجوش

Since you know not the secret of words, do not bray!

به طامات مجلس نیاراستم

With words of two meanings my prayer was fraught;

ز داد آفرین توبه‌اش خواستم

From the Author of Justice his penance I sought

که هر گه که باز آید از خوی زشت

When a man to abandon his vices contrives,

به عیشی رسد جاودان در بهشت

In Paradise, doubtless, with joy he arrives.

همین پنج روز است عیش مدام

The 'five days'" resemble the pleasure of wine;

به ترک اندرش عیشهای مدام

When abandoned, the soul gains the pleasure divine."

حدیثی که مرد سخن ساز گفت

To repeat what was said by the subtle-tongued man,

کسی ز آن میان با ملک باز گفت

A friend from their midst to the king's presence ran.

ز وجد آب در چشمش آمد چو میغ

The king's eyes from rapture filled, cloud-like, with tears,

ببارید بر چهره سیل دریغ

And a torrent of grief on his features appears.

به نیران شوق اندرونش بسوخت

By the fire of desire his bad conscience was burned;

حیا دیده بر پشت پایش بدوخت

From shame his sad eyes on his insteps were turned.

بر نیک محضر فرستاد کس

At regret's portal knocking, he made someone go

در توبه کوبان که فریاد رس

To the man of kind heart, saying, "Soother of woe!

قدم رنجه فرمای تا سر نهم

Oh come, that my head I may prostrate to-day!

سر جهل و ناراستی بر نهم

My ignorant head that has erred from the way! "

نصیحتگر آمد به ایوان شاه

The soldiers in rows stood protecting the gate;

نظر کرد در صفه بارگاه

The orator reached the king's palace in state.

شکر دید و عناب و شمع و شراب

He saw sugar and jujubes, and candles and wine;

ده از نعمت آباد و مردم خراب

A town full of blessings and men drunk as swine.

یکی غایب از خود، یکی نیم مست

One was senseless, another half-drunk tried to stand;

یکی شعر گویان صراحی به دست

One was singing a song with a cup in his hand.

ز سویی بر آورده مطرب خروش

The clamour of minstrels arose from one rink;

ز دیگر سو آواز ساقی که نوش

From another the cup-bearer's voice, crying, " Drink! "

حریفان خراب از می لعل رنگ

And the harper's head, harp-like from sleep, sought his breast

سر چنگی از خواب در بر چو چنگ

Among the companions of noble degree,

نبود از ندیمان گردن فراز

The narcissus alone open-eyed you could see.

به جز نرگس آن جا کسی دیده باز

The harp and the cymbal in unison bound,

دف و چنگ با یکدگر سازگار

They shiver the harps and they sever the strings,

بر آورده زیر از میان ناله زار

From the middle of discord produced a shrill sound.

بفرمود و در هم شکستند خرد

The king had them broken in pieces, like pegs,

مبدل شد آن عیش صافی به درد

And pure-looking pleasure was changed into dregs.

شکستند چنگ و گسستند رود

They shiver the harps and they sever the strings,

به در کرد گوینده از سر سرود

And turn out the songster while loudly he sings.

به میخانه در سنگ بر دن زدند

The jars in the wine cellar smashed they right small;

کدو را نشاندند و گردن زدند

The gourds they demolished and broke one and all.

می لاله گون از بط سرنگون

Harps lying inverted wine flowing a flood;

روان همچنان کز بط کشته خون

You'd have said from a goose newly killed ran the blood.

خم آبستن خمر نه ماهه بود

Jars pregnant with wine were by no means expert;

در آن فتنه دختر بینداخت زود

But in casting their loads in the strife were alert

شکم تا به نافش دریدند مشک

They ripped the wine bags to the navel in height;

قدح را بر او چشم خونی پر اشک

The jars' bloody eyes were in tears at the sight.

بفرمود تا سنگ صحن سرای

He ordered; the palace-yard stones they out-threw,

بکندند و کردند نو باز جای

And the court of the palace they wholly renew;

که گلگونه خمر یاقوت فام

For the ruby-like wine's red, indelible stain,

به شستن نمی‌شد ز روی رخام

They in vain tried to wash from the marble again.

عجب نیست بالوعه گر شد خراب

If the drains became ruined, no wonder! for they

که خورد اندر آن روز چندان شراب

Drank wine to excess in the course of that day.

دگر هر که بربط گرفتی به کف

Wherever one held in his fingers a harp,

قفا خوردی از دست مردم چو دف

Like a drum, he was beaten by men's fingers sharp.

وگر فاسقی چنگ بردی به دوش

If a profligate carried a lute on his back,

بمالیدی او را چو طنبور گوش

His ear, like a tambour, got many a whack.

جوان سر از کبر و پندار مست

The youth who with pride and wild thoughts had been fired,

چو پیران به کنج عبادت نشست

Like a saint, to the nook of devotion retired.

پدر بارها گفته بودش به هول

His father had oft spoken words meant to scare:

که شایسته رو باش و پاکیزه قول

Let your conduct be pure and your language be fair! "

جفای پدر برد و زندان و بند

He bore his sire's harshness; the fetters and jail,

چنان سودمندش نیامد که پند

Compared with advice, were of little avail.

گرش سخت گفتی سخنگوی سهل

If the speaker said words that were harsh or were kind,

که بیرون کن از سر جوانی و جهل

Saying, "Folly and childishness cast from your mind! "

خیال و غرورش بر آن داشتی

His fancies and arrogance reached such a height,

که درویش را زنده نگذاشتی

That he left not a Dervish alive in his sight.

سپر نفکند شیر غران ز جنگ

The thundering lion submits not in war;

نیندیشد از تیغ بران پلنگ

But reflects when he hears the keen sword, the guitar.

به نرمی ز دشمن توان کرد دوست

By mildness, a foe to a friend you may change;

چو با دوست سختی کنی دشمن اوست

When you treat a friend badly, the friend you estrange.

چو سندان کسی سخت رویی نکرد

The person who, anvil-like, hardens his face,

که خایسک تأدیب بر سر نخورد

Must his head 'neath the hammer of chastisement place

به گفتن درشتی مکن با امیر

When you speak, you should never abuse the Ameer!

چو بینی که سختی کند، سست گیر

When you find he is harsh, very gentle appear!

به اخلاق با هر که بینی بساز

By the virtues! conciliate all you may see;

اگر زیردست است اگر سرفراز

Whether humble in rank or of lofty degree!

که این گردن از نازی بر کشد

For the one lifts his head, though retiring in mood

به گفتار خوش، و آن سر اندر کشد

By words that are kind, and the other's subdued.

به شیرین زبانی توان برد گوی

With sweetness of speech you can bear off the ball;

که پیوسته تلخی برد تندخوی

The hot-tempered carries off grief, and that's all.

تو شیرین زبانی ز سعدی بگیر

Accept you from Sádi sweet speech, while 'tis nigh!

ترش روی را گو به تلخی بمیر

To the sour-visaged man, say, "In misery die!"

❧◉❧◉❧

حکایت فروشنده عسل
Story of a honey seller

شکر خنده‌ای انگبین می‌فروخت

A charmer was selling his honey one day,

که دلها ز شیرینیش می‌بسوخت

So that hearts by his sweetness were burning away;

نباتِ میان بسته چون نیشکر

An idol with loins like the sugar-cane bound;

بر او مشتری از مگس بیشتر

The buyers more numerous than flies stood around.

گر او زهر برداشتی فی‌المثل

If he, for example, could poison command,

بخوردندی از دست او چون عسل

They'd have eaten it, honey-like, out of his hand

گرانی نظر کرد در کار او

An envier cast a long look at his trade,

حسد برد بر گرم بازار او

And envied the prosperous market he made.

دگر روز شد گردِ گیتی دوان

Next day he went round the wide world at a pace,

عسل بر سر و سرکه بر ابروان

With honey on's head and a vinegar face.

بسی گشت فریادخوان پیش و پس

He wandered, lamenting before and behind,

که ننشست بر انگبینش مگس

But not even a fly to his honey inclined.

شبانگه چو نقدش نیامد به دست

At night, when he found that no money he earned,

به دلتنگ رویی به کنجی نشست

He sat in a corner with face much concerned —

چو عاصی ترش کرده روی از وعید

Visage soured, like a culprit's awaiting his doom;

چو ابروی زندانیان روز عید

Like prisoners' eyebrows on Eed-day, all gloom.

زنی گفت بازی کنان شوی را

A wife to her husband remarked with a smile:

عسل تلخ باشد ترش روی را

To a sour visage honey seems bitter as bile."

حرامت بود نان آن کس چشید

It is unlawful for you to partake of one's bread,

که چون سفره ابرو به هم در کشید

Who winkles his brows, like a table-cloth spread.

مکن خواجه بر خویشتن کار سخت

Act not harshly, oh master, regarding your own!

که بدخوی باشد نگونسار بخت

For a spiteful man's fortune becomes overthrown.

گرفتم که سیم و زرت چیز نیست

Gold and silver, I grant, are as nothing to you;

چو سعدی زبان خوشت نیز نیست؟

But you have not, like Sádi, a pleasant tongue, too.

◈◉◈◉◈

حکایت در معنی تواضع نیکمردان

Story on the humility of good men

شنیدم که فرزانه‌ای حق پرست

I have heard that a sage, fearing God for God's sake,

گریبان گرفتش یکی رند مست

Had his collar caught fast by a wild, tipsy rake.

از آن تیره دل مرد صافی درون

From that sinner the man, of interior pure,

قفا خورد و سر بر نکرد از سکون

Raised his head not, though blows he was forced to endure.

یکی گفتش آخر نه مردی تو نیز؟

Someone said to him, "You are a man, too, at least!

تحمل دریغ است از این بی تمیز

It is a pity to bear with this dissolute beast."

شنید این سخن مرد پاکیزه خوی

The good-natured person heard all he could say,

بدو گفت از این نوع با من مگوی

And answered him, "Talk not to me in that way!

درد مست نادان گریبان مرد

The ignorant drunkard will men's raiment tear;

که با شیر جنگی سگالد نبرد

Who to fight with a fierce, warlike lion would dare?"

ز هشیار عاقل نزیبد که دست

It becomes not a sage who can caution command,

زند در گریبان نادان مست

To fix on a weak drunkard's collar his hand.

هنرور چنین زندگانی کند

A virtuous person so passes his days,

جفا بیند و مهربانی کند

That oppression he bears and with kindness repays."

حکایت در معنی عزت نفس مردان

Story on magnanimity

سگی پای صحرانشینی گزید

A dog bit the foot of a desert recluse.

به خشمی که زهرش ز دندان چکید

With such fury, that blood from its fangs dropped profuse.

شب از درد بیچاره خوابش نبرد

The helpless one slept not at night, being pained;

به خیل اندرش دختری بود خرد

In his household a daughter unmarried remained.

پدر را جفا کرد و تندی نمود

She was harsh to her father and showed temper hot;

که آخر تو را نیز دندان نبود؟

Saying, " You, too, at least, have got teeth, have you not?

پس از گریه مرد پراکنده روز

After weeping, the man of unfortunate day,

بخندید کای بابک دلفروز

Said, smiling, "Oh mistress with heart-lighting ray!

مرا گر چه هم سلطنت بود و بیش

Although I was also superior in Power,

دریغ آمدم کام و دندان خویش

I restrained my desire and my teeth at that hour.

محال است اگر تیغ بر سر خورم

Did a sword cleave my head, yet, I never could think

که دندان به پای سگ اندر برم

That my teeth in the foot of a dog I should sink.

287

توان کرد با ناکسان بد رگی

Towards no-bodies, exercise meanness you can;

ولیکن نیاید ز مردم سگی

But a dog never yet has come out of a man."

❮◉❯❮◉❯

حکایت خواجه نیکوکار و بنده نافرمان
Story of a beneficent master and his stubborn slave

بزرگی هنرمند آفاق بود

In the world there existed a virtuous sage,

غلامش نکوهیده اخلاق بود

With a vile-natured servant, the curse of the age.

از این خفرگی موی کالیده‌ای

He was thus: — Ill-conditioned with coarse, tangled hair;

بدی، سرکه در روی مالیده‌ای

Vile; with vinegar rubbed on his face, I declare!

چو ثعبانش آلوده دندان به زهر

His teeth, like a dragon's, with poison bestained;

گرو برده از زشت رویان شهر

The prize from the ugliest townsman he gained

مدامش به روی آب چشم سبل

From his bleared eyes the tears down his face always fell,

دویدی ز بوی پیاز بغل

And there came from his arm-pits an oniony smell.

گره وقت پختن بر ابرو زدی

When cooking, his eye-brows he screwed into knots;

چو پختند با خواجه زانو زدی

Bored his master when others were minding their pots.

دمادم به نان خوردنش هم نشست

While his master was eating he always sat by;

وگر مردی آبش ندادی به دست

Would not hand him a drink, even were he to die!

نه گفت اندر او کار کردی نه چوب

On him neither talking nor blows had effect;

شب و روز از او خانه در کند و کوب

Night and day was the house in a state of neglect

گهی خار و خس در ره انداختی

Now rubbish and thorns in the way he would throw,

گهی ماکیان در چه انداختی

And again to cast fowls down the well was not slow.

ز سیماش وحشت فراز آمدی

From his forehead fierce terror came down to his face;

نرفتی به کاری که باز آمدی

When sent out, never anxious his steps to retrace.

کسی گفت از این بندهٔ بد خصال

Someone said, " From a slave whose base mind you detect,

چه خواهی؟ ادب، یا هنر، یا جمال؟

Can you manners and merits and beauty expect?

نیرزد وجودی بدین ناخوشی

Life is not worth a copper with such a vile boor

که جورش پسندی و بارش کشی

Why favour his harshness? his load why endure?

منت بندهٔ خوب و نیکو سیر

A good-natured slave for your use, without fail

به دست آرم، این را به نخاس بر

I will buy j send this slave to the market for sale!

وگر یک پشیز آورد سر مپیچ

If he fetches one Dang, do not turn round and jeer!

گران است اگر راست خواهی به هیچ

For if truly you ask me — at nothing he's dear! "

شنید این سخن مرد نیکو نهاد

The good-natured man to this speech turned his head;

بخندید کای یار فرخ نژاد

Oh happy of birth! he then, smilingly, said:

بد است این پسر طبع و خویش ولیک

The boy's person and nature are bad enough, still,

مرا زاو طبیعت شود خوی نیک

My nature through him becomes charged with goodwill.

چو زاو کرده باشم تحمل بسی

Since I've borne on account of him very much care,

توانم جفا بردن از هر کسی

The oppression of others I'm able to bear.

مروت ندانم که بفروشمش

I think it unmanly that him I should sell,

بدیگر کسی عیب بر گویمش

For unto another his faults I would tell.

چو من در بلایش تحمّل کنم

Since to suffer his crosses I feel myself fit,

بسی به بود گر تحوّل کنم

It is better by far than to cause him to flit."

چو خود را پسندی کسی را پسند

Since yourself you admire, to another be kind!

تو در زحمتی دیگری را مبند

If you're troubled, on others, distress do not bind!

تحمل چو زهرت نماید نخست

Forbearance, like poison, at first to you shows,

ولی شهد گردد چو در طبع رست

But it changes to honey when in you it grows.

❁◉❁◉❁

حکایت معروف کرخی و مسافر رنجور
Story of Maruf-Karkhi and the sick traveler

کسی راه معروف کرخی بجست

No man in the path of Maruf-Karkhi sped,

که بنهاد معروفی از سر نخست

Who first did not cast foolish pride from his head.

شنیدم که مهمانش آمد یکی

I have heard that a certain one came as his guest,

ز بیماریش تا به مرگ اندکی

Who from sickness had closely approached his last rest:

سرش موی و رویش صفا ریخته

The hair of his head and his face was all grey;

به موییش جان در تن آویخته

By a hair was his life held from slipping away.

شب آنجا بیفکند و بالش نهاد

He alighted at night and his pillow he laid,

روان دست در بانگ و نالش نهاد

And quickly a noise of lamenting he made.

نه خوابش گرفتی شبان یک نفس

All the night, for a moment, sleep closed not his eyes;

نه از دست فریاد او خواب کس

Not a person could sleep, on account of his cries.

نهادی پریشان و طبعی درشت

With a nature distracted and temperament soured,

نمی‌مرد و خلقی به حجت بکشت

He lived, and his harshness a people devoured.

ز فریاد و نالیدن و خفت و خیز

From his weeping and wailing, and fidgety plight,

گرفتند از او خلق راه گریز

The household was forced to take refuge in flight.

ز دیار مردم در آن بقعه کس

Out of all the male inmates that dwelling contained,

همان ناتوان ماند و معروف و بس

Maruf and that helpless one only remained

شنیدم که شبها ز خدمت نخفت

For nights, in attendance, he slept not at all,

چو مردان میان بست و کرد آنچه گفت

And with loins girt obeyed like a slave every call.

شبی بر سرش لشکر آورد خواب

Sleep brought its strong army one night to his brain

که چند آورد مرد ناخفته تاب؟

For how long can a man without sleeping remain?

به یک دم که چشمانش خفتن گرفت

The instant that sleep caused his eyelids to close,

مسافر پراکنده گفتن گرفت

In the stranger distracted a tempest arose: —

که لعنت بر این نسل ناپاک باد

"May curses," he said, "seize this draggle-tailed kind!

که نامند و ناموس و زرقند و باد

Their name and their fame are deception and wind!

پلید اعتقادان پاکیزه پوش

With high aspirations and clothes clean and new,

فریبندهٔ پارسایی فروش

They're deceivers, and sellers of piety, too.

چه داند لت انبانی از خواب مست

What knows the coarse glutton, in drunken repose,

که بیچاره‌ای دیده بر هم نبست؟

Of the sufferer Powerless his starved eyes to close? "

سخنهای منکر به معروف گفت

He spoke to Maruf words devoid of respect,

که یک دم چرا غافل از وی بخفت

Saying, " Why did you slumber and show me neglect? "

فرو خورد شیخ این حدیث از کرم

Out of kindness, the sage bore the words he let fall;

شنیدند پوشیدگان حرم

In the private apartments the women heard all!

یکی گفت معروف را در نهفت

To Maruf one among them in secret thus spoke:

شنیدی که درویش نالان چه گفت؟

Did you hear what the wailing wretch said, to provoke?

برو زاین سپس گو سر خویش گیر

Go and say, 'Your own journey henceforth you must hie!

گرانی مکن جای دیگر بمیر

Your curses remove, in another place die! '

نکویی و رحمت به جای خود است

Both goodness and mercy are right in their place,

ولی با بدان نیکمردی بد است

But kindness to those who are wicked, is base.

سر سفله را گرد بالش منه

Neath the head of a wretch, a soft pillow don't put!

سر مردم آزار بر سنگ به

For the head of a tyrant a stone best will suit.

مکن با بدان نیکی ای نیکبخت

Do not favour the wicked; oh fortunate hand!

که در شوره نادان نشاند درخت

Only fools will plant trees in a dry, barren land.

نگویم مراعات مردم مکن

That you ought not to care for mankind, I don't say;

کرم پیش نامردمان گم مکن

But, before the debased, throw not mercy away!

به اخلاق نرمی مکن با درشت

Be not soft, through good nature, with harsh-mannered folk!

که سگ را نمالند چون گربه پشت

The back of a dog, like a cat's, you don't stroke.

گر انصاف خواهی سگ حق شناس

Ask you justice? the dog that some gratitude shows,

به سیرت به از مردم ناسپاس

Surpasses the man who no thankfulness knows.

به برفاب رحمت مکن بر خسیس

Do not serve with iced water those hardened in vice!

چو کردی مکافات بر یخ نویس

When you've done it, the recompense write upon ice!

ندیدم چنین پیچ بر پیچ کس

So cross-grained a person I never have seen;

مکن هیچ رحمت بر این هیچ کس

Do not pity a creature so worthless and mean

بخندید و گفت ای دلارام جفت

He smiled and replied, "Oh my heart-soothing spouse!

پریشان مشو زاین پریشان که گفت

Do not suffer his ravings your temper to rouse!

گر از ناخوشی کرد بر من خروش

If from sorrow his conduct was noisy and rough;

مرا ناخوش از وی خوش آمد به گوش

To my ear his displeasure came pleasant enough.

جفای چنین کس نباید شنود

Of such a man's fury one should not be shy,

که نتواند از بی‌قراری غنود

For his restlessness suffers not sleep to come nigh."

چو خود را قوی حال بینی و خوش

When you find yourself strong and your happiness sure

به شکرانه بار ضعیفان بکش

In gratitude, weak people's burden endure!

اگر خود همین صورتی چون طلسم

If you the same shape as a talisman show,

بمیری و اسمت بمیرد چو جسم

You die, and your name like your body will go.

وگر پرورانی درخت کرم

And if you're a trainer of mercy's fair tree,

بر نیکنامی خوری لاجرم

As fruit, a good name you will certainly see.

نبینی که در کرخ تربت بسی است

In Karkh you see tombs in great numbers around,

به جز گور معروف، معروف نیست

But excepting Maruf's, none is eminent found.

به دولت کسانی سر افراختند

By Fortune! those people have gained high renown,

که تاج تکبر بینداختند

Who have cast from their temples vain-glory's false crown.

تکبر کند مرد حشمت پرست

The pomp-loving person exhibits his pride;

نداند که حشمت به حلم اندر است

He knows not that pomp may in mildness reside.

حکایت در معنی سفاهت نااهلان

Story on the meanness of the worthless and the forbearance of the worthy

طمع برد شوخی به صاحبدلی

A " sauce-box" his wants to a pious man brought,

نبود آن زمان در میان حاصلی

Who happened himself at the time to have nought

کمربند و دستش تهی بود و پاک

Of money his girdle and hand showed no trace,

که زر برفشاندی به رویش چو خاک

Or else he'd have thrown it like dust in his face.

برون تاخت خواهندهٔ خیره روی

To the outside the vile-visaged beggar then ran,

نکوهیدن آغاز کردش به کوی

And to scold and abuse in the street thus began:

که زنهار از این کژدمان خموش

Of these silent-tongued scorpions," he shouted, "beware!

پلنگان درندهٔ صوف پوش

They are fierce, tearing tigers who woollen clothes wear.

که چون گربه زانو به دل برنهند

AVith their knees on their bosoms so cat-like, they stay,

وگر صیدی افتد چو سگ در جهند

And spring like a dog if a chance comes their way.

سوی مسجد آورده دکان شید

Their mart of deceit to the Musjid they brought,

که در خانه کمتر توان یافت صید

For within their own houses less plunder they got.

ره کاروان شیرمردان زنند

Those who rob caravans are a lion-like race,

ولی جامه مردم اینان کنند

But the raiment of men in such hands meet disgrace.

سپید و سیه پاره بر دوخته

Black patches and white they together have sewn

به سالوس و پنهان زر اندوخته

With deceit, and in secret their riches have grown.

زهی جو فروشان گندم نمای

Well done barley sellers, exhibiting wheat!

جهانگرد شبکوک خرمن گدای

World wanderers! night birds, who men's harvests eat!

مبین در عبادت که پیرند و سست

Take no heed that in worship they're feeble and old,

که در رقص و حالت جواند و چست

For in dancing and pleasure they're youthful and bold!

عصای کلیمند بسیار خوار

Like Moses' famed rod, they devour a great deal,

به ظاهر چنین زرد روی و نزار

And then show how distressed and afflicted they feel.

نه پرهیزگار و نه دانشورند

They do not abstain and their wisdom is Nil;

همین بس که دنیا به دین می‌خورند

It's enough that the faith brings of Earth's joys their fill.

عبایی بلیلانه در تن کنند

A cloak like Balil's they draw over their breast,

به دخل حبش جامهٔ زن کنند

And in garments most costly their women are dress'd.

ز سنت نبینی در ایشان اثر

Of the Prophet's great law not a trace do they show,

مگر خواب پیشین و نان سحر

But siestas and morning repasts, they all know.

شکم تا سر آکنده از لقمه تنگ

Their stomachs with morsels are stuffed, seized as dues,

چو زنبیل دریوزه هفتاد رنگ

Like the beggar's patched wallet of seventy hues."

نخواهم در این وصف از این بیش گفت

I care not to further enlarge on this case

که شنعت بود سیرت خویش گفت

For to talk of your own disposition is base.

فروگفت از این شیوه نادیده گوی

The speaker untruthful denounced in this style;

نبیند هنر دیدهٔ عیبجوی

The fault-seeking eye only sees what is vile.

یکی کرده بی آبرویی بسی

When a man has a great many others disgraced;

چه غم داردش ز آبروی کسی؟

What cares he when any one's honour's effaced?

مریدی به شیخ این سخن نقل کرد

To the Sheikh a disciple reported the lies;

گر انصاف پرسی، نه از عقل کرد

If the truth you require, such an act was not wise.

بدی در قفا عیب من کرد و خفت

A foe at my back told my faults and reposed,

بتر زاو قرینی که آورد و گفت

Much worse is the friend who brought all and disclosed.

یکی تیری افکند و در ره فتاد

Someone shot forth an arrow which fell on the road,

وجودم نیازرد و رنجم نداد

It hurt not my body nor sorrow bestowed;

تو برداشتی و آمدی سوی من

You lifted it up and came quickly to me,

همی در سپوزی به پهلوی من

And prick at my ribs with it, heartless and free.

بخندید صاحبدل نیکخوی

The good-natured pietist smilingly said:

که سهل است از این صعب تر گو بگوی

It is easy to utter much more on this head!

هنوز آنچه گفت از بدم اندکی است

So far but a speck of my sins he can show;

از آنها که من دانم از صد یکی است

But one in a hundred of all that I know.

ز روی گمان بر من اینها که بست

Those faults which to me in suspicion he bound,

من از خود یقین می‌شناسم که هست

I myself know for certain within me are found

وی امسال پیوست با ما وصال

For the first time this year, he before me appears;

کجا داندم عیب هفتاد سال؟

Does he know of my faults during seventy years?

به از من کس اندر جهان عیب من

Than myself, none knows better the sins I have done

نداند به جز عالم الغیب من

In this world, but the All-wise, Invisible One."

ندیدم چنین نیک پندار کس

A right thinking man I have never yet seen,

که پنداشت عیب من از این است و بس

Who thought that excepting one fault he was clean.

به محشر گواه گناهم گر اوست

Is my sins' witness he, at the last trumpet's swell;

ز دوزخ نترسم که کارم نکوست

I fear not the Fire for my footing is well.

گرم عیب گوید بد اندیش من

If my enemy wishes my faults to pourtray,

بیا گو بر نسخه از پیش من

Bid him take, from before me, the copy away.

کسان مرد راه خدا بوده‌اند

Those persons have been the pure men of God's road,

که برجاس تیر بلا بوده‌اند

Who themselves as the butt of Calamity showed.

زبون باش چون پوستینت درند

Be silent, until they the skin off you tear!

که صاحبدلان بار شوخان برند

For the pious, the burdens of wantons must bear.

گر از خاک مردان سبویی کنند

If a goblet they make from the ashes of men,

به سنگش ملامت کنان بشکنند

With stones, the revilers will break it again.

◈◈◈◈

حکایت گستاخی درویش و بخشش پادشاه
On the Impudence of Dervishes and the Clemency of Kings

ملک صالح از پادشاهان شام

A prince of Damascus, King Salih by name,

برون آمدی صبحدم با غلام

With his slave about dawn from his residence came.

بگشتی در اطراف بازار و کوی

The suburbs and streets and bazaars he went round;

به رسم عرب نیمه بر بسته روی

Like an Arab in style, half his face was upbound.

که صاحب نظر بود و درویش دوست

An observer he was and a friend of the poor;

هر آن کاین دو دارد ملک صالح اوست

Whoever is these is a Salih, I'm sure.

دو درویش در مسجدی خفته یافت

Two poor men lying down in a mosque met his sight;

پریشان دل و خاطر آشفته یافت

Heart-distracted he found them and restless in plight.

شب سردشان دیده نابرده خواب

From the cold of the night sleep had closed not their eyes;

چو حربا تأمل کنان آفتاب

They, chameleon-like, longed for the sun to arise.

یکی زآن دو می گفت با دیگری

One unto the other proceeded to say:

که هم روز محشر بود داوری

"A Judge, too, will come on the Last Judgment Day.

گر این پادشاهان گردن فراز

If all the proud monarchs of lofty degree,

که در لهو و عیشند و با کام و ناز

Who pleasures and mirth and desires sated see,

در آیند با عاجزان در بهشت

With the sufferers should unto Paradise go,

من از گور سر بر نگیرم ز خشت

My head I'd not raise from my brick tomb below.

بهشت برین ملک و مأوای ماست

The Paradise high is our dwelling-place meet;

که بند غم امروز بر پای ماست

For to-day are griefs fetters attached to our feet.

همه عمر از اینان چه دیدی خوشی

What pleasure from them during life did you share,

که در آخرت نیز زحمت کشی؟

That at last you should also their miseries bear?

اگر صالح آنجا به دیوار باغ

Were Salih to come to this garden retreat,

بر آید، به کفشش بدرم دماغ

With my slippers, the brains from his head I would beat!

چو مرد این سخن گفت و صالح شنید

When he uttered these words, to which Salih gave ear,

دگر بودن آنجا مصالح ندید

To remain, did not useful to Salih appear.

دمی رفت تا چشمهٔ آفتاب

Off he went for a time, till the fountain sun-rise

ز چشم خلایق فرو شست خواب

Washed slumber away from the multitude's eyes.

دوان هر دو را کس فرستاد و خواند

He sent for and summoned both men in hot haste;

به هیبت نشست و به حرمت نشاند

Majestic he sat and with honour them placed.

بر ایشان ببارید باران جود

A shower of bounty upon them he rained,

فرو شستشان گرد ذل از وجود

And washed from their bodies the filth that remained.

پس از رنج سرما و باران و سیل
After suffering from cold, rain, high floods, and all that,
نشستند با نامداران خیل
'Midst renowned cavaliers, they in dignity sat.

گدایان بی جامه شب کرده روز
As beggars, quite naked they shivered all night;,
معطر کنان جامه بر عود سوز
With censers they perfumed their clothes at daylight!

یکی گفت از اینان ملک را نهان
One privately thus to the monarch did say:
که ای حلقه در گوش حکمت جهان
Oh thou, whose commands all the world must obey!

پسندیدگان در بزرگی رسند
Only persons of merit to eminence rise;
ز ما بندگانت چه آمد پسند؟
What appeared in us slaves that seemed good in your eyes?"

شهنشه ز شادی چو گل بر شکفت
From gladness the king like a rose raised his head;
بخندید در روی درویش و گفت
He smiled in the face of the beggars and said:

من آن کس نیم کز غرور حشم
The man I am not, who from pride and display,
ز بیچارگان روی در هم کشم
Would in wrath, from the helpless my face turn away.

تو هم با من از سر بنه خوی زشت
Put you, too, on my account malice aside!
که ناسازگاری کنی در بهشت
Or you'll wrangle in Heaven when there you abide!

من امروز کردم در صلح باز
The portal of concord I've opened to-day;
تو فردا مکن در به رویم فراز
Shut it not in my face on the morrow, I pray! "

چنین راه اگر مقبلی پیش گیر
If accepted you are, keep before you the way;
شرف بایدت دست درویش گیر
And if honour you wish, be the poor beggar's stay!

بر از شاخ طوبی کسی بر نداشت

None bore fruit from the branch of the Tuba away,

که امروز تخم ارادت نکاشت

Who sowed not the seed of true longing, to-day.

ارادت نداری سعادت مجوی

If you're void of belief, don't for happiness strain!

به چوگان خدمت توان برد گوی

With the club of devotion, the ball you will gain.

تو را کی بود چون چراغ التهاب

When will you to lantern-like burning attain?

که از خود پری همچو قندیل از آب؟

Like a water-filled lamp, only self, you contain.

وجودی دهد روشنایی به جمع

A body imparts a bright light to the rest,

که سوزیش در سینه باشد چو شمع

Which burns like a candle within its own breast.

〈◉〉〈◉〉

حکایت در محرومی خویشتن بینان

Story on the disappointment of the conceited

یکی در نجوم اندکی دست داشت

Of Astrology someone a smattering had,

ولی از تکبر سری مست داشت

But his head was because of his vanity mad.

بر کوشیار آمد از راه دور

From a far distant land he reached Koshiyar's side,

دلی پر ارادت، سری پر غرور

With a heart full of longing and head full of pride.

خردمند از او دیده بردوختی

On his face the philosopher shut both his eyes,

یکی حرف در وی نیاموختی

Nor taught him an atom regarding the skies.

چو بی بهره عزم سفر کرد باز

When portionless, back he determined to go,

بدو گفت دانای گردن فراز

The eminent sage gave advice to him, so:

تو خود را گمان بردهای پر خرد

"You thought yourself full of Astrologer's lore!

انائی که پر شد دگر چون برد؟

Can a jug that is brimful contain any more?

ز دعوی پری زان تهی میروی

Come free from pretensions, that full you may be

تهی آی تا پر معانی شوی

You are full of yourself and go empty from me."

ز هستی در آفاق سعدی صفت

In this world, as does Sádi, all self-love resign!

تهی گرد و باز آی پر معرفت

And return again full of the knowledge divine.

◀◉▸◀◉▸

حکایت تواضع برای حفظ جان
Story on gratitude for safety

به خشم از ملک بندهای سربتافت

From a monarch a slave ran in anger away;

فرمود جستن کسش در نیافت

He ordered a search, none could find where he lay.

چو بازآمد از راه خشم و ستیز

When again he returned, free from anger and strife,

به شمشیر زن گفت خونش بریز

The king bade the swordsman deprive him of life.

به خون تشنه جلاد نامهربان

The blood-thirsty headsman, by pity unwrung,

برون کرد دشنه چو تشنه زبان

Like the thirsty put forward the dagger's sharp tongue.

شنیدم که گفت از دل تنگ ریش

I have heard that the man, sad and wounded, thus said:

خدایا بحل کردمش خون خویش

Oh God, I forgive him my blood he's to shed!

که پیوسته در نعمت و ناز و نام

For always, in comfort, caresses and fame,

در اقبال او بودهام دوستکام

I happy have been 'neath his prosperous name.

302

مبادا که فردا به خون منش

God forbid that hereafter, because of this blow,

بگیرند و خرم شود دشمنش

They should seize him and give much delight to his foe."

ملک را چو گفت وی آمد به گوش

When the ears of the king heard this generous speech,

دگر دیگ خشمش نیاورد جوش

Not again did the pot of his wrath boiling reach.

بسی بر سرش داد و بر دیده بوس

He frequently kissed both his head and his eyes;

خداوند رایت شد و طبل و کوس

In the monarch his banner and kettle-drum rise.

به رفق از چنان سهمگن جایگاه

With kindness, from such a terrific abyss,

رسانید دهرش بدان پایگاه

Time brought him to such a good station as this.

غرض زین حدیث آن که گفتار نرم

The design of this tale is — that soft speaking can

چو آب است بر آتش مرد گرم

Quench like water the fire of a hot-tempered man.

تواضع کن ای دوست با خصم تند

Be civil! oh friend, to a hot-tempered foe,

که نرمی کند تیغ برنده کند

For by softness the edge of the sabre will go!

نبینی که در معرض تیغ و تیر

Where the arrow and sword are employed, don't you know

بپوشند خفتان صد تو حریر

They wear silken vests of five score folds, or so?

حکایت در معنی تواضع و نیازمندی
Story on the humility and supplication of upright men

ز ویرانهٔ عارف ژنده پوش
From the hut of a saint, dressed in clothes patched and torn,

یکی را نباح سگ آمد به گوش
To the ear of a man a dog's barking was borne.

به دل گفت کوی سگ اینجا چراست؟
He said to himself, "What! a dog barking here? "

درآمد که درویش صالح کجاست؟
And to where the good Dervish was living, came near.

نشان سگ از پیش و از پس ندید
He no sign of a dog saw, before or behind;

به جز عارف آنجا دگر کس ندید
Except the recluse, no one else did he find.

خجل باز گردیدن آغاز کرد
Quite taken aback, he began to retire;

که شرم آمدش بحث این راز کرد
For about this strange case he felt shame to inquire.

شنید از درون عارف آواز پای
Within, the good man heard a footstep outside,

هلا گفت بر در چه پایی؟ در آی
And shouted, "Come in! at the door, why abide?

مپندار ای دیدهٔ روشنم
Oh light of my eyes! you must never suppose

کز ایدر سگ آواز کرد، این منم
That you heard a dog bark; no! from me it arose.

چو دیدم که بیچارگی می‌خرد
When I saw that by Him self-abasement was bought,

نهادم ز سر کبر و رای و خرد
I removed from my head pride and wisdom and thought.

چو سگ بر درش بانگ کردم بسی
Like a dog I have barked very much at His gate,

که مسکین تر از سگ ندیدم کسی
For I've seen naught to equal the dog's abject state."

چو خواهی که در قدر والا رسی
When a dignified rank you desire to obtain,

ز شیب تواضع به بالا رسی
At humility's foot you will excellence gain.

در این حضرت آنان گرفتند صدر
The chief seat in this Presence those persons will get,
که خود را فروتر نهادند قدر
Who lower than others their value have set

چو سیل اندر آمد به هول و نهیب
When a torrent bounds on, with a force that appals,
فتاد از بلندی به سر در نشیب
From the top to the bottom it speedily falls.

چو شبنم بیفتاد مسکین و خرد
Since dew falls in atoms, most humble in size,
به مهر آسمانش به عیوق برد
Observe how the sun bears it up to the skies!

حکایت حاتم اصم

Story on the deafness of Hatim and the humility of his nature

گروهی برآنند از اهل سخن
A number of eloquent men hold this view:
که حاتم اصم بود، باور مکن
"That Hatim is deaf, don't believe to be true! "

برآمد طنین مگس بامداد
One morning a buzzing arose from a fly,
که در چنبر عنکبوتی فتاد
That had stuck to the web of a spider nearby.

همه ضعف و خاموشیش کید بود
His weakness and silence were only a ruse;
مگس قند پنداشتتش قید بود
The fly thought him candy and fell to his noose.

نگه کرد شیخ از سر اعتبار
In order to profit, the chief took a view,
که ای پایبند طمع پای دار
Saying, "Captive through avarice, patience pursue!

نه هر جا شکر باشد و شهد و قند
Sugar, honey and candy are not everywhere;
که در گوشه‌ها دامیار است و بند
For in corners lie hidden the hunter and snare."

یکی گفت از آن حلقهٔ اهل رای

Of that circle of people of wisdom, one said:

عجب دارم ای مرد راه خدای

"Oh man of the road of the Lord! I'm misled.

مگس را تو چون فهم کردی خروش

How came you the fly's gentle buzzing to hear,

که ما را به دشواری آمد به گوش؟

That only quite faintly arrived at our ear?

تو آگاه گشتی به بانگ مگس

Since the buz of a fly was detected by you,

نشاید اصم خواندنت زین سپس

Henceforth, to be calling you deaf, will not do!

تبسم کنان گفت ای تیز هوش

He replied to him, smiling; " Oh thou with mind clear!

اصم به که گفتار باطل نیوش

To be deaf is far better than nonsense to hear.

کسانی که با ما به خلوت درند

The men who around me as confidants stay,

مرا عیب پوش و ثنا گسترند

Conceal all my faults and my merits display.

چو پوشیده دارند اخلاق دون

Since over my vices a curtain they stretch,

کند هستیم زیر، طبع زیون

It debases my life, and pride makes me a wretch.

فرا می‌نمایم که می‌نشنوم

That my hearing is faulty, I state as a blind,

مگر کز تکلف مبرا شوم

In the hope that from worry release I may find.

چو کالیو دانندم اهل نشست

When those seated around me consider me mad,

بگویند نیک و بدم هر چه هست

They tell what exists of my good and my bad.

اگر بد شنیدن نیاید خوشم

If hearing of sin brings no pleasure to me,

ز کردار بد دامن اندر کشم

From deeds that are evil, I keep my skirt free."

به حبل ستایش فرا چه مشو

With flattery's rope, down a well do not go!

چو حاتم اصم باش و عیبت شنو

Like Hatim be deaf, and your shortcomings know!

سعادت نجست و سلامت نیافت

He for happiness searched not, nor safety acquired,

که گردن ز گفتار سعدی بتافت

Who from treasuring Sádi discourses, retired.

ازین به نصیحتگری بایدت

To a better adviser than he you must go!

ندانم پس از وی چه پیش آیدت

What may happen you after he dies, I don't know!

◈◉◈◉◈

حکایت زاهد تبریزی
story of the pious man and the thief

عزیزی در اقصای تبریز بود

In Tibriz dwelt a man who was dear in God's sight;

که همواره بیدار و شب خیز بود

He was always awake, and a riser at night

شبی دید جایی که دزدی کمند

One night he observed where a robber, his noose

بپیچید و بر طرف بامی فکند

Had twisted and on to a roof had cast loose.

کسان را خبر کرد و آشوب خاست

He informed all the neighbours; a tumult arose;

ز هر جانبی مرد با چوب خاست

Men with sticks, from each quarter sprang up from repose

چو نامردم آواز مردم شنید

When the noise of the crowd reached the base robber's ear,

میان خطر جای بودن ندید

Midst danger, he saw that no refuge was near.

نهیبی از آن گیر و دار آمدش

On hearing the tumult, fear mastered him quite;

گریز به وقت اختیار آمدش

He bethought him in time to take refuge in flight.

ز رحمت دل پارسا موم شد

Pity softened, like wax, the religious man's heart,

که شب دزد بیچاره محروم شد

For the luckless night-thief had to, bootless, depart.

به تاریکی از پی فراز آمدش

By a path in the darkness he left him and then

به راهی دگر پیشباز آمدش

Returned by another before him, again.

که یارا مرو کآشنای توام

Saying, " Friend! I'm your chum! do not go, I entreat!

به مردانگی خاک پای توام

By bravery, I swear! I'm the dust of your feet.

ندیدم به مردانگی چون تو کس

I have never beheld one so powerful as you;

که جنگاوری بر دو نوع است و بس

In warfare the modes of proceeding are two: —

یکی پیش خصم آمدن مردوار

One facing your foe like a valorous man;

دوم جان به در بردن از کارزار

One running from battle with life, while you can.

بر این هر دو خصلت غلام توام

In both of these modes I'm your servant the same;

چه نامی که مولای نام توام؟

Which say you? for I am the slave of your name!

گرت رای باشد به حکم کرم

If such is your pleasure, the order convey!

به جایی که میدانمت ره برم

To a place I know well I will show you the way;

سرایی است کوتاه و در بسته سخت

A cottage it is, with the door fixed secure,

نپندارم آنجا خداوند رخت

And the owner will not be at home, I am sure.

کلوخی دو بالای هم بر نهیم

Two clods, one on top of the other, let's put;

یکی پای بر دوش دیگر نهیم

And I'll place upon each of your shoulders a foot.

به چندان که در دستت افتد بساز

Whatever arrives at your hand do not spurn

از آن به که گردی تهیدست باز

It is better than empty of hand to return."

به دلداری و چاپلوسی و فن

By condoling, cajoling and art's cunning grace,

کشیدش سوی خانهٔ خویشتن

He drew him along to his own dwelling place.

جوانمرد شبرو فرو داشت دوش

When the night-robber downwards his shoulders had bent,

به کتفش برآمد خداوند هوش

The possessor of mind on the top of them went.

به غلطاق و دستار و رختی که داشت

His chattels, including a turban and cap,

ز بالا به دامان او در گذاشت

From above he passed down to the night-robber's lap.

وز آنجا برآورد غوغا که دزد

Raised a clamour of, "Thieves!" from the place where he was,

ثواب ای جوانان و یاری و مزد

Reward! oh young men! and, your help in this cause!"

به در جست از آشوب دزد دغل

The base thief made a bound to the door in alarm,

دوان، جامهٔ پارسا در بغل

And escaped with the pious man's clothes 'neath his arm.

دل آسوده شد مرد نیک اعتقاد

Heart soothed was the person of excellent creed,

که سرگشته‌ای را برآمد مراد

For the poor, luckless wretch in his aim did succeed.

خبیثی که بر کس ترحم نکرد

The thief who had never to man mercy shown,

ببخشود بر وی دل نیکمرد

By the good-hearted pauper was pitied, alone.

عجب ناید از سیرت بخردان

It's not rare, in the nature of those who are wise,

که نیکی کنند از کرم با بدان

Out of pity, to favour the bad they despise.

در اقبال نیکان بدان می‌زیند

In good men's prosperity bad men have grown,

وگر چه بدان اهل نیکی نیند

Although wicked men have no goodness their own.

❖◉❖◉❖

حکایت در معنی احتمال از دشمن از بهر دوست
Story on an enemy oppressing a friend

یکی را چو سعدی دلی ساده بود

A person like Sádi who owned a pure heart,

که با ساده رویی در افتاده بود

A captive became to a smooth-faced one's art

جفا بردی از دشمن سختگوی

Oppression he bore from the harsh spoken foe;

ز چوگان سختی بخستی چو گوی

From Tyranny's club like a ball he would go.

ز کس چین بر ابرو نینداختی

He turned not from any one frowning away;

ز یاری به تندی نپرداختی

Nor practised rebellion in preference to play.

یکی گفتش آخر تو را ننگ نیست؟

Someone said, " You at least have no honour to show!

خبر زین همه سیلی و سنگ نیست؟

Of these buffets and load, not an atom you know! "

تن خویشتن سغبه دونان کنند

The ignoble, alone, of their bodies take care;

ز دشمن تحمل زبونان کنند

The weak, the affronts of the enemy bear.

نشاید ز دشمن خطا درگذاشت

To wink at the fault of a fool is not right,

که گویند یارا و مردی نداشت

For they'll say, " You possess neither manhood nor might."

بدو گفت شیدای شوریده سر

How well the demented enthusiast gave

جوابی که شاید نبشتن به زر

A reply, that in gold it were well to engrave:

دلم خانهٔ مهر یار است و بس

My heart's but the house of the love of my friend,

از آن می‌نگنجد در او کین کس

And cannot for others, then, hate comprehend."

چه خوش گفت بهلول فرخنده خوی

How well spoke Bahlul, ever happy in mood,

چو بگذشت بر عارفِ جنگجوی

When he passed by a grumbler who thought himself good:

گر این مدعی دوست بشناختی

If this claimant had known aught concerning the Friend,

به پیکار دشمن نپرداختی

He would not have dared with the foe to contend.

گر از هستی حق خبر داشتی

If regarding the presence of God he knew aught,

همه خلق را نیست پنداشتی

He'd have reckoned the whole of the creatures as naught.

◈◉◈◉◈

حکایت لقمان حکیم
Story of Lukman, the doctor, and the native of Baghdad

شنیدم که لقمان سیه‌فام بود

I have heard that Lukman in complexion was black,

نه تن‌پرور و نازک اندام بود

And in tending his ill-favoured body was slack.

یکی بندهٔ خویش پنداشتش

Someone thought him a runaway slave he once had,

زبون دید و در کار گل داشتش

And employed him in working among clay at Baghdad.

جفا دید و با جور و قهرش بساخت

In a year, for his master a mansion he reared;

به سالی سرایی ز بهرش بساخت

No one thought he was else than the slave he appeared.

چو پیش آمدش بندهٔ رفته باز

When before him arrived, then, the slave who had fled,

ز لقمانش آمد نهیبی فراز

The sight of Lukman filled the master with dread.

به پایش در افتاد و پوزش نمود

He fell at his feet and advanced pleas profuse;

بخندید لقمان که پوزش چه سود؟

Lukman smiled and said, " Are your pleadings of use?

به سالی ز جورت جگر خون کنم

From your harshness my liver turned to blood for a year;

به یک ساعت از دل به در چون کنم؟

Can that in an hour from my heart disappear?

ولی هم ببخشایم ای نیکمرد

And yet, oh good man! I'll forgive even thee,

که سود تو ما را زیانی نکرد

For the profit to you caused no, damage to me.

تو آباد کردی شبستان خویش

For yourself you constructed a statelier place;

مرا حکمت و معرفت گشت بیش

have gained greater skill and increase of God's grace.

غلامی است در خیلم ای نیکبخت

Oh fortunate man! I've a slave of my own,

که فرمایمش وقتها کار سخت

On whom heavy labour I often have thrown;

دگر ره نیازارمش سخت، دل

Not again will I trouble his heart in that way,

چو یاد آیدم سختی کار گل

When I think of the hardship of working among clay."

هر آن کس که جور بزرگان نبرد

The man who has never been wronged by the great,

نسوزد دلش بر ضعیفان خرد

Does not burn in his heart at the poor's wretched state.

نکو گفت بهرام شه با وزیر

In this manner Bihram his vizier once addressed:

که دشوار با زیردستان مگیر

Let your subjects not be by hard labour oppressed!

گر از حاکمان سختت آید سخن

If the words of a Ruler seem harsh unto you,

تو بر زیردستان درشتی مکن

Do not you towards subjects oppression pursue!

◈◉◈◉◈

حکایت جنید و سیرت او در تواضع
Story of Junaid of Baghdad, and the humility of his nature

شنیدم که در دشت صنعا جنید
I have heard that Junaid, in the plain of Sana

سگی دید برکنده دندان صید
Saw a dog that had lost evry tooth in his jaw.

ز نیروی سر پنجهٔ شیرگیر
His claws, lion-seizing, of strength were bereft;

فرومانده عاجز چو روباه پیر
Like a feeble, decrepit, old fox he was left

پس از غرم و آهو گرفتن به پی
After catching the deer and wild ram, in the chase,

لگد خوردی از گوسفندان حی
He was butted and spurned by the sheep of the place.

چو مسکین و بی طاقتش دید و ریش
When he saw the poor brute weak and wounded and sad,

بدو داد یک نیمه از زاد خویش
He gave him the half of the viands he had.

شنیدم که می‌گفت و خوش می‌گریست
I have heard he was saying, while shedding red tears:

که داند که بهتر ز ما هر دو کیست؟
Who knows which of us two the better appears?

به ظاهر من امروز از این بهترم
I am better to look at than this one, to-day,

دگر تا چه راند قضا بر سرم
But how long on my head will this good fortune stay?

گرم پای ایمان نلغزد ز جای
If my foot of belief does not slip from its place,

به سر بر نهم تاج عفو خدای
With the crown of God's pardon my head I will grace.

وگر کسوت معرفت در برم
If the robe of God's knowledge I do not possess,

نماند، به بسیار از این کمترم
Than this brute I am certainly very much less.

که سگ با همه زشت نامی چو مرد
For the dog with a name vile as any can tell,

مر او را به دوزخ نخواهند برد
They will never convey, like a man, unto Hell."

ره این است سعدی که مردان راه

The way is this, Sádi: The men of the road

به عزت نکردند در خود نگاه

Never have on themselves a sublime look bestowed.

از آن بر ملائک شرف داشتند

Than the angels a higher position they held,

که خود را به از سگ نپنداشتند

For they did not conceive that the dog they excelled

حکایت زاهد و بربط زن
Story of the holy man and the harper

یکی بربطی در بغل داشت مست

A tipsy bard held 'neath his arm a harp tight;

به شب در سر پارسایی شکست

On a pious man's head he destroyed it at night

چو روز آمد آن نیکمرد سلیم

The gentle, good soul when the morning began,

بر سنگدل برد یک مشت سیم

Brought a handful of coins to the hard-hearted man.

که دوشینه معذور بودی و مست

"Last night you were haughty and tipsy," he said,

تو را و مرا بربط و سر شکست

"And broke while excited your harp and my head.

مرا به شد آن زخم و برخاست بیم

My wound has recovered; my terror has flown;

تو را به نخواهد شد الا به سیم

But you cannot get well until money you own."

از این دوستان خدا بر سرند

For this reason the friends of the Lord are more pure,

که از خلق بسیار بر سر خورند

That they much on their heads from the people endure.

حکایت صبر مردان بر جفا
Story on the patience of man under the oppression of cowards

شنیدم که در خاک وخش از مهان

I have heard that in Wakhsh one of noble estate,

یکی بود در کنج خلوت نهان

Concealed in the nook of retirement did wait.

مجرد به معنی نه عارف به دلق

In heart a recluse, not a saint in rags dressed,

که بیرون کند دست حاجت به خلق

Who stretches to people the hand of request.

سعادت گشاده دری سوی او

Felicity's door was for him opened wide

در از دیگران بسته بر روی او

In his face, closed the doors of all others beside.

زبان آوری بی‌خرد سعی کرد

An ignorant sycophant tried all he could

ز شوخی به بد گفتن نیکمرد

To revile, out of rudeness, the man who was good.

که زنهار از این مکر و دستان و ریو

Beware of those subtle deceivers! " he said,

بجای سلیمان نشستن چو دیو

Who are seated, like demons, in Solomon's stead.

دمادم بشویند چون گربه روی

At all times, like cats, they are washing their face,

طمع کرده در صید موشان کوی

Yet eager to hunt all the mice in the place.

ریاضت کش از بهر نام و غرور

For Pride and Repute's sake, abstemious they are

که طبل تهی را رود بانگ دور

For a drum being empty is heard from afar."

همی گفت و خلقی بر او انجمن

While speaking, the people a multitude grew;

بر ایشان تفرج کنان مرد و زن

Men and women amusing themselves at the two.

شنیدم که بگریست دانای وخش

I have heard that the learned man of Wakhsh wept a deal,

که یارب مر این بنده را توبه بخش

Saying, " Lord! cause this person repentance to feel!

وگر راست گفت ای خداوند پاک

And if he speak truly, Oh God, the most pure!

مرا توبه ده تا نگردم هلاک

Vouchsafe me repentance, lest death I endure!

پسند آمد از عیب جوی خودم

If I ferreted out my own faults, it were well,

که معلوم من کرد خوی بدم

For my bad disposition can all of them tell."

گر آنی که دشمنت گوید، مرنج

If you're all that your enemy says, do not grieve!

وگر نیستی، گو برو بادسنج

And if you are not, say, " Oh wind weigher, leave! "

اگر ابلهی مشک را گنده گفت

That foetid is musk if a blockhead should say,

تو مجموع باش او پراکنده گفت

Be at ease! for he speaks in a meaningless way.

وگر می‌رود در پیاز این سخن

And although this condition in onions may grow,

چنین است گو گنده مغزی مکن

It is their nature, say, " Do not a foetid brain show!

نه آیین عقل است و رای و خرد

It accords not with wisdom and reason and thought,

که دانا فریب مشعبد خورد

That the learned by a juggler's deceit should be caught.

پس کار خویش آنکه عاقل نشست

He who wisely employed at his own work is found,

زبان بداندیش بر خود ببست

Has the backbiting tongue of his enemy bound.

تو نیکو روش باش تا بد سگال

Let your conduct be good, and consistent your walk,

نیابد به نقص تو گفتن مجال

That your foe of your faults may be powerless to talk!

چو دشوارت آمد ز دشمن سخن

Since severe to your heart comes the word of a foe,

نگر تا چه عیبت گرفت آن مکن

Do not harshness to those who are under you show!

جز آن کس ندانم نکو گوی من

I know of no person who speaks in my praise,

که روشن کند بر من آهوی من

Save the man who exposes my culpable ways.

❖◉❖◉❖

حکایت امیرالمؤمنین علی (ع) و سیرت پاک او

Story of Ali, the Commander of the Faithful (may god reward him and the humility of his nature!)

کسی مشکلی برد پیش علی

To Ali a man brought a subject abstruse,

مگر مشکلش را کند منجلی

In the hope that the difficult knot he would loose.

امیر عدوبند کشور گشای

The conquering, foe-subjugating Ameer,

جوابش بگفت از سر علم و رای

Full of wisdom and sense, his reply stated clear.

شنیدم که شخصی در آن انجمن

I have heard that a man at the conference said:

بگفتا چنین نیست یا باالحسن

Oh perfection of goodness! you've erred on this head! "

نرنجید از او حیدر نامجوی

The magnanimous lion raged not at the man,

بگفت ار تو دانی از این به بگوی

But replied, "State it better than this, if you can! "

بگفت آنچه دانست و بایسته گفت

He explained what he knew in an elegant way

به گل چشمهٔ خور نشاید نهفت

It becomes not to hide the sun's splendour with clay

پسندید از او شاه مردان جواب

The monarch of men liked his lucid reply,

که من بر خطا بودم او بر صواب

Saying, "He is correct, and in error was I.

به از ما سخنگوی دانا یکی است

He better explained; and the Maker is one!

که بالاتر از علم او علم نیست

And knowledge more noble than His there is none."

317

گر امروز بودی خداوند جاه

Had you been a person of. rank in those days,

نکردی خود از کبر در وی نگاه

From hauteur you would not have deigned him a gaze.

به در کردی از بارگه حاجبش

Your slaves would have quickly expelled him the hall,

فرو کوفتندی به ناواجبش

And beaten him down, for no reason at all

که من بعد بی آبرویی مکن

Saying, " Do not hereafter disgracefully walk!

ادب نیست پیش بزرگان سخن

It is rude in the presence of nobles to talk! "

یکی را که پندار در سر بود

If in any one's head self-conceit should appear,

مپندار هرگز که حق بشنود

Do not fancy that always the truth he will hear.

ز علمش ملال آید از وعظ ننگ

From his learning comes grief; at advice shame is shown

شقایق به باران نروید ز سنگ

Rain cannot cause tulips to spring from a stone

نبینی که از خاک افتاده خوار

Don't you see that from Earth, which humility shows,

بروید گل و بشکفد نوبهار

The spring season comes and the rose blossom blows.

مریز ای حکیم آستینهای در

Oh, philosopher, scatter your pearls not too free,

چو می‌بینی از خویشتن خواجه پر

When the buyer stuffed full of himself you can see!

به چشم کسان در نیاید کسی

A person seems little in other men's eyes,

که از خود بزرگی نماید بسی

Who to publish his greatness continually tries.

مگو تا بگویند شکرت هزار

Do not lecture that thousands of thanks you may gain!

چو خود گفتی از کس توقع مدار

When you've eulogized self, hope in others is vain!

❈◉❈◉❈

حکایت عمر فروانروای با ایمان
Story of Omar, Commander of the Faithful (May God reward him!)

گدایی شنیدم که در تنگ جای

Saint Omar? I've heard, in a rough, narrow road,

نهادش عمر پای بر پشت پای

On a poor beggar's instep by accident trode.

ندانست درویش بیچاره کاوست

Who he was, the poor beggar distressed did not know

که رنجیده دشمن نداند ز دوست

For a sufferer knows not a friend from a foe.

برآشفت بر وی که کوری مگر؟

You surely are blind! " in a passion, he cried

بدو گفت سالار عادل عمر

Saint Omar, the chief of the just, thus replied:

نه کورم ولیکن خطا رفت کار

"I'm not blind; yet a fault I've committed to-day,

ندانستم از من گنه در گذار

Without my intending; forgive me! I pray."

چه منصف بزرگان دین بوده‌اند

What judges the chiefs of religion were then,

که با زیردستان چنین بوده‌اند

Since they acted like this towards poor, subject men.

فروتن بود هوشمند گزین

In the man choosing wisdom, humility's found;

نهد شاخ پر میوه سر بر زمین

The branch bearing fruit bends its head to the ground.

بنازند فردا تواضع کنان

Those who practise abasement are happy at last;

نگون از خجالت سر گردنان

The heads of the haughty from shame are downcast.

اگر می‌بترسی ز روز شمار

If concerning the day of account you have fear,

از آن کز تو ترسد خطا در گذار

Overlook the defects of those dreading you here!

مکن خیره بر زیر دستان ستم

By oppression, oh Brave! make not subjects repine!

که دستی است بالای دست تو هم

For a hand, too, exists that is higher than thine.

حکایت به خواب دیدن مرد نیک کردار

Story of the good man seen in a dream

یکی خوب کردار خوش خوی بود

A beneficent man who a good nature had,

که بد سیرتان را نکو گوی بود

Spoke kindly of people whose natures were bad.

به خوابش کسی دید چون در گذشت

After death, by a man in a dream he was seen,

که باری حکایت کن از سرگذشت

Who said, " Kindly tell what your trials have been? "

دهانی به خنده چو گل باز کرد

A mouth like a rose, smiling sweetly, ope'd wide;

چو بلبل به صوتی خوش آغاز کرد

In a voice like the nightingale's notes, he replied:

که بر من نکردند سختی بسی

They did not address me with harshness of tone,

که من سخت نگرفتمی بر کسی

For harshness to any I never had shown."

◆◉◆◉◆

حکایت ذوالنون مصری

Story of Zunun of Egypt (on him be mercy)

چنین یاد دارم که سقای نیل

I thus recollect that the clouds did not deign

نکرد آب بر مصر سالی سبیل

For the space of a year upon Egypt to rain.

گروهی سوی کوهساران شدند

To the mountainous regions a multitude fled;

به فریاد خواهان باران شدند

Lamenting and praying for showers they sped

گرستند و از گریه جویی روان

They wept, and from weeping the tears, flood-like, fell,

نیامد مگر گریهٔ آسمان

In the hope that the sky would perchance weep, as well

320

به ذوالنون خبر برد از ایشان کسی

One of these, to Zunun the intelligence bore,

که بر خلق رنج است و زحمت بسی

That the people were grieved and distressed very sore.

فرو ماندگان را دعایی بکن

For those in affliction, do thou intercede,

که مقبول را رد نباشد سخن

Since the words of the righteous avail when there's need."

شنیدم که ذوالنون به مدین گریخت

I have heard that Zunun to Medain quickly ran,

بسی بر نیامد که باران بریخت

And very soon after the raining began.

خبر شد به مدین پس از روز بیست

The news to Medaina in twenty days crept,

که ابر سیه دل بر ایشان گریست

That the black-hearted clouds on the people had wept.

سبک عزم باز آمدن کرد پیر

The old man soon resolved to return back again,

که پر شد به سیل بهاران غدیر

For the pools were all filled by the torrents of rain.

بپرسید از او عارفی در نهفت

A pious man, privately, asked on this head:

چه حکمت در این رفتنت بود؟ گفت

In your going, what virtue existed? " He said:

شنیدم که بر مرغ و مور و ددان

"I had heard that on birds, ants and animals, all,

شود تنگ روزی به فعل بدان

Through the deeds of the wicked, great hardships, would fall

در این کشور اندیشه کردم بسی

In this land, I have thought of it well in my mind,

پریشان‌تر از خود ندیدم کسی

And a man more distressed than myself, could not find.

برفتم مبادا که از شر من

I hurried away, lest through my sinful state,

ببندد در خیر بر انجمن

On the face of the crowd had been shut welfare's gate."

تو آنگه شوی پیش مردم عزیز

By your own fellow men you'll be highly esteemed,

که مر خویشتن را نگیری به چیز

When yourself as of little account you have deemed

بزرگی که خود را به خردی شمرد

To the great man who reckoned his merits as small,

به دنیا و عقبی بزرگی برد

In this world and the next will supremacy fall.

از این خاکدان بنده‌ای پاک شد

From this Earth went the Slave in a sanctified state,

که در پای کمتر کسی خاک شد

Who before his inferiors was humble in gait.

الا ای که بر خاک ما بگذری

Oh thou wandering over my ashes, take care!

به خاک عزیزان که یاد آوری

By the dust of the holy, in memory bear!

که گر خاک شد سعدی، او را چه غم؟

That if changed into dust why should Sádi be sad,

که در زندگی خاک بوده‌ست هم

Since in life he abundant humility had?

به بیچارگی تن فرا خاک داد

Unresisting his body to dust he resigned,

وگر گرد عالم برآمد چو باد

Although he had circled the world, like the wind.

بسی برنیاید که خاکش خورد

In a very short time, Earth will make him its own,

دگر باره بادش به عالم برد

And then by the wind through the world he'll be blown.

مگر تا گلستان معنی شکفت

Observe: Since the garden of meaning upsprung,

بر او هیچ بلبل چنین خوش نگفت

So sweetly as this, not a Bulbul has sung!

عجب گر بمیرد چنین بلبلی

It would be strange were a nightingale such to take wing,

که بر استخوانش نروید گلی

And a rose from the bones of his corpse not to spring.

❖◉❖◉❖

5

باب پنجم

(CHAPTER V.)

 در رضا

ON RESIGNATION

سرآغاز

In begin

شبی زیت فکرت همی سوختم

I was burning the oil of reflection one night,

چراغ بلاغت می افروختم

And Rhetoric's lamp I had kindled up bright.

پراکنده گویی حدیثم شنید

To my sayings a frivolous talker gave ear;

جز احسنت گفتن طریقی ندید

Save expressing approval, no way he saw clear.

هم از خبث نوعی در آن درج کرد

From a word, too, detracting, he could not refrain,

که ناچار فریاد خیزد ز درد

For groaning unconsciously rises from pain:

که فکرش بلیغ است و رایش بلند

His thoughts are mature and his judgment is nice,

در این شیوهٔ زهد و طامات و پند

On the topics of piety, mystics, advice;

نه در خشت و کوپال و گرز گران

Not on spears, iron maces, and truncheons of weight,

که این شیوه ختم است بر دیگران

For these are fit subjects for others to state."

نداند که ما را سر جنگ نیست

He knows not that I have no liking for fight,

وگر نه مجال سخن تنگ نیست

Else to speak on these matters my Power is not slight.

توانم که تیغ زبان بر کشم

The sword of the tongue I can draw from its case,

جهانی سخن را قلم در کشم

And a world of grandiloquence quickly efface.

بیا تا در این شیوه چالش کنیم

Come, let us this topic of war undertake!

سر خصم را سنگ، بالش کنیم

For the head of the foe a stone-pillow make.

سعادت به بخشایش داورست

Felicity dwells in God's favour alone;

نه در چنگ و بازوی زور آورست

In war and the arm of the strong, it's unknown.

324

چو دولت نبخشد سپهر بلند

If the high sphere of Heav'n give not wealth, be aware

نیاید به مردانگی در کمند

That it will not by manliness come to your snare

نه سختی رسید از ضعیفی به مور

The ant although weak does not hardship sustain;

نه شیران به سرپنجه خوردند و زور

By their Powerfulness, lions their food do not gain.

چو نتوان بر افلاک دست آختن

Since the hand is unable to reach to the skies,

ضروری است با گردشش ساختن

One is bound to submit to the changes that rise.

گرت زندگانی نبشته‌ست دیر

If Fate has inscribed that your life will be long,

نه مارت گزاید نه شمشیر و شیر

The snake, sword and tiger can do you no wrong.

وگر در حیاتت نمانده‌ست بهر

And if of your life not a part should remain,

چنانت کشد نوشدارو که زهر

The antidote kills you, the same as the bane.

نه رستم چو پایان روزی بخورد

When Rustam his last daily morsel had gnawed,

شغاد از نهادش برآورد گرد؟

Was dust from his body not brought by Shighad?

حکایت سرباز جنگاور
Story of a bold soldier

مرا در سپاهان یکی یار بود

In great Isphahan, a companion had!,

که جنگاور و شوخ و عیار بود

Who was warlike and bold and uncommonly sly.

مدامش به خون دست و خنجر خضاب

His hand and his sword were with blood always dyed;

بر آتش دل خصم از او چون کباب

Like flesh on the fire, hearts of foes through him fried.

ندیدمش روزی که ترکش نبست

Not a day did I see him with quiver unlashed;

ز پولاد پیکانش آتش نجست

From his steel arrow-heads every day the fire flashed.

دلاور به سرپنجهٔ گاوزور

He was brave, and his strength was exceedingly great;

ز هولش به شیران در افتاده شور

From dread of him, tigers were restless in state.

به دعوی چنان ناوک انداختی

Such reliance in shooting his shafts he would show,

که عذرا به هر یک یک انداختی

That he failed not to smite with each arrow a foe.

چنان خار در گل ندیدم که رفت

I have not seen a thorn pierce a flower so quick,

که پیکان او در سپرهای جفت

As the heads of his arrows pierced shields that were thick.

نزد تارک جنگجویی به خشت

He smote not an enemy's head with his spear,

که خود و سرش را نه در هم سرشت

That he did not cause helmet and head to adhere.

چو گنجشک روز ملخ در نبرد

In battle, like sparrows among locusts in flight;

به کشتن چه گنجشک پیشش چه مرد

Men and sparrows, for slaughter, were one in his sight

گرش بر فریدون بدی تاختن

If upon Faridun an attack he had made,

امانش ندادی به تیغ آختن

No time he'd have left him to flourish his blade.

پلنگانش از زور سرپنجه زیر

By the strength of his fingers were leopards subdued;

فرو برده چنگال در مغز شیر

He his nails in the brains of fierce tigers imbrued.

گرفتی کمربند جنگ آزمای

He would seize by the girdle one used to the fray,

وگر کوه بودی بکندی ز جای

And were he a mountain, would dash him away.

زره پوش را چون تبرزین زدی

On a man clad in mail when his battle-axe fell,

گذر کردی از مرد و بر زین زدی

He passed through the man and smote saddle as well.

نه در مردی او را نه در مردمی

In valour and generous qualities shown,

دوم در جهان کس شنید آدمی

His equal on earth, no one ever had known.

مرا یک دم از دست نگذاشتی

For a moment he let me not out of his sight,

که با راست طبعان سری داشتی

For with men of good nature he gathered delight.

سفر ناگهم زان زمین در ربود

From that country a journey soon called me away,

که بیشم در آن بقعه روزی نبود

For it had not been fated that there I should stay.

قضا نقل کرد از عراقم به شام

From Irak into Sham I was carried by Fate;

خوش آمد در آن خاک پاکم مقام

In that sanctified land I was happy in state.

دگر پر شد از شام پیمانه‌ام

In Sham, then, I finished my measure of toil,

کشید آرزومندی خانه‌ام

And a longing I felt for my own native soil.

قضا را چنان اتفاق اوفتاد

By chance, it occurred that while journeying back,

که بازم گذر بر عراق اوفتاد

I again had to pass through the land of Irak.

شبی سر فرو شد به اندیشه‌ام

One night, with my head hanging down in deep thought,

به دل برگذشت آن هنر پیشه‌ام

To my mind was that skillful one's memory brought.

نمک ریش دیرینه‌ام تازه کرد

The salt of remembrance renewed my old sore,

که بودم نمک خورده از دست مرد

For oft had I eaten his salt, long before.

به دیدار وی در سپاهان شدم

To great Isphahan to behold him I went;

به مهرش طلبکار و خواهان شدم

Out of friendship, on searching and asking intent.

جوان دیدم از گردش دهر، پیر

I saw that Time's changes had made the youth old;

خدنگش کمان، ارغوانش زریر

His straight figure bent and his red hue, like gold;

چو کوه سپیدش سر از برف موی

His snowy-haired head like a white-crested hill;

دوان آبش از برف پیری به روی

From the snow of old age down his face the tears rill.

فلک دست قوت بر او یافته

The sky having mastery over him found,

سر دست مردیش بر تافته

Soon twisted the hand of his manliness round.

بدر کرده گیتی غرور از سرش

The world from his head having ostracised pride,

سر ناتوانی به زانو برش

Infirmity's head, on his knees must abide.

بدو گفتم ای سرور شیر گیر

I exclaimed, " Oh great chief! who with lions engaged,

چه فرسوده کردت چو روباه پیر؟

What has polished you down like a fox that is aged?"

بخندید کز روز جنگ تتر

Since the Tartar invasion," he smilingly said,

بدر کردم آن جنگجویی ز سر

I have driven strife-seeking away from my head.

زمین دیدم از نیزه چو نیستان

The ground filled with spears, like a cane-break, I watched,

گرفته علمها چو آتش در آن

With their banners of scarlet, like fire-brands attached.

بر انگیختم گرد هیجا چو دود

Like smoke, I excited the dust-clouds of war;

چو دولت نباشد تهور چه سود؟

But what Vantage gives bravery when Fortune's afar?

من آنم که چون حمله آوردمی

I am he, who, whenever an onset I made,

به رمح از کف انگشتری بردمی

A ring from the palm with my spear I conveyed.

ولی چون نکرد اخترم یاوری

But because in my ' star ' no assistance I found,

گرفتند گردم چو انگشتری

Like a ring, they immediately circled me round!

غنیمت شمردم طریق گریز

The path of retreat I esteemed as a friend;

که نادان کند با قضا پنجه تیز

For the foolish alone will with Fortune contend.

چه یاری کند مغفر و جوشنم

What succour do helmet and armour bestow,

چو یاری نکرد اختر روشنم؟

When my planet refuses assistance to show?

کلید ظفر چون نباشد به دست

When you hold not possession of Victory's key,

به بازو در فتح نتوان شکست

Conquest's door by your arm cannot broken up be.

گروهی پلنگ افکن پیل زور

A host came, leopard-felling, of elephant might;

در آهن سر مرد و سم ستور

Iron-clad the horse-hoofs and the head of each wight.

همان دم که دیدیم گرد سپاه

As soon as the dust of this army we spied,

زره جامه کردیم و مغفر کلاه

To put on our armour and helmets we hied.

چو ابر اسب تازی برانگیختیم

Like clouds, we urged forward our Arabs, amain,

چو باران بلارک فرو ریختیم

And brought our swords down, like a torrent of rain.

دو لشکر به هم بر زدند از کمین

Both armies together from ambushment crashed;

تو گفتی زدند آسمان بر زمین

You'd have said that the sky on the earth they had dashed.

ز باریدن تیر همچو تگرگ

From the raining of arrows, like hail, among the foes,

به هر گوشه برخاست طوفان مرگ

The whirlwind of death, in each corner arose.

به صید هژبران پرخاش ساز

In hunting the lions accustomed to war,

کمند اژدهای دهن کرده باز

The mouth of the dragon like noose was ajar.

زمین آسمان شد ز گرد کبود

From the dust, azure coloured, the earth became sky,

چو انجم در او برق شمشیر و خود

And the helmets and swords flashed like stars twinkling high.

سواران دشمن چو دریافتیم

As soon as the enemy's horse came in sight,

پیاده سپر در سپر بافتیم

With our shields knit together, dismounted we fight

چه زور آورد پنجهٔ جهد مرد

What strength can the hand of man's labouring show,

چو بازوی توفیق یاری نکرد؟

If the arm of God's grace does not succour bestow?

نه شمشیر گندآوران کند بود

Not blunt were the swords of these brave men of war;

که کین آوری ز اختر تند بود

But fierce was the spite of their rancorous star.

کس از لشکر ما ز هیجا برون

Not a man of our army came out from the fray,

نیامد جز آغشته خفتان به خون

With doublet unmoistened with blood, on that day.

چو صد دانه مجموع در خوشه‌ای

Like a hundred grains, joined in one cluster, we start;

فتادیم هر دانه‌ای گوشه‌ای

We were scattered, each grain in a corner apart

به نامردی از هم بدادیم دست

We through cowardice further resistance forsook;

چو ماهی که با جوشن افتد به شست

Like the fish clothed in mail which succumbs to the hook.

کسان را نشد ناوک اندر حریر

The shafts of those men into silk did not go,

که گفتم بدوزند سندان به تیر

Who, I've said, with their arrows an anvil could sew.

چو طالع ز ما روی بر پیچ بود

When Fortune averted her face from our field,

سپر پیش تیر قضا هیچ بود

Against the arrows of Fate, of what use was a shield? "

◈◉◈◉◈

حکایت تیرانداز اردبیلی

Story of the archer and the youth clothed in felt

یکی آهنین پنجه در اردبیل

There dwelt in Ardbil, once, a man of strong thew,

می بگذرانید پیلک ز پیل

Who could pierce with his arrows a spade through and through.

نمد پوشی آمد به جنگش فراز

To fight him a man clothed in felt came from far

جوانی جهان سوز پیکار ساز

A strife-raising youth and promoter of war

به پرخاش جستن چو بهرام گور

He was like Bihram-Ghor, in his search for a fray;

کمندی به کتفش بر از خام گور

On his shoulder a noose of wild ass's skin lay.

به پنجاه تیر خدنگش بزد

Fifty arrows of poplar he shot at this foe;

که یک چوبه بیرون نرفت از نمد

Through the armour of felt not an arrow would go.

درآمد نمدپوش چون سام گرد

Like the hero Dastan the brave youth joined the fight;

به خم کمندش درآورد و برد

In the coil of his noose snared his enemy tight

به لشکرگهش برد و در خیمه دست

To the door of his tent, in the camp-pitching ground,

چو دزدان خونی به گردن ببست

His hands to his neck, like a robber's, he bound.

شب از غیرت و شرمساری نخفت

He slept not, from pride and from shame, all the night;

سحرگه پرستاری از خیمه گفت

A slave shouted out from a tent, at daylight:

تو کآهن به ناوک بدوزی و تیر

As the felt-clad one's prisoner, why are you here,

نمدپوش را چون فتادی اسیر؟

Who can penetrate iron with arrows and spear?

شنیدم که می‌گفت و خون می‌گریست

I have heard he wept blood, and thus said in reply:

ندانی که روز اجل کس نزیست؟

"Don't you know you can't live when the Fates bid you die?

من آنم که در شیوهٔ طعن و ضرب

I am he who in using the sword and the dart,

به رستم در آموزم آداب حرب

Could the tactics of war unto Rustam impart.

چو بازوی بختم قوی حال بود

When the arm of my fortune was strong in degree,

ستبری پیلم نمد می‌نمود

A thick iron spade seemed like felt unto me.

کنونم که در پنجه اقبیل نیست

But now that good luck from my fingers has strayed,

نمد پیش تیرم کم از پیل نیست

Felt in front of my shafts, is as good as a spade."

به روز اجل نیزه جوشن درد

When Death comes, a spear will pierce armour, indeed,

ز پیراهن بی اجل نگذرد

But will not pierce a shirt, if it is not decreed.

کرا تیغ قهر اجل در قفاست

He who has the fell sabre of death at his rear,

برهنه‌ست اگر جوشنش چند لاست

Will be nude, though his armour should triple appear.

ورش بخت یاور بود، دهر پشت

And should Fortune befriend -and Time's aid he obtain,

برهنه نشاید به ساطور کشت

Though naked, he cannot by dagger be slain.

نه دانا به سعی از اجل جان ببرد

The sage by his striving escaped not from fate,

نه نادان به ناساز خوردن بمرد

And the fool did not die from the rubbish he ate.

حکایت طبیب و کرد
Story of the Physician and the Peasant

شبی کردی از درد پهلو نخفت

A peasant one night could not sleep from an ache

طبیبی در آن ناحیت بود و گفت

In his side. A physician who practised there spake:

از این دست کاو برگ رز می‌خورد

From his habit of eating vine leaves this ache springs;

عجب دارم ار شب به پایان برد

Twill be strange, if the night to a finish he brings

که در سینه پیکان تیر تتار

For a Tartar's hard arrow-head, stuck in the chest,

به از ثقل مأکول ناسازگار

Is better than eating what will not digest.

گر افتد به یک لقمه در روده پیچ

xIn a twist of the gut should a morsel be caught, '

همه عمر نادان بر آید به هیچ

The whole of the life of the fool comes to naught."

قضا را طبیب اندر آن شب بمرد

It occurred that the doctor expired that same night;

چهل سال از این رفت و زنده‌ست کرد

Forty years have elapsed and the swain is all right.

حکایت سقط شدن خر
Story of the Ass's Skull

یکی روستایی سقط شد خرش

The unfortunate ass of a villager died;

علم کرد بر تاک بستان سرش

He its skull as a charm to a vine sapling tied.

جهاندیده پیری بر او بر گذشت

An experienced old man chanced to pass near the head;

چنین گفت خندان به ناطور دشت

To the vineyard protector he, smiling, thus said:

مپندار جان پدر کاین حمار

Oh life of your father! don't think this ass' bone,

کند دفع چشم بد از کشتزار

Can the evil eye drive from the field you have sown!

که این دفع چوب از سر و گوش خویش

For the stick from his own head and ears, though he tried,.

نمی‌کرد تا ناتوان مرد و ریش

He repelled not, and helpless and wounded he died.

چه داند طبیب از کسی رنج برد

What knows the physician of people diseased,

که بیچاره خواهد خود از رنج مرد؟

Since he himself, helpless, by Death will be seized. "

◈◉◈◈◉◈

حکایت دینار گمشده
Story of the lost dinar

شنیدم که دیناری از مفلسی

A Dinar, I have heard, from a needy man fell,

بیفتاد و مسکین بجستش بسی

And the poor fellow searched all around for it well

به آخر سر ناامیدی بتافت

His head in despair he averted at last;

یکی دیگرش ناطلب کرده یافت

It was found by another, unsought for, who passed.

به بدبختی و نیکبختی قلم

With good and bad fortune the pen travelled round,

بگردید و ما همچنان در شکم

And we in the womb of the mother still bound.

نه روزی به سرپنجگی می‌خورند

Mankind by their strength daily food do not eat,

که سرپنجگان تنگ روزی ترند

For the strong, the most needy, you often will meet

◈◈◈

حکایت توبیخ پسر توسط پدر
Story of the father chastising his son

فرو کوفت پیری پسر را به چوب

With a stick an old man beat his son on the head;

بگفت ای پدر بی‌گناهم مکوب

"I am guiltless, oh father! don't beat me! " he said;

توان بر تو از جور مردم گریست

At the harshness of men I can weep before you;

ولی چون تو جورم کنی چاره چیست؟

But if you treat me harshly what then can I do? "

به داور خروش، ای خداوند هوش

The possessor of wisdom to God sends his cry,

نه از دست داور برآور خروش

But does not complain of the Maker on high.

◈◈◈

حکایت مرد درویش و همسایهٔ توانگر
Story of the Beggar and his wife

بلند اختری نام او بختیار
A fortunate person, whose name was Bakhtyar,
قوی دستگه بود و سرمایه‌دار
Was exalted in rank and had wealth on a par.

چو درویش بیند توانگر به ناز
He alone possessed money and stores in the place;
دلش بیش سوزد به داغ نیاز
All the others were poor and showed grief in their face.

زنی جنگ پیوست با شوی خویش
A woman presumed with her husband to fight,
شبانگه چو رفتش تهیدست، پیش
Because he came home empty-handed at night.

که کس چون تو بدبخت، درویش نیست
Like you," she exclaimed, "there's no poor, blighted thing!
چو زنبور سرخت جز این نیش نیست
Like the wasp, you are only possessed of a sting!

بیاموز مردی ز همسایگان
From your neighbours some manliness try to acquire!
که آخر نیم قحبهٔ رایگان
For at any rate, I'm not a wife without hire.

کسان را زر و سیم و ملک است و رخت
Gold and silver and property others possess;
چرا همچو ایشان نه‌ای نیکبخت؟
Why don't you, like them, smiling Fortune caress? "

بر آورد صافی دل صوف پوش
The pure-hearted man in a woollen robe dressed,
چو طبل از تهیگاه خالی خروش
Like a drum, brought a cry from his desolate breast:

که من دست قدرت ندارم به هیچ
"No power have I over things that exist;
به سرپنجه دست قضا بر مپیچ
With your fingers, the strong hand of Fate do not twist!

نکردند در دست من اختیار
On my hand of selecting, the Fates placed a bar,
که من خویشتن را کنم بختیار
Else I'd have created myself a Bakhtyar."

حکایت مرد فقیر و همسر زشتش
Story of the poor man and his ugly wife

یکی پیر درویش در خاک کیش
A man who in Kish suffered poverty's yoke,

چه خوش گفت با همسر زشت خویش
To his vile-visaged wife, thus, with truthfulness spoke:

چو دست قضا زشت رویت سرشت
Since ugly is writ by Fate's hand on your face,

میندای گلگونه بر روی زشت
On your cheeks void of beauty, rose-pink do not place! "

که حاصل کند نیکبختی به زور؟
Who is able to master good fortune by might?

به سرمه که بینا کند چشم کور؟
To the eyes of the blind, who with salve can give sight?

نیاید نکوکار از بد رگان
Good works the malevolent never have shown,

محال است دوزندگی از سگان
And union among dogs is a thing quite unknown.

همه فیلسوفان یونان و روم
The whole of the Sages of Greece and of Rome,

ندانند کرد انگبین از زقوم
Could not honey extract from the thorny Zakom.

ز وحشی نیاید که مردم شود
A wild beast is not likely to change into man;

به سعی اندر او تربیت گم شود
Instruction is lost on it, strive as you can.

توان پاک کردن ز زنگ آینه
One can polish a mirror that rusty has grown,

ولیکن نیاید ز سنگ آینه
But a mirror can never be made out of stone.

به کوشش نه روید گل از شاخ بید
Effort makes not a rose from a willow. to grow;

نه زنگی به گرمابه گردد سپید
A warm-bath will not whiten a negro like snow.

چو رد می‌نگردد خدنگ قضا
Since nought can the arrow of destiny brave,

سپر نیست مر بنده را جز رضا
Resignation's the shield that is left to God's slave.

حکایت کرکس با زغن
Story of the vulture and the kite

چنین گفت پیش زغن کرکسی
In this manner a vulture conversed with a kite:

که نبود ز من دوربین‌تر کسی
No bird has like me such a far-reaching sight"

زغن گفت از این در نشاید گذشت
We must settle this point! " said the kite, in reply.

بیا تا چه بینی بر اطراف دشت
On the desert's expanse, tell me what you can spy? "

شنیدم که مقدار یک روزه راه
I have heard that a day's journey distant, or so,

بکرد از بلندی به پستی نگاه
He looked from above on the desert below;

چنین گفت دیدم گرت باور است
And said, "I can see, if you credit the feat,

که یک دانه گندم به هامون بر است
That on yonder vast plain there is one grain of wheat! "

زغن را نماند از تعجب شکیب
The kite was of patience bereft, from surprise;

ز بالا نهادند سر در نشیب
They directed their heads to the plains from the skies.

چو کرکس بر دانه آمد فراز
When the vulture arrived at the grain on the ground,

گره شد بر او پاینده‌ای دراز
In a long, stretching snare he was twisted and bound.

ندانست از آن دانه‌ای خوردنش
From eating that grain he was little aware,

که دهر افکند دام در گردنش
That Fate would entangle his neck in a snare.

نه آبستن در بود هر صدف
Not always in pearl shells are pearls found to lie;

نه هر بار شاطر زند بر هدف
An archer can't always transfix the bull's eye.

زغن گفت از آن دانه دیدن چه سود
Said the kite, "What acquire you from seeing that grain,

چو بینایی دام خصمت نبود؟
When no sight of the snare of your foe you obtain? "

شنیدم که می‌گفت و گردن به بند

I have heard that he said, with his neck in the noose,

نباشد حذر با قدر سودمند

Against Fate's decrees, caution proves of no use."

اجل چون به خونش بر آورد دست

When Death caused his hand for his murder to rise,

قضا چشم باریک بینش ببست

Fate instantly darkened his clear seeing eyes.

در آبی که پیدا نگردد کنار

In a sea where the opposite coast is concealed,

غرور شناور نیاید به کار

The swimmer's proud boast will no benefit yield.

حکایت شاگرد منسوج باف

Story of the gold-cloth weaver's apprentice

چه خوش گفت شاگرد منسوج باف

How nicely a weaver's apprentice did state

چو عنقا بر آورد و پیل و زراف

While sketching giraffes, birds and elephants great

مرا صورتی بر نیاید ز دست

A single design does not come from my hand,

که نقشش معلم ز بالا نبست

That the 'Teacher above has not previously planned."

گرت صورت حال بد یا نکوست

If your outward appearance be hideous, or fine,

نگارندهٔ دست تقدیر، اوست

Has. it not been portrayed by the Artist Divine?

در این نوعی از شرک پوشیده هست

In this person some hid infidelity see,

که زیدم بیازرد و عمروم بخست

Who declares, "Zaid afflicted and Omar smote me."

گرت دیده بخشد خداوند امر

If the Lord of command will vouchsafe to you eyes,

نبینی دگر صورت زید و عمر

Not again will you see Zaid and Omar arise.

نپندارم ار بنده دم در کشد

If a man remain silent, I do not suppose

خدایش به روزی قلم در کشد

That his means of subsistence the Maker will close.

جهان آفرینت گشایش دهاد

May the Maker of Earth keep it open for thee!

که گر وی ببندد نشاید گشاد

If He closes food's portal it cannot ope'd be.

◈◉◈◈◉◈

حکایت شتر

Story of the camel and her colt

شتر بچه با مادر خویش گفت

The colt of a camel its mother addressed

بس از رفتن، آخر زمانی بخفت

After traveling, "Oh, come! for a time let us rest! "

بگفت ار به دست منستی مهار

She replied, "If the halter had been in my sway,

ندیدی کسم بارکش در قطار

In the train 'neath a load none had seen me today."

قضا کشتی آنجا که خواهد برد

Wherever Fate wills she the vessel can bear,

وگر ناخدا جامه بر تن درد

Though the Captain should tear all his clothes in despair

مکن سعدیا دیده بر دست کس

Oh Sádi! on others' hands cast not your eyes!

که بخشنده پروردگار است و بس

For God is the giver and He should suffice.

اگر حق پرستی ز درها بست

If you worship the Lord you need no other door;

که گر وی براند نخواند کست

If He drive you away none will bid you come more.

گر او تاجدارت کند سر بر آر

If He give you good luck, raise your head in the air!

وگر نه سر نا امیدی بخار

Go! scratch, if He does not, the head of despair!

گفتار اندر اخلاص و برکت آن و ریا و آفت آن

Remarks on sincerity and its blessing, and on hypocrisy and its calamity

عبادت به اخلاص نیت نکوست

Devotion is good when its object is plain,

وگر نه چه آید ز بی مغز پوست؟

What good, else, can come from a skin without brain?

چه زنار مغ در میانت چه دلق

What's the belt of the gueber? the tattered, old cloak?

که در پوشی از بهر پندار خلق

When you wear them to tickle the fancies of folk

مکن گفتمت مردی خویش فاش

Do not publish your bravery, I've told you, at least;

چو مردی نمودی مخنث مباش

When you've shown you're a man, do not act like a beast

به اندازهٔ بود باید نمود

One should merit display, in accordance with facts

خجالت نبرد آن که ننمود و بود

He is never ashamed who in this manner acts.

که چون عاریت بر کنند از سرش

For when from one's head the lent turban they tear.

نماید کهن جامه‌ای در برش

On his breast there remains an old garment to wear.

اگر کوتهی پای چوبین مبند

Do not use wooden stilts if your stature be small.

که در چشم طفلان نمایی بلند

That in juvenile eyes you may seem to be tall!

وگر نقره اندوده باشد نحاس

If a coating of silver on copper you pass,

توان خرج کردن بر ناشناس

You may foist it with ease on an ignorant ass.

منه جان من آب زر بر پشیز

On coppers, my life, liquid gold do not place!

که صراف دانا نگیرد به چیز

For the wise bankers treat them as worthless and base.

زر اندودگان را به آتش برند

The coins that are gilt, in the furnace they throw;

پدید آید آنگه که مس یا زرند

Which is copper; which gold, they immediately know.

ندانی که بابای کوهی چه گفت

Don't you know what a chief of the mountain monks spake

به مردی که ناموس را شب نخفت؟

To the man, who for fame every night kept awake?

برو جان بابا در اخلاص پیچ

Oh soul of your father, in purity strive!

که نتوانی از خلق رستن به هیچ

For you cannot from people advantage derive.

کسانی که فعلت پسندیده‌اند

Those men who in love with your actions have been,

هنوز از تو نقش برون دیده‌اند

Have only your outward appearance yet seen.

چه قدر آورد بنده حوردیس

What price will a Houri like maiden bring in,

که زیر قبا دارد اندام پیس؟

Who beneath her fine dress has a foul, leprous skin?

نشاید به دستان شدن در بهشت

You cannot in Heav'n by deceit get a place,

که بازت رود چادر از روی زشت

For the veil will retire from your sinister face."

حکایت بچه روزه دار

Story of a child who kept a fast

شنیدم که نابالغی روزه داشت

I have heard that a tender aged child kept a fast;

به صد محنت آورد روزی به چاشت

With toil he held out till the morning repast.

به کتابش آن روز سائق نبرد

The teacher removed him from school the same day,

بزرگ آمدش طاعت از طفل خرد

For it seemed to him grand that an infant should pray.

پدر دیده بوسید و مادر سرش

His papa kissed his eyes and his mother his head;

فشاندند بادام و زر بر سرش

And over him, almonds and money they shed.

چو بر روی گذر کرد یک نیمه روز

When half of the day in this manner had passed,

فتاد اندر او ز آتش معده سوز

In his stomach the hot hunger pangs raised a blast.'

به دل گفت اگر لقمه چندی خورم

He said in his heart, " If some morsels I chew,

چه داند پدر غیب یا مادرم؟

My parents won't know what in secret I do."

چو روی پسر در پدر بود و قوم

As the boy for his father and tribe conscience showed,

نهان خورد و پیدا به سر برد صوم

He feasted in private and fasted abroad.

که داند چو در بند حق نیستی

Who knows that communion with God you don't share,

اگر بی وضو در نماز ایستی؟

When without an ablution you stand to say prayer?

پس این پیر از آن طفل نادان تر است

The old man is more foolish than that child can be,

که از بهر مردم به طاعت در است

Who engages in worship, for people to see.

کلید در دوزخ است آن نماز

That prayer is the key of the portal of hell,

که در چشم مردم گزاری دراز

Over which in men's presence a long time you dwell.

اگر جز به حق می‌رود جاده‌ات

If your path does not lead to the Maker alone,

در آتش فشانند سجاده‌ات

Your carpet for prayer into Hell will be thrown!

نکو سیرتی بی تکلف برون

One of good disposition in coarse garments clad

به از نیکنامی خراب اندرون

Surpasses the pietist inwardly bad.

به نزدیک من شبرو راهزن

A prowling night-robber is better, I vote,

به از فاسق پارسا پیرهن

Than the profligate dressed in a pious man's coat.

یکی بر در خلق رنج آزمای

To the man who seeks payment for trouble below,

چه مزدش دهد در قیامت خدای؟

What wages will God at the Judgment bestow?

ز عمرو ای پسر چشم اجرت مدار

Do not hope to get wages from Umar, oh son!

چو در خانهٔ زید باشی به کار

When your work, in the mansion of Zaid has been done.

نگویم تواند رسیدن به دوست

I say that one cannot arrive at the Friend,

در این ره جز آن کس که رویش در اوست

Unless, as a searcher, this way he should wend.

ره راست رو تا به منزل رسی

Pursue the right road that the goal you may find!

تو در ره نه‌ای، زین قبل واپسی

You are not on the road, so you're fallen behind!

چو گاوی که عصار چشمش ببست

You resemble the wine-presser's ox with eyes bound;

دوان تا به شب، شب همان جا که هست

In the same place from morning to night going round.

کسی گر بتابد ز محراب روی

Were a person to turn from the Kiblah his sight,

به کفرش گواهی دهند اهل کوی

His neighbours would vouch for his infidel plight.

تو هم پشت بر قبله‌ای در نماز

You, too, have your back to the Kiblah in prayer,

گرت در خدا نیست روی نیاز

If to God you a suppliant face do not bear.

درختی که بیخش بود برقرار

Take care of the tree with a permanent root,

بپرور، که روزی دهد میوه بار

For some day it will yield you abundance of fruit!

گرت بیخ اخلاص در بوم نیست

If you have not sincerity's root in your ground,

از این بر کسی چون تو محروم نیست

One like you is not baulked though this fruit is not found.

هر آن کافکند تخم بر روی سنگ

Whoever sows seed on the face of a stone,

جوی وقت دخلش نیاید به چنگ

Not a grain at the season of reaping will own.

منه آبروی ریا را محل

To hypocrisy give not the honour of place!

که این آب در زیر دارد وحل

For this water has mud lying under its face.

چو در خفیه بد باشم و خاکسار

When in heart I am thoroughly wicked and mean,

چه سود آب ناموس بر روی کار؟

What's the gain from fame's splendour in works that are seen?

به روی و ریا خرقه سهل است دوخت

By hypocrisy's aid a patched garb's eas'ly sewed;

گرش با خدا در توانی فروخت

But will you be able to sell it to God?

چه دانند مردم که در جامه کیست؟

What mortal can tell who is inside a coat?

نویسنده داند که در نامه چیست

A writer can tell what is writ in a note!

چه وزن آورد جایی انبان باد

What weight has a large, leather bag, full of wind,

که میزان عدل است و دیوان داد؟

When Justice and Equity's balance we find?

مرائی که چندین ورع می‌نمود

The hypocrite showing how much he abstained,

بدیدند و هیچش در انبان نبود

Was unmasked and his leather bag "nothing" contained.

کنند ابره پاکیزه‌تر ز آستر

The outside they make than the lining more clean,

که آن در حجاب است و این در نظر

For the latter is covered the former is seen.

بزرگان فراغ از نظر داشتند

The wise for the purpose of show were not dressed,

از آن پرنیان آستر داشتند

So linings of rich, painted silk they possessed.

ور آوازه خواهی در اقلیم فاش

If you wish that your fame through the country should go,

برون حله کن گو درون حشو باش

Your outside adorn! stuff the inside with tow!

به بازی نگفت این سخن بایزید

Bayizid did not jest when he uttered this speech:

که از منکر ایمن‌ترم کز مرید

" I'm with scoffers more safe than with those whom I teach."

کسانی که سلطان و شاهنشهند

All those who are sultans and kingly in line,

سراسر گدایان این درگهند

Are beggars entirely at this holy shrine.

طمع در گدا، مرد معنی نبست

A religious man's hope in the beggar's not bound;

نشاید گرفتن در افتاده دست

It is wrong to assist up the vile from the ground.

همان به گر آبستن گوهری

If you're pregnant with pearls, act like this! and 'tis well;

که همچون صدف سر به خود در بری

Keep your head in yourself, like the pearl bearing shell.

چو روی پرستیدنت در خداست

When in worship your face to the Lord is inclined,

اگر جبرئیلت نبیند رواست

If Gabriel should fail to observe you, don't mind!.

تو را پند سعدی بس است ای پسر

Oh son, Sádi's counsel for you is as clear

اگر گوش گیری چو پند پدر

As a father's advice, if you only give ear!

گر امروز گفتار ما نشنوی

If you do not attend to our sayings to-day,

مبادا که فردا پشیمان شوی

God forbid, lest to-morrow you penitent stay!

❁◉❁◉❁

6

باب ششم

(CHAPTER VI.)

در قناعت

ON CONTENTMENT

سرآغاز

In begin

خدا را ندانست و طاعت نکرد

He knew not the Lord and from worship abstained,

که بر بخت و روزی قناعت نکرد

Who repined at the portion in life he obtained.

قناعت توانگر کند مرد را

By contentment a man becomes wealthy and great;

خبر کن حریص جهانگرد را

This news to the greedy world-wanderer state!

سکونی به دست آور ای بی ثبات

Oh rover! acquire an established abode,

که بر سنگ گردان نروید نبات

For a rolling stone gathers no moss on the road!

مپرور تن ار مرد رای و هشی

Do not pamper your body, if wary and wise!

که او را چو می‌پروری می‌کشی

For when you indulge it you cause its demise.

خردمند مردم هنر پرورند

Philosophers nurture the virtues with care;

که تن پروران از هنر لاغرند

Those who pamper the body, of virtues are bare.

کسی سیرت آدمی گوش کرد

With a character human the person was filled,

که اول سگ نفس خاموش کرد

Who, to start with, the dog of concupiscence stilled.

خور و خواب تنها طریق دد است

Beasts of prey care for eating and sleeping, alone,

بر این بودن آیین نابخرد است

And to follow this habit the foolish are prone.

خنک نیکبختی که در گوشه‌ای

Oh happy is he, who, in corner retired,

به دست آرد از معرفت توشه‌ای

Has supplies for the road, from God's knowledge, acquired!

بر آنان که شد سر حق آشکار

Those whom God has informed of the secret of grace,

نکردند باطل بر او اختیار

Have not chosen the follies of life in its place.

وليکن چو ظلمت نداند ز نور

And yet, when one knows not the darkness from light,

چه دیدار دیوش چه رخسار حور

Fiend and cheek of a Houri are one in his sight

تو خود را از آن در چه انداختی

You could not the road from the pit again tell,

که چه را ز ره باز نشناختی

And, therefore, you cast yourself into a well.

بر اوج فلک چون پرد جره باز

Can the male falcon fly to the sky's highest height,

که در شهپرش بستهای سنگ آز؟

When with greed's heavy weight you have pinioned him tight?

گرش دامن از چنگ شهوت رها

If his skirt from the talons of lust you set free,

کنی، رفت تا سدرةالمنتهی

His flight to the mansion of Gabriel will be.

به کم کردن از عادت خویش خورد

If the amount you're accustomed to eat you curtail,

توان خویشتن را ملک خوی کرد

You'll the nature of angels acquire without fail

کجا سیر وحشی رسد در ملک

When will a wild beast to the angels come nigh,

نشاید پرید از ثری بر فلک

Since from Earth unto Heaven it is helpless to fly?

نخست آدمی سیرتی پیشه کن

First, the qualities special to man exercise!

پس آن گه ملک خوبی اندیشه کن

Let your thoughts to the nature of angels then rise.

تو بر کرهٔ توسنی بر کمر

You are up on the back of a spirited colt;

نگر تا نپیچد ز حکم تو سر

Take care! lest away from your hand it should bolt!

که گر پالهنگ از کفت در گسیخت

If it parted the reins from your palm, without doubt

تن خویشتن کشت و خون تو ریخت

It would kill its own body, and pour your blood out.

به اندازه خور زاد اگر مردمی

Be mod' rate in eating! if human you are;

چنین پر شکم، آدمی یا خمی؟

With your stomach so full, are you man, or a jar?

درون جای قوت است و ذکر و نفس

Your inside's for thinking of God, breath and food;

تو پنداری از بهر نان است و بس

You suppose that for viands alone, it is good.

کجا ذکر گنجد در انبان آز؟

Where's his room for reflection? from sordid desire,

به سختی نفس می‌کند پا دراز

He can only, with very great effort, respire!

ندارند تن پروران آگهی

Those who cherish the body, the fact do not know,

که پر معده باشد ز حکمت تهی

That the men with stuffed stomach no wisdom can show.

دو چشم و شکم پر نگردد به هیچ

The eye and the stomach can never be cloyed.

تهی بهتر این رودهٔ پیچ پیچ

Far better, indeed, were the twisted gut void.

چو دوزخ که سیرش کنند از وقید

When Hell's yawning furnace with fuel they fill,

دگر بانگ دارد که هل من مزید؟

It reiterates loud, " Is there any more still?"

همی میردت عیسی از لاغری

Your Jesus is dying of weakness, alas!

تو در بند آنی که خر پروی

You are occupied solely in feeding His ass.

به دین، ای فرومایه، دنیا مخر

From buying the world with the Faith, wretch, refrain!

تو خر را به انجیل عیسی مخر

With the Gospel of Jesus don't buy the ass grain!

مگر می‌نبینی که دد را و دام

I The wild beasts of prey, you may not be aware,

نینداخت جز حرص خوردن به دام؟

From their love of devouring are drawn to the snare.

پلنگی که گردن کشد بر وحوش

The leopard that stretches his neck after beasts,

به دام افتد از بهر خوردن چو موش

Is entrapped like a mouse, from his liking for feasts.

چو موش آن که نان و پنیرش خوری

When of one's bread and cheese, like a mouse, you eat part,

به دامش در افتی و تیرش خوری

You fall to his snare and are hit by his dart.

◈◉◈◉◈

حکایت شانه عاج حاجی
Story, of the Haji's ivory comb

مرا حاجیی شانهٔ عاج داد

A Haji once gave me an ivory comb;

که رحمت بر اخلاق حجاج باد

Mercy rest on the virtues of Hajis, who roam)

شنیدم که باری سگم خوانده بود

I had heard that he dared once to call me a dog;

که از من به نوعی دلش مانده بود

For at something I said, was his mind set agog.

بینداختم شانه کاین استخوان

This bone," I said — casting the comb on the ground

نمی‌بایدم دیگرم سگ مخوان

Does not suit me! henceforth do not call me a hound!

میندار چون سرکهٔ خود خورم

If I drink my own vinegar, do not suppose,

که جور خداوند حلوا برم

That I care to endure the confectioner's blows! "

قناعت کن ای نفس بر اندکی

Let a little, oh spirit, your wish satisfy!

که سلطان و درویش بینی یکی

That the Sultan and beggar as one, you may spy!

چرا پیش خسرو به خواهش روی

In front of a monarch, your wishes, why bring?

چو یک سو نهادی طمع، خسروی

When you've set aside greed, you yourself are a king!

351

وگر خود پرستی شکم طبله کن

If you worship yourself, make your stomach a gong!

در خانهٔ این و آن قبله کن

And pray at each door, as you travel along.

❖◉❖◉❖

حکایت مرد طماع و پسرش
Story of the covetous man and his son

یکی بر طمع پیش خوارزمشاه

I have heard that a person of covetous sight,

شنیدم که شد بامدادی پگاه

Went to Kharazam's king at the first dawn of light.

چو دیدش به خدمت دوتا گشت و راست

When his son had observed that in paying respect,

دگر روی بر خاک مالید و خاست

He bowed, kissed the ground and again stood erect;

پسر گفتش ای بابک نامجوی

He said, "Oh magnanimous father, give ear!

یکی مشکلت می‌پرسم بگوی

I've a difficult question for you to make clear.

نگفتی که قبله‌ست سوی حجاز

You have stated that Mecca's your worshipping place;,

چرا کردی امروز از این سو نماز؟

Why in praying, to-day, turned you elsewhere your face? "

مبر طاعت نفس شهوت پرست

Your spirit, lust-worshipping, do not obey!

که هر ساعتش قبلهٔ دیگر است

For each hour, at a different shrine it will pray.

مبر ای برادر به فرمانش دست

On its order, oh brother, extend not a hand!

که هر کس که فرمان نبردش برست

He was rescued, who did not obey its command.

قناعت سرافرازد ای مرد هوش

Oh wise man! by contentment the head is raised high;

سر پر طمع بر نیاید ز دوش

The head, full of greed, on the shoulder must lie!

طمع آبروی توقر بریخت
The fair fame of honour is scattered by greed;

برای دو جو دامنی در بریخت
A skirt ful of pearls strewn for two grains of seed!

چو سیراب خواهی شدن ز آب جوی
When you wish your thirst quenched at a rivulet nice,

چرا ریزی از بهر برف آبروی؟
Why squander your fame for the sake of some ice?

مگر از تنعم شکیبا شوی
Perhaps you are pleased with your comforts in store!

وگرنه ضرورت به درها شوی
If not, you must travel from door unto door!

برو خواجه کوتاه کن دست آز
Go, sir! make the base hand of avarice short!

چه می‌بایدت ز آستین دراز؟
What occasion have you in long sleeves to disport?

کسی راکه درج طمع در نوشت
He whose record of av'rice is folded from sight,

نباید به کس عبد و خادم نبشت
To no one, "Your slave!" or "Your servant!" should write.

توقع براند ز هر مجلست
Out of every assembly by greed you are turned;

بران از خودش تا نراند کست
Drive it out of yourself, that you may not be spurned!

حکایت مرد بیمار
Story of the pious sick man

یکی را تب آمد ز صاحبدلان
In one of the pious an ague began;

کسی گفت شکر بخواه از فلان
Someone said, "Ask conserve from a certain rich man!"

بگفت ای پسر تلخی مردنم
He answered, " The harshness of dying, oh son!

به از جور روی ترش بردنم
Is better than scowls from a sour-visaged one."

شکر عاقل از دست آن کس نخورد

Of that person's conserve, the wise man did not eat,

که روی از تکبّر بر او سرکه کرد

Who had shown him a vinegar face from conceit.

مرو از پی هر چه دل خواهدت

Do not follow whatever your heart may desire!

که تمکین تن نور جان کاهدت

For tending the body abates your soul's fire.

کند مرد را نفس اماره خوار

Inordinate appetite makes a man low;

اگر هوشمندی عزیزش مدار

Do not show it affection, if wisdom you know!

اگر هرچه باشد مرادت خوری

If whatever may be its desire, you should eat,

ز دوران بسی نامرادی بری

From the changes of Time, disappointment you'll meet.

تنور شکم دم به دم تافتن

If the store of the stomach is always kept hot,

مصیبت بود روز نایافتن

Misfortune arises when nought can be got.

به تنگ بریزاندت روی رنگ

The hue of your face disappears in distress,

چو وقت فراخی کنی معده تنگ

When in plentiful times you your stomach oppress.

کشد مرد پرخواره بار شکم

The man always eating, the stomach's load bears;

وگر در نیابد کشد بار غم

If he eats not, he carries a burden of cares.

شکم بنده بسیار بینی خجل

The stomach's slave, greatly abashed you will find;

شکم پیش من تنگ بهتر که دل

A void stomach is better, I think, than void mind.

❮◉❯❮◉❯

حکایت در مذلت بسیار خوردن
Story on the depravity of gluttons

چه آوردم از بصره دانی عجب
Do you know of the wonders from Basra I brought?
حدیثی که شیرین تر است از رطب
Far sweeter than dates, some remarks I have got.

تنی چند در خرقه راستان
A few of us, decked in the garb of the true,
گذشتیم بر طرف خرماستان
Passed a district where dates in luxuriance grew.

یکی در میان معده انبار بود
The stomach of one of our number was great;
ز پر خواری خویش بس خوار بود
A glutton he was, from the bushels' he ate.

میان بست مسکین و شد بر درخت
The poor creature got ready and climbed up a tree,
وز آنجا به گردن در افتاد سخت
And down again heavily, headlong, fell he.

نه هر بار خرما توان خورد و برد
One cannot eat dates, aye, and bear them away;
لت انبان بد عاقبت خورد و مرد
The glutton, ill-starred, ate and lifeless he lay.

رئیس ده آمد که این را که کشت؟
The village chief coming, "Who killed him?" he cried;
بگفتم مزن بانگ بر ما درشت
Do not shout at us harshly like that!" I replied;

شکم دامن اندر کشیدش ز شاخ
His stomach neath's skirt dragged him down from a branch;
بود تنگدل رودگانی فراخ
Narrow-minded is he who is spacious in paunch."

شکم بند دست است و زنجیر پای
The hand's bonds, is the stomach, and chain of the feet;
شکم بنده نادر پرستد خدای
A stomach's slave pious, you rarely will meet.

سراسر شکم شد ملخ لاجرم
The locust's all stomach and therefore, no doubt,
به پایش کشد مور کوچک شکم
The small-bellied ant, by the leg pulls it out.

برو اندرونی به دست آر، پاک

Depart and an inside of pureness acquire!

شکم پر نخواهد شد الّا به خاک

The stomach can never be filled, but with mire.

◈◈◈

حکایت صوفی و دینارش
story of the Sufi and his dinars

شکم صوفیی را زبون کرد و فرج

By his belly and lust, was a Sufi subdued,

دو دینار بر هر دوان کرد خرج

For he foolishly spent two Dinars on their food.

یکی گفتش از دوستان در نهفت

One among his companions addressed him aside,

چه کردی بدین هر دو دینار؟ گفت

Saying, "How did you spend the Dinars? "He replied:

به دیناری از پشت راندم نشاط

a From my back, I with one of them pleasure released;

به دیگر، شکم را کشیدم سماط

With the other, I spread for my stomach a feast.

فرومایگی کردم و ابلهی

With baseness and foolishness, now, I am stained;

که این همچنان پر نشد وآن تهی

For the latter's not full and the former is drained."

غذا گر لطیف است و گر سرسری

If a food is nice-flavoured, or coarse and ill-dressed,

چو دیرت به دست اوفتد خوش خوری

When it reaches you late, you will eat it with zest.

سر آنگه به بالین نهد هوشمند

The sage his tired head on the pillow will lay,

که خوابش به قهر آورد در کمند

When sleep in its noose bears him fiercely away.

مجال سخن تا نیابی مگوی

While you cannot speak fluently, speak not at all!

چو میدان نبینی نگه دار گوی

Till you see a clear plain, take good care of the ball!

به بی رغبتی شهوت انگیختن

Let your talk and your walk, while to choose you are free,

به رغبت بود خون خود ریختن

Be neither above nor below your degree!

⟨◉⟩⟨◉⟩

حکایت در عزت قناعت

Story of the holy man and the sugar-cane

یکی نیشکر داشت بر طبقری

One had pieces of sugar-cane heaped on a plate,

چپ و راست گردیده بر مشتری

And went hither and thither, on buyers to wait

به صاحبدلی گفت در کنج ده

In the village he said to a God-fearing man:

که بستان و چون دست یابی بده

"Take a little and pay me the price when you can! "

بگفت آن خردمند زیبا سرشت

The sage of good origin gave, on his part,

جوابی که بر دیده باید نبشت

An answer that ought to be graved on the heart:

تو را صبر بر من نباشد مگر

Perhaps you might fail to have patience with me;

ولیکن مرا باشد از نیشکر

But without sugar-cane I can very well be.

حلاوت ندارد شکر در نیش

The sugar in cane can no sweetness possess,

چو باشد تقاضای تلخ از پیش

When bitter exacting must after it press."

⟨◉⟩⟨◉⟩

حکایت مرد روشن ضمیر و هدیه امیر
Story of the wise man and the ameer's gift

یکی را ز مردان روشن ضمیر

The Cathay Ameer sent a rich, silken dress

امیر ختن داد طاق حریر

To a sage, who a luminous mind did possess.

ز شادی چو گلبرگ خندان شکفت

He donned it and kissing the ground and his hands,

نپوشید و دستش ببوسید و گفت

Said, "A thousand Well dones 'on the king of all lands!:

چه خوب است تشریف میر ختن

How fine is this dress, from the Tartar Ameer!

وز او خوب تر خرقهٔ خویشتن

Yet my own ragged garment to me is more dear! "

گر آزاده‌ای بر زمین خسب و بس

If you're free; on the ground you should slumber, and then,

مکن بهر قالی زمین بوس کس

Do not kiss for a carpet the ground before men!

◈◉◈◉◈

حکایت مرد سر میز پادشاه
Story of the man at the King's table

یکی نان خورش جز پیازی نداشت

One had only an onion to eat with his bread;

چو دیگر کسان برگ و سازی نداشت

With life's dainties he was not, like other men, fed.

کسی گفتش ای سغبهٔ خاکسار

A lunatic shouted, "Oh indigent wretch!

برو طبخی از خوان یغما بیار

Go and ready-cooked meat from the public tray fetch!

بخواه و مدار ای پسر شرم و باک

Demand thou, oh sir! and for no one show dread!

که مقطوع روزی بود شرمناک

For cut off is the timid petitioner's bread."

قبا بست و چابک نوردید دست

He put on his cloak and with hands ready, stood;

قبایش دریدند و دستش شکست

They fractured his fingers and tore up his hood.

همی گفت و بر خویشتن می‌گریست

I have heard he was saying and shedding red tears:

که مر خویشتن کرده را چاره چیست؟

Oh my spirit! what help for what's self-done appears?

بلا جوی باشد گرفتار آز

The Captive of Avarice, evil pursues;

من و خانه من بعد و نان و پیاز

Henceforth my own house, bread and onions, I'll use.

جوینی که از سعی بازو خورم

The barley loaf I by my own arm can eat,

به از میده بر خوان اهل کرم

Is better than charity loaves made of wheat."

چه دلتنگ خفت آن فرومایه دوش

How distressed was the sleep of that base one, last night,

که بر سفرهٔ دیگران داشت گوش

Who on other men's tables had fastened his sight!

حکایت گربه پیرزن

Story of the old woman's cat

یکی گربه در خانهٔ زال بود

A cat in the house of an old woman dwelt,

که برگشته ایام و بد حال بود

Who changes of time and condition had felt.

دوان شد به مهمان سرای امیر

To the banqueting hall of a ruler it went;

غلامان سلطان زدندش به تیر

Through its body the slaves of the chief arrows sent

چکان خونش از استخوان، می‌دوید

It was running, with blood from its bones dripping rife;

همی گفت و از هول جان می‌دوید

It was saying, and running from fear of its life:

اگر جستم از دست این تیر زن

"If I from the hand of this archer can flee,

من و موش و ویرانهٔ پیرزن

With the mouse of the old woman's hut I'll agree."

نیرزد عسل، جان من، زخم نیش

The honey repays not the wound of the sting;

قناعت نکوتر به دوشاب خویش

With contentment, date-juice more enjoyment will bring.

خداوند از آن بنده خرسند نیست

The Lord with that servant is not satisfied,

که راضی به قسم خداوند نیست

Who sulks at the share which the Lord has supplied.

◖◉◗◖◉◗

حکایت مرد کوته نظر و زن عالی همت
Story of the short-sighted man and the woman of noble spirit

یکی طفل دندان برآورده بود

An infant the whole of his milk-teeth had got;

پدر سر به فکرت فرو برده بود

The father hung down his sad head in deep thought.

که من نان و برگ از کجا آرمش؟

Saying, " Where can I get food and clothes for my son?

مروت نباشد که بگذارمش

It would not be manly to leave him and run! "

چو بیچاره گفت این سخن، نزد جفت

When the wretch made this statement in front of his wife,

نگر تا زن او را چه مردانه گفت

Hear how bravely replied the help-meet of his life

مخور هول ابلیس تا جان دهد

Do not fear for the Devil! for while the child lives,

همان کس که دندان دهد نان دهد

He who gave him the teeth also food to him gives!

تواناست آخر خداوند روز

The Omnipotent God has the Power, after all,

که روزی رساند، تو چندین مسوز

To give us our food; in this way, do not bawl!

نگارندهٔ کودک اندر شکم

He Who sketches the child in the uterine cell,

نویسنده عمر و روزی است هم

Is the Writer of life and subsistence, as well.

خداوندگاری که عبدی خرید

When a lord buys a slave he will food to him give;

بدارد، فکیف آن که عبد آفرید

How much more will He, then, Who bade the slave live?

تو را نیست این تکیه بر کردگار

Your reliance upon the Creator is less,

که مملوک را بر خداوندگار

Than that which a slave on his lord should possess."

شنیدی که در روزگار قدیم

Have you heard that in ages, a long time ago,

شدی سنگ در دست ابدال سیم

In the hands of the saints, stone to silver would grow?

نپنداری این قول معقول نیست

You cannot suppose that the saying's unwise:

چو قانع شدی سیم و سنگت یکی است

When content, stone and silver are one in your eyes."

چو طفل اندرون دارد از حرص پاک

When the heart of a child knows no envy or lust,

چه مشتی زرش پیش همت چه خاک

In his eyes, what's a handful of gold, or of dust?

خبر ده به درویش سلطان پرست

Make the Dervish who worships the monarch aware,

که سلطان ز درویش مسکین ترست

That the king than the pauper more sorrow must bear!

گدا را کند یک درم سیم سیر

With one paltry Direm the beggar is pleased;

فریدون به ملک عجم نیم سیر

Faridun was half-glad when all Persia he seized

نگهبانی ملک و دولت بلاست

Guarding kingdom and wealth is a dangerous game;

گدا پادشاه است و نامش گداست

The beggar's a king, although beggar's his name.

گدایی که بر خاطرش بند نیست

The beggar without any care on his heart,

به از پادشاهی که خرسند نیست

Is better than kings who in joy have no part

بخسبند خوش روستایی و جفت

The peasant slept happy along with his spouse,

به ذوق که سلطان در ایوان نخفت

With a joy that no king in a palace could rouse.

اگر پادشاه است و گر پینه دوز

If one is a king, and should one cotton sew,

چو خفتند گردد شب هر دو روز

When they sleep, both their nights into daylight will go.

چو سیلاب خواب آمد و مرد برد

When sleep's flood arrives and bears man in its train,

چه بر تخت سلطان، چه بر دشت کرد

What's the king on the throne? what's the Kurd on the plain?

چو بینی توانگر سر از کبر مست

When you see a rich man who is crazy in head,

برو شکر یزدان کن ای تنگدست

Depart and thank God that you barely have bread!

نداری بحمدالله آن دسترس

Praised be God! that in you no ability lies,

که برخیزد از دستت آزار کس

That affliction on one, from your hand should arise!

◈◉◈◈◉◈

حکایت رباخوار

OF the Usurer and his son

رباخواري از نردباني فتاد

From a staircase a usurer tumbled, one day;

شنیدم که دم در نفس جان بداد

I have heard that his soul at the time passed away.

پسر چند روزي گرستن گرفت

His son for a little lamented him sore,

دگر با حریفان نشستن گرفت

And then joined his frolicsome friends, as before.

بخواب اندرش دید و پرسید حال

He saw him one night in a dream and thus said :

که چون رستي از حشر و نشر و سوال ؟

" At the judgment and questioning, how have you sped?"

بگفت اي پسر! قصه بر من مخوان

" The story, oh son! do not ask me to tell!

بدوزخ در افتادم از نردبان

From the staircase I tumbled, at once, into Hell."

⟨◉⟩⟨◉⟩

حکایت صاحبدل نیکمرد
Story of the good man and his house

شنیدم که صاحبدلی نیکمرد

I have heard that a man who was good and upright,

یکی خانه بر قامت خویش کرد

For himself built a dwelling becoming his height.

کسی گفت می‌دانمت دسترس

Someone said, "I'm aware that with means you're supplied

کز این خانه بهتر کنی، گفت بس

To build a house statelier." " Stop! "he replied;

چه می‌خواهم از طارم افراشتن؟

What desire for arched ceilings comes into my mind?

همینم بس از بهر بگذاشتن

This same is sufficient, for leaving behind."

مکن خانه بر راه سیل، ای غلام

In the way of a flood, oh youth, build not a seat!

که کس را نگشت این عمارت تمام

For to no one was such a house ever complete.

نه از معرفت باشد و عقل و رای

It's against sense and reason and knowledge of God,

که بر ره کند کاروانی سرای

That a traveler should build up an inn on the road.

⟨◉⟩⟨◉⟩

حکایت شیخی که پادشاه شد
Story of the holy man who became King

یکی سلطنت ران صاحب شکوه

There once was a monarch of pomp and renown,

فرو خواست رفت آفتابش به کوه

Whose "sun" to the mountain desired to go down.

به شیخی در آن بقعه کشور گذاشت

He abandoned his realm to a saint of that place,

که در دوره قائم مقامی نداشت

For no living successor was left of his race.

چو خلوت نشین کوس دولت شنید

When the holy recluse heard the big drum of state,

دگر ذوق در کنج خلوت ندید

He cared not again in retirement to wait.

چپ و راست لشکر کشیدن گرفت

He began to manoeuvre his troops left and right;

دل پردلان زو رمیدن گرفت

The hearts of brave men were alarmed at the sight

چنان سخت بازو شد و تیز چنگ

So strong grew his arm and so brave had he got,

که با جنگجویان طلب کرد جنگ

That with war-seeking people encounter he sought.

ز قوم پراکنده خلقی بکشت

Of the foe, disunited, a number he killed.

دگر جمع گشتند و هم رای و پشت

The remainder assembled, with one spirit filled.

چنان در حصارش کشیدند تنگ

They circled him round in a fortress so tight,

که عاجز شد از تیرباران و سنگ

That the raining of arrows and stones cowed him quite.

بر نیکمردی فرستاد کس

To an eminent saint he made someone repair;

که صعبم فرومانده، فریاد رس

Saying, "I am distressed! oh reliever of care,

به همت مدد کن که شمشیر و تیر

With your prayers assist! for the arrow and sword,

نه در هر وغایی بود دستگیر

Do not always, in battle, assistance afford."

چو بشنید عابد بخندید و گفت

When the worshipper heard this, he smiled, and then said

چرا نیم نانی نخورد و نخفت؟

Why did he not sleep on a half loaf of bread?

ندانست قارون نعمت پرست

Karun the wealth-worshipper, was not aware,

که گنج سلامت به کنج اندر است

That the treasure of peace hugs the corner of prayer."

گفتار در صبر بر ناتوانی به امید بهی

Remarks on patience in weakness and hope of better days

کمال است در نفس مرد کریم

In a generous man's spirit perfection is bred;

گرش زر نباشد چه نقصان و بیم؟

If no money he owns, what's the harm or the dread?

مپندار اگر سفله قارون شود

Were a miser with Croesus in riches to range,

که طبع لئیمش دگرگون شود

Do not think that his miserly spirit would change!

وگر درنیابد کرم پیشه، نان

If a liberal person obtains not his bread,

نهادش توانگر بود همچنان

His spirit is rich, just as if he were fed.

مروت زمین است و سرمایه زرع

The giving's the ground and the means, the sown field;

بده کاصل خالی نماند ز فرع

Bestow! that the root fertile branches may yield.

خدایی که از خاک مردم کند

I would wonder where God, who makes man out of clay,

عجب باشد ار مردمی گم کند

To make his humanity vanish away.

ز نعمت نهادن بلندی مجوی

In hoarding up wealth, do not strive to excel!

که ناخوش کند آب استاده بوی

For water when stagnant emits a bad smell.

به بخشندگی کوش کآب روان

In munificence labour! for water that flows,

به سیلش مدد می‌رسد ز آسمان

By the favour of Heav'n to a mighty flood grows!

گر از جاه و دولت بیفتد لئیم

If a miser should fall from his wealth and estate,

دگر باره نادر شود مستقیم

Very rarely again will his riches be great.

وگر قیمتی گوهری غم مدار

If you are a jewel of worth, do not fret!

که ضایع نگرداندت روزگار

For Time will not cause your existence to set

کلوخ ار چه افتاده بینی به راه

A clod may be lying exposed on the way;

نبینی که در وی کند کس نگاه

Yet I do not see any one heed to it pay.

و گر خردهٔ زر ز دندان گاز

f a clipping of gold should escape from the shears,

بیفتد، به شمعش بجویند باز

With a candle they search for it, till it appears.

به در می‌کنند آبگینه ز سنگ

From the heart of a stone they can crystal obtain;

کجا ماند آیینه در زیر زنگ؟

Where under the rust does a mirror remain?

هنر باید و فضل و دین و کمال

The manners must please and exhibit much grace,

که گاه آید وگه رود جاه و مال

For coming and going are Fortune and Place.

❖◉❖❖◉❖

حکایت در معنی آسانی پس از دشواری
Story on repose after difficulty

شنیدم ز پیران شیرین سخن
By the veterans of affable speech, I've been told,

که بود اندر این شهر پیری کهن
That there dwelt in this city a man very old.

بسی دیده شاهان و دوران و امر
He had seen many monarchs and times and decrees,

سرآورده عمری ز تاریخ عمرو
And had lived since the days of the great Amralis.

درخت کهن میوهای تازه داشت
The withered, old tree had a fruit, fresh and sweet,

که شهر از نکویی پرآوازه داشت
With the fame of whose beauty the town was replete.

عجب در زنخدان آن دل فریب
In the chin of that charmer a wonder was shown,

که هرگز نبودهست بر سرو سیب
For an apple has never on cypress-tree grown.

ز شوخی و مردم خراشیدنش
On account of his mirth and the torture he spread,

فرج دید در سر تراشیدنش
His father found pleasure in shaving his head.

به موسی، کهن عمر کوته امید
The old life of short hope, with a razor's keen blade,

سرش کرد چون دست موسی سپید
The head of his son like the sun's surface made.

ز سر تیزی آن آهنین دل که بود
From its sharpness, the steel that from stone, once, hac sprung,

به عیب پریرخ زبان برگشود
On the fault of the fairy-cheek fastened its tongue.

به مویی که کرد از نکوییش کم
The razor that against his rare beauty transgressed,

نهادند حالی سرش در شکم
Had its head, then, within its own belly depressed.

چو چنگ از خجالت سر خوبروی
Like a harp, very bashful, the pretty-faced head

نگونسار و در پیشش افتاده موی
Hung down, and the fallen hair around it was spread.

یکی را که خاطر در او رفته بود

To a person, whose heart had inclined to the child,

چو چشمان دلبندش آشفته بود

When his heart-fettered eyes grew distracted and wild,

کسی گفت جور آزمودی و درد

Someone said, "You have suffered oppression and pain;

دگر گرد سودای باطل مگرد

Do not flit round this fanciful passion again!

ز مهرش بگردان چو پروانه پشت

Turn your back, like the moth, from his love that appears,

که مقراض، شمع جمالش بکشت

For his candle of beauty's extinguished with shears."

برآمد خروش از هوادار چست

The lover astute gave a harrowing yell;

که تردامنان را بود عهد سست

Saying, "Fickle engagements with profligates dwell

پسر خوش منش باید و خوبروی

It is right that the son be good-natured and fair;

پدر گو به جهلش بینداز موی

Let the father in ignorance cut off his hair!

مرا جان به مهرش برآمیخته‌ست

My soul with his friendship is thoroughly mixed;

نه خاطر به مویی در آویخته‌ست

My heart to his hair's not suspended or fixed"

چو روی نکو داری انده مخور

When you own a good face, let not sorrow remain!

که موی ار بیفتد بروید دگر

For although the hair falls it will grow in again.

نه پیوسته رز خوشهٔ تر دهد

The vine will not always a ripe cluster show;

گهی برگ ریزد، گهی بر دهد

It may either throw leaves or to fruit it may go.

بزرگان چو خور در حجاب اوفتند

Great men drop 'neath a veil, like the sun's brilliant ball;

حسودان چو اخگر در آب اوفتند

Like a live coal in water the envious fall

برون آید از زیر ابر آفتاب

The sun by degrees from the cloud will arise,

به تدریج و اخگر بمیرد در آب

And under the water the live ember dies.

ز ظلمت مترس ای پسندیده دوست

Oh agreeable friend, for the darkness don't care!

که ممکن بود کاب حیوان در اوست

Who knows but the water of life may be there?

نه گیتی پس از جنبش آرام یافت؟

Did not Earth, after trembling, composure acquire?

نه سعدی سفر کرد تا کام یافت؟

Did not Sádi make journeys to gain his desire?

دل از بی مرادی به فکرت مسوز

At defeated desires, burn your head not with thought!

شب آبستن است ای برادر به روز

Night pregnant with daylight, oh brother, you've got!

369

7

باب هفتم

(CHAPTER VII)

در عالم تربیت

ON TRAINING AND

INSTRUCTION

سرآغاز
In begin

سخن در صلاح است و تدبیر و خوی
Of rectitude, counsels and manners I tell;
نه در اسب و میدان و چوگان و گوی
Not on battle-fields, polo and studs do I dwell.

تو با دشمن نفس هم‌خانه‌ای
With the foe, lustful passion, why housed are you found?
چه در بند پیکار بیگانه‌ای؟
To a stranger's forced labour, how can you be bound?

عنان بازپیچان نفس از حرام
From unlawful affairs those who twist passion's reins,
به مردی ز رستم گذشتند و سام
In bravery, pass Rustam and Sam, for their pains.

کس از چون تو دشمن ندارد غمی
No one cherishes fear for a foeman like you;
که با خوبشتن بر نیائی همی
For you have not the strength your own self to subdue.

تو خود را چو کودک ادب کن به چوب
Like a boy, teach respect to yourself with the cane!
به گرز گران مغز مردم مکوب
A man, with a ponderous mace, do not brain!

وجود تو شهری است پر نیک و بد
Your body's a town, full of good and bad gear;
تو سلطان و دستور دانا خرد
You're the sultan, and wisdom's the polished vizier.

همانا که دونان گردن فراز
In this city, resembling the arrogant mean,
درین شهر گیرند سودا و آز
Are haughtiness, passion and avarice seen.

رضا و ورع: نیکنامان حر
Contentment and chasteness are good men and true;
هوی و هوس: رهزن و کیسه بر
In envy and lust, thieves and cut-purses view!

چو سلطان عنایت کند با بدان
When the Sultan to vile-minded men favour shows,
کجا ماند آسایش بخردان؟
In people of wisdom, where lodges repose?

تو را شهوت و حرص و کین و حسد

Lust and avarice, malice and envy, full rife,

چو خون در رگانند و جان در جسد

Are like blood in your veins, in your body, the life.

گر این دشمنان تربیت یافتند

If foes of this stamp have indulgence obtained,

سر از حکم و رأی تو بر تافتند

By your order and counsel they will not be reined.

هوی و هوس را نماند ستیز

From passion and lust flees the courage to fight,

چو بینند سر پنجه عقل تیز

When intellect's fingers are sharp in their sight

نبینی که شب دزد و اوباش و خس

Don't you see that the night-thief, the rake and the mean,

نگردند جائی که گردد عسس

Do not loiter about where the night-watch is seen?

رئیسی که دشمن سیاست نکرد

The chief who to punish his enemy failed,

هم از دست دشمن ریاست نکرد

Was unable to rule, for his foe's hand prevailed.

نخواهم در این نوع گفتن بسی

This subject I care not to further pursue,

که حرفی بس ار کار بندد کسی

For if one is observant, a letter will do.

◈◉◈◉◈

گفتار اندر فضیلت خاموشی
On the Excellence of Silence and the Sweetness of Self-denial

اگر پای در دامن آری چو کوه

If you draw in your feet 'neath your skirt, mountain-wise,

سرت ز آسمان بگذرد در شکوه

Past the heavens in grandeur your head will arise.

زبان درکش ای مرد بسیار دان

Oh man of great knowledge, have little to say!

که فردا قلم نیست بر بی زبان

For the dumb will be saved on the Last Judgment Day!

صدف وار گوهرشناسان راز

Those knowing the gems of God's mystery well,

دهان جز به لؤلؤ نکردند باز

Do not open their mouths, but for pearls, like the shell.

فراوان سخن باشد آکنده گوش

The garrulous man has so plugged up his ears,

نصیحت نگیرد مگر در خموش

That excepting in silence no counsel he hears.

چو خواهی که گویی نفس بر نفس

When your wish is perpetual talking, of course,

حلاوت نیابی و گفتار کس

No relish you'll get from another's discourse

نباید سخن گفت ناساخته

To make unconsidered remarks is not meet;

نشاید بریدن نینداخته

It is wrong to reply till the speech is complete!

تأمل کنان در خطا و صواب

Those reflecting on error and rectitude, rise

به از ژاژخایان حاضر جواب

Superior to prattlers, with ready replies.

کمال است در نفس انسان سخن

Since speech is a perfect attainment in man,

تو خود را به گفتار ناقص مکن

Do not make yourself faulty by talk! if you can.

کم آواز هرگز نبینی خجل

Him ashamed you won't see who has little to say;

جوی مشک بهتر که یک توده گل

Better one grain of musk than a hillock of clay.

حذر کن ز نادان ده مرده گوی

Beware of the fool with the talk of ten men!

چو دانا یکی گوی و پرورده گوی

Like a wise man speak once and effectively, then!

صد انداختی تیر و هر صد خطاست

You have shot five-score arrows and errant they flew;

اگر هوشمندی یک انداز و راست

Shoot one if you're wary and let it be true!

چرا گوید آن چیز در خفیه مرد

Why mentions a man as a secret, the tale

که گر فاش گردد شود روی زرد؟

Which if publicly uttered would make his cheeks pale?

مکن پیش دیوار غیبت بسی

Do not slander too freely in front of a wall!

بود کز پسش گوش دارد کسی

For it may be that someone behind it hears all!

درون دلت شهربند است راز

Your mind's a town wall, all your secrets around,

نگر تا نبیند در شهر باز

Take care that the door, opened wide, is not found!

از آن مرد دانا دهان دوخته ست

The sage sewed his mouth up because he assumed,

که بیند که شمع از زبان سوخته ست

That the candle by means of its tongue is consumed.

حکایت سلطان تکش و حفظ اسرار
On Keeping Secrets

تکش با غلامان یکی راز گفت

Tagash told his attendants a secret and said:

که این را نباید به کس باز گفت

Do not mention a word to a soul on this head! "

به یک سالش آمد ز دل بر دهان

It reached not the mouth from the heart for a year;

به یک روز شد منتشر در جهان

Through the world in a day it became very clear.

بفرمود جلاد را بی دریغ

Tagash, pitiless, ordered the headsman to go,

که بردار سرهای اینان به تیغ

And sever their heads with the sword, at a blow.

یکی ز آن میان گفت و زنهار خواست

Of the number, one said and protection desired:

مکش بندگان کاین گناه از تو خاست

Do not murder your slaves! for their fault you inspired.

تو اول نبستی که سرچشمه بود

You stopped it not, first, as a fountain concealed,

چو سیلاب شد پیش بستن چه سود؟

Why uselessly stem, now, the torrent revealed? "

تو پیدا مکن راز دل بر کسی

Do not show to a man what lies hid in your mind!

که او خود نگوید بر هر کسی

For he, surely, will tell it to all he can find.

جواهر به گنجینه داران سپار

Trust your gems to the keepers of treasure and pelf!

ولی راز را خویشتن پاس دار

But, take very good care of a secret yourself!

سخن تا نگویی بر او دست هست

While the word is not spoken you have it in hand;

چو گفته شود یابد او بر تو دست

When spoken, it brings you within its command.

سخن دیو بندی است در چاه دل

Is not speech a fiend, chained in the well of the mind?

به بالای کام و زبانش مهل

On the palate and tongue, do not leave it entwined!

توان باز دادن ره نره دیو

For the nude, filthy fiend you can open the way,

ولی باز نتوان گرفتن به ریو

But again, cannot seize him with hocussing play.

تو دانی که چون دیو رفت از قفس

You know when a fiend from his cage gets away,

نیاید به لا حول کس باز پس

He will never return, though " la-houl " you should say.

یکی طفل بر گیرد از رخش بند

A child may a roan-coloured charger unloose;

نیاید به صد رستم اندر کمند

Not for Rustams, five-score, will it come to the noose.

مگوی آن که گر بر ملا اوفتد

Do not mention that, which, if revealed unto all,

وجودی از آن در بلا اوفتد

Into bitter misfortune a person would fall!

به دهقان نادان چه خوش گفت زن

How well said a wife to her ignorant swain

به دانش سخن گوی یا دم مزن

With knowledge discourse! or else, silence maintain!

◈◉◈◉◈

حکایت در معنی سلامت جاهل در خاموشی
On the Impunity of the Ignorant under the Screen of Silence

یکی خوب خلق خلق پوش بود

A good-natured man who in tatters was dressed,

که در مصر یک چند خاموش بود

For a season in Egypt strict silence professed.

خردمند مردم ز نزدیک و دور

Men of wisdom from near and from far, at the sight,

به گردش چو پروانه جویان نور

Gathered round him like moths seeking after the light

تفکر شبی با دل خویش کرد

One night he communed with himse lf, in this way:

که پوشیده زیر زبان است مرد

"Beneath the tongue's surface the man hidden lay;

اگر همچنین سر به خود در برم

If I carry my head for myself, in this plan,

چه دانند مردم که دانشورم؟

How can people discover in me a wise man? "

سخن گفت و دشمن بدانست و دوست

He spoke, and his friends and his foes all could see,

که در مصر نادان تر از وی هم اوست

That the greatest of blockheads in Egypt was he!

حضورش پریشان شد و کار زشت

His admirers dispersed, and his trade lost its note;

سفر کرد و بر طاق مسجد نبشت

He journeyed, and over a mosque's arch he wrote:

در آیینه گر خویشتن دیدمی

"Could I have myself in a looking-glass seen,

به بی دانشی پرده ندریدمی

Not in ignorance would I have riven my screen.

چنین زشت از آن پرده برداشتم

So ugly, the veil from my features I drew,

که خود را نکو روی پنداشتم

For I thought that my face was most charming to view

کم آواز را باشد آوازه تیز

The fame of the man talking little is high;

چو گفتی و رونق نماندت گریز

When you talk, and your glory has fled; you, too, fly!

تو را خامشی ای خداوند هوش

Oh sensible person! in silence serene

وقار است و، نا اهل را پرده پوش

You have honour, and people unworthy, a screen.

اگر عالمی هیبت خود مبر

If you've learning, you should not your dignity lose!

وگر جاهلی پردهٔ خود مدر

If you're ignorant, tear not the curtain you use!

ضمیر دل خویش منمای زود

The thoughts of your heart do not quickly display!

که هر گه که خواهی توانی نمود

For you're able to show them whenever you may.

ولیکن چو پیدا شود راز مرد

But when once a man's secret to all is revealed,

به کوشش نشاید نهان باز کرد

By exertion it cannot again be concealed.

قلم سر سلطان چه نیکو نهفت

How well did the pen the king's secret maintain!

که تا کارد بر سر نبودش نگفت

For it said not a word till the knife reached its brain.

بهایم خموشند و گویا بشر

The beasts are all dumb and man's tongue is released;

زبان بسته بهتر که گویا به شر

A nonsensical talker is worse than a beast!

چو مردم سخن گفت باید به هوش

A speaker should talk in a sensible strain;

وگر نه شدن چون بهایم خموش

If he can't; like the brutes, he should silence maintain

به نطق است و عقل آدمی‌زاده فاش

By reason of speech Adam's children are known;

چو طوطی سخنگوی نادان مباش

Do not grow like the parrot, a prater, alone!

❖◉❖◉❖

حکایت اثرات گستاخی

Story on the effects of impertinence

یکی ناسزا گفت در وقت جنگ

A man spoke impertinent words in a fray;

گریبان دریدند وی را به چنگ

They tore with their ringers his collar away.

قفا خورده عریان و گریان نشست

Well-beaten and naked he, weeping, sat down;

جهاندیده‌ای گفتش ای خودپرست

Said a man of experience, "Oh self-loving clown!

چو غنچه گرت بسته بودی دهن

If your mouth like a rose-bud unopened had been,

دریده ندیدی چو گل پیرهن

Your shirt, rose-like, riven you would not have seen."

سراسیمه گوید سخن بر گزاف

The madman speaks words that in boasting abound;

چو طنبور بی مغز بسیار لاف

Like the drum that is empty, he makes a great sound

نبینی که آتش زبان است و بس

A burning is only a flame, don't you see!

به آبی توان کشتنش در نفس؟

That at once with some water extinguished can be.

اگر هست مرد از هنر بهره‌ور

If a person be blessed, through the merit he bears,

هنر خود بگوید نه صاحب هنر

Not the man but the merit its presence declares.

اگر مشک خالص نداری مگوی

If the musk you possess be not real, do not tell!

ورت هست خود فاش گردد به بوی

If it is, it will make itself known by the smell.

به سوگند گفتن که زر مغربی است

What need to swear gold is the purest of gold?

چه حاجت؟ محک خود بگوید که چیست

For the touch-stone will, surely, its nature unfold!

بگویند از این حرف گیران هزار

There are critics a thousand who, after this plan,

که سعدی نه اهل است و آمیزگار

Say that SddVs a worthless and reticent man.

روا باشد ار پوستینم درند

It is meet that to tear my poshteen they should strain!

که طاقت ندارم که مغزم برند

But I cannot endure them to harry my brain.

⟨◉⟩⟨◉⟩

حکایت عضد و مرغان خوش آواز
Story of King Azd and his sick son

عضد را پسر سخت رنجور بود

The son of King Azd lay afflicted in bed;

شکیب از نهاد پدر دور بود

From the mind of the father all patience had fled

یکی پارسا گفتش از روی پند

A pious man giving advice said, that he

که بگذار مرغان وحشی ز بند

Should all' the wild birds from their cages set free.

قفسهای مرغ سحر خوان شکست

He released all the warblers of sweet, morning strain;

که در بند ماند چو زندان شکست؟

When the prison is ope'd who would captive remain?

نگه داشت بر طاق بستان سرای

He preserved in the arch of the garden retreat,

یکی نامور بلبل خوش‌سرای

A wonderful Bulbul? that piped very sweet.

پسر صبحدم سوی بستان شتافت

In the morning, the son to the summer-house hied,

جز آن مرغ بر طاق ایوان نیافت

And that bird, all alone, in the cupola spied.

بخندید کای بلبل خوش نفس

He smiled, saying, "Bulbul! your notes are so choice,

تو از گفت خود مانده‌ای در قفس

In the cage you remain on account of your voice."

ندارد کسی با تو ناگفته کار

With your words while unspoken no man has to do;

ولیکن چو گفتی دلیلش بیار

When spoken, be ready to prove they are true!

چو سعدی که چندی زبان بسته بود

As Sádi for some time in silence remained,

ز طعن زبان آوران رسته بود

From the taunts of his critics he freedom obtained.

کسی گیرد آرام دل در کنار

That man to his bosom takes comfort of heart,

که از صحبت خلق گیرد کنار

Who lives from communion with people apart

مکن عیب خلق، ای خردمند، فاش

Exposing men's failings, oh wise man! avoid!

به عیب خود از خلق مشغول باش

Be with faults of your own, not of others, employed!

چو باطل سرایند مگمار گوش

When they sing out of harmony, do not give ear!

چو بی‌ستر بینی بصیرت بپوش

Shut your eyes when you see an unveiled one appear!

حکایت مرید و چنگ
Story of the scholar and the minstrel's harp

شنیدم که در بزم ترکان مست

I have heard that, in company with tipsy young folk,

مریدی دف و چنگ مطرب شکست

A scholar a minstrel's small drum and harp broke.

چو چنگش کشیدند حالی به موی

Like a harp, he was dragged by the hair through the place

غلامان و چون دف زدندش به روی

By the slaves, and was tambour-like thumped on the face.

شب از درد چوگان و سیلی نخفت

He was sleepless all night, from the pain of the blows

دگر روز پیرش به تعلیم گفت

His tutor rebuked him next day when he rose:

نخواهی که باشی چو دف روی ریش

"If you wish not to be, tambourine-like, face sore,

چو چنگ، ای برادر، سر انداز پیش

Oh brother; hold, harp-like, your face down before!

حکایت خویشتن دار

An Example

دو کس گرد دیدند و آشوب و جنگ

Two people saw dust and confusion and strife;

پراکنده نعلین و پرنده سنگ

Shoes everywhere scattered and stones flying rife.

یکی فتنه دید از طرف بر شکست

One viewed the disturbance and broke from the way;

یکی در میان آمد و سر شکست

One joined and his head became smashed in the fray.

کسی خوشتر از خویشتن دار نیست

Than the abstinent, none can more happiness share,

که با خوب و زشت کسش کار نیست

For one's good or one's evil is not his affair!

تو را دیده در سر نهادند و گوش

Your eyes and your ears to the head are consigned;

دهان جای گفتار و دل جای هوش

For speech, there's the mouth, and for reason, the mind.

مگر باز دانی نشیب از فراز

If you, haply, the downs from the ups recognize,

نگویی که این کوته است، آن دراز

Do not say this is short, or that long, in your eyes!

حکایت در فضیلت خاموشی و آفت بسیار سخنی
On the Comfort of Silence and the Misfortune of Garrulity

چنین گفت پیری پسندیده هوش

Thus spoke an old man of agreeable mind:

خوش آید سخنهای پیران به گوش

To the ear the remarks of the aged come kind

که در هند رفتم به کنجی فراز

To a corner of India I went from the throng;

چه دیدم؟ چو یلدا سیاهی دراز

What saw I? A black like a wintry night, long.

در آغوش وی دختری چون قمر

A moon-visaged maiden was in his embrace;

فرو برده دندان به لبهاش در

In her lips he had buried his teeth to their base.

چنان تنگش آورده اندر کنار

He hugged to his bosom the damsel so tight,

که پنداری اللیل یغشی النهار

You'd have said that the day was concealed by the night

مرا امر معروف دامن گرفت

My 'evident duty' took hold of my skirt;

فضول آتشی گشت و در من گرفت

His excess became fire and forthwith me begirt.

طلب کردم از پیش و پس چوب و سنگ

I searched all around for a stick or a stone,

که ای نا خدا ترس بی نام و ننگ

Saying, 'Godless, base wretch, to whom shame is unknown!

به تشنیع و دشنام و آشوب و زجر

With shouts and reproaches, with threats and abuse,

سپید از سیه فرق کردم چو فجر

The' light ' from the' dark like the dawn, I produce.

شد آن ابر ناخوش ز بالای باغ

From over the garden that demon cloud flew;

پدید آمد آن بیضه از زیر زاغ

From under the raven the egg came in view.

ز لا حولم آن دیو هیکل بجست

By my saying ' la-houla that ogre-shape fled;

پری پیکر اندر من آویخت دست

The fairy-faced maid clung to me, in his stead.

که ای زرق سجادهٔ دلق پوش

Oh canter! she said, in hypocrisy clad!

سیه‌کار دنیاخر دین‌فروش

You world-buying, faith-selling sinner, so bad!

مرا عمرها دل ز کف رفته بود

For ages, my heart has escaped from my clutch

بر این شخص و جان بر روی آشفته بود

To this man, and my soul is in love with him much.

کنون پخته شد لقمه خام من

And now that my raw morsel, cooked, by me lay,

که گرمش به در کردی از کام من

Steaming hot, from my palate you drove it away

تظلم برآورد و فریاد خواند

She complained of oppression and harshness and said:

که شفقت بر افتاد و رحمت نماند

Compassion has fallen and mercy has fled.

نماند از جوانان کسی دستگیر

Among the young men no protectors remain,

که بستاندم داد از این مرد پیر؟

Who might my revenge from this dotard obtain;

که شرمش نیاید ز پیری همی

For in his old age, shame has failed to appear,

زدن دست در ستر نامحرمی

Since he pulls off one's veil, whom he should not go near

همی کرد فریاد و دامن به چنگ

With my skirt in her grasp she her grievance proclaimed;

مرا مانده سر در گریبان ز ننگ

My head hanging down on my bosom, ashamed.

برون رفتم از جامه در دم چو سیر

From my garment, at once, like a garlic I sprung;

که ترسیدم ار جور برنا و پیر

For I dreaded the threats of the old and the young.

برهنه دوان رفتم از پیش زن

Away from the woman, quite naked, I fly —

که در دست او جامه بهتر که من

For better my skirt in her fingers, than I.

پس از مدتی کرد بر من گذار

When a time had elapsed, to my dwelling she came,

که می‌دانیم؟ گفتمش زینهار

And said, 'Do you know me?' I answered, 'For shame!

که من توبه کردم به دست تو بر

On account of your conduct repentant I've grown,

که گرد فضولی نگردم دگر

And in future will leave foolish meddling alone.'

کسی را نیاید چنین کار پیش

To no one will such an adventure appear,

که عاقل نشیند پس کار خویش

Who sits wisely at work in his own proper sphere.

از آن شنعت این پند برداشتم

On account of this baseness the lesson I glean,

دگر دیده نادیده انگاشتم

That, henceforth, what I see I shall reckon unseen."

زبان در کش ار عقل داری و هوش

Have you wisdom and reason and judgment and sense?

چو سعدی سخن گوی ور نه خموش

Like Sádi instruct, or maintain silence, hence!

◈◉◈◉◈

حکایت در خاصیت پرده پوشی و سلامت خاموشی
On the Advantage of Screening

یکی پیش داود طائی نشست

A certain one sat before David of Tai,

که دیدم فلان صوفی افتاده مست

Saying, "So and so Sufi I saw tipsy lie;

قی آلوده دستار و پیراهنش

His turban and shirt stained with vomited food,

گروهی سگان حلقه پیرامنش

A number of dogs in a ring round him stood."

چو پیر از جوان این حکایت شنید

When the good-natured man heard this tale to a close,

به آزار از او روی در هم کشید

On his face angry frowns at the speaker arose.

زمانی بر آشفت و گفت ای رفیق

He was wroth for a little and said, 'Oh my friend'!

به کار آید امروز یار شفیق

To-day a kind comrade will prove a Godsend.

برو زآن مقام شنیعش بیار

Go! and bring him away from that horrible place!

که در شرع نهی است و در خرقه عار

For by law it's forbid; to our sect, it's disgrace!

به پشتش در آور چو مردان که مست

On your back, man-like, bring him, for drunkards they say,

عنان سلامت ندارد به دست

Do not hold in their ringers the reins of the way! "

نیوشنده شد زین سخن تنگدل

These words made the hearer look wretchedly blank;

به فکرت فرو رفت چون خر به گل

Like an ass in the mire, in reflection he sank.

نه زهره که فرمان نگیرد به گوش

He could not evade the injunction he got;

نه یارا که مست اندر آرد به دوش

And he loathed to convey on his shoulders a sot.

زمانی بپیچید و درمان ندید

He writhed for a time but no remedy saw,

ره سر کشیدن ز فرمان ندید

Nor means from the order his head to withdraw.

میان بست و بی اختیارش به دوش

He got ready and carried him off, without choice,

در آورد و شهری بر او عام جوش

On his shoulders; the city roughs making a noise.

یکی طعنه می‌زد که درویش بین

One cursing them shouted, " These Dervishes heed!

زهی پارسایان پاکیزه دین

How good are their piety, chasteness and creed! "

یکی صوفیان بین که می خورده‌اند

See the wine-drinking Sufis" another one cried,

مرقع به سیکی گرو کرده‌اند

Who have pawned their patched garments for wine, fortified!"

386

اشارت کنان این و آن را به دست

People pointed their fingers as onwards they slunk,

که آن سرگران است و این نیم مست

Saying, "This one's top-heavy and that one half drunk! "

به گردن بر از جور دشمن حسام

A sword on the neck, struck by tyrannous foe,

به از شنعت شهر و جوش عوام

Is more just than town jeers and the rage of the "low."

بلا دید و روزی به محنت گذاشت

Misfortune he bore; passed a troublesome day;

به ناکام بردش به جایی که داشت

Without choice, he conveyed him to where his home lay.

شب از فکرت و نامرادی نخفت

From reflection and shame, he was sleepless that night;

دگر روز پیرش به تعلیم گفت

Next morning Tai smiling remarked, at his plight:

مریز آبروی برادر به کوی

"In the street, you should never a brother defame!

که دهرت نریزد به شهر آبروی

For Time, in the city will treat you the same! '

❖◉❖◉❖

گفتار اندر غیبت و خللهایی که از وی صادر شود

Story about evil speaking

بد اندر حق مردم نیک و بد

Regarding a man who is good or is bad,

مگوی ای جوانمرد صاحب خرد

Do not speak any evil! oh sensible lad!

که بد مرد را خصم خود می‌کنی

For you make a bad man your own foe, to begin,

وگر نیکمردست بد می‌کنی

And if he be good, you commit a great sin!

تو را هر که گوید فلان کس بدست

Whoever informs you that so and so's vile,

چنان دان که در پوستین خودست

You may safely infer is himself bad, the while.

که فعل فلان را بباید بیان

For, so and so's acts he feels bound to disclose,

وز این فعل بد می‌برآید عیان

And from this wicked action his backbiting shows.

به بد گفتن خلق چون دم زدی

When you speak ill of men, in expressing your view,

اگر راست گویی سخن هم بدی

You do wrong even if you should state what is true!

مقالات مردان ز مردی شنو

The sayings of men, through their manliness, hear!

نه از سعدی و سهروردی شنو

To Sádi or Saharward? do not give ear

مرا پیر دانای مرشد شهاب

My enlightened old tutor, Sahab, to me gave

دو اندرز فرمود بر روی آب

Two bits of advice, on the face of the wave!

یکی آنکه بر خود خودبین مباش

The first was, "Conceited of self do not be! "

دگر آنکه بر غیر بدبین مباش

The second was, "Evil in others, don't see!

داستان در حال بازگشت

Story on backbiting

زبان کرد مردی به غیبت دراز

In slandering, a man let his tongue freely go;

بدو گفت داننده‌ای سرفراز

A distinguished philosopher spoke to him, so:

که یاد کسان پیش من بد مکن

Those you mention to me, don't with vileness connect!

مرا بدگمان در حق خود مکن

Regarding yourself, do not mal'e me suspect!

گرفتم ز تمکین او کم ببود

That his dignity suffered abatement, I own;

نخواهد به جاه تو اندر فزود

Thereby, to your honour no increase is shown."

حکایت غیبت و دزدی
Story on backbiting and robbery

کسی گفت و پنداشتم طیبت است
A person remarked, and I thought it was good,

که دزدی بسامان تر از غیبت است
That better than backbiting, robbery stood.

بدو گفتم ای یار آشفته هوش
I replied, "Oh companion, with intellect crazed!

شگفت آمد این داستانم به گوش
At hearing you talk, I am greatly amazed!

به ناراستی در چه بینی بهی
What good do you see in a criminal case,

که بر غیبتش مرتبت می‌نهی؟
That you higher than backbiting give it a place? "

بلی گفت دزدان تهور کنند
Very well!" he replied, "thieves show rashness, enough;

به بازوی مردی شکم پر کنند
By the strength of their manhood their stomachs they stuff.

ز غیبت چه می‌خواهد آن ساده مرد
But not. so, the backbiting, meritless wight;

که دیوان سیه کرد و چیزی نخورد
Who blackened his book and secured no delight! "

حکایت سعدی و استادش
Story of Sádi and his tutor

مرا در نظامیه ادرار بود
I once a Nizamiah scholarship gained;

شب و روز تلقین و تکرار بود
Day and night were debates and instruction maintained.

مر استاد را گفتم ای پر خرد
To the tutor I said, "Oh thou, wise in our days!

فلان یار بر من حسد می‌برد
My friend, so and so, for me envy displays.

چو من داد معنی دهم در حدیث
When I give the true meaning of any nice text,
بر آید به هم اندرون خبیث
The heart of that wicked companion is vexed."

شنید این سخن پیشوای ادب
To this tale the promoter of learning gave heed;
به تندی برآشفت و گفت ای عجب
He grew angry and said, "What a wonder, indeed!

حسودی پسندت نیامد ز دوست
An envious friend's not approved in your sight;
که معلوم کردت که غیبت نکوست؟
I know not who taught you that sland'ring was right!

گر او راه دوزخ گرفت از خسی
If he chooses, through baseness, the pathway to hell,
از این راه دیگر تو در وی رسی
By a different road you will reach there," as well."

◈◉◈◉◈

حکایت حجاج ستمگر
Story of the tyrant Hajaj

کسی گفت حجاج خون‌خواره‌ای است
Hajaj" someone said, "is a tyrant well known;
دلش همچو سنگ سیه پاره‌ای است
His heart is as hard as a piece of black stone;

نترسد همی ز آه و فریاد خلق
Of the sighs and complaints of mankind, without dread;
خدایا تو بستان از او داد خلق
Oh God, bring the people's revenge on his head! "

جهاندیده‌ای پیر دیرینه زاد
An experienced person of very great age,
جوان را یکی پند پیرانه داد
To the youth gave a bit of advice, very sage:

کز او داد مظلوم مسکین او
They'll seek justice from him, for the poor he oppressed,
بخواهند و از دیگران کین او
And from them, for the hatred of him they expressed.

تو دست از وی و روزگارش بدار
From him and his service, withhold you your hand!

که خود زیر دستش کند روزگار
For Time will itself bring him under command.

نه بیداد از او بهره‌مند آیدم
Do not fancy that I sympathize with his ways!

نه نیز از تو غیبت پسند آیدم
Or bestow upon you, for your backbiting, praise."

به دوزخ برد مدبری را گناه
Sin bears the unfortunate person to Hell,

که پیمانه پر کرد و دیوان سیاه
Who has made his cup full and his book black, as well.

دگر کس به غیبت پیش می‌دود
Another, by backbiting, runs at his rear,

مبادا که تنها به دوزخ رود
Lest to Hell, by himself, his lone course he should steer

حکایت پارسا و کودک
Story of the holy man and the youth

شنیدم که از پارسایان یکی
I have heard that among the religious, one had

به طیبت بخندید با کودکی
In pleasantry joked with a good-looking lad

دگر پارسایان خلوت نشین
The other good men, who in solitude dwell,

به عیبش فتادند در پوستین
Discussed in his absence his shortcomings well.

به آخر نماند این حکایت نهفت
This story at length with rapidity spread;

به صاحب نظر باز گفتند و گفت
To the man who was pious they told it; he said:

مدر پرده بر یار شوریده حال
Do not rend a friend's cover, love-stricken in plight;

نه طیبت حرام است و غیبت حلال
Good humour's not wrong, nor is backbiting right!"

حکایت روزه در حال طفولیت

Story on purification before prayer

به طفلی درم رغبت روزه خاست

In my childhood, a longing to fast filled me quite;

ندانستمی چپ کدام است و راست

I could not distinguish the left from the right

یکی عابد از پارسایان کوی

An adorer among the good men of the place,

همی شستن آموختم دست و روی

Taught me all about washing the hands and the face.

که بسم الله اول به سنت بگوی

First, repeat, "In God's name? as the prophet commands!

دوم نیت آور، سوم کف بشوی

Next determine a vow! wash the palms of your hands!

پس آن گه دهن شوی و بینی سه بار

After that, wash your mouth and nose thrice, with despatch!

مناخر به انگشت کوچک بخار

The nostrils with both little fingers, then, scratch!

به سبابه دندان پیشین بمال

With the forefinger, afterwards, rub the front teeth;

که نهی است در روزه بعد از زوال

For a tooth-brush is wrong when the sun sinks beneath.

وز آن پس سه مشت آب بر روی زن

Dash a handful of water, then, thrice in your face!

ز رستنگه موی سر تا ذقن

From the hair of the head to the chin, is the place.

دگر دستها تا به مرفق بشوی

After that, wash your arms to the elbows in height

ز تسبیح و ذکر آنچه دانی بگوی

In worshipping God, all you know, then, recite!

دگر مسح سر، بعد از آن غسل پای

You should next rub your head! wash, thereafter, your feet;

همین است و ختمش به نام خدای

"In the name of the Lord" the ablution's complete.

کس از من نداند در این شیوه به

No person knows better than I the good rule;

نبینی که فرتوت شد پیر ده؟

The village old man is a doting, old fool.

بگفتند با دهخدای آنچه گفت

This remark reached the ear of the old, village lord;

فرستاد پیغامش اندر نهفت

He was angry and said, 'Oh thou sinner, abhorred!

که ای زشت کردار زیبا سخن

Of unspeakable words, first, your mouth you should scour!

نخست آنچه گویی به مردم بکن

Then, wash it of things you're forbid to devour! "

نه مسواک در روزه گفتی خطاست

It was wrong to brush teeth, you said, during a fast;

بنی آدم مرده خوردن رواست؟

Is eating dead men, then, a lawful repast?

دهن گو ز ناگفتنیها نخست

Of unspeakable words, first, your mouth you should scour

بشوی آن که از خوردنیها بشست

Then, wash it of things you're forbid to devour!

کسی را که نام آمد اندر میان

When, in talking, the name of a person you state,

به نیکوترین نام و نعتش بخوان

His name and his fame in the best way relate!

چو همواره گویی که مردم خرند

If you say, "Men are asses," whenever you can,

مبر ظن که نامت چو مردم برند

Do not think they will give you the name of a man!

چنان گوی سیرت به کوی اندرم

So speak of my character inside the street,

که گفتن توانی به روی اندرم

That the words you can state to myself, when we meet.

وگر شرمت از دیدهٔ ناظر است

If you blush when you see the inspector appear,

نه ای بیبصر، غیب دان حاضر است؟

Oh thou, sightless! is God, the Omniscient not here?

نیاید همی شرمت از خویشتن

No shame on account of yourself comes to thee;

کز او فارغ و شرم داری ز من؟

For you're careless of God and ashamed before me.

حکایت سرزنش غیبت
Story of the slanderer's reproof

طریقت شناسان ثابت قدم

Some resolute men, knowing God in their heart,

به خلوت نشستند چندی به هم

Were seated, conversing together, apart.

یکی زان میان غیبت آغاز کرد

One among them began to revile and deride;

در ذکر بیچارهای باز کرد

And in slandering a helpless one, ope'd the door wide.

کسی گفتش ای یار شوریده رنگ

Another addressed him, "Oh prejudiced friend!

تو هرگز غزا کردهای در فرنگ؟

Did you ever in war with crusaders contend? "

بگفت از پس چار دیوار خویش

He replied, " From behind the four walls that I own;

همه عمر ننهادهام پای پیش

In my lifetime, a foot to the front I've not shown."

چنین گفت درویش صادق نفس

The pure-hearted Dervish his answer thus gave:

ندیدم چنین بخت برگشته کس

"I have never beheld such an infamous knave!

که کافر ز پیکارش ایمن نشست

For while infidels sit from his warring secure,

مسلمان ز جور زبانش نرست

Musalmans must his tongue's fiery venom endure!

◈◉◈◉◈

دیوانه و غیبت
Of the madman and backbiting

چه خوش گفت دیوانهٔ مرغزی

How well did a madman of Marghaz recite

حدیثی کز او لب به دندان گزی

A truth, that should make one his under lip bite!

من ار نام مردم بزشتی برم

"If I mention in enmity any one's name

نگویم به جز غیبت مادرم

When speaking, I only my mother defame;

که دانند پروردگان خرد

For philosophers, cherishing wisdom, agree

که طاعت همان به که مادر برد

That a mother's devotion's the best that can be."

رفیقی که غایب شد ای نیک نام

Oh thou of good name should a friend pass from view,

دو چیزست از او بر رفیقان حرام

Two things all his friends are forbidden to do:

یکی آن که مالش به باطل خورند

One is, foolishly wasting his money, and then,

دوم آن که نامش به غیبت برند

Reviling his name in the presence of men.

هر آن کو برد نام مردم به عار

Whoever advances men's names with disgrace,

تو خیر خود از وی توقع مدار

On his speaking with fairness, no hope you need place.

که اندر قفای تو گوید همان

When you turn your own back, about you he relates,

که پیش تو گفت از پس مردمان

What in other men's absence, before you he states.

کسی پیش من در جهان عاقل است

In this world he, in my estimation, is wise,

که مشغول خود وز جهان غافل است

Who can mind his own business and earth's joys despise.

⟨◉⟩⟨◉⟩

گفتار اندر کسانی که غیبت ایشان روا باشد

Story on persons you may backbite

سه کس را شنیدم که غیبت رواست

Three persons, I've heard, you may justly backbite;

وز این درگذشتی چهارم خطاست

When these you've exceeded, the fourth is not right

یکی پادشاهی ملامت پسند

The first is a king, to oppression inclined,

کز او بر دل خلق بینی گزند

Through whom you see ruin on everyone's mind;

حلال است از او نقل کردن خبر

It is lawful to mention the news everywhere,

مگر خلق باشند از او بر حذر

That respecting him, people may exercise care.

دوم پرده بر بی حیایی متن

Next; a veil on a wretch, void of shame, do not weave!

که خود می‌درد پرده بر خویشتن

For with his own fingers his screen he will reave!

ز حوضش مدار ای برادر نگاه

In reviling him, brother, you sin not one whit!

که او می‌درافتد به گردن به چاه

For headlong he tumbles, down into a pit!

سوم کژ ترازوی ناراست خوی

Third; the teller of falsehoods who deals in false weight;

ز فعل بدش هرچه دانی بگوی

Whatever you know of his wrong doings, state!

❖◉❖◉❖

حکایت دزد و سیستانی

story of the robber and the grocer

شنیدم که دزدی درآمد ز دشت

A robber came out of the desert one day,

به دروازهٔ سیستان برگذشت

And passed by the gate of Sistan? on his way.

چو چیزی خرید او ز بقال کوی

From a grocer, who tended a stall in the street,

ز مأکول و طعمی که بایستش اوی

He purchased some victuals and dainties, to eat

بدزدید بقال از او نیم دانگ

The grocer purloined from him half of a " Dang";

برآورد دزد سیهکار بانگ

The thief, of dark deeds, thus commenced to harangue

خدایا تو شبرو به آتش بسوز
"Consume Thou! oh God! the night-robber, I pray!
که ره می‌زند سیستانی به روز
For the Sistani robs in the broad light of day."

❖◉❖◉❖

حکایت اندر نکوهش غمازی و مذلت غمازان
Story of the Sufi and the Slanderer

یکی گفت با صوفیی در صفا
Said a man to a Sufi, with sanctity blest,
ندانی فلانت چه گفت از قفا
You know not what someone behind you expressed?

بگفتا خموش، ای برادر، بخفت
He said, " Silence! oh brother! and sleep it away!
ندانسته بهتر که دشمن چه گفت
It is best not to know what your enemies say! '

کسانی که پیغام دشمن برند
Those people who carry the words of a foe,
ز دشمن همانا که دشمن ترند
Than enemies, truly, more enmity show.

کسی قول دشمن نیارد به دوست
The remarks of a foe, to a friend no one bears,
جز آن کس که در دشمنی یار اوست
Excepting the man who his enmity shares.

نیارست دشمن جفا گفتنم
A foe cannot speak with such harshness to me,
چنان کز شنیدن بلرزد تنم
That from hearing, my body should shivering be!

تو دشمن‌تری کآوری بر دهان
You are worse than a foe I with your lips you unfold
که دشمن چنین گفت اندر نهان
The same that the foe to you privately told! "

سخن چین کند تازه جنگ قدیم
A talebearer gives to old war a fresh life,
به خشم آورد نیکمرد سلیم
And urges a good, gentle person to strife.

397

از آن همنشین تا توانی گریز

Fly away from that comrade, while strength in you lies

که مر فتنهٔ خفته را گفت خیز

Who says unto sleeping sedition, "Arise!"

سیه چال و مرد اندر او بسته پای

A man in a pit, with his feet firmly bound,

به از فتنه از جای بردن به جای

Is better than spreading disturbance around.

میان دو تن جنگ چون آتش است

Between two, an encounter resembles a fire,

سخن‌چین بدبخت هیزم کش است

And the ill-omened tell-tale's the fuel supplier.

حکایت فریدون و وزیر و غماز
Story of Faridun's vizier

فریدون وزیری پسندیده داشت

Faridun had a praiseworthy man as vizier;

که روشن دل و دوربین دیده داشت

His mind was enlightened, his foresight was clear.

رضای حق اول نگه داشتی

First, the will of the Maker, his study he made,

دگر پاس فرمان شه داشتی

And, next, the commands of the king he obeyed.

نهد عامل سفله بر خلق رنج

A ruler debased, who racks subjects with pain,

که تدبیر ملک است و توفیر گنج

Thinks it ruling the land and the treasury's gain.

اگر جانب حق نداری نگاه

If you fix not your look towards God in each thing,

گزندت رساند هم از پادشاه

He brings you to grief at the hand of the king.

یکی رفت پیش ملک بامداد

In the morning, a person the king's presence sought,

که هر روزت آسایش و کام باد

Saying, "Peace and success, every day, be your lot!

غرض مشنو از من نصیحت پذیر

Do not listen to envy! to warning, give ear!

تو را در نهان دشمن است این وزیر

In secret your foe is your trusted vizier!

کس از خاص لشکر نمانده‌ست و عام

Among the high and the low in the army, none's known,

که سیم و زر از وی ندارد به وام

Who has not obtained from him money, on loan;

به شرطی که چون شاه گردن فراز

On condition that when the great king is no more,

بمیرد، دهند آن زر و سیم باز

All the gold and the silver, forthwith, they'll restore.

نخواهد تو را زنده این خودپرست

He, selfish, desires not to see you alive,

مبادا که نقدش نیاید به دست

Lest your living, should him of his money deprive! "

یکی سوی دستور دولت پناه

The king, at the empire-protecting vizier,

به چشم سیاست نگه کرد شاه

Gave a look, in which punishment showed very clear,

که در صورت دوستان پیش من

And said, "Like a friend, in my presence thou art!

به خاطر چرایی بد اندیش من؟

Why art thou my enemy, then, in thy heart? "

زمین پیش تختش ببوسید و گفت

The ground near the throne he saluted and spoke:

نشاید چو پرسیدی اکنون نهفت

"Since you've asked me the question, 'tis needless to cloak

چنین خواهم ای نامور پادشاه

Oh monarch, renowned! this design I've in view,

که باشند خلقت همه نیک خواه

That your subjects may all be well-wishers of you.

چو مرگت بود وعدهٔ سیم من

Since to pay back my coin on your death, they agree,

بقا بیش خواهندت از بیم من

They wish you long life, from their terror of me.

نخواهی که مردم به صدق و نیاز

Don't you wish that in prayer and sincereness, each one

سرت سبز خواهند و عمرت دراز؟

Should desire your head fresh, for your life a long run?

غنیمت شمارند مردان دعا

Men look upon prayer as a boon in their hearts;

که جوشن بود پیش تیر بلا

It is armour that shields from Calamity's darts."

پسندید از او شهریار آنچه گفت

At all he had mentioned, the king pleasure showed,

گل رویش از تازگی برشکفت

The rose of his face out of cheerfulness blowed.

ز قدر و مکانی که دستور داشت

Great Power and high rank the vizier held before;

مکانش بیفزود و قدرش فراشت

He augmented his rank and his power much more.

ندیدم ز غماز سرگشته‌تر

More perplexed than a slanderer, none have I met,

نگون طالع و بخت برگشته‌تر

More hapless, with fortune so greatly upset

ز نادانی و تیره رایی که اوست

By means of the folly and malice he shows,

خلاف افکند در میان دو دوست

Between two companions he enmity sows;

کنند این و آن خوش دگر باره دل

When the two again meet, they their friendship renew,

وی اندر میان کور بخت و خجل

And he is ashamed and abashed 'twixt the two.

میان دو کس آتش افروختن

Between two cordial friends to cause fire to arise,

نه عقل است و خود در میان سوختن

And you in betwixt them to burn, is not wise.

چو سعدی کسی ذوق خلوت چشید

Like Sádi y the man tastes retirement's delight,

که از هر که عالم زبان درکشید

Who, respecting both worlds, draws his tongue in from sight.

بگوی آنچه دانی سخن سودمند

Declare what you know, that may useful appear,

وگر هیچ کس را نیاید پسند

Though it may not fall sweet on a certain one's ear!

که فردا پشیمان برآرد خروش

For to-morrow, repentant, a cry he will raise,

که آوخ چرا حق نکردم به گوش؟

Saying: "Why was I deaf to the Truth, in my days? "

گفتار اندر پرورش زنان و ذکر صلاح و فساد ایشان
Story on the qualities of a good wife

زن خوب فرمانبر پارسا

A wife who is charming, obedient, and chaste,

کند مرد درویش را پادشا

Makes a king of the man knowing poverty's taste.

برو پنج نوبت بزن بر درت

Go! and boast by the beat of five drums at your gate,

چو یاری موافق بود در برت

That you have by your side an agreeable mate!

همه روز اگر غم خوری غم مدار

If, by day, sorrow trouble you, be not distressed!

چو شب غمگسارت بود در کنار

When, by night, a grief-soother reclines on your breast!

کرا خانه آباد و همخوابه دوست

When a man's house is thriving, his wife friendly too,

خدا را به رحمت نظر سوی اوست

Towards him is directed God's merciful view.

چو مستور باشد زن و خوبروی

When a lovely-faced woman is modest and nice,

به دیدار او در بهشت است شوی

Her husband on seeing her tastes Paradise.

کسی بر گرفت از جهان کام دل

The man in this world his heart's longing has found,

که یکدل بود با وی آرام دل

Whose wife and himself are in harmony bound.

اگر پارسا باشد و خوش سخن

If choice in her language and chaste in her ways,

نگه در نکویی و زشتی مکن

On her beauty or ugliness fix not your gaze!

زن زشت خو گر چه زیبا بود

For the heart by an amiable wife's more impressed,

کجا در درون دلش جا بود

Than by one of great personal beauty possessed;

زن خوش منش دل نشان تر که خوب

A sociable nature is hostile to strife,

که آمیزگاری ببوشد عیوب

And covers a number of faults in a wife.

ببرد از پری چهرهٔ زشت خوی

A demon-faced wife, if good-natured withal,

زن دیو سیمای خوش طبع، گوی

From a bad-tempered, pretty one bears off the ball.

چو حلوا خورد سرکه از دست شوی

She vinegar sips like liqueur from her spouse,

نه حلوا خورد سرکه اندوده روی

And eats not her sweetmeats with vinegar brows.

دلارام باشد زن نیک خواه

An agreeable wife is a joy to the heart,

ولیکن زن بد، خدایا پناه

But, oh God! from a wicked one keep me apart!

چو طوطی کلاغش بود هم نفس

As a parrot shut up with a crow shows its rage,

غنیمت شمارد خلاص از قفس

And deems it a boon to escape from the cage;

سر اندر جهان نه به آوارگی

So, to wander about on the Earth, turn your face!

وگرنه بنه دل به بیچارگی

If you do not, your heart upon helplessness place!

تهی پای رفتن به از کفش تنگ

Better bare-footed walk than in tight-shoes to roam

بلای سفر به که در خانه جنگ

Better travel's misfortune than fighting at home.

به زندان قاضی گرفتار به

In the magistrate's jail better captive to be,

که در خانه دیدن بر ابرو گره

Than a face, full of frowns, in your dwelling to see.

سفر عید باشد بر آن کدخدای

A journey is y Eed x to the head of the house,

که بانوی زشتش بود در سرای

Who has in his home a malevolent spouse.

در خرمی بر سرایی ببند

The door of delight on that mansion shut to!

که بانگ زن از وی برآید بلند

Whence issues with shrillness the voice of a shrew!

چو زن راه بازار گیرد بزن

The woman addicted to gadding, chastise!

وگرنه تو در خانه بنشین چو زن

If you don't; sit at home like a wife! I advise.

اگر زن ندارد سوی مرد گوش

If a wife disregard what her husband should say,

سراویل کحلیش در مرد پوش

In her breeches of stibial hue, him, array!

زنی را که جهل است و ناراستی

When a woman is foolish and false to your bed,

بلا بر سر خود نه زن خواستی

To misfortune, and not to a wife, you are wed.

چو در کیله یک جو امانت شکست

When a man in a measure of barley will cheat,

از انبار گندم فرو شوی دست

You may wash your hands clear of the store of his wheat.

بر آن بنده حق نیکویی خواسته است

The Lord had the good of that servant in view,

که با او دل و دست زن راست است

When he made his wife's heart and her hands to him true.

چو در روی بیگانه خندید زن

When a woman has smiled in the face of strange men,

دگر مرد گو لاف مردی مزن

Bid her husband not boast of his manhood again!

زن شوخ چون دست در قلیه کرد
When an impudent wife dips her hand in disgrace,.

برو گو بنه پنجه بر روی مرد
Go! and tell her to scratch her lord's cuckoldy face!

ز بیگانگان چشم زن کور باد
May the eyes of a wife, to all strangers be blind!

چو بیرون شد از خانه در گور باد
When she strays from her home — to the grave be consigned!

چو بینی که زن پای بر جای نیست
When you find that a wife is on fickleness bent,

ثبات از خردمندی و رای نیست
With wisdom and reasoning, rest not content!

گریز از کفش در دهان نهنگ
Fly away from her bosom! much better to face

که مردن به از زندگانی به ننگ
A crocodile's mouth, than to live in disgrace.

بپوشانش از چشم بیگانه روی
To conceal a wife's face from a stranger, you need;

وگر نشنود چه زن آنگه چه شوی
What are husband and wife, if she fails to give heed?

زن خوب خوش طبع رنج است و بار
A fine, buxom wife is a trouble and charge;

رها کن زن زشت ناسازگار
A wife who is ugly and cross, set at large!

چه نغز آمد این یک سخن زآن دو تن
How well this one saying two people expressed,

که بودند سرگشته از دست زن
Whose minds at the hands of their wives were distressed!

یکی گفت کس را زن بد مباد
One remarked, "May no man to a vixen be bound! "

دگر گفت زن در جهان خود مباد
Said the other, "On Earth may no women be found!

زن نو کن ای دوست هر نوبهار
Oh friend! take a bride evry spring that ensues!

که تقویم پاری نیاید بکار
For a past season's almanac no one will use.

زنان شوخ و فرمانده و سرکشند

Some wives are tyrannical, head-strong and bold,

ولیکن شنیدم که در بر خوشند

But are pleased when they share your embrace, I am told.

کسی را که بینی گرفتار زن

Oh Sádi, go to I do not jeer at his life!

مکن سعدیا طعنه بر وی مزن

When you see that a man is henpecked by his wife.

تو هم جور بینی و بارش کشی

You, too, are oppressed and her load you abide,

اگر یک سحر در کنارش کشی

If once you invite her to come to your side!

◈◉◈◈◉◈

حکایت زن و شوهر
Story of the Husband and Wife

جوانی ز ناسازگاری جفت

A youth on account of the shrew he had wed,

بر پیرمردی بنالید و گفت

In an aged man's presence lamented and said:

گران باری از دست این خصم چیر

"A load at the hand of this impudent foe

چنان می‌برم کآسیا سنگ زیر

I bear, like the mill-stone fixed, helpless, below."

به سختی بنه گفتش، ای خواجه، دل

Put up with her harshness, oh sir I "he replied;

کس از صبر کردن نگردد خجل

No man is ashamed if his patience be tried!

به شب سنگ بالایی ای خانه سوز

Oh scapegrace! at night you as upper stone sway,

چرا سنگ زیرین نباشی به روز؟

Why not serve as the under one, during the day?

چو از گلبنی دیده باشی خوشی

When you've culled from a rose-bush of pleasure a deal,

روا باشد ار بار خارش کشی

It is right that the pain of its thorns you should feel.

درختی که پیوسته بارش خوری

When you're always partaking of fruit from a tree;

تحمل کن آنگه که خارش خوری

When you taste of the prickles, long-suffering be!"

⟨◉⟩⟨◉⟩

گفتار اندر پروردن فرزندان
On the Instruction of Children

پسر چون ز ده برگذشتش سنین

Bid a boy, when ten years shall have passed o'er his head,

ز نامحرمان گو فراتر نشین

Live apart from the maids he may lawfully wed!

بر پنبه آتش نشاید فروخت

It is improper, a fire upon cotton to light,

که تا چشم بر هم زنی خانه سوخت

For the house, in a twink, is consumed in its might.

چو خواهی که نامت بماند به جای

When you wish that your name may be permanent here,

پسر را خردمندی آموز و رای

In knowledge and wisdom, your son you should rear!

که گر عقل و طبعش نباشد بسی

For should he be wanting in wisdom and mind,

بمیری و از تو نماند کسی

You die, and you leave no relation behind!

بسا روزگارا که سختی برد

The son often suffers a deal of mishap,

پسر چون پدر نازکش پرورد

When reared by the father in luxury's lap.

خردمند و پرهیزگارش بر آر

As a prudent and abstinent person, him, train!

گرش دوست داری به نازش مدار

And from petting him much, if you love him, refrain!

به خردی درش زجر و تعلیم کن

Chastise and instruct him, while still he's a lad;

به نیک و بدش وعده و بیم کن

Use favours and threats, in his good and his bad!

نوآموز را ذکر و تحسین و زه

For a learner, much better commending and praise,

ز توبیخ و تهدید استاد به

Than the threats and reproaches a tutor displays!

بیاموز پرورده را دسترنج

Teach the son you have nurtured to work with his hand!

وگر دست داری چو قارون به گنج

Even should you a treasure, like Korah's, command!

مکن تکیه بر دستگاهی که هست

In the wealth you possess you ought not to confide!

که باشد که نعمت نماند به دست

For the wealth you may have may not with you abide.

به پایان رسد کیسهٔ سیم و زر

A purse, full of money, may empty become;

نگردد تهی کیسهٔ پیشه ور

The purse of the artisan always shows some.

چه دانی که گردیدن روزگار

And how do you know that the changes of time,

به غربت بگرداندش در دیار

May not force him to wander in many a clime?

چو بر پیشهای باشدش دسترس

If a useful profession he has at command,

کجا دست حاجت برد پیش کس؟

When to men will he stretch a necessitous hand?

ندانی که سعدی مراد از چه یافت؟

You know not how Sádi obtained high degree?

نه هامون نوشت و نه دریا شکافت

He crossed not the desert, he ploughed not the sea;

به خردی بخورد از بزرگان قفا

When young, he had cuffs from his elders to brave;

خدا دادش اندر بزرگی صفا

When older the Lord to him piety gave!

هر آن کس که گردن به فرمان نهد

Whoever his neck in obedience will place,

بسی بر نیاید که فرمان دهد

Will himself give command, in a very short space.

هر آن طفل کاو جور آموزگار

The stripling who feels not the teacher's rebuff,

نبیند، جفا بیند از روزگار

Will endure at Time's hand bitter hardships enough.

پسر را نکو دار و راحت رسان

Your son, then, in goodness and comfort maintain!

که چشمش نماند به دست کسان

That in others, his hope may not have to remain.

هر آن کس که فرزند را غم نخورد

In rearing your son, if no trouble you take,

دگر کس غمش خورد و بدنام کرد

Someone else takes the trouble and makes him a rake.

نگه‌دار از آمیزگار بدش

From a wicked companion, protect him with care!

که بدبخت و بی ره کند چون خودش

For his vice and bad fortune he with him will share.

حکایت جشن و طرب
Story of a convivial party

شبی دعوتی بود در کوی من

In my quarter one night an invitement was made;

ز هر جنس مردم در او انجمن

Men assembled of every description and shade.

چو آواز مطرب در آمد ز کوی

When the voice of the minstrel arose from the street,

به گردون شد از عاشقان های و هوی

With shouts of approval the sky was replete.

پری‌چهره‌ای بود محبوب من

To a fairy-faced maiden — a sweetheart of mine

بدو گفتم ای لعبت خوب من

I said, "Oh my beautiful idol, divine!

چرا با رفیقان نیایی به جمع

Why do you not join the young men here to-night,

که روشن کنی بزم ما را چو شمع؟

And, candle-like, give to our gathering light? "

شنیدم سهی قامت سیم‌تن

I heard the erect, silver-bodied one say

که می‌رفت و می‌گفت با خویشتن

In sweet tones to herself, as she glided away:

محاسن چو مردان ندارم به دست

"I'm not graced, like a man, with a beard and moustache,

نه مردی بود پیش مردان نشست

So, for me to carouse with young men would be rash."

سیه نامه تر زآن مخنث مخواه

Do not wish him more vile than the "paederast" base,

که پیش از خطش روی گردد سیاه

Who is infamous ere the down shows on his face!

از آن بی حمیت بباید گریخت

Away from that wretch, it behoves one to haste,

که نامردیش آب مردان بریخت

Whose poltrpon'ry has man's reputation effaced.

پسر کاو میان قلندر نشست

If a son has in comp'ny with vagabonds been,

پدر گو ز خیرش فرو شوی دست

Of his welfare, the father may wash his hands clean!

دریغش مخور بر هلاک و تلف

At his ruin and death, from lamenting refrain!

که پیش از پدر مرده به ناخلف

Better die! Yore his father, than wicked remain!

گفتار اندر پرهیز کردن از صحبت احداث

Remarks on avoiding improper attachments

خرابت کند شاهد خانه کن

A beautiful mistress will ruin your life;

برو خانه آباد گردان به زن

Go and make your home thriving by wedding a wife!

نشاید هوس باختن با گلی

It's improper to squander your love on a rose

که هر بامدادش بود بلبلی

To whom, every morning, a nightingale goes.

چو خود را به هر مجلسی شمع کرد

Since, candle-like, every assembly she lit,

تو دیگر چو پروانه گردش مگرد

Do not you, like a moth, round her flame further flit!

زن خوب خوش خوی آراسته

Does the beautiful, affable woman adorned,

چه ماند به نادان نو خاسته؟

Resemble the ignorant youth who is scorned?

در او دم چو غنچه دمی از وفا

As a rosebud, fidelity breathe in her ear!

که از خنده افتد چو گل در قفا

And rose-like, all smiles, she will fall at your rear.

نه چون کودک پیچ بر پیچ شنگ

But not so the stripling, wrapped up in his pride

که چون مقل نتوان شکستن به سنگ

Who resembles hard fruit that a stone can't divide.

مبین دلفریبش چو حور بهشت

As a virgin of Paradise, view not his charms!

کز آن روی دیگر چو غول است زشت

He, too, has an aspect that ghoul-like alarms!

گرش پای بوسی نداردت پاس

If you kiss both his feet, he no care for you shows;

ورش خاک باشی نداند سپاس

If you kiss, too, his dust, he no thankfulness knows.

سر از مغز و دست از درم کن تهی

With your brains and your money you foolishly part,

چو خاطر به فرزند مردم نهی

When to any man's child you surrender your heart.

مکن بد به فرزند مردم نگاه

On another man's son, a bad look do not cast!

که فرزند خویشت برآید تباه

For your own may return to you ruined, at last.

◦ ◉ ◦ ◉ ◦

حکایت بازرگان و غلام
Story of the Merchant and his Slave

در این شهر باری به سمعم رسید
In this city, one time, to my hearing it got

که بازرگانی غلامی خرید
That a slave by an opulent merchant was bought

شبانگه مگر دست بردش به سیب
Perhaps, in the night, with the slave he made free;

بر درکشیدش به ناز و عتیب
For silvery chinned and heart-charming was he.

پریچهره هرچ اوفتادش به دست
Whatsoever the fairy-cheeked youth could obtain,

ز رخت و اوانیش در سر شکست
He broke, in revenge, on the fool's face and brain.

نه هر جا که بینی خطی دل فریب
Not always on seeing a heart-charming line,

توانی طمع کردنش در کتیب
Can your longing secure it for that book of thine.

گواکرد بر خود خدای و رسول
He called God and the prophet, as witnesses true,

که دیگر نگردم به گرد فضول
Saying, " Never again will I folly pursue."

رحیل آمدش هم در آن هفته پیش
Face wounded, head bandaged and broken in heart,

دل افگار و سر بسته و روی ریش
He was forced the same week on a journey to start.

چو بیرون شد از کازرون یک دو میل
When two or three miles out of Gazar he rode,

به پیش آمدش سنگلاخی مهیل
A wild, rocky mountain in front of him showed.

بپرسید کاین قله را نام چیست؟
He inquired, "What's the name of this hill, rising high,

که بسیار بیند عجب هر که زیست
That appears so prodigious to eVry one's eye? "

کسی گفتش این راه را وین مقام
Thus, answered a friend in his own caravan:

بجز تنگ ترکان ندانیم نام
Perhaps, you don't know of the Tangi Turkan?

سیه را یکی بانگ برداشت سخت

At his servant the man gave a bellow severe,

هم این جا که هستی بینداز رخت

Saying, " Wherefore proceed? let us pitch our tents here!

نه عقل است و نه معرفت یک جوم

Of wisdom and knowledge I'd not have a grain,

اگر من دگر تنگ ترکان روم

If the rage of the Turk I encountered again! "

در شهوت نفس کافر ببند

Shut the door of the passion of lust, so ingrate!

وگر عاشق لت خور و سر ببند

If a lover, bear kicks and then bandage your pate!

چو مر بندهای را همی پروری

When you make it your duty a slave boy to train,

به هیبت بر آرش کز او برخوری

Be strict! so that fruit from his work you may gain.

وگر سیدش لب به دندان گزد

If the master should fasten his teeth in his lips,

دماغ خداوندگاری بزد

The desire of becoming the master, he sips.

غلام آبکش باید و خشت زن

Make a slave carry water and work among bricks!

بود بندهٔ نازنین مشت زن

A slave who is pampered learns pugilists' tricks.

گروهی نشینند با خوش پسر

Some admirers are seated around a fair lad,

که ما پاکبازیم و صاحب نظر

Saying, "Saintly are we and in holiness clad."

ز من پرس فرسودهٔ روزگار

Ask me! — from the wearing of time in decay —

که بر سفره حسرت خورد روزهدار

For a "faster" regrets, when he sees the stored tray.

از آن تخم خرما خورد گوسپند

The goat, with the date-stones his appetite sates,

که قفل است بر تنگ خرما و بند

For a lock and a chain guard the sack, full of dates.

سر گاو عصار از آن در که است

The oil-presser's ox, upon straw has to feed,

که از کنجدش ریسمان کوته است

For a tether prevents him from touching the seed.

◈◉◈◉◈

گفتار اندر سلامت گوشه‌نشینی و صبر بر ایذاء خلق

On the Ill-natured Remarks of Worldly People

اگر در جهان از جهان رسته‌ای است،

If on Earth to escape from the world one's allowed,

در از خلق بر خویشتن بسته‌ای است

It is he who has fastened his door on the crowd.

کس از دست جور زبانها نرست

From the tyrannous hand of the times, none is free,

اگر خودنمای است وگر حق پرست

Whether boaster or servant of God he may be.

اگر برپری چون ملک ز آسمان

If you come from the sky, like an angel, on wings,

به دامن در آویزدت بدگمان

To the skirt of your garment your enemy clings.

به کوشش توان دجله را پیش بست

You can stem by exertion the Tigris' swift flow,

نشاید زبان بداندیش بست

But you cannot make silent the tongue of a foe.

فرا هم نشینند تردامنان

Vile profligates seated together declare:

که این زهد خشک است و آن دام نان

"This devotion is dry, that a bread-getting snare! "

تو روی از پرستیدن حق مپیچ

From God's holy worship avert not your face!

بهل تا نگیرند خلقت به هیچ

Let the people alone! lest they count you as base.

چو راضی شد از بنده یزدان پاک

When the pure holy God with His servant is pleased,

گر اینها نگردند راضی چه باک؟

What matter though men should remain unappeased?

بد اندیش خلق از حق آگاه نیست

No knowledge of God has the people's vile foe;

ز غوغای خلقش به حق راه نیست

From the din of the world he God's path cannot know.

از آن ره به جایی نیاورده‌اند

For this reason those reached not the goal they essayed,

که اول قدم بی غلط کرده‌اند

That the first step they travelled, a false step they made!

دو کس بر حدیثی گمارند گوش

To the words of the Prophet two persons give ear;

از این تا بدان، ز اهرمن تا سروش

They as diff rent as angels from devils appear;

یکی پند گیرد دگر ناپسند

One accepts the advice and the other declines;

نپردازد از حرف‌گیری به پند

He heeds not the text, from decrying the lines.

فرو مانده در کنج تاریک جای

Dejected and in a dark corner shut up,

چه دریابد از جام گیتی نمای؟

What can he obtain from the world-seeing cup?

مپندار اگر شیر و گر روبهی

And were you a tiger or fox, don't suppose,

کز اینان به مردی و حیلت رهی

That by courage or tricks you'd escape from these foes!

اگر کنج خلوت گزیند کسی

If a person the nook of retirement should choose —

که پروای صحبت ندارد بسی

Because with small favour he company views —

مذمت کنندش که زرق است و ریو

They defame him and call it mere canting and lies;

ز مردم چنان می گریزد که دیو

That from people, as if from the Devil, he flies.

وگر خنده روی است و آمیزگار

And if he be friendly and jovial-faced

عفیفش ندانند و پرهیزگار

They do not consider him template and chaste

غنی را به غیبت بکاوند پوست

The skin of the rich they by backbiting flay;

که فرعون اگر هست در عالم اوست

If a Pharaoh's on Earth, "This is he! " they will say.

وگر بینوایی بگرید به سوز

If an indigent man is in poverty stuck,

نگون بخت خوانندش و تیره‌روز

They say it's from sinning and badness of luck.

وگر کامرانی در آید ز پای

If a prosperous man tumbles down from his place,

غنیمت شمارند و فضل خدای

A boon they account it and God's proving grace:

که تا چند از این جاه و گردن کشی؟

By this grandeur how long will he stretch his neck out?

خوشی را بود در قفا ناخوشی

After pleasure, the torture of pain comes, no doubt! "

و گر تنگدستی تنک مایه‌ای

And should a distressed one, without stock in hand,

سعادت بلندش کند پایه‌ای

Be raised up by Fortune to wealth and command,

بخایندش از کینه دندان به زهر

Their poisonous teeth they snap at him from rage,

که دون پرور است این فرومایه دهر

Saying, "Cherish but wretches does this sordid age! "

چو بینند کاری به دستت در است

When they see that affairs in your hands are all right,

حریصت شمارند و دنیا پرست

You are greedy and worship the world, in their sight

وگر دست همت بداری ز کار

If from active employment your hand you withhold

گدا پیشه خوانندت و پخته خوار

They call you a beggar and parasite bold.

اگر ناطقی طبل پر یاوه‌ای

If you talk, you're a drum, full of whimsical din;

وگر خامشی نقش گرماوه‌ای

And if mute, you're to portraits on bath walls akin.

تحمل کنان را نخوانند مرد

They don't call him a man who some patience displays;

که بیچاره از بیم سر برنکرد

Saying, "Wretched! from terror his head he can't raise! "

وگر در سرش هول و مردانگی است

If manliness' awe in his head should appear,

گریزند از او کاین چه دیوانگی است؟

They fly from him, saying, "What madness is here? "

تعنت کنندش گر اندک خوری است

If he sparingly eats, they malign him, and say:

که مالش مگر روزی دیگری است

"His income, perhaps, is another man's pay."

وگر نغز و پاکیزه باشد خورش

And if he has good and luxurious fare,

شکم بنده خوانند و تن پرورش

They say he's a glutton, whose body's his care!

وگر بی تکلف زید مالدار

If a man who is rich does not cultivate style —

که زینت بر اهل تمیز است عار

Self-adornment in men of discretion is vile —

زبان در نهندش به ایذا چو تیغ

With their tongues, like a sword, to his damage, they whack,

که بدبخت زر دارد از خود دریغ

Saying, "Luckless! his gold from himself he keeps back."

وگر کاخ و ایوان منقش کند

And should he adorn his apartments and halls,

تن خویش را کسوتی خوش کند

And wrap himself up in magnificent shawls,

به جان آید از طعنه بر روی زنان

He is worried to death, on account of their taunts,

که خود را بیاراست همچون زنان

Saying, "Decked in the raiment of women he flaunts! "

اگر پارسایی سیاحت نکرد

If a pious man has not a journey essayed,

سفر کردگانش نخوانند مرد

Those say, "He's no man! "who have pilgrimage made.

که نارفته بیرون ز آغوش زن

He has never," they say, "left his sweetheart's embrace;

کدامش هنر باشد و رای و فن؟

Where for merit and wisdom and skill has he place? "

جهاندیده را هم بدرند پوست

They tear the man's skin who has many climes seen,

که سرگشتهٔ بخت برگشته اوست

Saying, "Wretched and luckless this person has been!

گرش حظ از اقبال بودی و بهر

Had his lines in prosperity's shadow been cast,

زمانه نراندی ز شهرش به شهر

Him, from city to city, the Fates had not passed! "

عزب را نکوهش کند خرده بین

The caviller slanders the bachelor swain,

که می‌رنجد از خفت و خیزش زمین

Saying, "Earth at his sleeping and waking's in pain."

وگر زن کند گوید از دست دل

If he marry, he says, "From the heart's strong desire,

به گردن در افتاد چون خر به گل

He headlong falls down, like an ass, in the mire."

نه از جور مردم رهد زشت روی

The ugly from tyrannous man cannot go,

نه شاهد ز نامردم زشت گوی

Nor the fair from the cowardly, filthy-tongued foe.

حکایت سرگذشت
Of the slave boy and his remarks

غلامی به مصر اندرم بنده بود

In Egypt a little slave boy I possessed,

که چشم از حیا در بر افکنده بود

Whose eyes, out of shame, were cast down on his breast.

کسی گفت: «هیچ این پسر عقل و هوش

Someone said, "Void of wisdom and sense he appears,

ندارد، بمالش به تعلیم گوش

You should give him instruction, by boxing his ears!

شبی بر زدم بانگ بر وی درشت

In accents severe, I one night at him cried;

هم او گفت: «مسکین به جورش بکشت

The poor fellow, killed by my harshness, replied:

گرت برکند خشم روزی ز جای

"If anger should cast you from station, one day!

سراسیمه خوانندت و تیره رای

You are crazed and demented, the people will say.

وگر بردباری کنی از کسی

And if from a person oppression you bear,

بگویند غیرت ندارد بسی

A high sense of honour you lack, they'll declare."

سخی را به اندرز گویند: «بس

They, advising a liberal man, say, "Give o'er!

که فردا دو دستت بود پیش و پس

Or, to-morrow, you'll stretch out your hands, hind and fore."

وگر قانع و خویشتن‌دار گشت

If content and denying of self you have grown,

به تشنیع خلقی گرفتار گشت

'Midst the taunts of the people, a captive you're thrown.

که همچون پدر خواهد این سفله مرد

For they'll say, " Like his father, the wretch will depart;

که نعمت رها کرد و حسرت ببرد

He abandoned the world and regret filled his heart."

که یارد به کنج سلامت نشست؟

In the corner of peace, who is able to sit,

که پیغمبر از خبث ایشان نرست

Since the prophet from villainous hands had to flit?

خدا را که ماند و انباز و جفت

Have you heard what the Christian believer did state

ندارد، شنیدی که ترسا چه گفت؟

o God — without equal and partner and mate?

رهایی نیابد کس از دست کس

"From the hands of his fellows, no man gets away,

گرفتار را چاره صبر است و بس

And patience alone is the prisoner's stay."

◈◉◈◉◈

حکایت عیبجو
Story on fault-finding

جوانی هنرمند فرزانه بود
There lived an accomplished, intelligent youth;

که در وعظ چالاک و مردانه بود
A skillful and manly expounder of Truth

نکونام و صاحبدل و حق پرست
God worshipping, pious and good among men;

خط عارضش خوشتر از خط دست
His cheek lines more choice than the lines from his pen.

قوی در بلاغات و در نحو چست
In rhetoric strong and in argument bright;

ولی حرف ابجد نگفتی درست
He pronounced not his Alphabet letters aright

یکی را بگفتم ز صاحبدلان
To one of the pious the view I expressed,

که دندان پیشین ندارد فلان
That such a one none of his front teeth possessed.

برآمد ز سودای من سرخ روی
In a rage at my boldness, his face became red;

کز این جنس بیهوده دیگر مگوی
Again do not utter such nonsense! "he said;

تو در وی همان عیب دیدی که هست
The one single fault in his speech you descry,

ز چندان هنر چشم عقلت ببست
To his numerous merits, you close wisdom's eye."

یقین بشنو از من که روز یقین
From me hear the truth! that upon the Last Day,

نبینند بد، مردم نیک بین
The man sees no ill who has looked the right way!

یکی را که فضل است و فرهنگ و رای
If a man be instructed, far-seeing and wise,

گرش پای عصمت بخیزد ز جای
And his virtuous feet from their place should arise,

به یک خرده مپسند بر وی جفا
For his one little fault, to oppression don't lean!

بزرگان چه گفتند؟ خذ ما صفا
What have the wise spoken? "Accept what is clean"

بود خار و گل با هم ای هوشمند
The thorn and the rose grow together, oh sage!
چه در بند خاری؟ تو گل دسته بند
Why cling to the thorns? With a nosegay engage!

که را زشت خویی بود در سرشت
The man in whose nature ill-will has its seat,
نبیند ز طاووس جز پای زشت
In the. peacock, sees only his big, ugly feet.

صفایی به دست آور ای خیره روی
Oh, thou void of discretion! make pureness thine own!
که ننماید آیینهٔ تیره، روی
For a mirror reflects not that dirty has grown.

طریقی طلب کز عقوبت رهی
To escape future punishment, seek for a way!
نه حرفی که انگشت بر روی نهی
Not a letter, on which you your finger may lay!

منه عیب خلق ای خردمند پیش
Oh wretch! do not faults of the people expose!
که چشمت فرو دوزد از عیب خویش
If you do; your own eyes to your faults it will close.

چرا دامن آلوده را حد زنم
Why should I reprove one whose skirt may be vile,
چو در خود شناسم که تردامنم؟
When by falsely construing, you back your own vice!

نشاید که بر کس درشتی کنی
With harshness to treat any man, is not nice,
چو خود را به تأویل پشتی کنی
When by falsely construing, you back your own vice!

چو بد ناپسند آیدت خود مکن
Since you deprecate evil, from evil, abstain!
پس آنگه به همسایه گو بد مکن
Bid your neighbour, thereafter, from evil refrain!

من ار حق شناسم وگر خود نمای
If I recognize truth, or if cant is my role!
برون با تو دارم، درون با خدای
My outside's with you and with God is my soul

چو ظاهر به عفت بیاراستم

Since in Chastity neatly adorned I appear,

تصرف مکن در کژ و راستم

With my error or rectitude don't interfere!

اگر سیرتم خوب و گر منکر است

If I'm good or I'm bad you must silence maintain!

خدایم به سر از تو داناتر است

For I'm bearer myself of my loss and my gain!

تو خاموش اگر من بهم یا بدم

If my nature be pure or depraved through and through,

که حمال سود و زیان خودم

God knows all my secrets much better than you.

کسی را به کردار بد کن عذاب

I expect no reward for my virtues from thee,

که چشم از تو دارد به نیکی ثواب

That for sinning such torture from you I should see.

نکوکاری از مردم نیک رای

For a good done by one of the pure-minded men,

یکی را به ده می‌نویسد خدای

The Lord in His kindness accredits him ten!

تو نیز ای عجب هر که را یک هنر

Oh strange! to ten faults in a person be blind,

ببینی، ز ده عیبش اندر گذر

In whom you should happen one virtue to find!

نه یک عیب او را بر انگشت پیچ

Do not twist round your finger his one little blot!

جهانی فضیلت بر آور به هیچ

And bring his unlimited merits to nought!

چو دشمن که در شعر سعدی، نگاه

When a foe upon Sádi's poetical lines,

به نفرت کند ز اندرون تباه

Looks with hate and a heart full of evil designs;

ندارد به صد نکتهٔ نغز گوش

To a hundred rare sayings he does not give ear,

چو زحفی ببیند بر آرد خروش

And on finding one fault, does not scruple to jeer.

جز این علتش نیست کان بد پسند

He has no higher object, for envy has torn

حسد دیده نیک بینش بکند

The just-seeing eyes from that object of scorn!

نه مر خلق را صنع باری سرشت؟

Has God not created his creatures with care?

سیاه و سپید آمد و خوب و زشت

There are ugly and handsome and coloured and fair!

نه هر چشم و ابرو که بینی نکوست

Not comely's each eyebrow and eye you perceive;

بخور پسته مغز و بینداز پوست

Eat pistachio kernels! the shells you can leave!

❖◉❖◉❖

8

(CHAPTER VIII.)

 در شکر بر عافیت

ON THANKS

سرآغاز
In begin

نفس می‌نیارم زد از شکر دوست
I cannot find words to give thanks to the Friend!
که شکری ندانم که در خورد اوست
For to suitably thank Him, I do not pretend.

عطایی است هر موی از او بر تنم
Every hair on my body's a gift from Him, free;
چگونه به هر موی شکری کنم؟
How can I give thanks for each hair that may be?

ستایش خداوند بخشنده را
All praise to the bountiful Maker, I sing!
که موجود کرد از عدم بنده را
Who caused, out of nothing, His servant to spring!

که را قوت وصف احسان اوست؟
Who with power to praise His great kindness is graced?
که اوصاف مستغرق شأن اوست
For His praises are all in His splendour embraced!

بدیعی که شخص آفریند ز گل
The Creator who fashioned from clay all mankind,
روان و خرد بخشد و هوش و دل
Gives spirit and wisdom and reason and mind;

ز پشت پدر تا به پایان شیب
From the loins of your father as far as the grave,
نگر تا چه تشریف دادت ز غیب
See what presents He from the Unseen to you gave!

چو پاک آفریدت بهُش باش و پاک
Since clean He created you, wise and pure stay!
که ننگ است ناپاک رفتن به خاک
For a shame it would be to return foul to clay!

پیاپی بیفشان از آیینه گرد
Incessantly wipe from a mirror the dust;
که مصقل نگیرد چو زنگار خورد
For it takes not a polish when eaten by rust!

نه در ابتدا بودی آب منی؟
Were you not liquid semen when first you began?
اگر مردی از سر به در کن منی
From your head cast conceit, if you claim to be man!

چو روزی به سعی آوری سوی خویش

When you earn by your labour your daily supply,

مکن تکیه بر زور بازوی خویش

On the strength of your arm do not, therefore, rely!

چرا حق نمی‌بینی ای خودپرست

The Lord, oh self-server! why do you not see?

که بازو به گردش درآورد و دست؟

Who can bring into motion your hand, except He?

چو آید به کوشیدنت خیر پیش

When good by your energy comes into view,

به توفیق حق دان نه از سعی خویش

To the favour of God, not your efforts, 'tis due.

به سرپنجگی کس نبرده‌ست گوی

No person has carried the ball off by force;

سپاس خداوند توفیق گوی

Give thanks unto God! of all favour the source.

تو قائم به خود نیستی یک قدم

On foot, you are Powerless to stand up alone;

ز غیبت مدد می‌رسد دم به دم

Invisible aid every moment is shown.

نه طفل زبان بسته بودی ز لاف؟

Was your tongue not from speaking in infancy tied?

همی روزی آمد به جوفش ز ناف

Through the navel your inside with.food was supplied;

چو نافش بریدند و روزی گسست

When they stopped the supply and divided the string,

به پستان مادر در آویخت دست

To the breast of the mother your hand had to cling

غریبی که رنج آردش دهر پیش

To a stranger afflicted with sickness by time,

به دارو دهند آبش از شهر خویش

They give water to cure from his own native clime.

پس او در شکم پرورش یافته‌ست

Hence the babe in the belly got nourishment good,

ز انبوب معده خورش یافته‌ست

And obtained, through the tube of the stomach, his food.

دو پستان که امروز دلخواه اوست

The mother's two breasts which to-day he adores,

دو چشمه هم از پرورشگاه اوست

Are likewise two fountains from God's endless stores.

کنار و بر مادر دلپذیر

A Heav'n are a good mother's bosom and lap;

بهشت است و پستان در او جوی شیر

In the bosom a. fountain of milk is the pap.

درختی است بالای جان پرورش

Her life-rearing stature resembles a tree.

ولد میوه نازنین بر برش

And the son a choice fruit on her breast, you can see

نه رگهای پستان درون دل است؟

Do the veins of the nipples not reach to the heart?

پس ار بنگری شیر خون دل است

Of the heart's blood, observe how the milk is a part!

به خونش فرو برده دندان چو نیش

His teeth in her blood, like a lancet, he sunk;

سرشته در او مهر خونخوار خویش

Him, the Lord made her love, who her life's blood had drunk.

چو بازو قوی کرد و دندان ستبر

When his arm becomes strong and his teeth stout appear,

براندایدش دایه پستان به صبر

On her nipples the nurse bitter aloes must smear.

چنان صبرش از شیر خامش کند

To this aloes and milk he is so disinclined,

که پستان شیرین فرامش کند

That desire for the sweet nipple fades from his mind.

تو نیز ای که در توبه‌ای طفل راه

Oh you, too, a penitent child of the way!

به صبرت فراموش گردد گناه

By Patience your sins in oblivion you lay.

❁◉❁◉❁

حکایت مادر و فرزندش
Story of the mother and her son

جوانی سر از رای مادر بتافت
A youth from his mother's wise counsels had turned;
دل دردمندش به آذر بتافت
Her sorrowing heart, like the demon-fire, burned.

چو بیچاره شد پیشش آورد مهد
In despair,, she his cradle in front of him brought;
که ای سست مهر فراموش عهد
Saying, " Oh weak of love, who have compacts forgot!

نه گریان و درمانده بودی و خرد
Were you, one time, not weeping and helpless and small;
که شبها ز دست تو خوابم نبرد؟
And for nights, at your hands I had no sleep at all?

نه در مهد نیروی حالت نبود
Did you have in the cradle the strength you have now?
مگس راندن از خود مجالت نبود؟
You could not repel a weak fly from your brow!

تو آنی کز آن یک مگس رنجهای
Are you not the same, whom a fly troubled then,
که امروز سالار و سرپنجهای
Who to-day are a powerful leader of men?

به حالی شوی باز در قعر گور
Again, yours will be such a state 'neath the clay,
که نتوانی از خویشتن دفع مور
That you can't from yourself drive the ant swarms away.

دگر دیده چون برفروزد چراغ
Will your eyes ever kindle their lustre again,
چو کرم لحد خورد پیه دماغ؟
When the worms of the tomb eat the pith of your brain? "

چو پوشیده چشمی ببینی که راه
Don't you see that a man who is blind of both eyes,
نداند همی وقت رفتن ز چاه
When he walks, can't the pit from the road recognize!

تو گر شکر کردی که با دیدهای
If God you have thanked for your eyes, it is right!
وگر نه تو هم چشم پوشیدهای
If you have not, your eyes also see not the light!

معلم نیاموختت فهم و رای

Neither reason nor sense did your tutor impart;

سرشت این صفت در نهادت خدای

The Maker created these gifts in your heart.

گرت منع کردی دل حق نیوش

If a truth-hearing mind God had kept back from you,

حقت عین باطل نبودی به گوش

As downright absurd, you'd have heard what was true!

❖◉❖◉❖

گفتار اندر صنع باری عز اسمه در ترکیب خلقت انسان
On Praising God for the Creation of Mankind

ببین تا یک انگشت از چند بند

To the number of joints in finger, give thought!

به صنع الهی به هم در فگند

Which with Euclid's precision together He brought.

پس آشفتگی باشد و ابلهی

It would therefore be folly and madness in one,

که انگشت بر حرف صنعش نهی

A finger to place on a work He has done.

تأمل کن از بهر رفتار مرد

On the gait of a man, let your thoughts be profound!

که چند استخوان پی زد و وصل کرد

How together some bones He has jointed and bound!

که بی گردش کعب و زانو و پای

Without moving the ankle, the knee and the toe,

نشاید قدم بر گرفتن ز جای

A step from the spot one's unable to go!

از آن سجده بر آدمی سخت نیست

A man without trouble can make himself prone,

که در صلب او مهره یک لخت نیست

For his back is not fashioned from one piece of bone.

دو صد مهره بر یکدگر ساخته‌ست

He has two hundred bones on each other so laid,

که گل مهره‌ای چون تو پرداخته‌ست

That a tall, clayey structure, like you, He has made!

رگت بر تن است ای پسندیده خوی
The veins of your body, oh you, of sweet looks!

زمینی در او سیصد و شصت جوی
Form a mead with three hundred and sixty rich brooks.

بصر در سر و فکر و رای و تمیز
In the head are established reflection and sight; There, too, are discretion and thinking aright.

جوارح به دل، دل به دانش عزیز
The body is dear, on account of the mind; And the mind, too, for knowledge most precious you find.

بهایم به روی اندر افتاده خوار
The brutes, being mean, have a down-hanging face;

تو همچون الف بر قدمها سوار
You're erect on your feet like an "Alif" in grace.

نگون کرده ایشان سر از بهر خور
He has placed their mouths downwards, to help them to feed;

تو آری به عزت خورش پیش سر
The food to your mouth, you with dignity lead.

نزیبد تو را با چنین سروری
It does not look well, when such pref rence is shown,

که سر جز به طاعت فرود آوری
That you bow your head down save to worship alone.

ولیکن بدین صورت دلپذیر
And yet with this form, that can pleasure inspire,

فرفته مشو، سیرت خوب گیر
Be not of dazzled! a good disposition acquire!

ره راست باید نه بالای راست
You require the straight road, not a stature that's straight;

که کافر هم از روی صورت چو ماست
For the scoffer is like us in figure and gait

تو را آن که چشم و دهان داد و گوش
Who gave you your ears and your mouth and your eyes!

اگر عاقلی در خلافش مکوش
Do not seek to contend against Him, if you're wise,

گرفتم که دشمن بکوبی به سنگ
I admit you don't batter your foe with a stone;

مکن باری از جهل با دوست جنگ
Do not fight with the Friend, out of rudeness alone!

خردمند طبعان منت شناس

Those of wise disposition who gratitude know,

بدوزند نعمت به میخ سپاس

Their wealth with the needle of thanksgiving sew.

حکایت اندر معنی شکر منعم
Story of the King and the Greek Physician

ملک زاده‌ای ز اسب ادهم فتاد

From a dark-coloured horse fell a king, used to war,

به گردن درش مهره بر هم فتاد

Displacing a bone of his neck by the jar.

چو پیلش فرو رفت گردن به تن

On his body his head like an elephant's shrunk;

نگشتی سرش تا نگشتی بدن

He could not look round without turning his trunk.

پزشکان بماندند حیران در این

The physicians perplexed could not give him release;

مگر فیلسوفی ز یونان زمین

But a doctor who came from the country of Greece,

سرش باز پیچید و رگ راست شد

Re-twisted his head, and his body grew straight;

وگر وی نبودی زمن خواست شد

Had the doctor not come, sad had been the king's state

دگر نوبت آمد به نزدیک شاه

When again he came near to the king with his train,

به عین عنایت نکردش نگاه

A look from the creature he did not obtain.

خردمند را سر فرو شد به شرم

The doctor, ashamed at the slight, hung his head;

شنیدم که می‌رفت و می‌گفت نرم

I have heard, that when leaving, in whispers he said:

اگر دی نپیچیدمی گردنش

"If his neck I had yesterday failed to replace,

نپیچیدی امروز روی از منش

He would not, to-day, have averted his face."

فرستاد تخمی به دست رهی

He sent him a seed by the hand of a slave;

که باید که بر عود سوزش نهی

On a censer to roast it, directions he gave.

ملک را یکی عطسه آمد ز دود

The king gave a sneeze, from the vapour it bore,

سر و گردنش همچنان شد که بود

And his head and his neck turned the same as before!

به عذر از پی مرد بشتافتند

With excuses, they followed the man all around,

بجستند بسیار و کم یافتند

And searched for him much, but no trace of him found.

مکن، گردن از شکر منعم مپیچ

Turn your neck not from thanking the Bountiful One!

که روز پسین سر بر آری به هیچ

Or your head will appear at the judgment undone.

گفتار اندر گزاردن شکر نعمتها

Remarks on Viewing the Works off God, the Most High.

شب از بهر آسایش توست و روز

For your comfort, the night and the day were begun,

مه روشن و مهر گیتی فروز

The moon shining bright and the world-warming sun.

سپهر از برای تو فراش وار

At the hardship don't burn, should you thirsty remain!

همی گستراند بساط بهار

For the pluvial cloud on its shoulder brings rain.

اگر باد و برف است و باران و میغ

Like a spreader of carpets, the sky overhead,

وگر رعد چوگان زند، برق تیغ

Commands Beauty's carpet for you to be spread.

همه کارداران فرمانبرند

If you've clouds and the rain and the wind and the snow

که تخم تو در خاک می‌پرورند

The roaring of thunder and lightning's bright glow;

اگر تشنه مانی ز سختی مجوش

To be workers obedient to orders they're found,

که سقای ابر آبت آرد به دوش

For they bring up the seed that you sow in the ground.

ز خاک آورد رنگ و بوی و طعام

Food, perfume, and colour He brought from the Earth, —

تماشاگه دیده و مغز و کام

The palate, the brain, and the eye's source of mirth.

عسل دادت از نحل و من از هوا

From the bee you have honey,' and manna from wind,

رطب دادت از نخل و نخل از نوی

Ripe dates from the palms, palms from seeds of their kind.

همه نخلبندان بخایند دست

All the gardeners gnaw at their hands in surprise,

ز حیرت که نخلی چنین کس نبست

For a date-tree like this none has caused to arise.

خور و ماه و پروین برای تواند

Sun and moon are for you, and the Pleiades, far,

قنادیل سقف سرای تواند

The lamps of the roof of your residence are.

ز خارت گل آورد و از نافه مشک

From thorns He brought roses and musk from the pod;

زر از کان و برگ تر از چوب خشک

Pure gold from the mine, and moist leaves from a rod.

به دست خودت چشم و ابرو نگاشت

Your eyebrows and eyes with His own hand He penned;

که محرم به اغیار نتوان گذاشت

For to strangers he could not relinquish his friend.

توانا که او نازنین پرورد

So powerful! he nurtures that delicate one;

به الوان نعمت چنین پرورد

With various bounties the work is thus done.

به جان گفت باید نفس بر نفس

From the soul every morning let praises be shown!

که شکرش نه کار زبان است و بس

For to render Him thanks is not tongue-work alone.

خدایا دلم خون شد و دیده ریش

Oh God! my heart bleeds, and my eyes become sore,

که می‌بینم انعامت از گفت بیش

For I find that Thy gifts than my praises are more.

نگویم دد و دام و مور و سمک

Not beasts, ants and fishes alone, I can tell,

که فوج ملائک بر اوج فلک

But the army of angels in Heaven, as well,

هنوزت سپاس اندکی گفته‌اند

As yet but a part of Thy praises have told;

ز بیور هزاران یکی گفته‌اند

But one, they have stated, in one hundredfold.

برو سعدیا دست و دفتر بشوی

Go! oh Sádi your hand and your record wash clean!

به راهی که پایان ندارد مپوی

Do not run on a road where no ending is seen!

در استفاده درست از زبان

On making a good use of tongue

شنیدم که پیری پسر را به خشم

A man rubbed the ears of a boy very hard,

ملامت همی کرد کای شوخ چشم

Saying, "Frivolous talker! with fortune ill-starred!

تو را تیشه دادم که هیزم شکن

I gave you an axe to cut firewood up fine;

نگفتم که دیوار مسجد بکن

I said not, The wall of the mosque undermine! "

زبان آمد از بهر شکر و سپاس

The tongue to give thanks and to praise with you got;

به غیبت نگرداندش حق شناس

For to backbite, the grateful man uses it not.

گذرگاه قرآن و پند است گوش

The Koran and advice have their way through the ear;

به بهتان و باطل شنیدن مکوش

False accusing and falsehood, take care not to hear!

دو چشم از پی صنع باری نکوست

Two eyes, for beholding God's wonders, are well,

ز عیب برادر فروگیر و دوست

Not on faults of a friend or a brother to dwell.

گفتار اندر بخشایش بر ناتوانان و شکر نعمت حق در توانایی
On Inquiring into the State of the Weak, and Thanking God for His Favours

نداند کسی قدر روز خوشی

No one knows of the worth of the days of delight,

مگر روزی افتد به سختی کشی

Unless he has, once, been in desperate plight.

زمستان درویش در تنگ سال

Before a rich person, how easy appear

چه سهل است پیش خداوند مال

Cold, winter and want, in a famine-struck year?

سلیمی که یک چند نالان نخفت

He who snake-bitten slept, after being distressed,

خداوند را شکر صحت نگفت

For curing him, thanks to the Master expressed.

چو مردانه‌رو باشی و تیز پای

Since in foot you are rapid, and manly in gait,

به شکرانه با کندپایان بپای

With slow moving travellers in thankfulness wait!

به پیر کهن بر ببخشد جوان

Do the young on the old many favours bestow?

توانا کند رحم بر ناتوان

Do the strong for the weak any sympathy show?

چه دانند جیحونیان قدر آب

Of water's worth, what do Jihoonians know?

ز واماندگان پرس در آفتاب

Ask of those left behind in the sun's parching glow!

عرب را که در دجله باشد قعود

What grief for the parch'd, in Zaroods desert wide,

چه غم دارد از تشنگان زرود

Has the Arab who sits by the Tigris' green side?

کسی قیمت تندرستی شناخت

The man knows the value of health, in his case,

که یک چند بیچاره در تب گداخت

Who, helpless, has melted in fever a space.

تو را تیره شب کی نماید دراز

When will the dark night appear long to your mind,

که غلطی ز پهلو به پهلوی ناز؟

Since, from side unto side, you can turn when inclined?

براندیش از افتان و خیزان تب

On the falling and rising of ague, reflect!

که رنجور داند درازای شب

For the man who is ill the long night can detect

به بانگ دهل خواجه بیدار گشت

The master awoke by the drum's sound at last;

چه داند شب پاسبان چون گذشت؟

Does he know how the night of the sentinel passed?

حکایت سلطان طغرل و هندوی پاسبان
Story of Sultan Toghral and the Slave guard

شنیدم که طغرل شبی در خزان

I have heard that Toghral, on a cold, wintry night,

گذر کرد بر هندوی پاسبان

Passed a slave-guard on duty and saw his sad plight.

ز باریدن برف و باران و سیل

From the falling of snow and the torrents of rain,

به لرزش در افتاده همچون سهیل

Like Canopus, he could not from trembling refrain.

دلش بر وی از رحمت آورد جوش

For the watchman, his heart out of pity grew hot,

که اینک قبا پوستینم بپوش

And he said, "Take this mantle of sheepskin, I've got!

دمی منتظر باش بر طرف بام

Near the roof for a moment, expecting it, stand!

که بیرون فرستم به دست غلام

And I'll send it without, by a slave stripling's hand."

در این بود و باد صبا بروزید

The wind in the meantime a hurricane blew,

شهنشه در ایوان شاهی خزید

As inside his palace the king slipped from view.

وشاق پری چهره در خیل داشت

He possessed in his household a fairy-faced slave,

که طبعش بدو اندکی میل داشت

To whose charms a good share of attention he gave.

تماشای ترکش چنان خوش فتاد

On beholding the maiden, such joy did he find,

که هندوی مسکین برفتش ز یاد

That the wretched slave sentry escaped from his mind.

قبا پوستینی گذشتش به گوش

The mantle of sheepskin went through the slave's ear;

ز بدبختیش در نیامد به دوش

From bad luck, on his shoulders it did not appear.

مگر رنج سرما بر او بس نبود

With the pain of the cold, was it little to cope,

که جور سپهر انتظارش فزود

That the tyrannous sky should have bidden him hope?

نگه کن چو سلطان به غفلت بخفت

Observe, when the king heedless slept on his bed,

که چوبک زنش بامدادان چه گفت

What the drummer, when daylight appeared, to him said:

مگر نیکبختت فراموش شد

Very likely Nek-Bakht on your thoughts did not rest,

چو دستت در آغوش آغوش شد؟

When you carried your hand to the fair maiden's breast!

تو را شب به عیش و طرب می‌رود

In enjoyment and pleasure, your night slips away,

چه دانی که بر ما چه شب می‌رود؟

How know you how our night dissolves into day? "

فرو برده سر کاروانی به دیگ

When the head of the trav'ller is over the pot,

چه از پا فرو رفتگانش به ریگ

What cares he concerning the sand-stayed one's lot?

بدار ای خداوند زورق بر آب

To your ships on the water, oh master, hold fast!

که بیچارگان را گذشت از سر آب

For the water has over the pauper's head passed!

توقف کنید ای جوانان چست

Oh active, young man! you should practise delay!

که در کارواند پیران سست

For feeble old men in the caravan stay.

تو خوش خفته در هودج کاروان

In the caravan litter, you sleep without qualm,

مهار شتر در کف ساروان

While the halter is held in the camel-man's palm.

چه هامون و کوهت، چه سنگ و رمال

What are deserts and hills, rocks and sand to your mind?

ز ره باز پس ماندگان پرس حال

Find the truth out from. those on the road left behind!

تو را کوه پیکر هیون می‌برد

A beast, like a mountain in form, bears you well,,

پیاده چه دانی که خون می‌خورد؟

Of the footman who eats his own blood, can you tell?

به آرام دل خفتگان در بنه

Those in comfort, asleep among the baggage, who wait,

چه دانند حال کم گرسنه؟

Do not know of the famishing stomach's sad state.

حکایت دو زندانی

Story of the two prisoners

یکی را عسس دست بر بسته بود

By the night-watch the hands of a person were bound;

همه شب پریشان و دلخسته بود

All the night he showed grief and affliction profound.

به گوش آمدش در شب تیره رنگ

It arrived at his ear, in that dark, dismal night,

که شخصی همی نالد از دست تنگ

That a man was bemoaning his famishing plight.

شنید این سخن دزد مغلول و گفت

The fettered thief heard the lamenting, and said:

ز بیچارگی چند نالی؟ بخفت

"How long will you blubber from grief? Go to bed

برو شکر یزدان کن ای تنگدست

Go thank the Almighty! oh destitute wight!

که دستت عسس تنگ بر هم نبست

That the night-watch with thongs have not tied your hands tight"

مکن ناله از بینوایی بسی

Do not weep much, although you have Poverty's plea,

چو بینی ز خود بینواتر کسی

When a person more poor than yourself you can see!

◈◉◈◈◉◈

حکایت مرد فقیر و جامه

Story of the poor man and his skin coat

برهنه تنی یک درم وام کرد

One, naked, a direm by borrowing got,

تن خویش را کسوتی خام کرد

And a coat of raw hide, as a cov'ring, he bought.

بنالید کای طالع بدلگام

Shedding tears, he exclaimed, " Headstrong fortune, self- willed!

به گرما بپختم در این زیر خام

Beneath this raw hide in a warm bath Tm grilled! "

چو ناپخته آمد ز سختی به جوش

While the fool, under torture, was fuming away,

یکی گفتش از چاه زندان: «خموش

From a dungeon one said to him, " Silence, I pray!

به جای آور، ای خام، شکر خدای

You ought to give thanks to the Giver divine,

که چون ما نه‌ای خام بر دست و پای

That your limbs are not fastened with thongs, like to mine! "

◈◉◈◈◉◈

حکایت جهود
Story of a saint mistaken for a jew

یکی کرد بر پارسایی گذر
A man passed a person possessing God's grace,

به صورت جهود آمدش در نظر
And thought him a Jew, by the cut of his face.

قفایی فرو کوفت بر گردنش
On the back of his neck, he inflicted a whack;

ببخشید درویش پیراهنش
The holy man gave him the shirt from his back!

خجل گفت کانچ از من آمد خطاست
Ashamed, he exclaimed, " What I've done is amiss!

ببخشای بر من، چه جای عطاست؟
Forgive me! what time for a favour is this"?

به شکرانه گفتا به سر بیستم
I brood not on evil," he, thankfully, said,

که آنم که پنداشتی نیستم
But I am not the man who came into your head ".

نکو سیرت بی تکلف برون
A nature refined and a form free from pride,

به از نیکنام خراب اندرون
Surpass a good name and a wicked inside.

به نزدیک من شبرو راهزن
The prowling night-robber seems better to me,

به از فاسق پارسا پیرهن
Than the profligate wretch you in pious garb see.

❖◉❖◉❖

حکایت مسکین
Story of the wretched man and the ass

ز ره باز پس ماندهای میگریست
A man left behind on the road, weeping, cried:

که مسکین تر از من در این دشت کیست؟
"Who more wretched than I in this plain can be spied"?

جهاندیده‌ای گفتش ای هوشیار

Oh void of discretion" a burdened ass spoke,

اگر مردی این یک سخن گوش دار

How long will you Heaven's oppression provoke?

برو شکر کن چون به خر بر نه‌ای

Go tender your thanks, since you ride not a beast,

که آخر بنی آدمی، خر نه‌ای

That you are not an ass under people, at least"!

◈◉◈◉◈

حکایت فقیه و مست

Story of the Pharisee and the Drunkard

فقیهی بر افتاده مستی گذشت

A divine passed a man lying drunk on the plain,

به مستوری خویش مغرور گشت

And, because of his sanctity, waxed very vain.

ز نخوت بر او التفاتی نکرد

He did not, from pride, the man's circumstance scan;

جوان سر برآورد کای پیرمرد

The youth raised his head, saying, "Oh aged man!

برو شکر کن چون به نعمت دری

Go and thankfulness show, that in favour you are!

که محرومی آید ز مستکبری

For when pride is at hand, disappointment's not far!

یکی را که در بند بینی مخند

Do not laugh, when you see one in manacles bound!

مبادا که ناگه درافتی به بند

Lest, suddenly, you may in fetters be found.

نه آخر در امکان تقدیر هست

It may be, at least, in the ruling of Fate,

که فردا چو من باشی افتاده مست؟

That, soon, you may fall into my drunken state!

تو را آسمان خط به مسجد نوشت

The sky has inscribed the word 'Mosque' to your name;

مزن طعنه بر دیگری در کنشت

Someone else, in a 'Fire-Temple do not defame

ببند ای مسلمان به شکرانه دست

In thanksgiving, oh Musulman, clasp your hands

که زنار مغ بر میانت نبست

That your loins are not girt by the Guebre's false bands.

نه خود می‌رود هر که جویان اوست

The searcher for Him, of himself does not move

به عنفش کشان می‌برد لطف دوست

The Friend's favour pulls him by force, in the groove.

نگر تا قضا از کجا سیر کرد

Observe to what length Fate has managed to fly!

که کوری بود تکیه بر غیر کرد

It is blindness on any but God to rely!

❖◉❖◉❖

نظر در اسباب وجود عالم
On the Pious Looking to God, not to Reasons

سرشته‌ست باری شفا در عسل

The Lord has created in plants means of cure,

نه چندان که زور آورد با اجل

Should life in the person afflicted endure.

عسل خوش کند زندگان را مزاج

The health of the living by honey's made sound;

ولی درد مردن ندارد علاج

For the torture of dying no cure can be found.

رمق مانده‌ای را که جان از بدن

In the mouth of the person is honey of worth,

برآمد، چه سود انگبین در دهن؟

Who has reached his last gasp and whose soul has gone forth?

یکی گرز پولاد بر مغز خورد

Someone's brain felt the weight of a steel-headed mace,

کسی گفت صندل بمالش به درد

Said another, "Rub sandal-wood oil on the place! "

ز پیش خطر تا توانی گریز

When in presence of danger, endeavour to run!

ولیکن مکن با قضا پنجه تیز

And the thought of contending with Fate you should shun!

درون تا بود قابل شرب و اکل
While the stomach is fit to digest drink and food,

بدن تازه روی است و پاکیزه شکل
The face remains fresh and the figure keeps good

خراب آنگه این خانه گردد تمام
The house in a ruinous pickle will be,

که با هم نسازند طبع و طعام
When the system and food don't together agree.

طبایع تر و خشک و گرم است و سرد
Moist and dry, hot and cold, are your nature's rich store,

مرکب از این چار طبع است مرد
And man's constitution consists of these four.

یکی زین چو بر دیگری یافت دست
When one of them over another prevails,

ترازوی عدل طبیعت شکست
The scale of your nature's equality fails.

اگر باد سرد نفس نگذرد
If you do not inspire the cool air at each breath,

تف معده جان در خروش آورد
By the heat of the chest life is harassed to death.

وگر دیگ معده نجوشد طعام
If the food by the pot of the stomach's not boiled,

تن نازنین را شود کار خام
The delicate body is speedily spoiled

در اینان نبندد دل، اهل شناخت
The hearts of the knowing to these are not bound,

که پیوسته با هم نخواهند ساخت
For in harmony always, they may not be found.

توانایی تن مدان از خورش
Do not think that the food gives the body its Power.

که لطف حقت می‌دهد پرورش
For God by His favour supports you each hour.

به حقش که گر دیده بر تیغ و کارد
By His truth! if your eyes you on sword and knife lay,

نهی، حق شکرش نخواهی گزارد
The thanks to Him due, you're unable to pay!

چو رویی به طاعت نهی بر زمین

When your face in devotion you rest on the dust,

خدا را ثناگوی و خود را مبین

Give praise to the Lord! on yourself do not trust!

گدایی است تسبیح و ذکر و حضور

With beggary, duty to God is allied;

گدا را نباید که باشد غرور

It becomes not the beggar to show any pride!

گرفتم که خود خدمتی کرده‌ای

I admit that you've rendered some service to God;

نه پیوسته اقطاع او خورده‌ای؟

Have you not always eaten the part He bestowed?

◈◉◈◉◈

درسابقه حکم ازل و توفیق خیر
Discourse on the Pre-eminence of God's Orders and Providence

نخست او ارادت به دل در نهاد

First, God to the heart the intention conveyed,

پس این بنده بر آستان سر نهاد

And then, on the threshold this slave his head laid

گر از حق نه توفیق خیری رسد

If the means to do good, from the Lord you don't gain,

کی از بنده چیزی به غیری رسد؟

When will other men good, through your efforts, obtain?

زبان را چه بینی که اقرار داد

In the tongue that acknowledged him, what do you see?

ببین تا زبان را که گفتار داد

On the Giver of speech, let your scrutiny be!

در معرفت دیدهٔ آدمی است

The doors of God's knowledge are man's seeing eyes,

که بگشوده بر آسمان و زمی است

Which are open so wide to the earth and the skies.

کیت فهم بودی نشیب و فراز

When would you the low and the lofty have known,

گر این در نکردی به روی تو باز؟

If He had not this door in your face open thrown?

443

سر آورد و دست از عدم در وجود

He the head and the hand from nonentity brought,

در این جود بنهاد و در وی سجود

And to them, adoration and almsgiving taught

وگرنه کی از دست جود آمدی؟

Had He not, would the hand have munificence spread?

محال است کز سر سجود آمدی

Adoration would never have come from the head!

به حکمت زبان داد و گوش آفرید

He gave, in His wisdom, a tongue, made the ear;

که باشند صندوق دل را کلید

As the key of the chest of the mind these appear!

اگر نه زبان قصه برداشتی

Had the tongue not for speaking an aptitude shown,

کس از سر دل کی خبر داشتی؟

Would a person the heart's hidden secrets have known?

وگر نیستی سعی جاسوس گوش

Had the spy of the ear not to effort inclined,

خبر کی رسیدی به سلطان هوش

When would news have been brought to the monarch the mind?

مرا لفظ شیرین خواننده داد

The pronouncer of sweet sounding words He gave me;

تو را سمع و ادراک داننده داد

The acute and intelligent ear He gave thee.

مدام این دو چون حاجبان بر درند

Like porters, these two always stand at the gate,

ز سلطان به سلطان خبر می‌برند

And from monarch to monarch the news they relate.

چه اندیشی از خود که فعلم نکوست؟

Why trouble yourself? saying, "Good, is my deed! "

از آن در نگه کن که توفیق اوست

From the other side look, for by Him 'tis decreed!

برد بوستانبان به ایوان شاه

To the halls of the monarch the gard'ner repairs,

به نوباوه گل هم ز بستان شاه

And a present of fruit from the king's garden bears!

حکایت سفر هندوستان و ضلالت بت پرستان
Story of Sádi's journey to Hindustan and the depravity of idolatry

بتی دیدم از عاج در سومنات
An ivory idol I saw at Somnat,

مرصع چو در جاهلیت منات
Begemmed, as in paganish times was Monat?

چنان صورتش بسته تمثالگر
So well had the sculptor its features designed,

که صورت نبندد از آن خوبتر
That an image more perfect no mortal could find.

ز هر ناحیت کاروانها روان
Caravans from each district were moving along;

به دیدار آن صورت بی روان
To look at that spiritless image they throng.

طمع کرده رایان چین و چگل
Kings of China and Chighil, like Sádi forsooth!

چو سعدی وفا ز آن بت سخت دل
From that hard-hearted idol were longing for truth.

زبان آوران رفته از هر مکان
Men of eloquence, gathered from every place,

تضرع کنان پیش آن بی زبان
Were beseeching in front of that dumb idol's face.

فرو ماندم از کشف آن ماجرا
I was helpless to clear up the circumstance, how

که حیی جمادی پرستد چرا؟
The Animate should to the inanimate bow?

مغی راکه با من سر و کار بود
To a pagan with whom I had something to do

نکوگوی و هم حجره و یار بود
A companion well spoken, a chum of mine, too —

به نرمی بپرسیدم ای برهمن
I remarked in a whisper, " Oh Brahmin, so wise!

عجب دارم از کار این بقعه من
At the scenes in this place I experience surprise!

که مدهوش این ناتوان پیکرند
About this helpless form they are crazed in their mind,

مقید به چاه ضلال اندرند
And in error's deep pit- are as captives confined.

نه نیروی دستش، نه رفتار پای

Its hands have no strength, and its feet have no pace;

ورش بفکنی بر نخیزد ز جای

And if thrown to the ground It would not rise from its place.

نبینی که چشمانش از کهرباست؟

Don't you see that its eyes are but amber, let in?

وفا جستن از سنگ چشمان خطاست

To seek for good faith in the blind is a sin!

بر این گفتم آن دوست دشمن گرفت

That friend at my speech to an enemy turned;

چو آتش شد از خشم و در من گرفت

He seized me and, fire-like, from anger he burned

مغان را خبر کرد و پیران دیر

He told all the pagans and temple old men;

ندیدم در آن انجمن روی خیر

I saw not my welfare in that meeting, then.

چو آن راه کژ پیششان راست بود

Since the crooked road seemed unto them to be right,

ره راست در چشمشان کژ نمود

The straight road very crooked appeared, in their sight;

چو که مرد ار چه دانا و صاحبدل است

For although a good man may be pious and wise,

ه نزدیک بی‌دانشان جاهل است

He's an ignorant fool in the ignorant's eyes.

فرو ماندم از چاره همچون غریق

I was helpless to aid, like a man being drowned;

برون از مدارا ندیدم طریق

Except in abasement no method I found.

چو بینی که جاهل به کین اندر است

When you see that a fool has malevolence shown,

سلامت به تسلیم و لین اندر است

Resignation and meekness give safety alone.

مهین برهمن را ستودم بلند

The chief of the Brahmins I praised to the skies:

که ای پیر تفسیر استا و زند

Of the Zind and Asta? oh expounder, most wise!

مرا نیز با نقش این بت خوش است

With this idol's appearance I'm satisfied, too;

که شکلی خوش و قامتی دلکش است

For the face and the features are charming to view.

بدیع آیدم صورتش در نظر

Its figure appears very choice in my sight;

ولیکن ز معنی ندارم خبر

But regarding the truth, I am ignorant, quite.

که سالوک این منزلم عن قریب

I am here as a traveler a very short while,

بد از نیک کمتر شناسد غریب

And a stranger knows seldom the good from the vile.

تو دانی که فرزین این رقعه‌ای

You're the queen of the chess-board and therefore aware;

نصیحتگر شاه این بقعه‌ای

And the monarch's adviser of this temple fair.

چه معنی است در صورت این صنم

To worship by mimicking, doubtless, is wrong;

که اول پرستندگانش منم

Oh happy the pilgrim whose knowledge is strong!

عبادت به تقلید گمراهی است

What truths in the figure of this idol lie?

خنک رهروی راکه آگاهی است

For the chief of its worshippers, truly, am I!"

برهمن ز شادی بر افروخت روی

The face of the old Brahmin glowed with delight;

پسندید و گفت ای پسندیده گوی

He was pleased and said, "Oh thou whose statements are right!

سؤالت صواب است و فعلت جمیل

Your question is proper, your action is wise —

به منزل رسد هر که جوید دلیل

Whoever seeks truth will to happiness rise.

بسی چون تو گردیدم اندر سفر

Like yourself, too, on many a journey I've been,

بتان دیدم از خویشتن بی خبر

And idols not knowing themselves I have seen,

جز این بت که هر صبح از اینجا که هست

Save this, which each morning, just where it now stands,

برآرد به یزدان دادار دست

To the great God of Justice upraises its hands!

وگر خواهی امشب همینجا بباش

And if you are willing, remain the night here!

که فردا شود سر این بر تو فاش

And to-morrow, the secret to you will be clear."

شب آنجا ببودم به فرمان پیر

At the chief Brahmin's bidding I tarried all night;

چو بیژن به چاه بلا در اسیر

In the well of misfortune, like Bizhan's x my plight.

شبی همچو روز قیامت دراز

The night seemed as long as the last Judgment Day;

مغان گرد من بی وضو در نماز

The pagans unwashed, round me feigning to pray.

کشیشان هرگز نیازرده آب

The priests very carefully water did shun

بغلها چو مردار در آفتاب

Their armpits like carrion exposed in the sun!

مگر کرده بودم گناهی عظیم

Perhaps a great sin I had done, long before,

که بردم در آن شب عذابی الیم

That I on that night so much punishment bore.

همه شب در این قید غم مبتلا

All the night I was racked in this prison of grief,

یکم دست بر دل، یکی بر دعا

With one hand on my heart, one in prayer for relief;

که ناگه دهل زن فرو کوفت کوس

When the drummer, with suddenness, beat his loud drum,

بخواند از فضای برهمن خروس

And the cock crowed the fate of the Brahmin, to come.

خطیب سیه پوش شب بی خلاف

Unresisted, the black-coated preacher, the Night,

بر آهخت شمشیر روز از غلاف

Drew forth from its scabbard, the sword of daylight.

فتاد آتش صبح در سوخته

On this tinder, the morning fire happened to fall,

به یک دم جهانی شد افروخته

And the world in a moment was brilliant to all.

تو گفتی که در خطهٔ زنگبار

You'd have said that all over the country of Zang

ز یک گوشه ناگه در آمد تتار

From a corner, the Tartars had suddenly sprung!

مغان تبه رای ناشسته روی

The pagans depraved, with unpurified face,

به دیر آمدند از در و دشت و کوی

Came from door, street and plain to the worshipping place.

کس از مرد در شهر و از زن نماند

The city and lanes were of people bereft;

در آن بتکده جای درزن نماند

In the temple, no room for a needle was left.

من از غصه رنجور و از خواب مست

I was troubled from rage and from sleeplessness dazed,

که ناگاه تمثال برداشت دست

When the idol its hands upwards, suddenly, raised.

به یک بار از ایشان برآمد خروش

All at once, from the people there rose such a shout,

تو گفتی که دریا بر آمد به جوش

You'd have said that the sea in a rage had boiled out.

چو بتخانه خالی شد از انجمن

When the temple became from the multitude free,

برهمن نگه کرد خندان به من

The Brahmin all smiles gazed intently at me:

که دانم تو را بیش مشکل نماند

I am sure that your scruples have vanished," he said,

حقیقت عیان گشت و باطل نماند

Truth has made itself manifest, falsehood has fled."

چو دیدم که جهل اندر او محکم است

When I saw he was slave to an ignorant whim,

خیال محال اندر او مدغم است

And that fancies absurd were established in him,

نیارستم از حق دگر هیچ گفت

Respecting the truth, I no more could reveal,

که حق ز اهل باطل بباید نهفت

For from scoffers, 'tis proper the truth to conceal.

چو بینی زبر دست را زور دست

When you find yourself under a tyrant's command,

نه مردی بود پنجهٔ خود شکست

It would scarcely be manly to break your own hand.

زمانی به سالوس گریان شدم

I wept for a time, that he might be deceived,

که من زآنچه گفتم پشیمان شدم

And said, "At the statement I made, I am grieved!

به گریه دل کافران کرد میل

At my weeping, the pagans' hearts merciful proved —

عجب نیست سنگ ار بگردد به سیل

Is it strange that a stone by the torrent is moved?

دویدند خدمت کنان سوی من

In attendance, they ran to me, very much pleased;

به عزت گرفتند بازوی من

And in doing me honour my hands they all seized.

شدم عذرگویان بر شخص عاج

Asking pardon, I went to the image of bone

به کرسی زر کوفت بر تخت ساج

In a chair made of gold, on a teak-timber throne —

بتک را یکی بوسه دادم به دست

A kiss to the hand of the idol I gave,

که لعنت بر او باد و بر بت پرست

Saying, "Curse it and eVry idolatrous slave!"

به تقلید کافر شدم روز چند

A pagan I was for a little, in name;

برهمن شدم در مقالات زند

In discussing the Zind, I a Brahmin became!

چو دیدم که در دیر گشتم امین

When myself, " one of trust? in the temple I found,

نگنجیدم از خرمی در زمین

I could scarcely from joy keep myself on the ground.

در دیر محکم ببستم شبی
I fastened the door of the temple one night,

دویدم چپ و راست چون عقربی
And, scorpion-like, ran to the left and the right

نگه کردم از زیر تخت و زبر
All under and over the throne I then pried,

یکی پرده دیدم مکلل به زر
And a curtain embroidered with gold I espied;

پس پرده مطرانی آذرپرست
A fire-temple prelate in rear of the screen,

مجاور سر ریسمانی به دست
With the end of a rope in his hand, could be seen!

به فورم در آن حال معلوم شد
The state of affairs I at once saw aright —

چو داود کآهن بر او موم شد
Like David when steel grew like wax in his sight.

که ناچار چون در کشد ریسمان
For, of course, he has only the rope to depress,

بر آرد صنم دست، فریادخوان
When the idol up-raises its hand for redress!

برهمن شد از روی من شرمسار
Ashamed was the Brahmin at seeing my face

که شنعت بود بخیه بر روی کار
For to have any secret exposed's a disgrace.

بتازید و من در پیش تاختم
He bolted and I in pursuit of him fell,

نگونش به چاهی در انداختم
And speedily tumbled him into a well;

که دانستم ار زنده آن برهمن
For I knew that the Brahmin escaping alive,

بماند، کند سعی در خون من
To compass my death would incessantly strive.

پسندد که از من بر آید دمار
And were I despatched he would happiness feel,

مبادا که سرش کنم آشکار
Lest, living, I might his base secret reveal.

چو از کار مفسد خبر یافتی

When you know of the business a villain has planned,

ز دستش برآور چو دریافتی

Put it out of his Power! when he falls to your hand.

که گر زنده‌اش مانی، آن بی هنر

For if to that blackguard reprieve you should give,

نخواهد تو را زندگانی دگر

He will not desire that you longer should live.

وگر سر به خدمت نهد بر درت

When in service he places his head at your gate,

اگر دست یابد ببرد سرت

If he can, he will surely your head amputate!

فریبنده را پای در پی منه

Your feet, in the track of a cheat, do not place!

چو رفتی و دیدی امانش مده

If you do, and discover him, show him no grace!

تمامش بکشتم به سنگ آن خبیث

I despatched the impostor with stones, without dread,

که از مرده دیگر نیاید حدیث

For tales are not told by a man when he's dead.

چو دیدم که غوغایی انگیختم

When I found that I caused a disturbance to spread,

رها کردم آن بوم و بگریختم

I abandoned that country and hastily fled.

چو اندر نیستانی آتش زدی

If a fire in a cane-brake you cause to arise,

ز شیران بپرهیز اگر بخردی

Look out for the tigers therein, if you're wise!

مکش بچهٔ مار مردم گزای

The young of a man-biting snake do not slay!

چو کشتی در آن خانه دیگر مپای

If you do, in the same dwelling-place do not stay!,

چو زنبور خانه بیاشوفتی

When you've managed a hive, full of bees, to excite,

گریز از محلت که گرم اوفتی

Run away from' the spot! or you'll suffer their spite.

به چابک‌تر از خود مینداز تیر

At one sharper than you, don't an arrow despatch!

چو افتاد، دامن به دندان بگیر

When you've done it, your skirt in your teeth you should catch!

در اوراق سعدی چنین پند نیست

No better advice SddVs pages contain:

که چون پای دیوار کندی مایست

When a wall's undermined, do not near it remain!"

به هند آمدم بعد از آن رستخیز

I travelled to Stnd after that Judgment Day;

وز آنجا به راه یمن تا حجیز

By Yemen and Mecca I, thence, took my way.

از آن جمله سختی که بر من گذشت

From the whole of the bitterness, Fate made me meet,

دهانم جز امروز شیرین نگشت

My mouth till to-day has not shown itself sweet.

در اقبال و تأیید بوبکر سعد

By the aiding of Bu-Bakar-SacPs fortune fair

که مادر نزاید چنو قبل و بعد

Whose like not a mother has borne nor will bear —

ز جور فلک دادخواه آمدم

From the sky's cruel harshness, for justice I sought;

در این سایه‌گستر پناه آمدم

In this shadow diffuser, a refuge I got

دعاگوی این دولتم بنده‌وار

Like a slave, for the Empire I fervently pray:

خدایا تو این سایه پاینده دار

"Oh God, cause this shadow for ever to stay!"

که مرهم نهادم نه در خورد ریش

He applied not the salve to my wound's need alone,

که در خورد انعام و اکرام خویش

But becoming the bounty and favour his own.

کی این شکر نعمت به جای آورم

Meet thanks for his favours, when could I repeat?

و گر پای گردد به خدمت سرم؟

Even if in his service my head changed to feet!

فرج یافتم بعد از آن بندها

When these miseries passed I experienced joy;

هنوزم به گوش است از آن پندها

Yet some of the subjects my conscience annoy.

یکی آن که هر گه که دست نیاز

One is — when the hand of petition and praise,

برآرم به درگاه دانای راز

To the shrine of the Knower of Secrets I raise,

به یاد آید آن لعبت چینیم

The thoughts of that puppet of China arise,

کند خاک در چشم خودبینیم

And cover with dust my self-valuing eyes;

بدانم که دستی که برداشتم

I know that the hand I stretched forth to the shrine,

به نیروی خود بر نیفراشتم

Was not lifted by any exertion of mine!

نه صاحبدلان دست بر می‌کشند

Men of sanctity do not their hands upward bring,

که سررشته از غیب در می‌کشند

But the Powers unseen pull the end of the string.

در خیر باز است و طاعت ولیک

Ope's the door of devotion and well-doing, still,

نه هر کس تواناست بر فعل نیک

Every man has not Power a good work to fulfil.

همین است مانع که در بارگاه

This same is a bar; for to Court to repair,

نشاید شدن جز به فرمان شاه

Is improper, except the king's order you bear.

کلید قدر نیست در دست کس

No man can the great key of destiny own,

توانای مطلق خدای است و بس

For absolute Power is the Maker's alone.

پس ای مرد پوینده بر راه راست

Hence, oh travelling man on the straight path Divine!

تو را نیست منت، خداوند راست

The favour is God, the Creator's, not thine.

چو در غیب نیکو نهادت سرشت

Since, unseen, He created your mind pure and wise,

نیاید ز خوی تو کردار زشت

From your nature no action depraved can arise.

ز زنبور کرد این حلاوت پدید

The sweetness produced by the bee, too, did make.

همان کس که در مار زهر آفرید

The same Who has poison produced in the snake,

چو خواهد که ملک تو ویران کند

When He wishes to change to a desert your land,

نخست از تو خلق پریشان کند

He first makes the people distressed at your hand;

وگر باشدش بر تو بخشایشی

And should His compassion upon you descend,

رساند به خلق از تو آسایشی

To the people through you He will comfort extend.

تکبر مکن بر ره راستی

That you walk the right road, do not boast, I advise I.

که دستت گرفتند و برخاستی

For the Fates took your hand and you managed to rise.

سخن سودمند است اگر بشنوی

By these words you will benefit if you attend;

به مردان رسی گر طریقت روی

You will reach pious men if their pathway you wend.

مقامی بیابی گرت ره دهند

You will get a good place if the Fates are your guide;

که بر خوان عزت سماطت نهند

On the table of honour, rich fare they'll provide.

ولیکن نباید که تنها خوری

And yet 'tis not right that you eat all alone,

ز درویش درمنده یاد آوری

For the poor, helpless Dervish some thought should be shown.

فرستی مگر رحمتی در پیم

Perhaps, you'll ask mercy for me when I die,

که بر کردهٔ خویش واثق نیم

For upon my own efforts I do not rely.

❖◉❖◉❖

9

در توبه و راه صواب

ON PENITENCE

سرآغاز
In begin

بیا ای که عمرت به هفتاد رفت
Oh come thou, whose age has to seventy crept!

مگر خفته بودی که بر باد رفت؟
Perhaps, since it went to the winds, you have slept.

همه برگ بودن همی ساختی
With provision for living your time you employed;

به تدبیر رفتن نپرداختی
Not a thought about dying your conscience annoyed.

قیامت که بازار مینو نهند
At the Judgment, when Paradise' Market proceeds,

منازل به اعمال نیکو دهند
They will stations assign in accordance with deeds.

بضاعت به چندان که آری بری
As much stock as you bring you will bear from this place,

وگر مفلسی شرمساری بری
And if you have naught you will carry disgrace.

که بازار چندان که آکندهتر
For the better the market is stocked, you will see

تهیدست را دل پراکندهتر
That the heart of the pauper more wretched will be.

ز پنجه درم پنج اگر کم شود
If two score and ten direms by five are reduced,

دلت ریش سرپنجهٔ غم شود
A wound in your heart by Griefs nails is produced.

چو پنجاه سالت برون شد ز دست
When two score and ten years shall have over you passed,

غنیمت شمر پنج روزی که هست
Consider a boon the "five days" that still last!

اگر مرده مسکین زبان داشتی
If a tongue had been left to the poor, helpless dead,

به فریاد و زاری فغان داشتی
Lamenting and weeping he thus would have said:

که ای زنده چون هست امکان گفت
Oh living! since power of speech in you shows,

لب از ذکر چون مرده بر هم مخفت
Like the dead on God's mention your lips do not close!

چو ما را به غفلت بشد روزگار

Since our opportunity passed in neglect,

تو باری دمی چند فرصت شمار

You should look upon this as your time to reflect! "

❖◉❖◉❖

حکایت پیرمرد و تحسر او بر روزگار جوانی

Story of the old man regretting the time of his youth

شبی در جوانی و طیب نعم

In the time of our youth and in pleasant delight,

جوانان نشستیم چندی بهم

A few of us gathered together one night;

چو بلبل، سرایان چو گل تازه روی

Like nightingales singing, fresh-faced, like the rose;

ز شوخی در افکنده غلغل به کوی

Our boisterous mirth broke the street's still repose.

جهاندیده پیری ز ما بر کنار

An experienced old man sat aloof from our play;

ز دور فلک لیل مویش نهار

From the sky's change, the night of his hair was bright day.

چو فندق دهان از سخن بسته بود

Like a filbert, his tongue from discoursing was tied;

نه چون ما لب از خنده چون پسته بود

Not like us with our lips smiling, pista-like, wide.

جوانی فرا رفت کای پیرمرد

A youth who approached him said, " Veteran, explain!

چه در کنج حسرت نشینی به درد؟

In the nook of repentance why sit you, in pain?

یکی سر برآر از گریبان غم

For once, raise your head from the collar of woe!

به آرام دل با جوانان بچم

And with youths, in composure of heart, gaily go! "

برآورد سر سالخورد از نهفت

From retirement, the man of old age raised his head;

جوابش نگر تا چه پیرانه گفت

Observe his reply how old man like, he said:

چو باد صبا بر گلستان وزد
Should the cool morning breeze through the rose-garden blow,

چمیدن درخت جوان را سزد
It becomes the young bushes to wave to and fro.

چمد تا جوان است و سرسبز خوید
The corn waves majestic while growing and green;

شکسته شود چون به زردی رسید
It will break when a yellow appearance is seen.

بهاران که بید آورد بید مشک
In the Spring when the wind wafts the musk-willow smell,

بریزد درخت گشن برگ خشک
The trees that are young shed their dry leaves, as well.

نزیبد مرا با جوانان چمید
It does not become me with youth to keep pace,

که بر عارضم صبح پیری دمید
For the breeze of old age has blown over my face.

به قید اندرم جره بازی که بود
The famous male falcon, once under my Power,

دمادم سر رشته خواهد ربود
Now severs the end of the cord, evry hour.

شما راست نوبت بر این خوان نشست
It is your turn to sit at the tray piled with fare,

که ما از تنعم بشستیم دست
For our hands we have washed, after eating our share.

چو بر سر نشست از بزرگی غبار
When on your head has settled the dust of old age,

دگر چشم عیش جوانی مدار
Do not hope you'll again in youth's pleasures engage!

مرا برف باریده بر پر زاغ
The snow has come down on my raven's dark wing;

نشاید چو بلبل تماشای باغ
Garden sporting, like Bulbuls, is not now the thing.

کند جلوه طاووس صاحب جمال
The peacock has beauty and proudly may walk;

چه می‌خواهی از باز برکنده بال؟
What can you expect from a broken- winged hawk?

مرا غله تنگ اندر آمد درو

My grain has been reaped and collected to thresh;

شما را کنون می‌دمد سبزه نو

Your verdure is growing up still, soft and fresh.

گلستان ما را طراوت گذشت

My rose garden's freshness has all disappeared;

که گل دسته بندد چو پژمرده گشت؟

Who would fashion a nose-gay from flow'rs that are seared?

مرا تکیه جان پدر بر عصاست

Oh soul of your father! a staff is my stay;

دگر تکیه بر زندگانی خطاست

To rely more on self would be out of the way!

مسلم جوان راست بر پای جست

It is safe for a stripling to spring to his feet,

که پیران برند استعانت به دست

But the aged, the help of their hands must entreat.

گل سرخ رویم نگر زر ناب

The rose of my face, see! like yellow gold shines.

فرو رفت، چون زرد شد آفتاب

When the sun becomes yellow it quickly declines.

هوس پختن از کودک ناتمام

The nursing of lust by an ignorant youth,

چنان زشت نبود که از پیر خام

Is less wicked than by an old lecher, forsooth

مرا می‌باید چو طفلان گریست

It behoves me to weep, out of shame, for each crime,

ز شرم گناهان، نه طفلانه زیست

Like a child, but not, child-like, to idle my time.

نکو گفت لقمان که نازیستن

Lukman said correctly, ' Much better be dead,

به از سالها بر خطا زیستن

Than let years of transgressing pass over your head! '

هم از بامدادان در کلبه بست

Better close the shop-door, from the dawning of day,

به از سود و سرمایه دادن ز دست

Than to cast both the stock and the profit away!

جوان تا رساند سیاهی به نور
Before the young man bears his darkness to light,
برد پیر مسکین سپیدی به گور
The poor aged man bears his sin out of sight.

❖◉❖◉❖

حکایت بالا رفتن سن
Story on advancing age

کهنسالی آمد به نزد طبیب
A man, full of years, to a doctor came nigh,
ز نالیدنش تا به مردن قریب
From his weeping he looked as if ready to die.

که دستم به رگ بر نه، ای نیک رای
He said, "Feel my pulse! oh intelligent man!
که پایم همی بر نیاید ز جای
For to step from this spot is much more than I can.

بدین ماند این قامت خفته‌ام
My motionless body just looks, you would say,
که گویی به گل در فرو رفته‌ام
As if I had mingled again with the clay."

برو، گفت دست از جهان در گسل
He answered, " Your hands from the World you should tear,
که پایت قیامت برآید ز گل
For your feet from the clay resurrection will bear.

اگر در جوانی زدی دست و پای
If you used hands and feet in your juvenile years,
در ایام پیری به هش باش و رای
Be wise and discreet when your old age appears!

چو دوران عمر از چهل درگذشت
When your life has exceeded two score years in length,
مزن دست و پا کآبت از سر گذشت
Do not dance and clap hands for impaired is your strength.

نشاط از من آن گه رمیدن گرفت
When my hair black as night, first began to get grey,
که شامم سپیده دمیدن گرفت
My enjoyment of pleasure departed away.

ببايد هوس كردن از سر به در

It is proper that lust from your heart you should send,

كه دور هوسبازى آمد به سر

When the time to enjoy it has come to an end.

به سبزه كجا تازه گردد دلم

When will greenness refresh my old heart, become sear,

كه سبزه بخواهد دميد از گلم؟

For verdure will soon from my ashes appear?

تفرج كنان در هوا و هوس

Amusing ourselves with excesses and lust,

گذشتيم بر خاك بسيار كس

We have passed over many a dead person's dust;

كسانى كه ديگر به غيب اندرند

Those who still in the womb of Futurity lie,

بيايند و بر خاك ما بگذرند

Will arrive and pass over our dust, when we die.

دريغا كه فصل جوانى برفت

Alas! that the season of youth slipped away!

به لهو و لعب زندگانى برفت

And that life has been squandered in amorous play!

دريغا چنان روح پرور زمان

Alas! that the soul-nursing time did not last!

كه بگذشت بر ما چو برق يمان

Like the lightning of Yemen it over us passed.

ز سوداى آن پوشم و اين خورم

In desire to eat " this" and in love "that" to wear,

نپرداختم تا غم دين خورم

I so lived that the Faith did not give me a care.

دريغا كه مشغول باطل شديم

Alas! that with falsehood our life has been spent;

ز حق دور مانديم و غافل شديم

From the Truth we stood far, and in negligence went!

چه خوش گفت با كودك آموزگار

How well to a stripling the schoolmaster said:

كه كارى نكرديم و شد روزگار

Our work is not done and the season has fled.

❁◉❁◉❁

گفتار اندر غنیمت شمردن جوانی پیش از پیری

On esteeming as a boon the strength of youth previous to the weakness of old age

جوانا ره طاعت امروز گیر

To-day, oh young man, in devotion engage!

که فردا جوانی نیاید ز پیر

For to-morrow, fresh youth will not come from old age.

فراغ دلت هست و نیروی تن

You have leisure of mind and your body has force;

چو میدان فراخ است گویی بزن

Hit straight at the ball when you have a wide course!

قضا روزگاری ز من در ربود

Fate deprived me of time, in a sorrowful hour,

که هر روزی از وی شبی قدر بود

Of which every day was the great "night of Power"

چه کوشش کند پیر خر زیر بار؟

What toil has an ass, become old, 'neath his load?

تو می‌رو که بر بادپایی سوار

Astride a good steed, you continue your road.

شکسته قدح ور ببندند چست

Though a cup that is smashed you may neatly restore

نیاورد خواهد بهای درست

Not again will it bring the same price as before.

کنون کاوفتادت به غفلت ز دست

As it fell from your hand out of negligence, then,

طریقی ندارد مگر باز بست

No course can you follow but patch it again.

که گفتت به جیحون در انداز تن؟

Yourself in the Oxus, who told you to cast?

چو افتاد، هم دست و پایی بزن

If you do, with your hands and your feet strike out fast!

به غفلت بدادی ز دست آب پاک

The water of cleansing you gave from your hand;

چه چاره کنون جز تیمم به خاک؟

What resource have you left, but to utilize sand

چو از چابکان در دویدن گرو

When you took not the prize from the swift in the race,

نبردی، هم افتان و خیزان برو

Even stumbling and rising, continue your pace!

گر آن بادپایان برفتند تیز

If those of swift foot are remarkably fleet;

تو بی دست و پای از نشستن بخیز

Get up you are palsied in hands and in feet.

◖◉◗◖◉◗

حکایت در معنی ادراک پیش از فوت

Story on making the most of time

شبی خوابم اندر بیابان فید

One night fickle sleep, in the desert of Faid,

فرو بست پای دویدن به قید

My feet from progressing with fetters had tied.

شتربانی آمد به هول و ستیز

A camel-man came, showing angry surprise,

زمام شتر بر سرم زد که خیز

And battered my head with his rope, saying, " Rise

مگر دل نهادی به مردن ز پس

Left behind, you perhaps are determined to die,

که بر می‌نخیزی به بانگ جرس؟

Since you do not get up when the bell sounds so high?

مرا همچو تو خواب خوش در سر است

Like you, I desire very much to sleep more;

ولیکن بیابان به پیش اندر است

But, alas! the lone desert lies stretched out before ".

تو کز خواب نوشین به بانگ رحیل

Since to rise from sweet slumber, no liking you showed

نخیزی، دگر کی رسی در سبیل

At the starting loud noise; can you get to the road?

فرو کوفت طبل شتر ساروان

The camel-man sounded his drum as he ran,

به منزل رسید اول کاروان

And first reached the stage, of the whole caravan.

خنک هوشیاران فرخنده بخت

Oh happy the sensible, fortunate folk!

که پیش از دهل‌زن بسازند رخت

Who packed their effects ere the drummer awoke

465

به ره خفتگان تا بر آرند سر

Those upon the road sleeping, their heads do not raise,

نبینند ره رفتگان را اثر

Till no trace of those travelling reaches their gaze.

سبق برد رهرو که برخاست زود

The traveler first rising, pre-eminence won;

پس از نقل بیدار بودن چه سود؟

What avails it to wake when the march has begun

چو شیبت در آمد به روی شباب

When your features of youth are overshadowed with grey,

شبت روز شد دیده بر کن ز خواب

Cast sleep from your eyes! for your night now is day.

من آن روز بر کندم از عمر امید

All hope from my life I was forced to expel

که افتادم اندر سیاهی سپید

On that day when my darkness to hoariness fell.

دریغا که بگذشت عمر عزیز

Alas! my dear life is, at last, on the wane,

بخواهد گذشت این دمی چند نیز

And soon will depart, too, the days that remain.

گذشت آنچه در ناصوابی گذشت

The time that has gone has in sinfulness passed;

ور این نیز هم در نیابی گذشت

And of this, too, you have not a moment to last

کنون وقت تخم است اگر پروری

Now's the time for the seed, if to tend it you care,

گر امید داری که خرمن بری

Or if you expect in the harvest to share!

به شهر قیامت مرو تنگدست

To the town " Resurrection you must not go poor!

که وجهی ندارد به حسرت نشست

For to sit and regret would not favour procure.

گرت چشم عقل است تدبیر گور

If you've got Wisdom's eyes, make arrangements to-day

کنون کن که چشمت نخورده‌ست مور

For the grave; ere the ants eat your eyeballs away.

به مایه توان ای پسر سود کرد

From stock, oh young man! you can profit obtain;

چه سود افتد آن را که سرمایه خورد؟

What profit can he who has wasted it gain?

کنون کوش کآب از کمر درگذشت

Strive, now, that the water has reached to your waist!

نه وقتی که سیلابت از سر گذشت

And not when the flood o'er your head flows in haste.

کنونت که چشم است اشکی ببار

Shed a shower of tears, now that eyes you have got!

زبان در دهان است عذری بیار

There's a tongue in your mouth, let excuses be brought!

نه پیوسته باشد روان در بدن

To the body, the soul will not always be bound;

نه همواره گردد زبان در دهن

The tongue in the mouth will not always go round.

ز دانندگان بشنو امروز قول

To the sayings of sages, to-day, lend your ear!

که فردا نگیرت بپرسد به هول

For to-morrow, you'll find yourself tried by Nakir

غنیمت شمار این گرامی نفس

You should count as a treasure this spirit, so dear;

که بی مرغ قیمت ندارد قفس

For a cage that is birdless will worthless appear.

مکن عمر ضایع به افسوس و حیف

To waste life in regretting, one cannot afford

که فرصت عزیز است و الوقت سیف

Opportunity's precious and Time is a sword!

◀◉▸◀◉▸

حکایت آماده شدن برای مرگ
Story on preparing for death

قضا زنده‌ای را رگ جان برید
Fate the reins of a mortal's existence had shorn

دگر کس به مرگش گریبان درید
On his dying, another his collar had torn.

چنین گفت بیننده‌ای تیز هوش
Thus said a beholder, with intellect clear,

چو فریاد و زاری رسیدش به گوش
When the weeping and wailing arrived at his ear:

ز دست شما مرده بر خویشتن
At your tyrannous hands, had the dead been allowed,

گرش دست بودی دریدی کفن
He'd have riven away from his body the shroud;

که چندین ز تیمار و دردم مپیچ
Saying, ' Writhe not so much out of sorrow for me,

که روزی دو پیش از تو کردم بسیچ
That provision I've made a few days before thee!

فراموش کردی مگر مرگ خویش
Perhaps you've forgotten your own dying day,

که مرگ منت ناتوان کرد و ریش
Since my death makes you wounded and weak in this way'!

محقق که بر مرده ریزد گلش
An observer who earth on a dead body strews,

نه بر وی که بر خود بسوزد دلش
Not for it, but himself, his heart fervency shows.

ز هجران طفلی که در خاک رفت
At the child's disappearance, which went back to clay,

چه نالی؟ که پاک آمد و پاک رفت
Why weep? he came pure, and he pure went away!

تو پاک آمدی بر حذر باش و پاک
Be careful and pure! you in purity came;

که ننگ است ناپاک رفتن به خاک
For returning polluted to dust, is a shame.

کنون باید این مرغ را پای بست
To the leg of this bird you must now tie a band;

نه آنگه که سررشته بردت ز دست
Not when it has wrested the string from your hand.

نشستی به جای دگر کس بسی
In the place of another, a long time you've sat;

نشیند به جای تو دیگر کسی
Another will sit in your place, for all that!

اگر پهلوانی و گر تیغزن
Whether famed as a wrestler or swordsman complete,

نخواهی به در بردن الا کفن
You can take with you only your white winding-sheet

خر وحش اگر بگسلاند کمند
If an ass of the desert should fracture the noose,

چو در ریگ ماند شود پای بند
And he sticks in the sand, why, his feet are not loose!

تو را نیز چندان بود دست زور
So long, too, a powerful hand you can wave,

که پایت نرفته‌ست در ریگ گور
As your feet do not sink in the dust of the grave.

منه دل بر این سالخورده مکان
Do not fasten your heart on this world for a home!

که گنبد نپاید بر او گردکان
For a walnut remains not, when thrown on a dome

چو دی رفت و فردا نیامد به دست
Since yesterday went, and to-morrow's not yours

حساب از همین یک نفس کن که هست
Make the most of the moment that life still ensures

❖◉❖◉❖

حکایت در معنی بیداری از خواب غفلت
Story of Jamshid and his deceased mistress

فرو رفت جم را یکی نازنین
Jamshed had a favourite mistress who died;

کفن کرد چون کرمش ابریشمین
A shroud, like the silkworm's, of silk he supplied.

به دخمه برآمد پس از چند روز
To her tomb, in a little time after, he went,

که بر وی بگرید به زاری و سوز
With fervour to weep o'er her corpse and lament

چو پوسیده دیدش حریرین کفن

When he saw that decay through her silk shroud had spread,

به فکرت چنین گفت با خویشتن

Absorbed in deep thought, to himself he thus said:

من از کرم برکنده بودم به زور

"I removed from the silkworm this substance by force;

بکندند از او باز کرمان گور

The worms of the grave take it back from her corse.

در این باغ سروی نیامد بلند

In this garden the cypress attains no great height,

که باد اجل بیخش از بن نکند

Ere the fierce wind of Fate roots it up from its site.

قضا نقش یوسف جمالی نکرد

Fate no picture with Joseph like beauty has hatched,

که ماهی گورش چو یونس نخورد

That, like Jonah, the fish of the grave has not snatched ".

حکایت دنیای بدون ما

On the world going on without us

دو بیتم جگر کرد روزی کباب

Two couplets quite roasted my liver one day,

که می‌گفت گوینده‌ای با رباب

That a minstrel with Rebeck sang sweet, in this way

دریغا که بی ما بسی روزگار

" Alas! that without us for many a year,

بروید گل و بشکفد نوبهار

The roses will grow and the tulips appear!

بسی تیر و دی ماه و اردیبهشت

Many Junes and Decembers and Aprils will pass,

برآید که ما خاک باشیم و خشت

While still we remain bricks and ashes, alas!

پس از ما بسی گل دهد بوستان

The garden will still yield its rose after us,

نشینند با یکدگر دوستان

And friends will, together, sit down and discuss.

حکایت پارسا"

Story of the pious man and his brick of Gold

یکی پارسا سیرت حق پرست

An ingot of gold to the hand of one fell.

فتادش یکی خشت زرین به دست

Who was pious in nature and worshipped God well.

سر هوشمندش چنان خیره کرد

It so greatly distracted his sensible head.

که سودا دل روشنش تیره کرد

That his madness of heart o'er his face darkness spread.

همه شب در اندیشه کاین گنج و مال

In the thought of his treasure and wealth, the night passe

در او تا زیم ره نیابد زوال

He said, "While I'm living it surely will last:

دگر قامت عجزم از بهر خواست

Again my weak body, for mere begging's sake,

نباید بر کس دوتا کرد و راست

Bent and straight, before people, I ought not to make.

سرایی کنم پای بستش رخام

I'll a palace, with basement of marble, erect;

درختان سقفش همه عود خام

And the roof will with aloes-wood rafters be decked.

یکی حجره خاص از پی دوستان

For my friends, I'll a private apartment complete

در حجره اندر سرا بوستان

Whose door will be inside a garden retreat

بفرسودم از رقعه بر رقعه دوخت

From sewing on patch upon patch, I am tired;

تف دیگدان چشم و مغزم بسوخت

While my eyes and my brain, others' burning has fired.

دگر زیردستان پزندم خورش

Henceforward will menials my victuals prepare

به راحت دهم روح را پرورش

I will cherish my soul by removing all care.

به سختی بکشت این نمد بسترم

This hard, felten blanket has murdered me quite;

روم زین سپس عبقری گسترم

I will go and arrange a rich bed from to-night ".

خیالش خرف کرد و کالیوه رنگ

Fancy caused him to dote, and look frenzied and wan;

به مغزش فرو برده خرچنگ چنگ

The crab sunk its claws in the brains of the man.

فراغ مناجات و رازش نماند

No leisure for prayer or God's study had he —

خور و خواب و ذکر و نمازش نماند

From sleeping and eating and worshipping free

به صحرا برآمد سر از عشوه مست

Head drunk from delusions, he came to a plain

که جایی نبودش قرار نشست

For nor rest nor composure with him did remain.

یکی بر سر گور گل می سرشت

At the head of a grave one was mixing up mire.

که حاصل کند زآن گل گور خشت

Some bricks from the dust of that grave to acquire.

به اندیشه لختی فرو رفت پیر

In deep thought with himself the old man hung his head;

که ای نفس کوته نظر پند گیر

Oh short-sighted soul! take a lesson! "he said

چه بندی در این خشت زرین دلت

Your heart on this brick, of pure gold, wherefore lay?

که یک روز خشتی کنند از گلت؟

For soon they will model a brick from your clay ".

طمع را نه چندان دهان است باز

The vast mouth of greed is not opened thus wide.

که بازش نشیند به یک لقمه آز

That its appetite should by one morsel be tied.

بدار ای فرومایه زین خشت دست

Withhold from this brick, oh, debased one, your hand!

که جیحون نشاید به یک خشت بست

For with one brick you cannot the Oxus withstand.

تو غافل در اندیشهٔ سود و مال

Absorbed in your profit and goods, you don't mind

که سرمایهٔ عمر شد پایمال

That the stock of your life has been cast to the wind!

بر این خاک چندان صبا بگذرد

Such breezes will over this dust of ours play,

که هر ذره از ما به جایی برد

That each atom of us will be wafted away.

غبار هوا چشم عقلت بدوخت

Your eyes were stitched up by the dust of desire

سموم هوس کشت عمرت بسوخت

Lust's scorching Simoom set your life's field on fire.

بکن سرمهٔ غفلت از چشم پاک

The black dust of neglect from your eyelids set free!

که فردا شوی سرمه در چشم خاک

For, to-morrow, black dust underground you will be.

◉ ◉

حکایت عداوت در میان دو شخص

Story on enmity between two persons

میان دو تن دشمنی بود و جنگ

Two persons, in hatred and fighting engaged,

سر از کبر بر یکدیگر چون پلنگ

And looked on each other, like leopards enraged.

ز دیدار هم تا به حدی رمان

To avoid -one another, so far did they fly,

که بر هر دو تنگ آمدی آسمان

That the Earth was too small for them, under the sky.

یکی را اجل در سر آورد جیش

At the head of one, Fate with his army arrived,

سرآمد بر او روزگاران عیش

And him of enjoying more pleasure deprived.

بداندیش او را درون شاد گشت

This, delight to the heart of his enemy gave;

به گورش پس از مدتی برگذشت

A short time thereafter, he passed by his grave.

شبستان گورش در اندوده دید

The cell of his tomb, he saw plastered with clay;

که وقتی سرایش زر اندوده دید

He had seen his gilt house on the previous day.

ز روی عداوت به بازوی زور

By the strength of his arm, with malicious intent,

یکی تخته برکندش از روی گور

He a slab from the face of the sepulchre rent.

سر تاجور دیدش اندر مغاک

He saw his crowned head lying inside the pit,

دو چشم جهان بینش آکنده خاک

And his world-seeing eyes filled entirely with grit.

وجودش گرفتار زندان گور

His body confined in the tomb-prison lay;

تنش طعمه کرم و تاراج مور

His corpse food for worms and the greedy ant's prey.

چنان تنگش آکنده خاک استخوان

From the sky's revolutions his full-moon-like face,

که از عاج پر توتیا سرمه دان

To a sharp-pointed crescent had now given place

ز دور فلک بدر رویش هلال

And towards him, time had such tyranny shown,

ز جور زمان سرو قدش خلال

That his cypress-like form, like a toothpick had grown.

کف دست و سرپنجۀ زورمند

The palms of his hands and his fingers of strength,

جدا کرده ایام بندش ز بند

By time had their pieces disjointed, at length.

چنانش بر او رحمت آمد ز دل

His heart for him sympathy showed, in such way,

که بسرشت بر خاکش از گریه گل

That the tears from his eyes wrought his dust into clay.

پشیمان شد از کرده و خوی زشت

He regretted the manner he served him from spite;

بفرمود بر سنگ گورش نبشت

On the slab of his grave he desired them to write:

مکن شادمانی به مرگ کسی

At any one's death, from rejoicing refrain!

که دهرت نماند پس از وی بسی

For after he dies you a moment remain ".

شنید این سخن عارف هوشیار

Someone heard the remark who with wisdom was stored,

بنالید کای قادر کردگار

And wept, saying, "Oh, Thou Omnipotent Lord!

عجب گر تو رحمت نیاری بر او

It were strange did Thy mercy to him not extend,

که بگریست دشمن به زاری بر او

Whose foe for him bitterly wept, like a friend ".

تن ما شود نیز روزی چنان

One day will our bodies in like manner turn

که بر وی بسوزد دل دشمنان

That our enemies' hearts, too, will over them burn.

مگر در دل دوست رحم آیدم

Perhaps the Friend's heart will to me mercy show,

چو بیند که دشمن ببخشایدم

When He sees me forgiven, at last, by my foe!

به جایی رسد کار سر دیر و زود

Such a state of the skull will immediately rise,

که گویی در او دیده هرگز نبود

That you'd say, it had never contained any eyes.

زدم تیشه یک روز بر تل خاک

I struck an earth mound with a pick-axe, one day;

به گوش آمدم ناله‌ای دردناک

A cry of distress, in my ears seemed to say:

که زنهار اگر مردی آهسته‌تر

Take a little more care, if you're manly, I pray!

که چشم و بناگوش و روی است و سر

There are ear-tips and eyes; face and head in this clay ".

❖◉❖◉❖

حکایت پدر و دختر

Story of a father and daughter

شبی خفته بودم به عزم سفر

In the thought of a journey, I slumbered one night,

پی کاروانی گرفتم سحر

And followed a large caravan at daylight

که آمد یکی سهمگین باد و گرد

A horrible dust-storm arose with the wind,

که بر چشم مردم جهان تیره کرد

And darkened the Earth in the eyes of mankind.

به ره در یکی دختر خانه بود

A maiden, who had on the way her abode,

به معجر غبار از پدر می‌زدود

From her father, with veil, wiped the dust of the road.

پدر گفتش ای نازنین چهر من

Oh my lovely-faced daughter! " the father expressed,

که داری دل آشفتهٔ مهر من

Whose heart out of love for me's greatly distressed!

نه چندان نشیند در این دیده خاک

Will not dust in these eyes soon so plenteous appear,

که بازش به معجر توان کرد پاک

That you cannot again with your veil wipe them clear?

تو را نفس رعنا چو سرکش ستور

Your affectionate soul, like an obstinate steed,

دوان می‌برد تا سر شیب گور

To the grave is conveying you onwards, with speed.

اجل ناگهت بگسلاند رکیب

Fate will suddenly shatter your stirrups, at last,

عنان باز نتوان گرفت از نشیب

And the reins you can't seize, when the grave holds you fast"

❧◉❧◉❧

موعظه و تنبیه

Admonition and Advice

خبر داری ای استخوانی قفس

Have you knowledge regarding your cage made of bone?

که جان تو مرغی است نامش نفس؟

For your life is a bird; as the spirit, 'tis known.

چو مرغ از قفس رفت و بگست قید

When a bird leaves its cage and confinement alive,

دگر ره نگردد به سعی تو صید

It will not be captive again, though you strive.

نگه دار فرصت که عالم دمی است

For a moment's the world, opportunity prize!

دمی پیش دانا به از عالمی است

A moment's preferred to the world by the wise.

سکندر که بر عالمی حکم داشت

Alexander, who held the whole world in his sway,

در آن دم که بگذشت و عالم گذاشت

At the moment he died could not bear it away;

میسر نبودش کز او عالمی

It was not allowed that his world they should seize,

ستاند و مهلت دهندش دمی

And grant him instead one short moment of ease.

برفتند و هر کس درود آنچه کشت

They have gone! What each sowed he will reap just the same;

نماند به جز نام نیکو و زشت

Nought remains now, excepting a good and bad name.

چرا دل بر این کاروانگه نهیم؟

Why should I set my heart on this traveler's home?

که یاران برفتند و ما بر رهیم

For our comrades have gone; on the road we still roam.

پس از ما همین گل دمد بوستان

The garden will yield that same rose after us,

نشینند با یکدگر دوستان

And friends will, together, sit down and discuss.

دل اندر دلارام دنیا مبند

By this sweetheart, the world, let your heart not be buoyed!

که ننشست با کس که دل بر نکند

For whoever she favoured his heart she destroyed.

چو در خاکدان لحد خفت مرد

When the tomb's niche becomes a poor man's sleeping place,

قیامت بیفشاند از موی گرد

Resurrection will wipe all the dust from his face.

سر از جیب غفلت برآور کنون

Raise your head up, this moment, from Apathy's breast!

که فردا نماند به حسرت نگون

Lest, to-morrow, regret makes it greatly distressed.

نه چون خواهی آمد به شیراز در

Don't you, entering Shiraz to take up your abode,

سر و تن بشویی ز گرد سفر

Wash your body and head from the dust of the road?

پس ای خاکسار گنه عن قریب

Hence, oh thou depraved habitation of sin!

سفر کرد خواهی به شهری غریب

To a strange city, soon, you'll your journey begin.

بران از دو سرچشمهٔ دیده جوی

From the founts of your eyes, cause a current to flow!

ور آلایشی داری از خود بشوی

And wash from yourself any filth you may show!

حکایت در عالم طفولیت
Story on the time of childhood

ز عهد پدر یادم آید همی

From the time of my father I memory retain,

که باران رحمت بر او هر دمی

May mercy in showers on him constantly rain!

که در طفلیم لوح و دفتر خرید

That a tablet, a book and a ring, golden-wrought,

ز بهرم یکی خاتم زر خرید

For my use, in the days of my childhood, he bought.

به در کرد ناگه یکی مشتری

A purchaser, suddenly, came and conveyed

به خرمایی از دستم انگشتری

The ring from my hand, and a date for it paid.

چو نشناسد انگشتری طفل خرد

When the worth of a ring to a child is unknown,

به شیرینی از وی توانند برد

With a sweetmeat a person can make it his own.

تو هم قیمت عمر نشناختی

You, too, failed to reckon your life as a boon,

که در عیش شیرین برانداختی

Since you've cast it away in sweet pleasures, so soon.

قیامت که نیکان بر اعلی رسند

When the good at the last Judgment Day mount on high,

ز قعر ثری بر ثریا رسند

And from under the earth to the Pleiades fly,

تو را خود بماند سر از ننگ پیش

Your own head will remain hanging forward from shame,

که گردت برآید عملهای خویش

For round you will press all the sins to your name.

برادر، ز کار بدان شرم دار

Oh brother! feel shame at the work of the bad!

که در روی نیکان شوی شرمسار

For in front of the good, you'll be humbled and sad

در آن روز کز فعل پرسند و قول

When the Fates ask of actions and what has been said,

اولوالعزم را تن بلرزد ز هول

The bodies of heroes will tremble from dread.

به جایی که دهشت خورند انبیا

To the place where the prophets in terror remain,

تو عذر گنه را چه داری؟ بیا

Come! and all your excuses for sinning explain!

زنانی که طاعت به رغبت برند

The woman who worships the Lord with delight,

ز مردان ناپارسا بگذرند

Is better than man who is godless in plight.

تو را شرم ناید ز مردی خویش

Respecting your manliness, rises no shame

که باشد زنان را قبول از تو بیش؟

That woman should over you preference claim?

زنان را به عذری معین که هست

The women because of a general law,

ز طاعت بدارند گه گاه دست

At seasons, their hands from devotions withdraw.

تو بی عذر یک سو نشینی چو زن

You sit like a woman, no plea have you got,

رو ای کم ز زن، لاف مردی مزن

Go! oh lower than woman! of manhood boast not!

مرا خود چه باشد زبان آوری

"What measure of eloquence centres in me? "

چنین گفت شاه سخن عنصری

Thus said the most eloquent man, Ansari,

مرا خود مبین ای عجب در میان

Oh strange! do not me with amazement behold!

ببین تا چه گفتند پیشینیان

Observe what my great predecessors have told!

چو از راستی بگذری خم بود

When you straightness exceed you to crookedness lean;

چه مردی بود کز زنی کم بود؟

In a man less than woman, what manhood is seen?

به ناز و طرب نفس پرورده گیر

In indulgence and mirth lustful appetite train,

به ایام دشمن قوی کرده گیر

And the enemy, shortly, more strength will obtain!

⟨◉⟩⟨◉⟩

حکایت مرد و گرگ
Story of the man and the wolf

یکی بچهٔ گرگ می‌پرورید

A man reared the cub of a wolf at his door;

چو پرورده شد خواجه بر هم درید

When reared, its protector in pieces it tore.

چو بر پهلوی جان سپردن بخفت

On resigning his spirit he laid down his head;

زبان آوری در سرش رفت و گفت

A man of experience passed him and said:

تو دشمن چنین نازنین پروری

"If you nurture a foe with such delicate care,

ندانی که ناچار زخمش خوری؟

Don't you know that, defenceless, his wounds you must bear?

نه ابلیس در حق ما طعنه زد

Has not Satan regarding us vented his spite?

کز اینان نیاید به جز کار بد؟

Saying, Wickedness only in these comes to light! '

فغان از بدیها که در نفس ماست

Alas! for the evils that in us unite;

که ترسم شود ظن ابلیس راست

I'm afraid the opinion of Satan is right! "

چو ملعون پسند آمدش قهر ما

When our chastisement pleased the accursed one, then,

خدایش بینداخت از بهر ما

The Lord, for our sakes, overthrew him again.

کجا سر برآریم از این عار و ننگ

When shall I my head from this baseness release?

که با او به صلحیم و با حق به جنگ

For with God I'm at war and with Satan at peace!

نظر دوست نادر کند سوی تو

The friend rarely looks the direction of you,

چو در روی دشمن بود روی تو

When yourself and the foe entertain the same view.

گرت دوست باید کز او بر خوری

If a friend you require who will friendship repay,

نباید که فرمان دشمن بری

You should not an enemy's order obey!

به سیم سیه تا چه خواهی خرید

How long with base coin will you buy at the mart,

که خواهی دل از مهر یوسف برید؟

And cut from the friendship of Joseph your heart?

روا دارد از دوست بیگانگی

The person approves of estrangement from friends,

که دشمن گزیند به همخانگی

Who to share the same house with the foe condescends.

ندانی که کمتر نهد دوست پای

A friend rarely places his foot, don't you know?

چو بیند که دشمن بود در سرای؟

In the house where he sees that there dwelleth a foe.

❖◉❖◉❖

حکایت سرکشی
Story of the Rebellious subject

یکی برد با پادشاهی ستیز
A subject engaged with a monarch in strife;
به دشمن سپردش که خونش بریز
To the foe he consigned him and said, " Take his life! "

گرفتار در دست آن کینه توز
Held fast in that harsh executioner's clutch,
همی گفت هر دم به زاری و سوز
To himself he was saying, with warmth weeping much,

اگر دوست بر خود نیازردمی
Had I brought not the wrath of the friend on my head,
کی از دست دشمن جفا بردمی؟
By the enemy, when would my blood have been shed? "

بتا جور دشمن بدردش پوست
The comrade incurring the Friend's wrath, let slide!
رفیقی که بر خود بیازرد دوست
The foe's ruthless harshness will tear off his hide.

تو از دوست گر عاقلی بر مگرد
Do not turn from the friend, if you claim to be wise,
که دشمن نیارد نگه در تو کرد
That the foe may not view you with sinister eyes.

تو با دوست یکدل شو و یک سخن
With the friend be united in word and in heart,
که خود بیخ دشمن برآید ز بن
That the enemy's root from its base may depart!

نپندارم این زشت نامی نکوست
This hideous aspersion I cannot commend:
به خشنودی دشمن آزار دوست
"In pleasing a foe to cause hurt to a friend! "

❁◉❁◉❁

حکایت کلاه بردار و ابلیس
Story of the Fraudulent Man and the Devil

یکی مال مردم به تلبیس خورد
A person, by fraud, people's property used;
چو برخاست لعنت بر ابلیس کرد
And on giving it up, he the Devil abused!

چنین گفتش ابلیس اندر رهی
On a highway, the Devil harangued him, one day:
که هرگز ندیدم چنین ابلهی
"I never have seen such a fool, I must say;

تو را با من است ای فلان، آشتی
In secret, between you and me there is peace;
به جنگم چرا گردن افراشتی؟
Why, in public, the sabre of warfare release? "

دریغ است فرمودهٔ دیو زشت
What a pity it is the vile demon's command,
که دست ملک بر تو خواهد نبشت
Will against you be writ by an angel's pure hand!

روا داری از جهل و ناپاکیت
You from foulness and ignorance seem to delight,
که پاکان نویسند ناپاکیت
That the holy the sins you've committed should write.

طریقی به دست آر و صلحی بجوی
Secure a good road and for peace seek with care!
شفیعی برانگیز و عذری بگوی
A Saviour obtain and excuses declare!

که یک لحظه صورت نبندد امان
One moment of respite for no one will stay,
چو پیمانه پر شد به دور زمان
When the measure is full, as time passes away.

وگر دست قدرت نداری به کار
If a strong hand in business you do not possess,
چو بیچارگان دست زاری بر آر
Like the helpless, put forward the hand of distress!

گرت رفت از اندازه بیرون بدی
And if beyond measure your wickedness went,
چو گفتی که بد رفت نیک آمدی
You'll be good when you say it has gone, and repent.

فرا شو چو بینی ره صلح باز

When the portal of peace you see open, advance!

که ناگه در توبه گردد فراز

For the door of repentance is shut at a glance!

مرو زیر بار گنه ای پسر

Oh son! do not walk under Sin's heavy load!

که حمال عاجز بود در سفر

For a porter gets weary and weak on the road.

پی نیک‌مردان بباید شتافت

It behoves one in rear of the pious to run;

که هر کاین سعادت طلب کرد یافت

For whoever enquired for this happiness, won.

ولیکن تو دنبال دیو خسی

But as you in pursuit of the vile demon strive,

ندانم که در صالحان چون رسی؟

I know not when you among the good will arrive.

پیمبر کسی را شفاعتگر است

That man's intercessor the Prophet will be,

که بر جادهٔ شرع پیغمبر است

Whom, walking the road of the Prophet, you see.

ره راست رو تا به منزل رسی

Pursue the straight road, till the wished stage you find!

تو بر ره نه ای زین قبل واپسی

You have strayed from the road and are therefore behind.

چو گاوی که عصار چشمش ببست

Like the ox, that, with eyes by the oil-presser bound,

دوان تا به شب، شب همانجا که هست

Through the whole of the night in the same place goes round.

⟨◉⟩⟨◉⟩

مرد آلوده و مسجد

Of the polluted man and the mosque

گل آلوده‌ای راه مسجد گرفت

To a mosque, one polluted with mud took the road,

ز بخت نگون بود اندر شگفت

Who because of misfortune bewilderment showed.

یکی زجر کردش که تبت یداک

Someone checking him said, " May your hands ruined be!

مرو دامن آلوده بر جای پاک

Skirt soiled, do not enter a place from filth free!

مرا رقتی در دل آمد بر این

Some sympathy entered my heart upon this,

که پاک است و خرم بهشت برین

For the Paradise lofty has pureness and bliss.

در آن جای پاکان امیدوار

In that place of the pure, who keep hope in their view,

گل آلودهٔ معصیت را چه کار؟

Has a man, skirt-polluted from sin, aught to do?

بهشت آن ستاند که طاعت برد

He who honestly worships will Paradise gain;

کرا نقد باید بضاعت برد

He who money possesses, choice goods will obtain.

مکن، دامن از گرد زلت بشوی

You must wash your skirt clean from the rubbish of vice,

که ناگه ز بالا ببندند جوی

For they'll shut off the stream, from above, in a trice.

مگو مرغ دولت ز قیدم بجست

Do not say, " Fortune's bird from my keeping has flown;

هنوزش سر رشته داری به دست

For the end of the string in your hand is still shown.

وگر دیر شد گرم رو باش و چست

Be quick-paced, and smart! if you've practised delay;

ز دیر آمدن غم ندارد درست

And coming late, right, need not cause you dismay.

هنوزت اجل دست خواهش نبست

Your hand of beseeching Death cared not to tie;

بر آور به درگاه دادار دست

Raise your hands to the shrine of the great God on high

مخسب ای گنه کار خوش خفته، خیز

Do not slumber! oh, negligent sinner, arise!

به عذر گناه آب چشمی بریز

In excuse for your sins, shed the tears from your eyes

چو حکم ضرورت بود کآبروی

When to scatter your fame comes the fated decree,

بریزند باری بر این خاک کوی

At least on the dust of this street let it be!

ور آبت نماند شفیع آر پیش

And if without name, let a pleader be shown,

کسی را که هست آبروی از تو بیش

Whose honour is higher esteemed than your own

به قهر ار براند خدای از درم

If the Lord should expel me, in wrath, from His gate,

روان بزرگان شفیع آورم

I'll bring as my pleaders the souls of the great!

حکایت وابستگی کودکان

Story on the dependence of children

همی یادم آید ز عهد صغر

I still recollect that in childhood I went,

که عیدی برون آمدم با پدر

One Eed, with my father, on sight-seeing bent.

به بازیچه مشغول مردم شدم

My attention was fixed on the people who played;

در آشوب خلق از پدر گم شدم

And, because of the crowd, from my father I strayed.

برآوردم از هول و دهشت خروش

I uttered a cry, full of terror and fear,

پدر ناگهانم بمالید گوش

When my father immediately tugged at my ear;

که ای شوخ چشم آخرت چند بار

Saying, "Oh, forward child! I oft told you, you know,

بگفتم که دستم ز دامن مدار

That your hand from my skirt, you were not to let go!

به تنها نداند شدن طفل خرد

A babe does not know how to travel alone,

که مشکل توان راه نادیده برد

For it is difficult walking a pathway unknown.

تو هم طفل راهی به سعی ای فقیر

In your efforts, you, too, are a child of the road;

برو دامن راه دانان بگیر

Go, and seize on the skirts of the people of God!

مکن با فرومایه مردم نشست

Do not sit and converse with a man who is mean!

چو کردی، ز هیبت فرو شوی دست

If you do, of all dignity wash your hands clean!

به فتراک پاکان درآویز چنگ

To pious men's saddle-straps cling with your hands!

که عارف ندارد ز دریوزه ننگ

For a saint's not ashamed who soliciting stands.

مریدان به قوت ز طفلان کمند

A disciple's less strong than a child of few years;

مشایخ چو دیوار مستحکمند

The teacher as strong as a rampart, appears.

بیاموز رفتار از آن طفل خرد

Take a lesson in walking from that infant small,

که چون استعانت به دیوار برد

Who when trying to walk, seeks the aid of a wall!

ز زنجیر ناپارسایان برست

He who sat in the circle of men who are chaste,

که در حلقهٔ پارسایان نشست

Free from profligates' fetters, enjoyed Freedom's taste.

اگر حاجتی داری این حلقه گیر

If you have a requirement, this circle embrace!

که سلطان ندارد از این در گزیر

For the sultan has no other way to get grace.

برو خوشه چین باش سعدی صفت

Like Sádi go out! and a gleaner become!

که گرد آوری خرمن معرفت

That you may, of the harvest of knowledge, glean some.

❖◉❖◉❖

حکایت مست خرمن سوز
Story of a drunken harvest-burner

یکی غله مرداد مه توده کرد

In the month of July, someone garnered his grain;

ز تیمار دی خاطر آسوده کرد

And cast further care for it out of his brain.

شبی مست شد و آتشی برفروخت

He got drunk, and a fire he enkindled, one night;

نگون بخت کالیوه، خرمن بسوخت

The unfortunate fool burned his harvest up quite.

دگر روز در خوشه چینی نشست

Next day, as a gleaner, his time he employed;

که یک جو ز خرمن نماندش به دست

For a grain was not left of his harvest, destroyed.

چو سرگشته دیدند درویش را

When they saw the poor man much afflicted in head,

یکی گفت پروردهٔ خویش را

A man to the son of his bosom, thus, said:

نخواهی که باشی چنین تیره روز

If you wish not, like him, to misfortune to turn,

به دیوانگی خرمن خود مسوز

Your harvest, through madness, take care not to burn! "

گر از دست شد عمرت اندر بدی

If your life from your hand has in wickedness flown,

تو آنی که در خرمن آتش زدی

You are he who a light on his harvest has thrown.

فضیحت بود خوشه اندوختن

To gather a harvest by gleaning's a shame,

پس از خرمن خویشتن سوختن

After giving the harvest you reaped to the flame.

مکن جان من، تخم دین ورز و داد

On the seed of the faith, oh, my life, do not trade!

مده خرمن نیکنامی به باد

Do not cast to the wind the good name you have made!.

چو برگشته بختی در افتد به بند

When a luckless man falls into bondage, through fate;

از او نیک‌بختان بگیرند پند

The fortunate men take a hint from his state.

تو پیش از عقوبت در عفو کوب

Ere Punishment reaches you, knock Pardon's door!

که سودی ندارد فغان زیر چوب

For under the rod it is useless to roar.

بر آر از گریبان غفلت سرت

Raise your head from the collar of negligence! lest,

که فردا نماند خجل در برت

To-morrow, some shame should remain in your breast.

❨◉❩❨◉❩

حکایت فراموشی حضور خدا

Story on forgetfulness of the presence of god

یکی متفق بود بر منکری

A certain one joined in committing a crime,

گذر کرد بر وی نکو محضری

A man of good countenance passed at the time;

نشست از خجالت عرق کرده روی

There he sat, and from shame beads of sweat on his face;

که آیا! خجل گشتم از شیخ کوی

He said, "Well! I'm ashamed 'fore the Sheikh of this place! "

شنید این سخن پیر روشن روان

The aged philosopher heard this remark

بر او بر بشورید و گفت ای جوان

He was vexed, and exclaimed, Oh, my youthful one, hark!

نیاید همی شرمت از خویشتن

Respecting yourself, are you callous to shame?

که حق حاضر و شرم داری ز من؟

For, God being present, you blushed when I came!

نیاسایی از جانب هیچ کس

Do not hope that through any one rest you will get;

برو جانب حق نگه دار و بس

Depart, and your hope on the Lord, only, set!

چنان شرم دار از خداوند خویش

In the presence of God, the same shame you should show,

که شرمت ز بیگانگان است و خویش

As in presence of strangers and people you know."

حکایت زلیخا با یوسف
Story of Joseph and Zulaikha

زلیخا چو گشت از می عشق مست
When Zulaikha became by the wine of love crazed,
به دامان یوسف در آویخت دست
Her hand to the skirt of poor Joseph she raised.

چنان دیو شهوت رضا داده بود
The demon of lust had encouraged so well,
که چون گرگ در یوسف افتاده بود
That, wolf-like, on Joseph she wantonly fell.

بتی داشت بانوی مصر از رخام
That, wolf-like, on Joseph she wantonly fell.
بر او معتکف بامدادان و شام
Which to worship, both morning and night she professed;

در آن لحظه رویش بپوشید و سر
That moment, she covered its head and its face,
مبادا که زشت آیدش در نظر
To prevent it from seeing her act of disgrace!

غم آلوده یوسف به کنجی نشست
Joseph sat in a corner, afflicted and grave,
به سر بر ز نفس ستمکاره دست
With a hand raised, himself from her ardour to save.

زلیخا دو دستش ببوسید و پای
Zulaikha kissed, fondly, his hands and his feet,
که ای سست پیمان سرکش درآی
Saying, "Fickle, and proud one! oh, come! I entreat!

به سندان دلی روی در هم مکش
With an anvil-like heart, be not frowning and coy!
به تندی پریشان مکن وقت خوش
Do not think of distress, in the moment of joy!"

روان گشتش از دیده بر چهره جوی
From his eyes, like a stream, the tears flowed down his face,
که برگرد و ناپاکی از من مجوی
Saying, "Turn thou, and bid me not share thy disgrace!

تو در روی سنگی شدی شرمناک
In front of a stone you exhibited shame;
مرا شرم باد از خداوند پاک
In presence of God should not I do the same?

چه سود از پشیمانی آید به کف

What good from repentance comes under your sway,

چو سرمایهٔ عمر کردی تلف؟

When Life's stock-in-trade you have squandered away?

شراب از پی سرخ رویی خورند

There are some who drink wine as it makes them feel glad;

وز او عاقبت زردرویی برند

The after effect, is to make them feel sad!

به عذرآوری خواهش امروز کن

With excuses, make known your requirements to-day

که فردا نماند مجال سخن

For, to-morrow, the power of speech will not stay.

حکایت کثیفی گربه

Story of the cat and its filth

پلیدی کند گربه بر جای پاک

A cat with its dirt a clean place will defile;

چو زشتش نماید بپوشد به خاک

And conceal it with dust when it sees it is vile.

تو آزادی از ناپسندیده‌ها

You are careless regarding your own evil ways;

نترسی که بر وی فتد دیده‌ها

Don't you fear lest they fall under other men's gaze?

براندیش از آن بندهٔ پرگناه

From that villanous slave, take a warning you may,

که از خواجه مخفی شود چند گاه

Who oft from his master has broken away;

اگر بر نگردد به صدق و نیاز

If he likes, he'll return, humbly begging, sincere;

به زنجیر و بندش بیارند باز

But fetters and chains will not make him appear.

به کین آوری با کسی بر ستیز

In revenge, with that person you safely can fight,

که از وی گزیرت بود یا گریز

From whom you've a cure, or a refuge in flight.

کنون کرد باید عمل را حساب

It behoves you, at present, your deeds to recall;

نه وقتی که منشور گردد کتاب

And not when the book becomes public to all.

کسی گر چه بد کرد هم بد نکرد

Though a person did evil, no evil was done,

که پیش از قیامت غم خود بخورد

If he grieved for himself, ere his last day had run.

گر آیینه از آه گردد سیاه

If the breath on a mirror makes dimness arise,

شود روشن آیینهٔ دل به آه

The heart's mirror adds to its brightness by sighs.

بترس از گناهان خویش این نفس

At the sins you have done, let alarm now appear!

که روز قیامت نترسی ز کس

So that, on the last day, not a soul you may fear.

حکایت سفر حبشه

Story on the consequences of Evil-doing

غریب آمدم در سواد حبش

As a stranger, at Habsh I arrived, on my way,

دل از دهر فارغ سر از عیش خوش

With my heart free from pain and my joyous head gay.

به ره بر یکی دکه دیدم بلند

By the side of the road I beheld a high mound,

تنی چند مسکین بر او پای بند

And on it some men who with fetters were bound;

بسیج سفر کردم اندر نفس

I instantly made preparations to fly;

بیابان گرفتم چو مرغ از قفس

Like a bird from its cage, to the desert I hie.

یکی گفت کاین بندیان شبروند

Someone said to me, "These are night-robbers, forsooth

نصیحت نگیرند و حق نشنوند

Who will neither take counsel nor listen to truth."

چو بر کس نیامد ز دستت ستم

If a man has not been by your actions oppressed,

تو را گر جهان شحنه گیرد چه غم؟

Should the world's guardian seize on you, don't be dis tressed!

نیاورده عامل غش اندر میان

A good man, as a prisoner, none has confined!

نیندیشد از رفع دیوانیان

Be afraid of the Lord! the Ameer do not mind!

وگر عفتت را فریب است زیر

If an agent has been in his dealings correct,

زبان حسابت نگردد دلیر

He feels not alarmed when by auditors checked.

نکونام را کس نگیرد اسیر

And if under his honesty cheating should lie,

بترس از خدای و مترس از امیر

His tongue in explaining accounts will be shy.

چو خدمت پسندیده آرم به جای

When a laudable service I'm able to show,

نیندیشم از دشمن تیره رای

I am free from concern for the dark-minded foe.

اگر بنده کوشش کند بندهوار

Should a slave be industrious, and humble appear,

عزیزش بدارد خداوندگار

His master will certainly reckon him dear.

وگر کند رای است در بندگی

And if, while at work, he should laziness show,

ز جانداری افتد به خربندگی

From a man to a load-bearing ass he will go.

قدم پیش نه کز ملک بگذری

Advance, that in rank you may angels surpass!

که گر باز مانی ز دد کمتری

If you tarry behind, you are worse than an ass.

❖◉❖◉❖

حکایت توبه

Story on penitence averting punishment

یکی را به چوگان مه دامغان

The King of Damghan, with a club, hit one blows,

بزد تا چو طبلش بر آمد فغان

Till his cries, like the sound of a kettle-drum, rose.

شب از بی قراری نیارست خفت

In the night-time, from writhing, he could not get rest;

بر او پارسایی گذر کرد و گفت

A pious man passed him and, thus, him addressed:

به شب گر ببردی بر شحنه، سوز

Had you brought the police an excuse over night,

گناه آبرویش نبردی به روز

Daylight had not looked on your infamous plight! "

کسی روز محشر نگردد خجل

At the Judgment, the person in shame will not pine,

که شبها به درگه برد سوز دل

Who brings his heart burning, at night, to the shrine.

هنوز ار سر صلح داری چه بیم؟

In the night of repentance ask God, if you're wise,

در عذرخواهان نبندد کریم

For forgiveness of sins that in day-time arise!

ز یزدان دادار داور بخواه

If you still think of peace, what's the fear for your state?

شب توبه تقصیر روز گناه

On implorers the Lord does not shut Pardon's gate!

کریمی که آوردت از نیست هست

It would be strange, were the bounteous Creator of all,

عجب گر بیفتی نگیردت دست

Not to lend you a hand if you happened to fall.

اگر بنده‌ای دست حاجت بر آر

If a slave of the Lord, raise your hands up in prayer!

وگر شرمسار آب حسرت ببار

Shed tears of repentance, if shame you should bear!

نیامد بر این در کسی عذر خواه

None has come to this door asking pardon, as yet,

که سیل ندامت نشستش گناه

Whose sins were not washed by the flood of regret.

نریزد خدای آبروی کسی

The Lord does not pour out the honour of one,

که ریزد گناه آب چشمش بسی

Whose sins cause the tears from his full eyes to run.

❁◉❁◉❁

حکایت مرگ پسر سعدی
Story on the death of Sádi's son

به صنعا درم طفلی اندر گذشت

At Sana, a young child of mine melted away;

چه گویم کز آنم چه بر سر گذشت

Of all that occurred to me, what shall I say?

قضا نقش یوسف جمالی نکرد

A Joseph-like picture the Fates never gave,

که ماهی گورش چو یونس نخورد

But was, Jonah-like, gulped by the fish of the grave.

در این باغ سروی نیامد بلند

In this garden, a cypress never reached any height,

که باد اجل بیخش از بن نکند

But the tempests of fate pulled its roots from their site.

عجب نیست بر خاک اگر گل شکفت

No wonder that roses will blow on the ground,

که چندین گل‌اندام در خاک خفت

When, beneath it, so many rose-bodies sleep sound!

به دل گفتم ای ننگ مردان بمیر

To my heart, I said, "Die, thou disgrace to mankind!

که کودک رود پاک و آلوده پیر

The child goes off pure, the old man, vile in mind! "

ز سودا و آشفتگی بر قدش

Out of love and distress, for his stature alone,

برانداختم سنگی از مرقدش

From his tomb I extracted a panel of stone.

ز هولم در آن جای تاریک و تنگ

On account of my dread, in that dark, narrow place,

بشورید حال و بگردید رنگ

My disconsolate state changed the hue of my face.

چو باز آمدم زآن تغیر به هوش

When I came to myself, from that horrible fear,

ز فرزند دلبندم آمد به گوش

From my darling, loved child, this arrived at my ear:

گرت وحشت آمد ز تاریک جای

"If this region of darkness produced in you fright,

به هش باش و با روشنایی در آی

Take care, when you enter, to carry a light!"

شب گور خواهی منور چو روز

If you wish that the night of the tomb should appear

از اینجا چراغ عمل برفروز

Bright as day, light the lamp of your actions while here!

تن کارکن می‌بلرزد ز تب

Shakes the husbandman's body, from fever and care,

مبادا که نخلش نیارد رطب

Peradventure the palms should not luscious dates bear.

گروهی فراوان طمع ظن برند

Some covetous men the opinion maintain,

که گندم نیفشانده خرمن برند

That, without sowing wheat, they'll a harvest obtain!

بر آن خورد سعدی که بیخی نشاند

He who planted the root, Sádi] on the fruit feeds!

کسی برد خرمن که تخمی فشاند

He will gather the harvest, who scattered the seeds!

❖◉❖◉❖

10

باب دهم

(CHAPTER X.)

 در مناجات و ختم کتاب

ON PRAYER

سرآغاز

In begin

بیا تا برآریم دستی ز دل

Let us raise up our hands from our hearts unto God;

که نتوان برآورد فردا ز گِل

For, to-morrow, we can't raise them up from the sod!

به فصل خزان در نبینی درخت

When the season of autumn arrives, you behold,

که بی برگ ماند ز سرمای سخت

That a tree remains leafless, because of the cold.

برآرد تهی دستهای نیاز

It raises its destitute hands to implore,

ز رحمت نگردد تهیدست باز

And does not retire without mercy in store.

مبندار از آن در که هرگز نبست

From the door that has never been shut, don't suppose

که نومید گردد بر آورده دست

That he who has stretched forth his hand, hopeless goes.

همه طاعت آرند و مسکین نیاز

All practise devotion, the poor supplicate;

بیا تا به درگاه مسکین نواز

At the shrine of the Kind-to-the-poor, come and wait!

چو شاخ برهنه برآریم دست

So that like the nude branch we our hands may sustain,

که بی برگ از این بیش نتوان نشست

For we can't without means any longer remain.

خداوندگارا نظر کن به جود

Oh, Lord! let Thy liberal glance on us rest!

که جرم آمد از بندگان در وجود

For the sins of Thy slaves have become manifest!

گناه آید از بندهٔ خاکسار

Sin comes from the slaves who humility show,-

به امید عفو خداوندگار

In the hope that the Lord will forgiveness bestow.

کریما به رزق تو پروردهایم

Oh, Kind One! we're reared by Thy daily supplies!

به انعام و لطف تو خو کردهایم

To Thy favour and gifts we're accustomed likewise!

گدا چون کرم بیند و لطف و ناز

When a beggar meets favour and kindness of heart,

نگردد ز دنبال بخشنده باز

From the heels of the giver he will not depart.

چو ما را به دنیا تو کردی عزیز

Since we in this world are beloved in Thy view,

به عقبی همین چشم داریم نیز

We have hope of the same in Futurity, too.

عزیزی و خواری تو بخشی و بس

Esteem and disgrace Thou alone canst bestow!

عزیز تو خواری نبیند ز کس

From none will Thy dear one humility know.

خدایا به عزت که خوارم مکن

By Thy honour, oh, God! do not make me defamed!

به ذل گنه شرمسارم مکن

At the baseness of sin, do not make me ashamed!

مسلط مکن چون منی بر سرم

Make not one like myself tyrannize over me!

ز دست تو به گر عقوبت برم

If I am to be punished, by Thee, let it be!

به گیتی بتر زین نباشد بدی

No evil is greater on Earth, I am sure,

جفا بردن از دست همچون خودی

Than harshness from one, like one's self, to endure.

مرا شرمساری ز روی تو بس

It suffices, that I in Thy presence feel shame,

دگر شرمسارم مکن پیش کس

Do not cause me to feel before others, the same!

گرم بر سر افتد ز تو سایه‌ای

If upon me should settle Thy shadow divine,

سپهرم بود کهترین پایه‌ای

The rank of the sky would be lower than mine.

اگر تاج بخشی سر افرازدم

It will raise up my head should Thou grant me a crown

تو بردار تا کس نیندازدم

Support me, that no one may tumble me down!

❖◉❖◉❖

حکایت شوریده دلفکار
Story on the madman's prayer, with remarks

تنم می‌بلرزد چو یاد آورم
My body still shakes, when I think of the prayers
مناجات شوریده‌ای در حرم
Of a madman, in Mecca's most sacred of squares.

همی‌گفت با حق به زاری بسی
He was saying to God, midst much wailing and cries:
میفکن که دستم نگیرد کسی
"Don't upset me! for no one will help me to rise!

به لطفم بخوان و مران از درم
If Thou call me with kindness, or drive me away;
ندارد به جز آستانت سرم
On Thy threshold, alone, my weak head I will lay."

تو دانی که مسکین و بیچاره‌ایم
That we are embarrassed and weak, Thou canst tell,
فرو مانده نفس اماره‌ایم
And crushed by inordinate passions, as well!

نمی‌تازد این نفس سرکش چنان
This passion refractory gallops not, such,
که عقلش تواند گرفتن عنان
That Wisdom can manage the reins in its clutch.

که با نفس و شیطان بر آید به زور؟
Who with devilish lust has the strength to contend?
مصاف پلنگان نیاید ز مور
Can an ant to encounter a leopard pretend?

به مردان راهت که راهی بده
By the men of Thy road, I swear, grant me a way!
وز این دشمنانم پناهی بده
And from all of those enemies, save me! I pray.

خدایا به ذات خداوندیت
Oh, God! by the nature in Thee that's divine!
به اوصاف بی مثل و مانندیت
By the virtues unequalled, unmatched that are Thine!

به لبیک حجاج بیت‌الحرام
By the phrase which the pilgrims to Mecca exclaim!
به مدفون یثرب علیه‌السلام
The entombed at Medina (peace be on his name!)

به تکبیر مردان شمشیر زن

By Allah- Akhbar shouted by Ghazies who strike;

که مرد وغا را شمارند زن

Who estimate warriors and women alike!

به طاعات پیران آراسته

By the fervent devotion of vet'rans arrayed!

به صدق جوانان نوخاسته

By the truthfulness youths newly-risen displayed!

که ما را در آن ورطهٔ یک نفس

In that gulf of "one breath, to preserve me assist!

ز ننگ دو گفتن به فریاد رس

From the shame of declaring that " two " can exist!

امید است از آنان که طاعت کنند

Those who practise devotion the hope entertain,

که بی طاعتان را شفاعت کنند

That they're able to plead for the many profane.

به پاکان کز آلایشم دور دار

By the holy! keep me from pollution away!

وگر زلتی رفت معذور دار

And if sin I've committed, forgive me, I pray!

به پیران پشت از عبادت دو تا

By the veterans, whose backs are bent double from prayer

ز شرم گنه دیده بر پشت پا

Who from shame for their sins at their insteps all stare,

که چشمم ز روی سعادت مبند

From the face of Felicity, seal not my eyes!

زبانم به وقت شهادت مبند

Let me speak, when the time to confess shall arise!

چراغ یقینم فرا راه دار

Hold Certainty's lamp on the road before me!

ز بد کردنم دست کوتاه دار

In the practice of sin, let my hand shortened be!

بگردان ز نادیدنی دیده‌ام

Turn my eyes from whatever' s unfit to be seen!

مده دست بر ناپسندیده‌ام

Do not give me control over things vile and mean!

من آن ذره‌ام در هوای تو نیست

That atom am I, on Thy love without claim;

وجود و عدم ز احتقارم یکی است

My presence or absence, in darkness, the same.

ز خورشید لطفت شعاعی بسم

From the sun of Thy favour, one ray suits my case;

که جز در شعاعت نبیند کسم

For, except in Thy rays, none can look on my face.

بدی را نگه کن که بهتر کس است

Look the way of a knave, that he may better be!

گدا را ز شاه التفاتی بس است

Regard from a king fills the beggar with glee.

مرا گر بگیری به انصاف و داد

If for justice and equity, me, Thou shouldst seize,

بنالم که عفوم نه این وعده داد

I shall weep; for Thy pardon did not promise these.

خدایا به ذلت مران از درم

Do not drive me, oh, God! from Thy door in disgrace!

که صورت نبندد دری دیگرم

For another, I cannot secure in its place.

ور از جهل غایب شدم روز چند

If through ignorance absent some days from Thy grace,

کنون کآمدم در به رویم مبند

I've returned, do not shut, now, the door in my face!

چه عذر آرم از ننگ تردامنی؟

From the shame of pollution, what plea shall I bring?

مگر عجز پیش آورم کای غنی

Better humbleness show, saying, " Absolute King!

فقیرم به جرم و گناهم مگیر

I'm a pauper; my sins by their guilt, do not test

غنی را ترحم بود بر فقیر

The rich show their pity for people distressed."

چرا باید از ضعف حالم گریست؟

To weep on account of my weakness is wrong;

اگر من ضعیفم پناهم قوی است

If I suffer from weakness, my refuge is strong!

خدایا به غفلت شکستیم عهد

We have broken our promise, oh God! through neglect;

چه زور آورد با قضا دست جهد؟

Who to battle against Thy decrees can expect?

چه برخیزد از دست تدبیر ما؟

From the hand of our counsels, what good can arise?

همین نکته بس عذر تقصیر ما

As a plea for our failings, this word will suffice:

همه هر چه کردم تو بر هم زدی

Whatever I've made, Thou hast cast from its site

چه قوت کند با خدایی خودی؟

How can Self ever cope with Divinity's might?

نه من سر ز حکمت به در می‌برم

Away from Thy orders my head I've not led;

که حکمت چنین می‌رود بر سرم

But Thy orders, like this, issue over my head! "

حکایت جواب سیه چرده

Story of the ugly man's astonishing reply

سیه چرده‌ای را کسی زشت خواند

A man called a dark-coloured person a fright,

جوابی بگفتش که حیران بماند

And received a reply that astonished him quite:

نه من صورت خویش خود کرده‌ام

No hand in portraying my features, I had,

که عیبم شماری که بد کرده‌ام

That fault you should find, saying, 'I have done bad.'

تو را با من از زشت رویم چه کار؟

What business have you with my beautiless face?

نه آخر منم زشت و زیبا نگار

Fm at least not the painter of wildness and grace."

از آنم که بر سر نبشتی ز پیش

Than what on my head Thou hast written before,

نه کم کردم ای بنده پرور نه بیش

Oh Protector of Slaves! I've not done less nor more.

تو دانایی آخر که قادر نیم
Thou, at least, art aware that no strength shows in me;
توانای مطلق تویی، من کیم؟
Thy power is absolute, who may I be?

گرم ره نمایی رسیدم به خیر
To safety I'll reach, if Thou show me the way;
وگر گم کنی باز ماندم ز سیر
On the road I'll be left, if Thou lead me astray.

جهان آفرین گر نه یاری کند
Creator of Earth! if Thou do not befriend,
کجا بنده پرهیزگاری کند؟
When will Thy poor servant to continence tend?

⟨◉⟩⟨◉⟩

حکایت درویش فقیر
Story of the poor dervish

چه خوش گفت درویش کوتاه دست
How aptly the indigent Dervish thus spoke —
که شب توبه کرد و سحرگه شکست
Who did penance at night, which at daybreak he broke

گر او توبه بخشد بماند درست
"If repentance to us He vouchsafe, it is right!
که پیمان ما بی ثبات است و سست
For unstable's our promise and wanting in might."

به حقت که چشمم ز باطل بدوز
By Thy Godhead! from lies sew my eyelids up well!
به نورت که فردا به نارم مسوز
By Thy light! do not burn me to-morrow in Hell!

ز مسکینیم روی در خاک رفت
My face from my poorness has gone to the ground;
غبار گناهم بر افلاک رفت
The dust of my sins in the Heav'ns may be found.

تو یک نوبت ای ابر رحمت ببار
For a little, oh cloud of compassion, rain some!
که در پیش باران نپاید غبار
For in presence of rain, dust will, surely, not come.

ز جرمم در این مملکت جاه نیست

From my sins, in this country no honour have!

ولیکن به ملکی دگر راه نیست

And yet, have no way to another to fly.

تو دانی ضمیر زبان بستگان

Of the state of the hearts of the dumb, Thou'rt aware;

تو مرهم نهی بر دل خستگان

Thou anointest the hearts of the wounded with care.

◈◉◈◉◈

حکایت بت پرست نیازمند
Story of the idolater and the idol

مغی در به روی از جهان بسته بود

From the world an idolater shut off his face,

بتی را به خدمت میان بسته بود

And to worship his idol was always in place.

پس از چند سال آن نکوهیده کیش

Fate, after some years, to that reprobate wretch

قضا حالتی صعبش آورد پیش

A difficult matter did suddenly fetch.

به پای بت اندر به امید خیر

At the idol's feet, hoping that good might be gained,

بغلطید بیچاره بر خاک دیر

On the dust of the temple he, helpless, complained:

که درمانده‌ام دست گیر ای صنم

"Oh, idol! I'm helpless; assistance I claim!

به جان آمدم رحم کن بر تنم

I am greatly exhausted, oh, pity my frame! "

بزارید در خدمتش بارها

He many a time in its presence bewailed,

که هیچش به سامان نشد کارها

But in getting his matter adjusted, he failed

بتی چون برآرد مهمات کس

Say, when will an idol one's business effect,

که نتواند از خود براندن مگس؟

That to drive off a fly from itself can't elect?

برآشفت کای پای بند ضلال

”Oh thou, on whose foot error’s fetter appears,

به باطل پرستیدمت چند سال

In folly, I’ve worshipped for several years!

مهمی که در پیش دارم برآر

The business that presses before me, complete!

و گر نه بخواهم ز پروردگار

If you don’t, the All-cherishing God, I’ll entreat! “

هنوز از بت آلوده رویش به خاک

He was still with the idol, his face smeared with dust,

که کامش برآورد یزدان پاک

When his wish was fulfilled by the God we all trust

حقایق شناسی در این خیره شد

A knower of truths at this work showed surprise;

سر وقت صافی بر او تیره شد

The time of his clearness seemed dark in his eyes.

که سرگشتهای دون یزدان پرست

For a mean and bewildered one worshipping God,

هنوزش سر از خمر بتخانه مست

Still drunk with the wine of the idol-abode —

دل از کفر و دست از خیانت نشست

Heart and head still with error and perfidy fraught,

خدایش برآورد کامی که جست

Through God, had accomplished the object he sought!

فرو رفت خاطر در این مشکلش

To this difficult matter his heart he resigned,

که پیغامی آمد به گوش دلش

When a message arrived at the ear of his mind:

که پیش صنم پیر ناقص عقول

In front of this idol, this foolish ‘one grieved,

بسی گفت و قولش نیامد قبول

And said rtiany words that had not been received;

گر از درگه ما شود نیز رد

Were he forced from my shrine, also, hopeless to plod,

پس آنگه چه فرق از صنم تا صمد؟

How far would it be from an idol to God? “

دل اندر صمد باید ای دوست بست

Your heart on the Lord, then, oh friend, you must bind

که عاجزترند از صنم هر که هست

All others, more feeble than idols, you'll find-

محال است اگر سر بر این در نهی

Place your head at this portal, and happen it can't,

که باز آیدت دست حاجت تهی

That your hand should return to you empty, from want

خدایا مقصر به کار آمدیم

Oh God I we have come, of our failures to tell;

تهیدست و امیدوار آمدیم

We have come to Thee sinners, and hopeful, as well

◄◉►◄◉►

حکایت مست و مسجد
Story of the drunkard at the mosque

شنیدم که مستی ز تاب نبید

I have heard that, excited with liquor, a man

به مقصورهٔ مسجدی در دوید

Within a Mosque's holiest sanctuary ran.

بنالید بر آستان کرم

He wept at the threshold of mercy, and said:

که یارب به فردوس اعلی برم

Oh God! into Paradise may I be led! "

مؤذن گریبان گرفتش که هین

The mosque-crier collared him, saying, " Take heed!

سگ و مسجد! ای فارغ از عقل و دین

Dog and mosque! Oh thou wanting in wisdom and creed!

چه شایسته کردی که خواهی بهشت؟

What have you done to ask for a Paradise place?

نمی‌زیبدت ناز با روی زشت

To ogle becomes not your beautiless face."

بگفت این سخن پیر و بگریست مست

Thus spoke the old man; and the drunkard wept sore,

که مستم بدار از من ای خواجه دست

Saying, "Master! I'm drunk, do not worry me more!

عجب داری از لطف پروردگار

You're amazed that the mercy of God has such scope,

که باشد گنهکاری امیدوار؟

That even a sinner may venture to hope!

تو را می‌گویم که عذرم پذیر

Not to you do I say — my excuses receive!

در توبه باز است و حق دستگیر

Wide's the door of repentance, and God will relieve!"

همی شرم دارم ز لطف کریم

At the kind Giver's favour I, too, suffer shame,

که خوانم گنه پیش عفوش عظیم

That before his forgiveness, great sins I can name.

کسی را که پیری در آرد ز پای

When age robs a person of strength, without doubt,

چو دستش نگیری نخیزد ز جای

If no one assists him, he can't move about.

من آنم ز پای اندر افتاده پیر

I am that aged man, who has fallen from place;

خدایا به فضل خودم دست گیر

Assist me, oh God! by Thy favour and grace!

نگویم بزرگی و جاهم ببخش

I do not say, " Greatness and rank give to me!"

فروماندگی و گناهم ببخش

But " From sorrow and sin, grant that I may be free! "

اگر یاری اندک زلل داندم

If a friend happen some of my failings to know,

به نابخردی شهره گرداندم

From folly, he makes them in public to go.

تو بینا و ما خائف از یکدگر

Thou hast vision! Alarm at each other we feel!

که تو پرده پوشی و ما پرده در

Thou secrets concealest! we secrets reveal!

برآورده مردم ز بیرون خروش

From the outside, the people have caused an uproar;

تو با بنده در پرده و پرده پوش

The slave's secrets Thou sharest and cover'st them o'er.

به نادانی ار بندگان سرکشند

If through foolishness slaves become arrogant, then,

خداوندگاران قلم در کشند

The masters will through their offence draw the pen.

اگر جرم بخشی به مقدار جود

If Thou pardon becoming Thy bounty's degree,

نماند گنهکاری اندر وجود

In existence a sinner there never will be.

وگر خشم گیری به قدر گناه

If befitting our errors Thy anger prevails,

به دوزخ فرست و ترازو مخواه

Despatch us to Hell, and don't ask for the scales!

گرم دست گیری به جایی رسم

I'll accomplish my wish, if Thou take my weak hand;

وگر بفکنی بر نگیرد کسم

And if Thou cast me down, none will help me to stand.

که زور آورد گر تو یاری دهی؟

Who will practise oppression, if Thou wilt befriend?

که گیرد چو تو رستگاری دهی؟

Who will seize me, if freedom to me Thou extend?

دو خواهند بودن به محشر فریق

Two sects there will be on the last Judgment Day;

ندانم کدامین دهندم طریق

I know not to which they will show me the way.

عجب گر بود راهم از دست راست

Twill be strange if my road to the right hand should be?

که از دست من جز کجی برنخاست

For crookedness only has risen from me.

دلم می‌دهد وقت وقت این امید

This hope my heart gives me, again and again,

که حق شرم دارد ز موی سپید

That God is ashamed of the grey hairs of men.

عجب دارم ار شرم دارد ز من

I wonder if He is ashamed about me?

که شرم نمی‌آید از خویشتن

As shame for myself, I'm unable to see.

نه یوسف که چندان بلا دید و بند

Did not Joseph, who heavy misfortunes endured, And for long in a prison was closely immured,

چو حکمش روان گشت و قدرش بلند

When his orders were current all over the land, And his dignity also became very grand,

گنه عفو کرد آل یعقوب را؟

Forgive Jacob's sons for the sins they had wrought?

که معنی بود صورت خوب را

For a face that is handsome with virtue is fraught

به کردار بدشان مقید نکرد

He did not confine them for having transgressed,

بضاعات مزجاتشان رد نکرد

And did not refuse the small stock they possessed.

ز لطفت همین چشم داریم نیز

This hope of Thy favour I too entertain;

بر این بی‌بضاعت ببخش ای عزیز

Oh God! to forgive a poor stockless one deign!

کس از من سیه نامه تر دیده نیست

None whose cry of distress is rejected on high,

که هیچم فعال پسندیده نیست

Has a record more black nor eyes moister than I!

جز این کاعتمادم به یاری تست

My hope in Thy aiding alone, do I place;

امیدم به آمرزگاری تست

And my trust is that I shall be saved by Thy grace.

بضاعت نیاوردم الا امید

No capital, saving fond hope, do I bear;

خدایا ز عفوم مکن ناامید

Of Thy pardon, oh God! do not make me despair!

MUSLIH-AL-DIN, better known under his poetical name of Sádi (acquired from his patron, the Persian king, Sád-Atabak), was born at Shiraz, in Persia, A.D. 1210. His father, Abdullah supposed to be a descendant of Ali, the- cousin and son-in-law of the "Prophet" was for some time in straitened circumstances; but having obtained a petty government appointment through an influential patron, his zeal, ability, and integrity raised him in the estimation of his superiors, gained for him promotion, and opened up a prospect of future advancement. Unfortunately, he died while Sádi was still a child, leaving him a trifling heritage, which soon disappeared, through the intrigues of false friends, and Sádi and his mother were obliged to live for a time on the bounty of a Saracen chief.

Sádi manifested from childhood, and maintained throughout life, a very religious disposition, and by his devoutness and attention to religious duties, acquired the title of Sheikh. He was passionately fond of learning, and, in pursuit of knowledge, determined to travel to Baghdad, at that time famed for its learned men and schools. On arrival at Baghdad his prospects were gloomy enough, as he was without money and a stranger. He was fortunate in relating his tale to a wealthy and benevolent inhabitant of the city, who sympathized with him, and provided for him at a private school. He worked hard, and when twenty-one years of age composed some verses of poetry, which he dedicated in verse to Shams-ud-din-Abdul-Farah, professor of Literature in the Nizamiah College, Baghdad. The professor was so well pleased with the verses, that he gave Sádi an allowance from his private purse and promised to assist him in his literary pursuits.

Soon afterwards Sádi gained admission to the Nizamiah College, and by his intelligence and industry, aided by able instructors, obtained a scholarship, which enabled him to pursue his- studies comfortably. He remained at Baghdad till he was sixty-four years of age, and acquired a great reputation as a poet, orator, and theologian.

Under the Caliph, Mutasim-Billah, youngest son of the celebrated Harun-ar-Rashid, the court of Baghdad had become corrupt, and the government feeble. The

Tartar chief, Halaku-Khan, had overrun the neighborhood, and hearing of the state of anarchy existing in Baghdad, besieged the city and, ultimately, captured it. His soldiers sacked the city and committed great excesses. 'Sádi was obliged to flee, and, in company with his tutor, Abdul-Kadir of Gilan, professor of Theology, made a pilgrimage to Mecca. It is stated that Sádi performed the pilgrimage to Mecca fourteen times on foot; and his writings show that he visited parts of Europe, Africa, and Asia, as far as India.

Sádi was twice married but does not appear to have been happy in his choice of wives, and his experience of married life led him to speak occasionally in disparaging terms of the fair sex. The story of his first marriage is amusing. He had been living for some time at Damascus and getting tired of the society of his friends there, wandered into the desert of Palestine. He was captured by Crusaders, and made to work, along with Jews, among the mud at the fortifications of Tripoli. A chief of Aleppo passing by, saw Sádi, and, recognizing him, inquired how he came to be there. The chief, on hearing his story, paid ten pieces of silver for his ransom, and took him with him to his own home at Aleppo. The chief had a daughter whom he gave to Sádi in marriage, with a dower of one hundred pieces of silver. She proved herself to be a vixen, and Sádi's home in consequence was not a Paradise. On one occasion she said to him, "Are you not the fellow whom my father bought from the Franks for ten pieces of silver ?" "Yes!" he said, "and sold to you for a hundred pieces!"

Sádi had a son and a daughter. The son, of whom he was very fond, died in childhood, and his untimely end was a source of great grief to him. His daughter afterwards became the wife of the celebrated poet Hafiz.

Sádi was held in great repute by his countrymen and found a liberal patron in the King of Persia, Sad-Atabak, who encouraged learning, and was fond of the society of learned men. He made Sádi Court poet, and Sádi's gratitude was shown in his almost fulsome praise of the monarch.

Sádi has written numerous works, in prose and verse, on moral, theological, and amatory subjects; and the best known and most read of his writings are the Gulistan in prose and verse, and the Bostdn in verse. He delighted in wit and repartee, and puns abound in his works. His moral and religious remarks show great depth of thought, correct observation, and knowledge of human nature. Judged by modern European ideas of propriety, he sometimes borders on the obscene in his remarks; but orientals do not guage their morality by European standards, and allowance must be made for Sádi accordingly. His style of writing is simple but vigorous, and the pride he occasionally displays in his conscious superiority in intelligence and eloquence over his neighbors is pardonable.

He is credited with having worked miracles, especially that of restoring to life a young lover, who had cast himself down from a tower, one hundred feet high, to the ground. If the young man survived the fall, it was certainly a miracle!

Sádi was modest in manner and could not tolerate vanity in others. He dressed modestly, was short in stature and not handsome; but a face beaming with intelligence and a long-flowing beard gave him an engaging and venerable appearance.

He closed his chequered life at Shiraz, the place of his birth, A.D. 1291, having reached the ripe age of one hundred and sixteen years. He is honoured as a saint by Mohamedans, and his tomb called the Sádiya in the vicinity of the town of Shiraz, is visited by numerous pilgrims and travelers.

زندگی نامه سعدی

تولد: ابومحمد مشرف‌الدین مصلح بن عبدالله بن مشرف، متخلص به سعدی، از شاعران پرآوازه ایران زمین، بر اساس استنباط صاحبنظران از آثارش در سال ۶۰۶ هجری قمری (۵۸۹ خورشیدی و ۱۲۱۰ میلادی) در شیراز چشم به جهان گشود. زمان تولد این شاعر، حکمران شیراز سومین پادشاه اتابکان بود. اتابکان علاوه بر شیراز، در دمشق، موصل، حلب، بین‌النهرین و آذربایجان نیز قدرتی داشتند.

سعدی در خانواده‌ای اهل علم و ادب دیده به جهان گشود. پدرش معلم دین و از کارکنان دربار اتابک و شاه سعد بن زنگی بود و بزرگترین مشوق سعدی برای یادگیری علم و دین بود. به این ترتیب از کودکی تحت تعلم و تربیت پدر قرار گرفت و به اطلاعات گسترده ای در زمینه تاریخ و ادبیات دست یافت تا اینکه در ۱۲ سالگی او را از دست داد و نزد جد مادری خود بنام مسعود بن مصلح الفارسی بزرگ شد.

واژه سعدی از نام اتابک مظفرالدین سعد، پسر ابوبکر، پسر سعد، پسر زنگی گرفته شده و برخی بر این باورند این شاعر به عنوان حق شناسی، تخلص سعدی را برای خود برگزیده و استاد سخن، پادشاه سخن، شیخ اجل و استاد، از القاب ویژه این شاعر بزرگ ایرانی به شمار می‌رود.

سفر و تحصیل

سعدی در دوران کودکی، مقدمات علوم ادبی و شرعی را در شیراز آموخت اما اوضاع نابسامان ایران در پایان دوران سلطان محمد خوارزمشاه و به‌ویژه حمله سلطان غیاث‌الدین خوارزمشاه به شیراز (سال ۶۲۰ هجری قمری)، سعدی را بر آن داشت که در روزگار جوانی شیراز را ترک کند و به بغداد برود.

او در نوجوانی تحت نظر اتابک به بغداد رفت و در مدرسه نظامیه بغداد مشغول به تحصیل شد و از حضور استادان بنام دوران خود از جمله ابوالفرج بن جوزی و شهاب‌الدین عمر سهروردی بهره برد. او در این دانشگاه که محل تربیت قاضی، فقیه و محدث اهل سنت بود دروسی از قبل صرف و نحو عربی، حدیث، فقه، اصول، طب، نجوم و فلسفه را فرا گرفت. سعدی پس از تحصیل در نظامیه، شغل واعظی پیشه می‌کند که مستلزم سفر به مناطق مختلف و ارائه خطابه و ارشاد مردم است.

سعدی برای کسب علم و دانش و تجربه به سمت دمشق، بعلبک، حجاز حرکت کرد. سعدی در مدت اقامت خود در دمشق بعلت دلگیری از دوستان از شغل خود کناره گیری کرده و سر به بیابان می گذارد اما در مسیر اسیر فرنگیان می شود. او مدتی بعنوان غنیمت در شهر طرابلس (لیبی فعلی) به کار اجباری گرفته می شود اما آنجا توسط یک تاجر باز خرید و آزاد می شود. گفته شده بعد از آزادی او توسط تاجر از بند مسیحیان، سعدی با دختر این تاجر ازدواج می کند و اتفاقا زنی بد خوی و ستیزه جوی نصیبش می شود.

بعد از جدایی از آن، بار دیگر در صنعا زنی اختیار کرده و از آن زن صاحب کودکی زیبا می شود اما کودک در عین طراوت پس از مدتی می میرد. بعد از این ماجرا سعدی سال ها بعد ازدواج کرده است.

سعدی به شهر های مختلفی در تمام نقاط دنیا پا گذاشت. نشانه هایی از سفر به هندوستان، ترکستان، آسیای صغیر، غزنین، آذربایجان، فلسطین، چین، یمن و آفریقای شمالی هم در سروده های وی یافت می‌شود. اما به نظر می‌رسد که بعضی از این سفرها داستان‌پردازی باشند و منطقاً پایه نمادین و اخلاقی داشته باشند. این جهانگردی به روایتی سی سال به طول انجامید.

تالیف آثار

سعدی در اواخر چهل سالگی به شیراز بازگشت و در خانقاه ابوعبدالله بن خفیف ساکن شد. در دوران ابوبکربن سعد بن زنگی حاکم فارس، شیراز پناهگاه دانشمندانی شده‌بود که از دَمِ تیغِ تاتار جان سالم به‌دربرده‌بودند. در دوران وی، سعدی مقامی ارجمند در دربار به‌دست آورده‌بود. در آن زمان، ولیعهد مظفرالدین ابوبکر به نام سعد بن ابوبکر، به سعدی ارادت بسیار داشت و در همین ایام سعدی دست به خلقت شاهکارهای جاودان خودبه نام بوستان و گلستان زد و آنها را به نام «اتابک» و پسرش سعد بن ابوبکر کرد.

همه آثار سعدی که شامل شعر و نثر می‌شود، در کتابی به نام کلیات سعدی جمع‌آوری شده است؛ اما در این میان دو آثار او به نام‌های بوستان و گلستان در دو کتاب مستقل آمده‌اند.

بوستان یا سعدی نامه: بوستان اولین اثر سعدی بوده که تالیف آن در سال ۶۵۵ هجری قمری به پایان رسید. این کتاب که یکی از شاهکارهای ادب فارسی به شمار می‌رود، در نسخه‌های قدیمی سعدی‌نامه نامیده می‌شد. سعدی، بوستان را در طی سفرهای خود به نقاط مختلف دنیا سروده شده است. این اثر که به نظم (شعر) و در قالب مثنوی است، از نظر وزن و قالب آن را حماسی به حساب می آورند. با این حال محتوای آن بیشتر در زمینه اخلاق و تربیت، سیاست و مسایل اجتماعی است و حدودا چهار هزار بیت شعر را شامل می‌شود.

بوستان با یک مقدمه نسبتاً طولانی شروع می‌شود که در حمد خداوند، ستایش پیامبر اسلام، بیان دلیل نگارش کتاب و مدح ابوبکر و سعد زنگی سروده‌شده‌است و شامل ۱۸۳ داستان و ده فصل در مورد فضیلت هایی مانند عدالت، مهربانی، عشق، حیا، آزادی خواهی، سخاوت، رضایت و خوشبختی و شیوه های وجدانی درویش است که به همه مردم برای داشتن زندگی بهتر و شادتر اشاره می کند.

حکایت‌های بوستان از نظر پیچیدگی و ساختار، یکسان نیستند؛ برخی از ساختار داستانی پیچیده‌تری برخوردارند و حوادث و اشخاص متعددی را در بر می‌گیرند، درحالی که برخی دیگر ساده و درحد حکایت‌واره‌اند. بوستان را می‌توان کتابی اخلاقی و آموزشی دانست که سعدی آرمان‌شهر خود را در آن توصیف می‌کند.

گلستان: گلستان شاهکار نویسندگی و بلاغت فارسی و یکی از تاثیرگذارترین کتاب‌های نثر در ادبیات فارسی است. سعدی این کتاب را در سال ۶۵۶ هجری قمری، به نثر آهنگین و آمیخته با نظم به تالیف درآورد. گلستان شامل هشت فصل به نام‌های سیرت پادشاهان، اخلاق درویشان، فضیلت قناعت، فوائد خاموشی، عشق و جوانی، ضعف و پیری، تاثیر تربیت و آداب صحبت است.

سعدی در این کتاب از پرداختن به تاریخ نگاری و تذکره نویسی پرهیز کرده و تمرکز خود را بر بیان امور مربوط به زندگی و منش اشخاص گذاشته است. گلستان را می توان گزارش سعدی از جامعه زمان خود پنداشت، که در آن اوضاع فرهنگی و اجتماعی مردم به صورت واقعی به تصویر کشیده شده است.

حکایت های گلستان، فراخور موضوع، کوتاه یا بلند می شود. در برخی از حکایت ها، شخصیت های خیالی یا واقعی ثالثی وجود دارند و ایفای نقش می کنند؛ اما در برخی از حکایت ها، نگارنده حاضر و ناظر است. برخی از این رخدادها، رخدادهای واقعی زندگی او و برخی صرفاً رخدادهای تخیای هستند.

کتاب گلستان نخستین بار در تبریز در سال ۱۸۲۲ میلادی به چاپ رسید. تا قبل از گلستان، هیچ کتاب دیگری به زبان فارسی با استفاده از دستگاه چاپ منتشر نشده بود. محمدعلی فروغی در سال ۱۳۱۶ خورشیدی گلستان را برای اولین بار، به طور علمی تصحیح کرد.پس از آن شرح‌ها، فرهنگ‌ها و تصحیح‌های مختلفی از گلستان منتشر شد که یکی از مهم‌ترین و دقیق‌ترین آنها، تصحیح دکتر غلامحسین یوسفی است که در سال ۱۳۶۸ عرضه گردید. قطعه مشهور بنی‌آدم در باب اول گلستان: "در سیرت پادشاهان" آمده است و با داشتن مضمون انسان دوستانه‌اش توجهی جهانی یافته است. در سال ۱۳۸۴، از سوی ایران، فرشی از استاد صیرفیان به سازمان ملل متحد اهدا و در آنجا نصب شد که شعر بنی‌آدم در آن نقش بسته بود.

این شعر در پیام فارسی که در مجموعه پیام‌های فضاپیمای ویجر (در مجموع، پیامهایی به ۵۵ زبان)برای فضاهای دوردست فرستاده شده‌است، به‌عنوان پیام بر گزیده شده‌است.

کلیات سعدی

غزلیات: سعدی حدود ۷۰۰ غزل دارد. محور بیشتر غزل‌های سعدی، عشق است و از معدود شاعرانی است که غزل‌های عاشقانه‌اش از ابتدا تا انتها عاشقانه باقی می‌ماند. علاوه بر غزل‌های عاشقانه، سعدی غزل‌های عارفانه و غزل‌های پندآموز نیز سروده‌است. در حالت کلی، غزلیات سعدی در چهار کتاب به نام‌های طیبات، بدایع، خواتیم و غزلیات قدیم جمع‌آوری شده است. سعدی غزلیات قدیم را در دوران جوانی سروده که سرشار از شور و شعف است. خواتیم مربوط به دوران کهنسالی و دربرگیرنده زهد و عرفان و اخلاقیات است. بدایع و طیبات، مربوط به

دوران میانسالی و پختگی سعدی‌اند؛ هم شور و شعف جوانی و هم زهد و عرفان را در بر می‌گیرند و به لحاظ هنری نسبت به دو کتاب دیگر برتری دارد.

هزلیات: در مجموعه آثار سعدی، سه رساله با نام‌های مطایبات، مضحکات و خبیثات دیده می‌شود که به مجموعه آنها هزلیات گفته می‌شود. مطایبات، مجموعه‌ای از لطیفه‌ها و داستان‌های جنسی است که در نگارش آنها از الفاظ جسورانه و بیان عریان و بی‌پروا استفاده شده‌است. خبیثات و مضحکات به نثر نوشته شده‌اند و در نسخه لرد گرینوی اثری از آنها نیست. گفته می‌شود سعدی به دستور عالی مقامان زمان خود، هزلیات را سروده است.

قصاید: شامل قصیده‌های فارسی و قصیده‌های عربی است. قصیده‌های فارسی در وصف ستایش پروردگار، مدح، اندرز، نصیحت بزرگان و پادشاهان قرن معاصر بوده که بسیار ارزشمند است.

قصیده‌های عربی حدود هفتصد بیت دارد که شامل موضوعات غنایی و مدح و اندرز و مرثیه می‌باشد. یکی از این قصیده‌ها، در مرثیه آخرین خلیفه عباسی، المستعصم بالله سروده‌شده‌است. سعدی اثر مستقلی به زبان عربی ندارد؛ اما برخی از اشعار او به زبان عربی سروده شده است. قصاید عربی سعدی شامل تعدادی قصیده، قطعه و تک بیت بوده و در سال ۱۳۹۰ در کتابی با نام اشعار عربی سعدی به‌همراه ترجمه فارسی آن‌ها، به چاپ رسید.

صاحبیه: صاحبیه، مجموعه‌ای از قطعات فارسی و عربی است که بیشتر آن‌ها در ستایش شمس‌الدین صاحب دیوان جوینی وزیر دانشمند دوست عصر اتابکان سروده شده و این اثر به همین علت به صاحبیه نام‌گذاری شده است. سعدی، علاوه بر گلستان، آثار دیگری نیز به نثر دارد، که عبارتند از مجالس پنج گانه، رساله عقل و عشق و نصیحه الملوک که شیوایی و جذابیت آن‌ها با دو کتاب معروف این شاعر، یعنی بوستان و گلستان برابری می‌کند.

مجالس پنجگانه: مجالس پنجگانه سعدی به نثر است و به خطابه‌ها و سخنرانی‌های او اطلاق می‌شود. محتوای این اثر سعدی به نصیحت و ارشاد مربوط می‌شود؛ اما از نظر نویسندگی سطح بسیار پایین‌تری از گلستان دارد.

نصیحه الملوک: محتوای این اثر سعدی در محوریت پند و اخلاق و چندین رساله دیگر به نثر در موضوعات مختلف است.

ملعمات و مثلثات و ترجیعات: این آثار سعدی در قالب‌های خاصی همانند ترجیع بند سروده شده است.

مراثی: مشتمل بر چند قصیده در مرثیه چند تن از رجال معاصر سعدی از جمله مستعصم آخرین خلیفه عباسی بوده که به فرمان هلاکو کشته شد. مراثی از چندین مرثیه در وصف ابوبکر بن سعد بن زنگی و سعد بن ابوبکر از اتابکان فارس و وزرای آن زمان هم تشکیل شده است.

همچنین در نسخه‌های چاپی پاکستان و هند کتاب شعر مثنوی دیگری با نام **کریما** به سعدی نسبت داده شده که اصالت این انتساب با توجه به قوی نبودن اشعار و موجود نبودن اسناد خطی از آن، محل شک است.

ویژگی آثار سعدی

سهل و ممتنع: معنی و مفهوم آثار سعدی به سادگی دریافته می‌شود و در ظاهر، نگارش چنین جملات یا ابیاتی ساده به‌نظر می‌رسد. اما در عمل، تقلید یا پدیدآوردن آثار مشابه، دشوار یا غیرممکن می‌شود.

ایجاز: کاستن عبارات بیهوده در شعر، نه تنها از زیبایی کلام نمی‌کاهد بلکه آن را در نظر خواننده زیبا تر و قابل فهم تر جلوه می‌دهد. از دیگر تکنیک‌های اصلی سعدی در به کارگیری ایجاز، حذف کردن بخشی از جمله است؛ به‌گونه‌ای که ذهن خواننده، ناخودآگاه بخش حذف‌شده را درج می‌کند و متوجه کمبود آن در جمله نمی‌شود.

موسیقی و وزن: موسیقی اشعار سعدی و آهنگین بودن آن‌ها، خواندن اشعار این شاعر را آسان تر می‌کند. او معمولا از اوزان عروضی در اشعارش استفاده می‌کند. هم چنین آرایه های ادبی که موجب آهنگین شدن اشعار می‌شود در آثار سعدی به وفور یافت می‌شود.

طنز و ظرافت: سعدی به عنوان استاد سخن، از طنازی‌های مخصوص به خود در آثارش بهره می‌جوید. لحن طنز آثار او، خشکی کلام را می گیرد و تاثیر گذاری بیشتری بر مخاطب خواهد داشت.

تأثیرگذاری بر زبان فارسی: کلام سعدی تاثیر انکارناپذیری بر زبان فارسی گذاشته‌است؛ به‌طوری‌که شباهت قابل توجهی بین زبان فارسی امروزی و زبان سعدی وجود دارد. آثار او مدت‌ها در مدرسه‌ها و مکتب‌خانه‌ها به‌عنوان منبع آموزش زبان فارسی تدریس می‌شده و بسیاری از ضرب‌المثل‌های رایج در زبان فارسی از آثار وی اقتباس شده‌است. به گفته ادوارد براون، ایران‌شناس مشهور بریتانیایی، طی شش قرن و نیم، هرجا به تحصیل زبان فارسی پرداخته شده، نخستین کتاب‌هایی که به دست محصل داده‌اند، آثار سعدی بوده‌است.

تکه‌های بسیاری از شعرها و حکایت‌های سعدی در فارسی امروز به‌صورت اصطلاح یا ضرب‌المثل به‌کارمی‌رود. بیش از ۴۰۰ عبارت از گلستان و بیش از ۸۰۰ مورد از غزل‌ها به عنوان ضرب‌المثل وارد زبان فارسی شده‌است.

تأثیرگذاری بر غرب: سعدی اولین شاعر ایرانی است که آثار او به یکی از زبان‌های اروپایی ترجمه شده است. آندره دو ریه در سال ۱۶۳۴ میلادی قسمت‌هایی از گلستان را به زبان فرانسوی ترجمه کرد. دو دهه پس از ترجمه او، یعنی در ۱۶۵۴، آدام اولئاریوس، ترجمهٔ کاملی از بوستان و گلستان را به زبان آلمانی منتشر کرد. ژان دو لا فونتن یکی از مشهورترین حکایت‌نویسان فرانسوی است که در برخی از آثار خود، بدون کم و کاست از حکایات سعدی اقتباس کرده‌است.

ولتر، نویسنده مشهور عصر روشنگری در فرانسه، در بخش‌هایی از رمان فلسفی صادق، تحت تأثیر گلستان سعدی بوده‌است. دنیس دیدرو از نویسندگان بزرگ قرن هفدهم فرانسه است که آثار سعدی را ستایش کرده است. به‌طور

خاص، باب اول گلستان (در سیرت پادشاهان) مورد توجه وی قرار داشته‌است. دیدرو نیز، دیباچه و برخی از حکایات گلستان را به زبان فرانسوی ترجمه کرده‌است.

گوته، شاعر بلندآوازه آلمانی، در خلق آثار خود به ادبیات شرقی و به‌طور خاص، ادبیات فارسی توجه ویژه‌ای داشت. گوته، سعدی را می‌شناخته و در خلق آثار خود از سعدی تأثیر می‌پذیرفته‌است. یکی از کتاب‌های وی با نام دیوان غربی–شرقی، اگرچه به‌طور کاملاً مشهود تحت تأثیر اشعار حافظ سروده‌شده و در هیچ کجای کتاب نامی از سعدی برده نشده؛ اما بخش‌هایی از آن نیز حاوی اشعاری است که از بوستان و گلستان سعدی اقتباس شده‌است. گوته، این دیوان خود را با نقل فارسی و ترجمه آلمانی یکی از اشعار گلستان به پایان می‌برد.

لازار کارنو، ریاضی‌دان مشهور فرانسوی، علاقه خیلی زیاد به سعدی، نام سعدی را به‌عنوان نام میانی فرزندان خود برگزید. فرزند وی نیکولا سعدی کارنو، پدر علم ترمودینامیک و نوه وی ماری فرانسوا سعدی کارنو، رئیس جمهور فرانسه در سال‌های ۱۸۸۷ تا ۱۸۹۴ است که نام میانی هردو به افتخار سعدی انتخاب شده‌است.

رالف والدو امرسون، شاعر آمریکایی قرن نوزدهم میلادی است. وی به فرهنگ و زبان‌های شرقی (از جمله فارسی و عربی) علاقه داشت و به واسطه مطالعه ترجمه آلمانی گلستان، با سعدی آشنا شد. وی مقالاتی در مورد سعدی نوشته و منتشر کرده‌است. در اشعار او نیز می‌توان عباراتی یافت که تحت تأثیر گلستان سعدی سروده‌شده‌است.

یادبود و بزرگداشت

سعدی پس از نگارش دو کتاب بوستان و گلستان در شیراز سکنا گزید و باقی عمر خود را صرف سرودن شعر و مراقبه کرد. در این زمان شهرت و آوازه او تا فرسنگ‌ها دورتر نیز رسیده و به عنوان شیخ لقب گرفته بود.

آرامگاه: برخی از مورخان معتقدند این شاعر گرانقدر در سال ۶۹۰ هجری قمری و در خانقاهی که اقامت داشت دیده از جهان فرو بست. امروزه آرامگاه سعدی را در شیراز خانقاه اقامت او در گذشته می‌دانند.

آرامگاه شاعر برجسته پارسی‌گوی معروف به سعدیه است و در شمال شرقی شیراز، در دامنه کوه فهندژ، انتهای خیابان بوستان و کنار باغ دلگشا واقع شده‌است. محل دفن سعدی، خانقاهی بود که او در سال‌های پایانی حیات خود در آن می‌زیست. این خانقاه، در نزدیکی سرچشمه‌های نهر رکن‌آباد واقع شده‌بود. این بنا در سال ۹۹۸ هجری قمری به حکم یعقوب ذوالقدر، حکمران فارس خانقاه شیخ تخریب شد.

در سال ۱۱۸۷ هجری قمری به دستور کریمخان زند، یک ساختمان آجری در آنجا بنا شد که شامل ۲ طبقه بود؛ طبقهٔ پایین دارای راهرویی بود که پلکان طبقه دوم از آنجا شروع می‌شد و مزار سعدی در محفظه‌ای چوبی در اتاق

شرقی راهرو قرار داشت. این بنا و محوطه آن در اثر مرور زمان رو به زوال گذاشت و در دهه ۱۳۲۰ عملاً به بنایی مخروبه، کثیف و زیستگاه مگس‌ها تبدیل شد. در این سال، با توجه به اتمام بنای حافظیه، و با تلاش‌های علی اصغر حکمت، طراحی و ساخت این عمارت جدید، بر عهده محسن فروغی، معمار ایرانی و علی صادق گذاشته شد؛ هرچند آندره گدار، معمار فرانسوی نیز بازدیدهایی از آن داشته‌است. کلنگ احداث این بنا در سال ۱۳۲۷ به دست اشرف پهلوی زده‌شد. این ساختمان با الهام از چهل ستون و با صرف هزینه ۹۸۰ هزار تومان، در سال ۱۳۳۱ آماده و در روز یازدهم اردیبهشت همان سال با حضور شاه وقت و دکتر حسابی، وزیر وقت فرهنگ افتتاح شد.

معماری بنای جدید سعدیه، با استفاده از عناصر معماری ایرانی صورت گرفته و در معماری آن از عناصر فارسی زیادی استفاده شده است ؛ این بنا از یک ایوان ستوندار بلند و یک رواق کشیده تشکیل شده‌است. رواق و ایوان به‌صورت (L) جانمایی شده‌اند. در محل برخورد ایوان و رواق، که مزار سعدی در آن قرار دارد، یک گنبد از کاشی فیروزه‌ای تعبیه شده‌است. آب قنات نیز در آبنمای موسوم به حوض ماهی در زیرزمین مجموعه جریان دارد. این مجموعه در آبان ۱۳۵۳ در فهرست آثار ملی ایران ثبت شد.

لغتنامه دهخدا به نقل از فرهنگ برهان قاطع نام موضعی که شیخ سعدی در آنجا آرمیده را «گازرگاه» نامیده و به نقل از فرهنگ آنندراج گازرگاه را حد شیراز نزدیک به مرقد شیخ مصلح‌الدین سعدی شیرازی دانسته است.

روز سعدی: مرکز سعدی‌شناسی، از سال ۱۳۸۱ خورشیدی، به‌منظور تجلیل از سعدی، روز اول اردیبهشت ماه (روز آغاز نگارش کتاب گلستان) را روز سعدی، اعلام کرد و در اول اردیبهشت ۱۳۸۹ خورشیدی، در «اجلاس شاعران جهان» در شیراز، نخستین روز اردیبهشت، از سوی نهادهای فرهنگی داخلی و خارجی، به‌عنوان «روز سعدی» نامگذاری شد.

پول ملی: سکه‌های پانصد ریالی برنزی ایران از سال ۱۳۸۷ خورشیدی به نقش آرامگاه سعدی مزین شده‌است. همچنین در سال ۱۳۸۹، طرح پشت اسکناس ده‌هزارتومانی (یکصدهزارریالی) نمایی از مقبرهٔ سعدی در شیراز می‌باشد.

مجسمه: در سال ۱۳۳۰، با ابتکار و پیگیری علی اصغر حکمت، رئیس وقت انجمن آثار ملی ایران، مجسمه بزرگی از سعدی ساخته و در میدان سعدی شیراز در نزدیکی دروازه اصفهان نصب و در سال ۱۳۳۱ همزمان با افتتاح آرامگاه سعدی، رونمایی شد. این مجسمه اثر ابوالحسن صدیقی، نقاش و مجسمه‌ساز برجستهٔ ایرانی است و از جنس سنگ مرمر ساخته‌شده‌است. کار ساخت این مجسمه که بیش از سه متر ارتفاع دارد، یک سال و نیم به طول انجامیده‌است. این مجسمه تا اواسط دهه ۱۳۷۰ در این میدان واقع بود اما با برچیده شدن میدان، مجسمه به میدان پیرنیا انتقال داده شد.

بوستان

سعدی

با ترجمه انگلیسی: G.S. Davie

گردآوری: حمید اسلامیان

Made in the USA
Monee, IL
30 June 2023

38164258R00286